AMERICAN MIDNIGHT

AMERICAN
MIDNIGHT

The Great War, A Violent Peace,
and Democracy's Forgotten Crisis

ADAM HOCHSCHILD

MARINER BOOKS
New York   Boston

Insert: p. 1—top: Getty; bottom left: Alamy; bottom right: Granger Historical Archives. p. 2—bottom: Getty. p. 3—top: St. Louis Post-Dispatch Archives; bottom: Alamy. p. 4—top and bottom: Alamy. p. 5—top: the Library of Congress. p. 6—top right: Ancestry.com; bottom: the National Archives. p. 7—top and bottom: Alamy. p. 8—top and bottom: Alamy. p. 9—top: © MMXXII Walter P. Reuther Library, Archives of Labor and Urban Affairs, Wayne State University. p. 10—top: Granger Historical Archives; bottom: Alamy. p. 11—top: Alamy; bottom: the Library of Congress. p. 12—top left and right: the Library of Congress; bottom left: Getty. p. 13—top: Alamy. p. 14—bottom: Getty. p. 15—top: Getty; bottom left and right: Alamy. p. 16—top left: the Library of Congress; bottom: Granger Historical Archives.

Portions of this book have appeared, in different form, in *The New Yorker, Mother Jones, The Washington Post Magazine*, and *The New York Review of Books*.

HarperCollins books may be purchased for educational, business, or sales promotional use. For information, please email the Special Markets Department at SPsales@harpercollins.com.

FIRST EDITION

Designed by Chloe Foster

Library of Congress Cataloging-in-Publication Data has been applied for.

ISBN 978-0-358-45546-2

22 23 24 25 26 LBC 6 5 4 3 2

For
Troy Duster, Russ Ellis, and Thelton Henderson

CONTENTS

Prologue: No Ordinary Times   1

PART I

1. Tears of Joy   15
2. Place a Gun upon His Shoulder   37
3. The Cardinal Goes to War   55
4. Enchanted by Her Beauty   71
5. Those Who Stand in Our Way   81
6. Soldiers of Darkness   93
7. Shoot My Brother Down   107
8. A Wily Con Man; A Dangerous Woman   119
9. The Water Cure   135
10. Nobody Can Say We Aren't Loyal Now!   149
11. Cut, Shuffle, and Deal   159
12. Cheerleaders   171
13. Peace?   181

PART II

14.　Another Savior Come to Earth　　　　　201

15.　World on Fire　　　　　219

16.　Sly and Crafty Eyes　　　　　233

17.　On the Great Deep　　　　　247

18.　I Am Not in Condition to Go On　　　　　259

19.　In a Tugboat Kitchen　　　　　273

20.　Men Like These Would Rule You　　　　　295

21.　Seeing Red　　　　　305

22.　A Little Man, Cool but Fiery　　　　　315

23.　Policeman and Detective　　　　　329

24.　Aftermath　　　　　339

Acknowledgments　　　　　359

Selected Bibliography　　　　　363

Notes　　　　　373

Index　　　　　407

AMERICAN MIDNIGHT

No Ordinary Times

NIGHT HAD FALLEN in the rugged oil-boom city of Tulsa, Oklahoma, when the squad of detectives appeared on a downtown street. They gathered outside a building whose ground-floor meeting hall had yellow curtains at the windows. Then they burst inside.

It was November 5, 1917, and the room they raided was the local headquarters of the Industrial Workers of the World. The IWW was the country's most militant labor union and was organizing the region's oil workers; for reasons obscure, its members were known to all as Wobblies. The detectives examined the premises suspiciously, looking into corners with flashlights, but found nothing more incriminating than 11 Wobblies reading or playing cards. They arrested the men, ordered them into a paddy wagon, and, for want of other offenses, charged them all with vagrancy. The worst that the *Tulsa Daily World*, the voice of the state's oil industry, could come up with the next day, looking for something damning to say about them, was, "Most of them were uncouth in appearance."

When the Wobblies were brought to court two days later, the police could not name any laws the men had violated, and none had a criminal record. Their attorney argued that they could not possibly be vagrants, or "loafers," as the prosecution charged, because they were employed. One had not lost a workday in ten months; another was the father of ten children and owned a mortgage-free home. However, when their trial ended late at night on November 9, Judge T. D. Evans found them all guilty and fined them $100 apiece (the equivalent of some $2,000 a hundred years later). This was a sum no Wobbly could afford and one that guaranteed that they would remain in jail.

By way of explaining his verdict, the judge cryptically declared, "These are no ordinary times."

Immediately after he sentenced the 11, bailiffs seized six other men in the courtroom, five of them Wobblies who had been defense witnesses, and locked them up as well. Shortly afterward, police ordered the entire group into three cars, supposedly to take them to the county jail. At a railroad crossing, however, the cars were suddenly surrounded by a large mob of men wearing long black robes and black masks and carrying rifles and revolvers. It was below freezing. "You could see the frost on the railroad ties," remembered one Wobbly. By now he and his comrades knew that in store for them was something worse than jail.

JUDGE EVANS WAS right: these were no ordinary times. Yet they are largely left out of the typical high school American history book. There's always a chapter on the First World War, which tells us that the United States remained neutral in that conflict until German submarines began sinking American ships. Then, of course, we sent General Pershing and his millions of khaki-clad doughboys to Europe in their distinctive, broad-brimmed, forest-ranger hats. They fought valiantly at Château-Thierry and Belleau Wood, helped win the war, and returned home to joyful ticker-tape parades. Turn the page and the next chapter begins with the Roaring Twenties: flappers, the Charleston, Prohibition, speakeasys, and Al Capone.

This book is about what's missing between those two chapters. It is a story of mass imprisonments, torture, vigilante violence, censorship, killings of Black Americans, and far more that is not marked by commemorative plaques, museum exhibits, or Ken Burns documentaries. It is a story of how a war supposedly fought to make the world safe for democracy became the excuse for a war against democracy at home.

The toxic currents of racism, nativism, Red-baiting, and contempt for the rule of law have long flowed through American life. People of my generation have seen them erupt in McCarthyism, in the rocks and insults hurled at Black children entering previously all-white schools, and in the demagoguery of politicians like Richard Nixon, George Wallace, and Donald Trump. By the time you read this, they may well have boiled up again in additional ways. My hope is that by examining closely an overlooked period in which they engulfed the country, we can understand them more deeply and better defend against them in the future. "The struggle of man against power," wrote Milan Kundera, "is the struggle of memory against forgetting."

Never was this raw underside of our nation's life more revealingly on display than from 1917 to 1921. For instance, twenty-first-century Americans are all too familiar with rage against immigrants and talk of fortifying the southern border, but this is nothing new: major candidates for both the Republican and Democratic Party presidential nominations in 1920 campaigned on promises of mass deportations. And some people, including the vice president of the United States, suggested going further: Why limit deportation merely to immigrants? Why not permanently expel troublemakers of every sort? Also during this period, army machine-gun nests appeared in downtown Omaha and tanks on the streets of Cleveland, and armed troops patrolled many other American cities, from Butte, Montana, to Gary, Indiana. The military crafted a secret 57-page contingency plan to put the entire country under martial law.

During those four years more than 450 people were imprisoned for a year or more by the federal government, and an estimated greater number by state governments, merely for what they wrote or said. For the same reason, or simply for belonging to fully legal organizations, thousands of Americans like those Tulsa Wobblies were jailed for shorter periods, anywhere from a few days to a few months.

Right-wing TV networks did not exist in 1917, but in that year was born a presidential tool even more powerful, a lavishly financed government propaganda agency that operated in every medium of the day: films, books, posters, newspaper articles, and a corps of 75,000 speakers who gave more than seven million talks everywhere from movie houses to revival tents. In addition, the federal government also attacked the press, both during and well after the First World War. It banned hundreds of issues of American newspapers and magazines from the mail (a fatal blow in an age before electronic media), permanently barring some 75 periodicals entirely.

These years also saw the birth of a nationwide group of vigilantes that, in size and power, dwarfed the militia groups in bulletproof vests that would flourish a century later. With more than a quarter-million members, that earlier organization became an official auxiliary of the Department of Justice. Men in its ranks would sport badges and military-style titles, cracking heads, roughing up protestors, and carrying out mass arrests. Tens of thousands of Americans would join smaller local groups as well; the masked vigilantes under those black hoods in Tulsa that night in November 1917 belonged to one called the Knights of Liberty.

WHEN THE POLICE cars stopped at the railroad crossing, "none of the policemen had a chance to reach for his gun," claimed the *Tulsa Daily World*, "as they were surrounded by armed men." The *World*'s managing editor, who clearly had been tipped off beforehand, was on the scene to observe, even bringing his wife with him. The newspaper had virtually called for something to happen, publishing an editorial that very afternoon saying, "The first step in the whipping of Germany is to strangle the I. W. W.'s. Kill 'em, just as you would kill any other kind of a snake. . . . It is no time to waste money on trials and continuances and things like that. All that is necessary is the evidence and a firing squad."

America's entry into the First World War earlier that year had provided business with a God-given excuse to stop workers from organizing. "Any man or any set of men," as the *World* put it, "who in any way restrict the production of oil to the extent of a fraction of a barrel are helping the German emperor."

The masked, robed members of the Knights of Liberty tied the hands of each Wobbly with rope, climbed into the police cars themselves, and ordered the drivers on, accompanied by additional carloads of black-clad men. By a ravine in the Osage Hills just outside town, the cars parked in a circle, their headlights shining on an oak tree. A bonfire crackled and flickered into the night sky.

The vigilantes stripped the Wobblies to the waist and made them remove their shoes. Then, one by one, they marched each man at gunpoint to the tree, tied him to it, and whipped him until his back bled. The lashing, according to one eyewitness, was done with double pieces of heavy rope soaked in saltwater; according to another, with a "blacksnake"—a long leather whip weighted with shot.

Then the vigilantes produced a pot of hot tar. As they brushed it onto each Wobbly's chest and bleeding back, from beneath his hood the group's leader intoned, "In the name of the outraged women and children of Belgium." (German atrocities there were a centerpiece of American war propaganda.) The mob next slit open pillows and rubbed handfuls of feathers onto the tar.

One member poured gasoline over a pile of shoes and clothing taken from the Wobblies, which contained their watches, pocketknives, money, and "everything that we owned in the world" in the words of one victim, and set it on fire. Finally, the Knights of Liberty told the barefoot Wobblies to run for it. To the accompaniment of volley after volley of rifle and pistol shots fired over their heads, they scattered into the frigid darkness.

Federal agents, the *World* reported the next day, "were making no apparent effort to discover the identity of the fifty black-robed and hooded men who held up the police cars . . . and had received no instruction from Washington as to what steps should be taken." These Wobblies survived, but many other victims of this grim period would not. On a barbed wire fence near the ravine, in the path of their flight, the newspaper reported, "pieces of clothing and flesh, and a profusion of feathers, were found entangled."

ALTHOUGH THIS BRUTAL time unfolded long before I was born, both my parents lived through it. They experienced it differently. To my mother, the daughter of a Princeton professor, Woodrow Wilson had been a familiar figure long before he was first elected president in 1912. His solemn gray eyes behind a pince-nez, a neatly folded hand-kerchief in his breast pocket, he doffed his top hat to women he met as he walked to work each day on the placid, leafy streets near her home. Wilson had been the university's president until elected governor of New Jersey in 1910 and continued to live in Princeton until voters sent him to the White House two years later. When a bell in a campus tower pealing nonstop proclaimed that news, my grandparents took their young daughters over to the Wilsons' spacious half-timbered Tu-dor house to join those who came to congratulate the couple.

A few years later, my 16-year-old mother shared the enthusiasm that swept the country as it entered the First World War, determined to defeat Kaiser Wilhelm II, that symbol of German militarism with his upswept mustache and love of bemedaled uniforms. She and her sisters rolled bandages for the Red Cross and moved pins on a map of Europe to show the positions of the armies. They were thrilled to see the flags of all the Allied nations hanging in the Princeton gymnasium, as well as the student cadets in puttees drilling on campus or donning leather helmets and goggles at a nearby new airfield. When a delegation of British officers visited town, hostesses vied to entertain them. Only af-ter the war's end did my horrified mother learn that it had claimed the lives of two beloved male cousins.

For my 24-year-old father, the war brought no cheering. Although his family was well off, they lived in fear. His parents were Jewish, his father an immigrant from Germany and his mother the daughter of immigrants, and the family spoke German at home. But you risked be-ing beaten up if someone heard you doing so on the street, for patriots now condemned the "kaiser's tongue." In New York City, where they lived, the Metropolitan Opera announced that it would cease perform-ing works in German. The American Defense Society, whose honorary head was ex-president Theodore Roosevelt, declared, "The sound of the German language . . . reminds us of the murder of a million help-less old men, unarmed men, women and children . . . the ravishment and murder of young girls." One wartime Sunday, spreading across five columns of the *New York Times*, which my father and grandfather read faithfully, was an article by a Johns Hopkins professor under the headline "Educator Says It Is a Barbarous Tongue." A few weeks later came a front-page *Times* story from nearby New Haven, where my father's brother was in college, headlined "Masked Patriots Beat Pro-German."

Some states warned citizens against speaking German even in private. In Shawnee, Oklahoma, a crowd burned German books to mark the Fourth of July. At least 19 ceremonial bonfires of such books were lit in Ohio alone; the public library in Columbus sold its German books for scrap paper. In McLean County, Illinois, a crowd of 300 surrounded the Evangelical German Lutheran Church and demanded that it cease using German or they would burn down the building. A Justice Department official on the scene ordered the church to comply. North Dakota, Delaware, Montana, and Louisiana banned the teaching of German in school. Iowa and Nebraska banned the use in public of *all* foreign languages.

"This is a nation," Theodore Roosevelt thundered, "not a polyglot boarding house." Organizations rushed to change their names: the German Savings Bank of Brooklyn, for instance, became the Lincoln Savings Bank. Only in researching this book did I realize that the Lenox Hill Hospital of my own New York City childhood, across the street from my pediatrician's office, had previously been the German Hospital and Dispensary, with a Kaiser Wilhelm Pavilion.

"It is the Christian duty of Americans," a Methodist minister declared, "to decorate convenient lamp posts with German spies and agents of the Kaiser, native or foreign-born." A Minnesota pastor was tarred and feathered because people overheard him praying in German with a dying woman. One of many patriotic lecturers touring the country with lurid tales of atrocities, a Congregational minister from Brooklyn told his audiences Germans were so inherently brutal that after the war ten million of their men should be sterilized.

Hysteria against Germans blended seamlessly with long-standing anti-Semitism. America barred Jews, either explicitly or in practice, from many clubs, businesses, law firms, college faculties, hotels, and more. The novelist Henry James was disgusted by the Jews he saw "swarming" on New York's Lower East Side, reminding him of "small, strange animals . . . snakes or worms . . . who, when cut into pieces, wriggle away contentedly and live in the snippet as completely as in the whole." In 1913, on evidence today considered fraudulent, Leo Frank, a young New York Jew working in Atlanta, had been convicted of raping and murdering a 13-year-old girl. Two years later, in the middle of the night, a mob broke into a prison, seized him, and lynched him. Half the 3,000 Jews living in Georgia left the state.

New York was not the Deep South, but a family with a name both German and Jewish still felt vulnerable. Several of my father's cousins would before long legally change their last name to one that sounded Anglo. On all sides were rallies, parades, and pageants urging people to buy war bonds. The city saw hundreds of thousands of men questioned by vigilantes who fanned out across town, intent on rounding up "slackers," as they were called, trying to avoid the draft. My father tried desperately to get into the army, hoping that a uniform could protect him and his family. He saved little of his correspondence, but to the end of his life kept a thick file of letters and telegrams about his repeated attempts in 1917 and 1918 to enlist in one or another branch of the military: cavalry, ordnance, artillery, intelligence. When severe nearsightedness prevented this, he was relieved that he could demonstrate his patriotism by going to work as a civilian volunteer in Washington for the War Department.

Popular songs reflected the vengeful mood:

If you don't like your Uncle Sammy
Then go back to your home o'er the sea,
To the land from where you came,
Whatever be its name.

Most Americans—almost certainly including my mother—were unaware of the violence underlying this feeling. If it mentioned them at all, the press often portrayed vigilantes beating up pacifists as patriots subduing rowdy malcontents. If the government banned an issue of a newspaper or magazine, or shut it down entirely, this was seldom announced. And no one was reporting from the prison at Camp Funston, Kansas, where conscientious objectors to military service were shackled to their cell bars on tiptoe for eight hours a day.

Most Americans were also unaware that hundreds of private detectives, undercover agents from the Bureau of Investigation (the predecessor to the FBI), and hundreds more agents from Military Intelligence were in the audiences for political meetings and were infiltrating perfectly legal organizations. In Tulsa, for example, the police seized those 11 Wobblies in their office and arrested six more sympathizers in the courtroom, for a total of 17. But when it came time to whip, tar, and feather them, there were only 16 victims. The 17th, a 29-year-old whose alias was John McCurry, was whisked out of the holding cell on a pretext because he had been working undercover for the Pinkerton National Detective Agency. Pinkerton's wide range of corporate clients included Oklahoma oil interests.

Such spying has a long history. I had my own brush with it as an opponent of the Vietnam War in the late 1960s and early 1970s. Although I was a most insignificant figure in that movement, when I later used the Freedom of Information Act to get the heavily redacted files on me compiled by the FBI, the CIA, and the army, I received more than 100 pages. Ever since, when writing history, I've been drawn to surveillance records. They often tell you, inadvertently, more about the minds of the watchers than of the watched. In this book, you will meet a remarkably prolific writer of such reports, who for years successfully posed as an outspoken crusader for left-wing causes.

Until 1917, surveillance in this country had been almost entirely the work of private detectives. Despite thousands of films and novels to the contrary, such detectives were not hard-boiled private eyes with hearts of gold who rescued kidnapped heiresses and solved other mysterious crimes. Rather, like that Pinkerton man in Tulsa, they were frontline troops in the long war American business waged on labor. But the para-

noia ignited by the First World War empowered government intelligence agencies, both military and civilian, to do their own spying and
infiltrating. Such surveillance remains part of American life to this day.

ALTHOUGH THE GOVERNMENT first used the war in Europe to jus-
tify the ferocity at home, the repression continued, and in some ways
grew worse, in the several years after the fighting ended, a time known
as the Red Scare. Deep tensions fueled it. During the very days those
Tulsa Wobblies were in jail, a group of radical Marxists known as Bolsheviks seized power in Russia, and many American business and political leaders feared that the Russian Revolution might spread to the
United States.

Other forces also fed the violence, and most of them are still with us:
a long-simmering nativism and hatred of immigrants; a military that
had picked up brutal habits waging war on guerrillas in Asia; the bitter
conflict between big business and organized labor that had raged for
decades; and, finally, a nostalgia among white southerners—and many
northerners—for the days when Blacks "knew their place."

Between 1917 and 1921 there was also, to be sure, some violence
from the left. Workers attacked strikebreakers with fists, knives, and
bricks. Anarchists planted bombs, killing several dozen people. For
many other acts of violence, however, it is unclear who was responsible.

The very afternoon before those Wobblies were arrested, for example, a 300-foot railroad bridge not far from Tulsa caught fire. The cause
of the flames "has not been discovered," reported the *Tulsa Democrat*,
"but it is thought to have been a part of an I. W. W. plot." The paper
cited no evidence, however, and in this period no prosecutor ever convicted an Oklahoma Wobbly of an act of political violence.

The greatest ferocity by far came from federal and state governments, businesses, and the vigilantes allied with them—and it was
backed at the very highest level. The corporate lawyer Elihu Root was
a former secretary of war, secretary of state, and senator from New
York. In August 1917, he had just returned from a trip abroad as a special emissary for President Wilson. "There are men walking about the

streets of this city tonight who ought to be taken out at sunrise tomorrow and shot for treason," he told a New York City audience. "There are some newspapers published in this city every day the editors of which deserve conviction and execution."

Such fierceness echoed across the country. Who, for instance, led the mob that tarred and feathered those Tulsa Wobblies? Two men: the city's police chief, Ed Lucas, and W. Tate Brady, one of its most prominent business figures. Brady's holdings included a lumberyard, a coal mine, commercial real estate, and the first hotel in town with baths. The IWW office, in fact, was on West Brady Street. Just a few days before the arrests, the volatile Brady, no stranger to the use of force, had attacked and beaten up a rival property owner who had rented that space to the IWW. The son of a Confederate veteran, Brady had moved to Oklahoma when white settlers were still staking out land in what was then Indian Territory. Later, he would join the Ku Klux Klan and, with his business profits, build a mansion modeled on the Virginia home of the Confederate general Robert E. Lee.

Key figures in these years took pride in other violent parts of the American past as well. One, who would come very close to being nominated for president, was a veteran of both the Indian Wars and the brutal campaign against Philippine independence fighters. Another Philippine War veteran headed the Military Intelligence operation that would spy on American civilians at home.

This was not, however, merely a time of villains and victims. There were plenty of heroes as well, who belong in any pantheon of Americans who fought for justice and defied bigotry. One was a feisty, outspoken woman who had a dramatic confrontation with her persecutor in the galley of a tugboat crossing New York Harbor. Another gave a speech from the one place where the police could not silence her—the top of a telephone pole. A third was a little-known but iron-principled bureaucrat who scored a decisive victory over someone who would intimidate other government officials for half a century to come: J. Edgar Hoover. And a US senator's bravery led him to receive nooses in the mail and be hanged in effigy at the university that was his alma mater.

Looming over this entire story is one of the most enigmatic of American presidents. A visionary internationalist, he staked his political fortune on his hopes for the League of Nations, where countries would settle their disputes by negotiation instead of warfare. Yet he presided over the greatest assault on American civil liberties in the last century and a half. And, despite his skill as an orator and writer, he showed few regrets over that contradiction.

Let us start with him, on the day this dark era began.

PART I

1

Tears of Joy

ON THE PIVOTAL day of his presidency, Woodrow Wilson tried to clear his mind by playing golf. He was anything but skilled at the game, for he once required 26 strokes to complete a single hole. However, his close friend Dr. Cary Grayson, a navy physician, recommended any exercise that might strengthen the president's shaky health and ease his high blood pressure. So, despite a smattering of light rain, Wilson fulfilled his doctor's orders, trying not to fret about the speech he was to give that evening, one that, he knew, would define his two terms in the White House.

It was the morning of April 2, 1917. Wilson's companion on the golf links in Virginia, across the river from Washington, was his second wife, Edith. She was his partner in much else as well, sitting in on meetings with ambassadors, sorting and discussing the vast flow of documents that came across the presidential desk, coding and decoding telegrams, and sometimes even serving as his intermediary with cabinet members.

After the president had lost his first wife, the mother of his adult children, to kidney disease three years earlier, Dr. Grayson had introduced him to Edith Bolling Galt, a widow 16 years his junior. With the wild enthusiasm of a much-younger man, he seemed transformed by the vivacious, slightly plump Edith, whose face was as round and cheerful as his own was long and somber—an undertaker's face, people often said. The morning after what was apparently his first night with her, on a sleeper train taking them to a honeymoon getaway, a Secret Service agent had seen the 58-year-old Wilson dancing a jig while singing a popular vaudeville tune:

Oh, you beautiful doll! You great big beautiful doll!
Let me put my arms around you, I can hardly live without you.

The president would not be dancing much longer. Several years later, a stroke would suddenly render him barely able to speak or move, leaving vastly more power than Americans knew in the hands of his wife, as she concealed his condition from the country. But for now, Edith Wilson remained merely a quiet presence in her husband's life.

Before they headed for the golf course the morning of April 2, the president had sent to the government printer a sealed envelope containing the speech he was to give to both houses of Congress the same evening. He had typed it himself on his Hammond portable. Although even his own cabinet members did not know exactly what Wilson was going to say, everyone knew what the topic of his legendary eloquence would be: the terrible conflict that by now had engulfed almost all of Europe, with the fighting spreading to Africa and Asia as well.

Like an immense whirlpool, what newspapers referred to as the "Great War" seemed to be sucking the United States into its grasp. It was mass-production slaughter on an unimaginable scale, with an estimated five million soldiers killed in less than three years of fighting so far, and an even larger number wounded. The previous year, 1916, had been the most violent that history had yet seen, with vast, monthslong battles at the Somme and Verdun in France and in a huge Russian offensive on the other side of Europe. At the Somme, more than 19,000 British soldiers had been killed in a single day as they walked into German machine-gun fire. In Russia alone, six million people would eventually take to the roads as refugees, many of them desperately hungry.

Pressure for the United States to join the war had been building since the fighting began in 1914. If the country did so, however, it would be unprecedented, for in the nation's entire existence, no American soldiers had ever fought in Europe. George Washington had famously warned his people not to "entangle our peace and prosperity in the toils of European ambition," and for many Americans, that prospect was still unthinkable.

If the country made this momentous step, which side would it join? Certainly not that of Germany and its chief partner, the Austro-Hungarian Empire, the powers blamed, with some reason, for starting the war. Many Americans were outraged by reports—some exaggerated, some true—that the Germans had shot civilians, pillaged farms, and conscripted forced laborers in occupied Belgium. The American public also was shocked by the burning of that country's famous university library at Louvain, with its priceless collection of medieval manuscripts; by German zeppelins bombing London; and by the great massacres of Christian Armenians by Germany's ally, Ottoman Turkey.

No—if the United States joined, it would be on the side of the Allies: Britain, France, Russia, Italy, and a number of smaller countries. Americans felt great sympathy for France, which was suffering ferocious combat on its own soil. Deep ties of history and language bound the United States to Britain, reinforced by a sophisticated British propaganda campaign that flooded the American press with articles, interviews, and cartoons; distributed millions of books and pamphlets; and sent speakers touring the United States with graphic tales of British bravery and German cruelty. Shrewd British propagandists even translated and published the writings of the most extreme German militarists, knowing Americans would be dismayed by them.

By contrast, German lobbying in America was hobbled: In the middle of the night, a few hours after Britain declared war, a specially equipped British ship waiting in the English Channel had lowered its grapple at the right spot to retrieve and cut all five undersea telegraph cables linking Germany to other parts of the world, including the United States. Vigilant British control of the remaining transatlantic cables ensured that no stories that reflected badly on the Allies reached American newspapers.

Britain and France were desperate for American support. Already at least 35,000 young Americans eager for battle had volunteered for the armed forces of Canada, among the Allies from the beginning. Others had enlisted in the French Foreign Legion, and several thousand Americans had gone to Europe as nurses and ambulance drivers for the Allies. Many more had donated millions to support them and to send food to occupied Belgium. Dozens of eager fliers had joined the elite Lafayette Escadrille, a unit of volunteer American fighter pilots in the French air force. Their fragile biplanes were painted with the head of a Native American in a feathered war bonnet.

Even so, millions of other Americans wanted no part of the conflict. Wilson had won reelection as the Democratic candidate in 1916 on the slogan "He kept us out of war." Although the president was careful never to utter those words himself, his campaign was so convincing that he gained the support of many pacifists. Nowhere was antiwar feeling stronger than in the Socialist Party, whose members had long dreamed of a workers' commonwealth that transcended national borders. In an implicit bow to Wilson, Eugene V. Debs, the perennial Socialist presidential candidate and an ardent opponent of war, chose not to run for president in 1916, and many of his followers voted for Wilson.

But had he really kept us out of war? A newspaper cartoon captured the truth: a walking Uncle Sam is wearing sandwich boards; the one covering his chest reads, "Peace on Earth, Goodwill Toward Men"; the one on his back, "War Ammunition for $ale, Orders Filled Promptly."

The United States might not officially be at war, but it was selling the Allies vast quantities of oil, barbed wire, rifle ammunition, and artillery shells, plus the steel, copper, and other materials needed to make more weapons. This cornucopia of supplies included $700 million worth of explosives alone. Workers in Canada assembled American parts and materials into submarines for Britain's Royal Navy. Midwestern farmers sold tens of thousands of horses and mules to replace those that had perished pulling artillery pieces and supply wagons at the front in France and Belgium, and also reaped good prices supplying much of the beef, pork, wheat, and other food that kept the British and French fed. American business was making millions selling goods to other Allied nations as well: everything from boots for Russian Cossacks to 500,000 canteens for Greece.

Theoretically, factories and farmers in "neutral" America were equally free to sell whatever they wanted to Germany and Austria-Hungary, but this was impossible. A blockade of British warships and minefields cut off those countries from all shipping. Not even medical supplies were allowed through.

Germany had greatly inflamed American public opinion in 1915 when one of its submarines torpedoed the British passenger liner *Lusitania* on its way from New York to Liverpool. Nearly 1,200 people lost their lives, including 128 Americans. Politicians in Washington and across the country furiously denounced German perfidy and the murder of innocent women and children. They ignored, however, the fact that the *Lusitania* was also carrying 173 tons of munitions, including artillery shells and 4.2 million rifle bullets.

Now, almost hour by hour as Woodrow and Edith Wilson played their morning golf game on April 2, momentum to join the fighting was escalating, fueled by two recent events even more galvanizing than the sinking of the *Lusitania*.

The first of these had come on February 1, 1917, when Germany declared unlimited submarine warfare. Previously the supplies and food the United States sold the Allies were generally safe from attack if they traveled on American ships, but now any vessel heading for Allied ports could be a target for German torpedoes. When the Germans quietly offered to negotiate exceptions for some American ships, Wilson ignored them. As American freighters and their sailors began to fall victim to German submarines, he cut off diplomatic relations with Germany.

Then, on March 1, front pages across the country carried the text of a shocking telegram—gleefully intercepted and decoded by British intelligence—that German foreign minister Arthur Zimmermann had sent to his country's ambassador in Mexico. It asked him to urge that nation into the war on the German side, in return for which Germany would reward it with its "lost territory in Texas, New Mexico, and Arizona." Lost territory! In an America where several decades of dramatically increased immigration had already left nativists inflamed, the Zimmermann telegram ignited fury. The War Department put troops at the Mexican border on alert and sent soldiers to guard railway tunnels in the Sierra Nevada Mountains. A private rifle club in San Diego offered to protect the city. The movie mogul Cecil B. De Mille put 75 men armed with rifles and a machine gun at the service of Los Angeles.

While his fellow Americans were succumbing to war fever, Wilson had long acted as if the United States, and he himself, were morally superior to the squabbling countries of the Old World. Two years earlier, speaking to a group of Civil War veterans, he had made a statement that would have raised many an eyebrow elsewhere in the world: "We created this Nation not to serve ourselves, but to serve mankind."

As late as January 1917, still seeming to speak from a lofty perch above the great conflict in Europe, he had called for the war to end in a "peace without victory," declaring that "victory would mean peace forced upon the loser, a victor's terms imposed upon the vanquished. It would be accepted in humiliation, under duress, at an intolerable sacrifice, and would leave a sting, a resentment."

It would be a dramatic change for Wilson to now ask Congress to join that very war, although by the time he headed home from his golf game, many Americans were sure he would do so. But just how would the country go to war? The United States had only a small standing military, while the armies now hurling themselves against each other across the Atlantic were swollen by conscription and altogether totaled in the tens of millions. Only once before, during the Civil War, had the United States tried a draft, and it had been met with violent protests that left well over 100 people killed.

Many thought, therefore, that if the president called for his country to take part in the war, it might be in some limited fashion—restricted, say, to naval attacks on German submarines. As recently as February, after all, Wilson had publicly opposed conscription. Would he reverse himself so soon?

APRIL 2 WAS a Monday, and over the weekend in his second-floor White House study the president had outlined and drafted his address to Congress: first in shorthand, then making corrections, and finally typing. That much is certain. But an oft-repeated story having to do with the speech is more likely legend.

Wilson was agonized about the decision he faced, his admirers are fond of saying. In the words of an authorized biographer partly subsidized by his widow, "The necessity of leading his people into war continued to occasion the President the acutest anguish. . . . The doubts that besieged him were all but overwhelming." As he finished writing his speech, the story goes, he sent for a trusted friend to whom he could bare his soul, Frank Cobb, the editor of the New York *World*. It was supposedly 1:00 a.m. on April 2 when Cobb finally reached the White House and found the president in his study, at his typewriter.

"I'd never seen him so worn down," Cobb was quoted as saying years later. "He looked as if he hadn't slept, and he said he hadn't. . . . For nights, he said, he'd been lying awake. . . . He tapped some sheets before him and said that he had written a message and expected to go before Congress with it as it stood. He said he couldn't see any alternative, that he had tried every way he knew to avoid war. 'What else can I do?' he asked."

Then, according to Cobb, Wilson brilliantly foresaw the years ahead.

> He said war would overturn the world we had known. . . .
> "Once lead this people into war," he said, "and they'll forget
> there ever was such a thing as tolerance. To fight you must
> be brutal and ruthless, and the spirit of ruthless brutality
> will enter into the very fibre of our national life, infecting
> Congress, the courts, the policeman on the beat, the man in
> the street . . ."

He thought the Constitution would not survive it; that free speech and the right of assembly would go. He said a nation couldn't put its strength into a war and keep its head level; it had never been done. "If there is any alternative, for God's sake, let's take it," he exclaimed.

In the words of another admiring biographer, "This was possibly the most anguished cry from the heart ever uttered in the White House by a president."

But did he really utter that cry?

Cobb made no surviving notes about his visit. And then there's the question of when he visited. White House logbooks show no appearance by Cobb that weekend. They do, however, show him visiting two weeks earlier, on March 19, 1917, but at 3:30 p.m., not 1:00 a.m. Furthermore, if the dramatic monologue Cobb describes took place on March 19, the papers he saw could not have been Wilson's speech to Congress, which he didn't start drafting until some ten days later.

The uncertainties only multiply. Cobb's account of the conversation was given to two colleagues six years later, when he was fatally ill. Neither of them made any notes. When one, seven months afterward, published his recollection of what Cobb told them, neither Cobb nor Wilson was able to confirm it, because they were both dead.

AFTER HIS MORNING golf game, the president had a quiet early lunch. His meals, on Dr. Grayson's advice, were always balanced and not too rich, with ice cream as the only sweet. Wilson then summoned his private secretary, Joseph Tumulty—today he would be called chief of staff—who was seldom far from the president's elbow. Despite his unassuming, cherubic looks, Tumulty was an experienced veteran of New Jersey machine politics who had helped Wilson navigate his stint as governor of that state. The president asked Tumulty to notify the House and Senate that he was ready to address a joint session as soon as they were prepared to receive him.

Meanwhile, great stacks of letters and telegrams, far more than clerks could sort, were piling up at the White House, making dramatically clear that public opinion had turned toward war. On the previous day, even sermons in Washington's pulpits reflected this. The rector of the Church of the Epiphany declared that war with Germany would be "a holy war." In the Vermont Avenue Christian Church, a speaker said that "if we stand idly by . . . we are a lot of fat-frying, profit-taking cowards." In the McKinley Memorial Colored Baptist Church, the minister promised, "We will be loyal to the Stars and Stripes."

By Wilson's side for most of the day was his closest adviser, Colonel Edward House. With his elegant three-piece suit and trim, dignified white mustache, the dapper House had no official title. Even the "colonel" was an honorific, bestowed on him by a governor of his native Texas. The title was at odds with his appearance, which was anything but military: he was shorter than the president, extremely thin, and had a voice barely louder than a whisper. Sensitive to cold, he often sat with a blanket over his knees. Although a wealthy investor, House had discovered that his real love was politics—not talking to voters, but quietly making deals, managing campaigns, and advising where to dispense patronage, while always remaining backstage. "Take my word for it," a US senator once said of him, "he can walk on dead leaves and make no more noise than a tiger."

When Texas came to feel too small to House, he moved his family to New York. In 1911, he met Wilson, then the governor of New Jersey. The two hit it off and, by the time Wilson was elected president on the Democratic ticket the following year, House was operating on the national political stage. He shrewdly declined an offer of a cabinet post; with no managerial distractions, he could devote himself fully to whispering in the president's ear and to doing just the kind of quiet, behind-the-scenes horse-trading with members of Congress that the Olympian and intellectual Wilson considered beneath him.

The bald, diminutive House, with his soft voice and receding chin, appeared the most self-effacing of men, but he wielded enormous influence. Sometimes the president even came to New York to consult him, staying in the colonel's apartment and taking drives out of the city with him, followed by carloads of Secret Service men and reporters. "It was House who had picked him out, shaped him as a politician, built the altar for him and placed him there above it to be worshipped," later wrote British prime minister David Lloyd George.

In Wilson's ten-man cabinet, House won positions for five friends. When he and the president were in different cities, they communicated in a code all their own, although it would not have been hard to break: the secretaries of war and of the navy, for instance, were "Mars" and "Neptune." "My dear friend," Wilson told House only a few weeks after the two first met, "We have known one another always."

Although Edith Wilson resented her husband's close attachment to House, the president had great faith in the colonel. After the war began, he sent him on two long trips to Europe to consult with monarchs and prime ministers on both sides and gauge the chances of stopping the bloodshed. The two of them were both ardent Anglophiles, but at this point Wilson was still playing the role of the neutral leader, above the fray.

Both House and Wilson had long felt that the path to putting the president's stamp on history led through the war now under way— whether by joining the fighting, crafting the peace that ended it, or both. "This is the part I think you are destined to play in this world tragedy, and it is the noblest part that has ever come to a son of man," House had written to Wilson a year and a half earlier. Today at last, it appeared, the president would be going onstage to play that role.

House had arrived from New York just as the Wilsons were leaving for golf, but even he did not know the exact contents of the president's speech—and possibly fretted that Edith Wilson knew more than he. Cabinet members knew how close he was to the president, and during the day one of them had telephoned to ask him exactly what Wilson planned to say. But since House was reluctant to reveal his ignorance, he merely said of the speech that "I thought it would meet every expectation." Later, back from golf, the president read his text aloud to House. The colonel pronounced it a masterpiece. In his quiet voice, he made only one suggestion, that Wilson delete a reference to not negotiating with Germany "until the German people have a government we can trust," since this seemed to be urging Germans to stage a revolution, much too radical an idea. Wilson agreed.

As the two men talked, waiting for word on when Congress would be ready, feelings throughout the country over the prospect of war continued to mount. Civil War and Spanish-American War veterans addressed patriotic rallies, while Socialist Party orators decried the spilling of workers' blood in a war among capitalist powers. Three days earlier, a meeting in Berkeley of 136 professors at the University of California had turned into an angry dispute. Most favored war, but a vocal minority of 21 did not, and telegrams from the two rival factions added to the overflowing piles of messages at the White House.

These tensions were visible that very afternoon on the rain-drenched streets of Washington. Pouring into Union Station were trains carrying pacifists coming to demonstrate against war. Also arriving, brandishing thousands of American flags, were trains full of "Pilgrims for Patriotism," a hastily organized group whose moving spirits included the combative Theodore Roosevelt, who as president had doubled the size of the US Navy and sent its "Great White Fleet" steaming around the world in a show of American might. Exasperated with Wilson, Roosevelt had written to his friend Massachusetts senator Henry Cabot Lodge a few weeks earlier, saying, "If he does not go to war with Germany I shall skin him alive."

The day's most notable clash occurred when a group of pacifists visited Lodge, an acerbic Boston Brahmin with a white beard. Lodge was an enthusiastic proponent of war who thought Wilson weak-willed, snorting contemptuously at the president's call for "peace without victory" of a few months earlier. When the senator stepped into the hallway outside his office to meet the pacifist delegation, its spokesman, Alexander Bannwart, a former minor-league baseball player, attacked Lodge's enthusiasm for war.

The senator was furious. "National degeneracy and cowardice are worse than war!" he told Bannwart, who retorted, "Anyone who wants to go to war is a coward! You're a damned coward!" This was too much for the 67-year-old Lodge, who shouted, "You're a damned liar!" and punched Bannwart, 36, to the floor. Bannwart fought back, slamming Lodge against a closed door. Office workers, police, and even a passing Western Union messenger joined the melee in defense of the senator. Lodge triumphantly yelled, "I'm glad I hit him first!" but it was the bloodied Bannwart whom the police hauled away in a paddy wagon.

The other unusual event in Congress that afternoon was the seating of its first woman. The United States was still several years away from ratifying the constitutional amendment that would allow all women to vote, but women could do so in many states, including Montana, where voters had just elected the pacifist social worker Jeannette Rankin to the House of Representatives. Her colleagues greeted her with a standing ovation as she entered the chamber carrying a bouquet of yellow and purple flowers from fellow suffragists. Despite their quickness to line up and shake her hand, most of Rankin's fellow representatives were eager for war. And so was the House chaplain, who opened the session with a prayer: "God of the Ages. . . . We abhor war and love peace. But if war has been, or shall be forced upon us, we pray that the heart of every American citizen shall throb with patriotic zeal."

WORD CAME THAT Congress would be ready to hear the president at 8:30 p.m. After a quick dinner, the Wilsons, several visiting family members, and Colonel House departed for the Capitol, along with the ever-present duo of Tumulty and Dr. Grayson. As they were chauffeured out the White House gate, more than a thousand prowar demonstrators sang "The Star-Spangled Banner" and, in homage to the first southerner elected president since the Civil War, "Dixie." As darkness fell, the gusty rain grew harder and lightning flashed. Even so, men and women lined the brightly lit Pennsylvania Avenue, hoping to catch a glimpse of the black presidential Pierce-Arrow limousine with its distinctive long hood. They waited in vain, for the Secret Service routed it along side streets.

All afternoon people had been trying to wangle a place in the visitors' galleries of the House of Representatives to hear Wilson's speech. The flag-topped Capitol dome was majestically lit to a brilliant white against the dark sky by a brand-new array of 119 400-watt floodlights, their beams cutting through rain and mist. Soldiers, Secret Service agents, and uniformed and plainclothes police officers were on guard, some on roofs. Through the windows of his limousine, the president could see cavalrymen in dress uniforms, with drawn sabers that glittered under the lights, protecting the entrance to the Capitol. They were thoroughly soaked after riding into the city from their base in Virginia.

In the House chamber, members were at their places in the semi-circular array of desks. On chairs beneath the rostrum sat the nine justices of the Supreme Court, several of whom Wilson had chosen, most notably Louis Brandeis. The first Jew to serve on the court, he was an outspoken friend of labor and opponent of trusts and monopolies. Business interests had waged a bitter fight against his appointment, resorting to anti-Semitism.

Brandeis was the president's boldest choice for any position, and his very presence in the House chamber that night was a reminder that Wilson had been elected first governor and then president as a reformer. He was, in fact, the last president of the Progressive Era, the two decades or so when many American leaders in both major parties promised solutions—some meaningful, some not—to the vast chasm between rich and poor created by the country's rapid industrialization. Progressives wanted to remake a nation where some lived in grand mansions but far too many in tenements where half a dozen people might share a single room. In the few years ahead, several notable progressives now in the Wilson administration would resign in despair; one would use his position brilliantly to defy the jingoism around him; and Brandeis would find himself in key dissents from the conservative majority of his Supreme Court colleagues.

Filling the seats immediately behind the justices came the members of the other chamber, the United States Senate. As they filed into the room, all but a handful of senators carried or wore on their breast pockets small American flags. Senator Lodge's face was slightly swollen from the exchange of punches earlier in the day. Leading the senators was the vice president, Thomas Marshall. An easygoing Indiana politician, he was considered by Wilson "a small-calibre man." Finding his opinions ignored, Marshall did not even attend the twice-a-week cabinet meetings. A family once had two sons, he liked to tell people. One of them was lost at sea, the other became vice president. Neither was ever heard from again.

To one side of the chamber were the members of Wilson's cabinet, and behind them, in an almost unprecedented appearance on the floor of Congress that signaled the importance of the evening's speech, diplomats from around the world in formal evening dress. At 8:30 p.m., the clatter of cavalry hoofs clearing a path through the crowd outside heralded Wilson's arrival.

The president's august, solemn figure then disappeared from public view for a few minutes. A journalist followed him into a small room high in the Capitol. "He walked to a little fireplace over which hung a large mirror. In it was the reflection of a face which Dante might have borrowed. The features were twisted with pain . . . the flesh deeply drawn and flushed. He placed his left elbow on the mantel and looked steadfastly . . . at his distorted countenance in the glass. . . . Then the President raised his hands, the left to his brow, the right to his chin, violently moulding it into place and smoothing the deep corrugations of his forehead. . . . Then he turned and strode into the hallway leading to the House of Representatives."

THE NINE JUSTICES rose to lead a deafening two-minute ovation. "Never had he been greeted as he was tonight," reported the Associated Press. "The public galleries were crowded to suffocation," remembered one cabinet member, "while people sat on the steps and stood in the doorways." In the gallery's front row sat Edith Wilson. The president briefly glanced up and seemed to catch his wife's eyes. Also with the White House party in the gallery was a bright, ambitious young official who, though relatively junior in rank, was adroit at getting himself included in the presidential entourage on occasions like this, the assistant secretary of the navy, Franklin D. Roosevelt.

No one who had come to hear Wilson could forget that he was the first president to earn a doctorate and to head a major university. He had spent decades as a college professor—in an age when someone in that role was not a performer struggling to draw students' attention away from their cell phones, but a source of moral authority, like a member of the clergy. One observer described him as he now stood before Congress: "His pale, immobile face, his protruding chin, his long thin nose firmly supporting eyeglasses, his carefully brushed hair, his slender figure seemingly elongated by a close-fitting frock coat, his dark gray trousers painstakingly creased, his ease, the manner of one conscious of his commanding place and of the importance of what others were now to hear from his lips;—yes, he was the schoolmaster from head to foot."

As the cheering died away, Wilson began speaking. His voice had a tremor, and the Supreme Court justices sitting close below him could see his hands shake slightly as he turned the pages of his text. "I have called the Congress into extraordinary session," he began, "because there are serious, very serious, choices of policy to be made, and made immediately."

Those listening could hear the occasional broad vowels—in Wilson's voice "might" sometimes sounded like "m-ah-t"—of a southerner. Paradoxically, that was as deep a part of him, perhaps deeper, than his identity as a progressive. He had been born in Virginia, to a minister father who preached that the Bible sanctified slavery. By the time he was two, his father had become pastor of a congregation in Augusta, Georgia, where he would serve as a chaplain to Confederate troops and convert his church into a hospital for their wounded. When Wilson was eight, his entire appalled family watched as Union soldiers led Jefferson Davis, president of the defeated Confederacy, through the streets of Augusta on his way to prison.

The family was dismayed by Reconstruction's promise of full citizenship to Black Americans. "Universal suffrage is at the foundation of every evil in this country," Wilson wrote in his diary as a young man. Even as a historian and president of Princeton, he took a startlingly benign view of slavery, asserting, for instance, "Slavery itself was not so dark a thing as it was painted. . . . The domestic slaves, at any rate, and almost all who were much under the master's eye, were happy and well cared for." After being elected president, he once paid a visit to Stratford Hall, the plantation house where General Robert E. Lee was born, and he told "darky stories" about naive Blacks to the fellow white southerners of his cabinet.

This Wilson was in stark contrast to the man who saw himself as an idealistic reformer—and who actually did things like appointing the crusading trustbuster Brandeis to the Supreme Court. Still, he was always most comfortable among the southern accents of people like Colonel House of Texas, Dr. Grayson of Virginia, and both of his wives—the first from Georgia, the second, Edith, from Virginia, where her grandparents had owned a slave plantation.

As Wilson's speech continued, he methodically reviewed the German U-boat attacks on US ships, ignoring, like most Americans, the arms and strategic supplies these "neutral" vessels were carrying to Germany's enemies. The torpedoing of such ships, he sternly declared, was beyond "all restraints of law or of humanity." His rapt listeners did not interrupt him until he said, "There is one choice we cannot make, we are incapable of making: we will not choose the path of submission. . . ."

"There was more of the sentence," reported the *New York Times*, "but Congress neither knew it nor would have waited to hear if it had known. Chief Justice White, with an expression of joy and thankfulness on his face . . . raised his hands high in the air, and brought them together with a heartfelt bang; and House, Senate, and galleries followed him with a roar like a storm. It was a cheer so deep and so intense and so much from the heart that it sounded like a shouted prayer." From this moment on, Wilson's voice grew firmer and stronger.

The stout, jowly Edward Douglass White of Louisiana had grown up on his family's sugar plantation and been cared for by enslaved servants. As a teenager, he had fought for the Confederate cause and been taken prisoner by Union troops. A staunch right-winger on every issue from segregation to the rights of labor, the chief justice was no admirer of Wilson's progressive side. Yet the president's call for war stirred him deeply. Was it the memory of his youth on Civil War battlefields? Was it the prospect, in this new war, of now at last being on the winning side? We can only guess. At the word "submission," the secretary of agriculture, who was sitting close to him, wrote of White, "He was on his feet instantly leading the Supreme Court and the entire assembly. His face . . . worked almost convulsively and great tears began to roll down his cheeks."

IF THERE WAS a single moment that epitomized the frenzy unleashed in these years, it was when the chief justice of the United States leapt to his feet and wept tears of joy at the certainty of war. That frenzy would only grow as time passed. More cheers interrupted the president as he continued. At one point, the French ambassador, thrilled at the prospect of such a mighty country coming to France's aid, turned and embraced the nearest American, the secretary of commerce, who was sitting next to him.

Going to war would, of course, require a massive reorientation of the US economy, producing billions of dollars' worth of manufacturing contracts. Wilson skipped over this in a few sentences. But we can be reasonably sure that among the visitors influential enough to have wangled passes to the gallery above him were at least a few of the Chamber of Commerce officials from around the country who had come to Washington for a special meeting, according to a passing mention in a newspaper, to discuss "how they could be of national service in this time of peril." They knew how much benefit the economy was already reaping as the warring powers across the Atlantic spent themselves deep into debt and the United States became the world's creditor. Already, in a 1915 speech, a J. P. Morgan partner had enthusiastically anticipated the day when the dollar would replace the British pound as the world's benchmark currency.

As Wilson went on, his voice now stronger, buoyed by the cheering, it became clear that he was calling for a war effort without limits and with a draft, for he proposed to raise an army "chosen upon the principle of universal liability to service." This massive body of men would be fighting, he said, "for the ultimate peace of the world and for the liberation of its peoples." Then he spoke the words that would in his mind define the next few years: "The world must be made safe for democracy."

"This sentence might have passed without applause," noted the *Times*, "but Senator John Sharp Williams was one man who instantly seized the full and immense meaning of it. Alone he began to applaud . . . and one after another followed his lead until the whole host broke forth in a great uproar." Williams, of Mississippi, like Chief Justice White, had grown up on a plantation. This was a curious point for him to lead the cheering, because more than 50 percent of his state's population enjoyed no democracy. They were Black, and almost all of them were not allowed to vote. There had been 50 recorded lynchings of Black Americans the previous year, and over a 60-year period, Mississippi would have the highest per capita rate of lynchings in the country. Wilson was a leading figure of the Progressive Era when it came to the eight-hour day, child labor, regulation of business, and the graduated income tax, but Williams knew there was no danger of his wanting to make the Deep South safe for democracy.

As Wilson continued, it was in the tone of voice that presidents would use for a century to come: "We have no selfish ends to serve. We desire no conquest, no dominion. . . . We fight without rancor and without selfish object, seeking nothing for ourselves." The United States was built on land bloodily wrested from its native inhabitants, some of it within his own lifetime, but Wilson's image of his country as a shining example of selflessness had deep appeal to Americans who have always wanted to believe there was something uniquely virtuous about their country. Seldom would any later president depart from such rhetoric.

Wilson, however, did not share with his audience information that would have revealed less righteous-sounding motives for going to war. Only a month earlier, his ambassador to London had telegraphed Washington a warning that if the country did not enter the conflict, not only might the Allies collapse, but with them any chance that Americans who had bought British and French war bonds would ever get their money back. By this point Britain alone owed the United States more than $2.7 billion—as a percentage of US gross domestic product, equal to roughly a trillion dollars a century later.

In Europe, the ambassador reported, conditions were "most alarming to the American financial and industrial outlook." Britain and France were running out of gold to pay for the American supplies and munitions they bought, risking "almost a cessation of transatlantic trade. This will, of course, cause a panic [a recession] in the United States." Huge new credits to the Allies from Washington would be needed to avert this, but "unless we go to war with Germany our Government of course cannot make such a direct grant of credit. . . . Perhaps our going to war is the only way in which our present preeminent trade position can be maintained and a panic averted."

Everyone listening to the president in the House chamber that evening knew the nation he led was an uneasy melting pot whose ingredients were far from melted. Roughly 14 percent of the population were foreign-born and many more had immigrant parents. On the president's mind at the moment were "the millions of men and women of German birth and native sympathy who live amongst us." He assured his audience that "they are, most of them . . . true and loyal Americans." This drew a cheer, but, significantly, a far larger one accompanied what followed. "A particularly vociferous outburst greeted the declaration," reported the Associated Press, that "'if there should be disloyalty, it will be dealt with with a firm hand of stern repression.'"

WILSON BROUGHT HIS 36-minute address to a close by again painting the war in highly moral colors: "There are, it may be, many months of fiery trial and sacrifice ahead of us. . . . Civilization itself seeming to be in the balance. But the right is more precious than peace. . . . America is privileged to spend her blood and her might for the principles that gave her birth." He finished with a flourish that would have pleased his father and grandfather, Presbyterian ministers both. "God helping her, she can do no other." (Not lost on devout listeners was the echo of Martin Luther's famous refusal to recant his beliefs: "Here I stand; God helping me, I can do no other.")

From the House floor to the farthest reaches of the galleries, said the *Times*, the audience "cheered him as he has never been cheered in the Capitol in his life." Chief Justice White was "pounding the arm of his chair like a boy at a football match," wrote another journalist. Even the man who never had a kind word for Wilson, the irascible Henry Cabot Lodge, came up and warmly shook his hand.

Some, however, did not join the cheering. Wisconsin's Robert "Fighting Bob" La Follette, the strongest progressive voice in the Senate, had already spoken out about how going to war would stifle his and others' long crusade for the rights of workers, Blacks, and the poor. "Bob, they'll crucify you," a labor leader friend had warned. A series of cartoons pillorying him had already appeared in the New York *World*, one showing a German mailed fist pinning an Iron Cross on the senator's lapel. (Decades later, the cartoonist would apologize to La Follette's children.)

At five feet, five inches, La Follette was one the shortest US senators. But he made up for it with a distinctive upswept forelock that gave him the highest head of hair among them; a hat with an unusually tall crown protected it when he was outdoors. Now, as Wilson slowly made his way out of the chamber, receiving congratulations, La Follette was conspicuous in a different way. He stood silently amid those applauding, arms crossed, chewing gum.

As the presidential party returned to the White House, it passed streetcars on tracks, black Model T Fords with cloth roofs, and rain-slicked sidewalks that would soon be filled with newsboys shouting "Extra! Extra!" Telegraph operators' keys clicked furiously as tens of thousands of words flooded wires from Washington to newsrooms all over the country and across the Atlantic. For the next morning's *New York Herald*, an artist drew an image of a stern and resolute Uncle Sam confronting the kaiser, the monarch's sword dripping blood and his jackbooted foot on the back of a bleeding woman representing Europe.

When the news of Wilson's call for war reached New York's Metropolitan Opera House after the second act of *The Canterbury Pilgrims*, cheers exploded and the orchestra broke into "The Star-Spangled Banner." When the third act finally began, Margarethe Arndt-Ober, the contralto singing the role of the Wife of Bath, collapsed on her back in a dead faint, hitting the stage with an audible thump. She was German and would shortly be fired by the Metropolitan.

Back in the White House, there took place, it is said, another scene that has made its way into dozens of histories and biographies. Wilson was silent on his limousine ride home from the Capitol, but then he supposedly sat for some time with his faithful secretary, Joe Tumulty, in the Cabinet Room. "Think what it was they were applauding," the pale and exhausted president told him. "My message today was a message of death for our young men. How strange it seems to applaud that." They talked for much longer, until finally, Tumulty declared, "the President drew his handkerchief from his pocket, wiped away great tears that stood in his eyes, and then laying his head on the Cabinet table, sobbed as if he had been a child."

A poignant picture. But the memoirs of neither Colonel House nor Mrs. Wilson record anything about the president going off with Tumulty. House, subtly emphasizing his own closeness to Wilson, says that the two of them and the president's wife and daughter gathered upstairs in the White House after the speech "and talked it over as families are prone to do after some eventful occasion." The only person to mention Wilson's sobbing was Tumulty. Like many people in later years, he was eager to stress how constantly he had been at the side of the noble president. But even though they worked in adjoining offices, the highly formal Wilson usually communicated with Tumulty by written notes.

Furthermore, Tumulty was on shaky ground at that moment. Several months previously, Wilson had asked him to resign and take a lesser position outside the presidential orbit. Both House and the easily jealous Edith Wilson, who considered Tumulty "common," were wary of the power wielded by this lowly Jersey City Irish Catholic from a family of 11 children. Wilson had relented only when Tumulty begged to remain in his job and a mutual friend had lobbied on his behalf. With all this having just happened, he was an unlikely confidant for the president to leave his family for a long, confessional talk with, at the massive table in the Cabinet Room.

Behind the reserved and even haughty face he showed to the public, Wilson was indeed a man capable of strong emotions. Eloquent, deeply felt letters testify to his love for each of his wives and his three daughters, and after the First World War was over, he was clearly shaken when he visited military hospital wards filled with the maimed men he had sent into battle. But this was still two years off. The coming months would indeed be filled with pain and tragedy. The part of it that happened on the battlefields of Europe, Wilson would take to heart. About the suffering that would occur inside the United States he would remain, to all appearances, unmoved.

Place a Gun upon His Shoulder

A T I:I5 P.M. on April 6, 1917, four days after Wilson's address to Congress, the president's 35-year-old naval aide, Byron Mc-Candless, grabbed two short-handled semaphore signaling flags, rushed outside the White House, and began sending a message. Across the street sat a grand edifice topped by a wedding cake roof with skylights and rotundas of stained glass. Today the Eisenhower Executive Office Building, it was then the State, War, and Navy Building and at one of its windows a fellow officer was waiting. He watched the flags spell out W-A-R. Then he ran down a hallway to give the news to waiting radio and telegraph operators, who rapidly tapped in Morse code to relay word to navy bases and ships at sea. The Senate and House of Representatives had voted for war as Wilson had asked and the president had just signed the resolution Congress had sent him.

Of course, McCandless could have as easily picked up a telephone to relay the news—the White House was equipped with the latest models, from which you took an earphone off a hook while speaking into a mouthpiece on a foot-high stand. But the two high-spirited young men, Naval Academy classmates, deliberately celebrated this moment in a way resonant with maritime tradition. And celebration was the spirit in which most Americans marked their country's entry, at last, into the greatest war the world had yet seen.

For several years, they had watched newsreels of British and French soldiers charging enemy trenches (always gaining ground, never losing it) and fighter pilots dueling in the skies. The combat looked glamorous, not deadly, and nobody stopped to wonder if the film had been shot at the front or far behind the lines. Now young men rushed to army, navy, and marine corps recruiting offices. In Chicago alone, nearly 600 signed up in a single day. In Kansas City, Missouri, a 33-year-old former National Guardsman named Harry S. Truman reenlisted in his artillery unit. A cartoon in the *Brooklyn Daily Eagle* showed a soldier in a broad-brimmed hat, his hand on a huge cannon labeled "America," in a line of other cannons with the names of France, England, Russia, Italy, and Belgium, all defending a high bluff labeled "Democracy."

One evening later that month, as church bells chimed midnight in New York, a young woman on horseback dressed in the uniform of George Washington's Continental army galloped down brightly lit Broadway from Times Square to 34th Street, reenacting the ride of Paul Revere. She was followed by two cars of trumpeters, calling on young men to enlist. Soon the city's Union Square became the site of a navy recruiting station in the shape of a 200-foot-long battleship, the USS *Recruit*, complete with wooden gun turrets, a smokestack, film showings, and a 36-piece band on deck playing John Philip Sousa marches.

People across the county began singing a new tune whose chorus ran:

> *America, I raised a boy for you.*
> *America, you'll find him staunch and true,*
> *Place a gun upon his shoulder,*
> *He is ready to die or do.*
> *America, he is my only one; My hope, my pride and joy,*
> *But if I had another, he would march beside his brother;*
> *America, here's my boy.*

Fervor spread through communities large and small. "The hopes of Missoula county high school for a victory in the interscholastic track meet have dropped," reported a Montana newspaper on April 11, "as several of the track squad have announced their intentions of leaving school in order to enlist."

When the New York Yankees played the opening game of their 1917 season, they marched out of their clubhouse in military formation, bats on their shoulders like rifles. On hand to toss out the first ball was Major General Leonard Wood, one of the country's best-known soldiers, with a mustache, bushy eyebrows, and a fierce, blue-eyed gaze that fit the part. In a legendary campaign in the twilight of the Indian Wars, he had won the Congressional Medal of Honor by walking and riding more than 4,000 miles, some of it back and forth across the Mexican border, enduring a tarantula bite and broiling heat, to help track down and accept the surrender of the defiant Apache chief Geronimo.

Some years later, Wood's close friend Theodore Roosevelt, who shared his belief that battle was good for the soul, was under Wood's command in the storied Rough Riders cavalry in the Spanish-American War. The unit's exploits were brief—its famous charge up a Cuban hill lasted less than an hour—but were embellished to a triumphal glow by the friendly war correspondents whom both men skillfully cultivated. Wood later served as military governor of Cuba and then presided over a notoriously bloody campaign against Islamic rebels resisting American rule in the Philippines. Like Roosevelt, he had been eager for the United States to enter the war in Europe and was exasperated that it had hesitated so long. As the baseball crowd in New York cheered him, he was anticipating the chance to again command soldiers in combat. He surely never imagined that two years later the people he would be leading troops against would be his own.

IT IS CURIOUS, this explosion of martial ferocity. After all, no one had attacked the United States. Nothing had happened that resembled the German invasion of Belgium three years earlier, or the Japanese attack on Pearl Harbor a quarter century later that would draw America into the next world war. The small number of Americans killed by German submarines had voluntarily been passengers or sailors on ships—

almost all of which carried munitions—in the waters of a war zone where they knew they would be at risk. Germany had even bought advertisements in dozens of American newspapers warning people not to travel on the most famous of these ships, the *Lusitania*. Yet across the land people were thrilled by the idea that the country was somehow defending itself.

In keeping with the pretense that the United States was an innocent victim drawn into the conflict against its will, Wilson had asked the Senate and House not exactly to declare war on Germany, but to declare that the United States "formally accept the status of belligerent which has . . . been thrust upon it" by the German submarine attacks. Congress complied, its war resolution echoing Wilson's "thrust upon."

But if anyone had thrust war upon the country, it was the United States itself, by becoming a bastion of the British and French military effort. Allied purchases had made American industry boom, putting millions of unemployed people to work, igniting an unbroken economic expansion that would last nearly four years, increasing the gross national product by more than 25 percent, and rescuing the nation from a 1914 recession so severe that the New York Stock Exchange had shut down for four months. Wilson was fully aware of this, for, like almost all twentieth-century American presidents, he had plenty of ties to Wall Street and the corporate world. Treasury Secretary William G. McAdoo (who was also the president's son-in-law), for instance, was a former railroad president, and Cleveland Dodge, a lifelong friend, adviser, and heavy campaign contributor, was vice president of the giant Phelps, Dodge mining empire and a director of the National City Bank and the Winchester Repeating Arms Company.

Thanks to the war, assembly lines had been moving again for several years now, and American shipyards were running at full capacity. The Allies had 1,600 purchasing agents stationed in the United States. Mostly British, some were posted in American factories making sure machine guns, artillery shells, more than 400,000 rifles, and other arms all met standards. By the time the United States entered the war, the British government was spending 40 percent of its military budget in

America. Socialist Party leaders and other critics spoke out strongly against these arms sales, but with little impact. As would be the case for more than a century to come, military spending produced jobs and profits. "Let 'em shoot!" the *Nashville Banner* remarked in 1915. "It makes good business for us!"

Still, despite the patriotic fever that now swept the county, the debate in Congress over going to war had not been without dissent. It cut across party lines, for both the Democrats and Republicans of this era had progressive and conservative wings. Six senators, representing both parties, had voted against declaring war, "six men with nerve straining to hold back a crazy steamroller with their bare hands," the novelist John Dos Passos later called them.

The most outspoken of the six was Robert La Follette, the man who had stood with his arms crossed, chewing gum, after Wilson's April 2 speech. For his opposition, he had been compared to Judas Iscariot and Benedict Arnold in a public lecture in New York, and had seen himself burned in effigy in Massachusetts. In a passionate, three-hour speech to the Senate, he was particularly outraged by Wilson's claim that this was "a war upon a government only"—because, La Follette pointed out, the Allied naval blockade prevented Germany and Austria-Hungary from importing medicine and food. "There are no words strong enough," he said, "to voice my protest. . . . If we are to enter upon this war . . . let us throw pretense to the winds, let us be honest, let us admit that this is a ruthless war against not only Germany's army and her navy but against her civilian population."

And, he asked pointedly, if this was a war for democracy, why was it that "the President has not suggested that we make our support of Great Britain conditional to her granting home rule to Ireland, or Egypt, or India?" He accused Wilson of hypocrisy for treating Germany's submarine attacks as a great evil while making conspicuously little protest against Britain's sowing the North Sea with mines to cut off shipping to Germany. A friend in the Senate press gallery watched La Follette speak "to an audience that dwindled when senator after senator rose from his seat and vanished. . . . At the end of his speech . . . he stood in silence, tears running down his face." His look of despair was "like that of a person who had failed to keep his child from doing itself an irreparable harm."

The accusations he had made against the president were nothing compared with those then hurled against La Follette by Mississippi senator John Sharp Williams, the man who had led the cheering when Wilson swore to "make the world safe for democracy." His voice rising to a shout, Williams called La Follette "pro-German, pretty nearly pro-Goth, and pro-Vandal . . . and anti-American." The senator's speech, Williams said, would be better given in the German Reichstag.

As La Follette walked from the Senate chamber to his office after casting his vote, a spectator handed him a rope. Soon he began receiving nooses in the mail, which he wryly showed off to visitors. Protestors burned him in effigy again, this time in Texas, and hanged him in effigy at his alma mater, the University of Wisconsin. All but two of that campus's faculty members signed a petition denouncing him. The university's president, a college classmate and once a friend, called his ideas "dangerous to the country." One of his cousins changed his last name, ashamed of being a La Follette. Theodore Roosevelt called him "a shadow Hun." A cartoon showed the senator, with his distinctive forelock, putting a German helmet on a woman's figure labeled "Wisconsin." The year and a half to come would plunge him into deep despair.

IN THE HOUSE OF REPRESENTATIVES, the vote for war, again not divided on party lines, was 373 to 50. One of the 50 was Jeannette Rankin, the sole woman member. She had been lobbied fiercely by rival factions of the suffrage movement, one of them pacifist, the other eager to show that women could be as war minded as men. "I want to stand by my country," she said in the end, "but I cannot vote for war."

As soon as Congress voted, the administration began putting the United States on a war footing. Newsreel photographers cranked their bulky cameras atop tripods as President Wilson received a succession of cabinet ministers, generals, and special envoys from Britain, France, and the other Allied powers. Members of these delegations also spoke to Congress and to the Army War College, visited West Point, placed wreaths on the graves of Washington and Lincoln, and everywhere pleaded for the United States to send troops to Europe, lots of them, soon. Americans began to realize that the Allied military situation was not as rosy as they had thought.

Since the draft would take hundreds of thousands of young men away from their work on farms, the government urged patriotic citizens to grow "victory gardens." These appeared in backyards, on porches, on rooftops, and even along the banks of the Potomac River where it ran past Washington. The YMCA opened canteens and recreation centers for soldiers. Women began knitting, eventually producing 22 million socks, sweaters, and other items for hospitals and another 16.5 million for soldiers and refugees. The press labeled those who failed to pick up their knitting needles as "slackers in petticoats."

To increase the food it planned to ship overseas, the administration called for women to be "kitchen soldiers" and to ensure that their families had at least one "meatless" meal a day, and a "sweetless" and a "wheatless" day each week. The food saved would go to Europe. This gave rise to a poem that appeared in newspapers around the country, which began:

My Tuesdays are meatless,
My Wednesdays are sweetless,
I'm getting more eatless each day.
My home, it is heatless,
My bed, it is sheetless,
They're all sent to the Y. M. C. A.

Daylight Saving Time was born, to decrease the need for electricity. Edith Wilson, in a blue-and-white uniform and apron, volunteered to serve coffee and sandwiches to soldiers passing through a Washington railroad depot, her effervescent good cheer making for admiring news stories. She also supervised a flock of sheep on the presidential lawn.

The "White House wool" they produced—rolled by her and the president's daughters while he held the yarn—was auctioned off to raise $100,000 for the Red Cross.

Wilson seemed to take it for granted that an all-out mobilization for war would further empower exactly those titans of industry whom his generation of progressives had tried, for the most part rather timidly, to restrain or regulate. He abandoned those ideals with remarkable swiftness. Although enforcement of antitrust laws was anemic to begin with, he thought that pursuing it at all could disrupt the war effort, and so, as his attorney general put it, "we let the cases go to sleep until the war was over." To his navy secretary, the president said, "War means autocracy. . . . We shall be dependent upon the steel, oil and financial magnates. They will run the country."

And they did. An array of new agencies, councils, and commissions brought to powerful posts in the capital men from corporate and financial executive suites. They included several high officials of J. P. Morgan & Co., already a lynchpin of the war economy. The giant investment bank had holdings in more than a dozen major military contractors, had floated loans to Britain and France, and won the lucrative contract to be the purchasing agent for the river of war supplies flowing to those two countries, collecting a 1 percent commission on everything purchased; 2 percent on some goods. In Washington a new War Industries Board began setting priorities for the manufacture of everything from destroyers to bullets.

In its rush to increase production, the board set prices at levels that gave incentives to even the most inefficient of companies. For big corporations, this meant an unbelievable windfall. For example, between 1914 and 1918, Du Pont, which made gunpowder and much more, quadrupled its assets and increased the dividends it paid by a factor of 16. The war was also particularly lucrative for makers of the material used in almost every weapon, steel.

The American steel industry's annual return on investment would soar from 7.4 percent in 1915 to 20 percent in 1918—and even that figure understated profits hidden by various accounting tricks. The US

Steel Corporation's annual income increased more than tenfold from 1914 to 1917, and its profits eightfold. Bethlehem Steel's stock price rose 17 times over during the war; in 1917 it paid shareholders a 200 percent dividend. It didn't hurt that many officials of the War Industries Board came from the steel business.

The huge expansion of the military also created a demand for canned food for the troops, allowing four major meatpacking firms to increase their sales to 150 percent of the prewar level, while seeing their profits soar 400 percent. There was little coordination in government purchasing, and the army and navy sometimes found themselves bidding against each other for the same goods, much to the delight of suppliers.

Much profiteering like this never showed up on corporate balance sheets. When, for instance, the government tried to limit profits by buying weapons with "cost plus" contracts—a device still enriching the arms industry today—the "cost" sometimes included massive bonuses for executives or rent for facilities that the company paid to a subsidiary. When the New York Shipbuilding Company won a cost-plus contract, it doubled its president's salary. Standard Steel Car, a manufacturer of railroad cars, built a rent-free hotel for executives and employees, charging all expenses to the government. When he saw the prices of equipment for troop transports and other ships, Treasury Secretary McAdoo acidly remarked that the machinery must be made of silver rather than iron and steel.

Ever since the fighting began in 1914, wealthy Americans had been profiting from it in other ways as well. In the decades before the war, European capital had financed much of America's industrial expansion. But Europeans, now desperate to raise money for arms, had been selling those American stocks and bonds, and Americans buying them, sometimes at fire-sale prices. And with their competitors across the Atlantic disrupted by war, US companies could easily muscle in on some of their overseas business, especially with Latin America.

Most of the money for military purchases that now began to fatten corporate ledgers came from "Liberty Bonds" sold to the public. The president signed a bill authorizing the issuing of $5 billion worth of these, starting at $50 apiece. More such bond issues would follow, adding up to the largest amount of money any government had yet borrowed in history. Charlie Chaplin made a movie short in which he used an oversize mallet labeled "Liberty Bonds" to knock out the kaiser. He and other stars toured the country promoting the bonds, and nearly a third of all Americans bought at least one. A song mocked people who didn't:

> *If you're going to be a sympathetic miser*
> *You're no better than one who loves the Kaiser . . .*

The composer John Philip Sousa wrote a "Liberty Bond March," and pastors gave Liberty Bond sermons. Police in St. Louis, Missouri, allowed drivers to buy a bond instead of paying a speeding ticket. The tax deductions and other financial incentives that came with the bonds, however, benefited banks and the wealthy far more than those too poor to pay income tax. However enthusiastic Americans felt about the war effort, paying for it and profiting from it only widened the country's already severe gap between rich and poor—something that would have explosive results.

"IT IS A fearful thing," Wilson had declared in his April 2 speech, "to lead this great peaceful people into war." Across the land, the press echoed him. "The Kaiser will discover that a peaceful nation roused to anger," said the *Alaska Daily Empire*, "is a deadly enemy." In Nevada, the *Goldfield News and Weekly Tribune* spoke of how war had come to a "country at peace." Magazine covers, sermons, and speeches from small-town bandstands evoked the image of the farm boy leaving a tranquil field, or the friendly blacksmith his shop, to reluctantly go to war.

But were Americans really a "peaceful people"? One reason military feeling so quickly swept the county was that it had fought several recent wars, and their memory was fresh. Before he surrendered to Leonard Wood only 31 years earlier, Geronimo had been pursued by thousands of US troops; four years later came the notorious massacre of Lakota Indians at Wounded Knee, South Dakota, and since then the Southwest had seen more skirmishes in the Indian Wars. The Spanish-American War of 1898, with fighting in two hemispheres, brought the United States new territories scattered across the world, including the Philippines, where a much-longer and more deadly war began, against nationalists battling to prevent their islands from becoming an American colony. Although it officially ended in 1902, sporadic fighting continued for some years afterward, leaving hundreds of thousands of Filipinos dead. Veterans of these wars would play major roles in the strife that roiled the United States starting in 1917, with revealing traces of the Philippine War, in particular, running through the period like a red thread. General Wood was a veteran of all three of these conflicts.

Another set of hostilities that made it hard to call the country peaceful was violence against immigrants, or, more precisely, certain kinds of immigrants. In the nineteenth century, for instance, prominent Protestant ministers denounced "Popery," pamphlets spread tales of orgies in nunneries and priests with harems, and a Boston mob burned down a Catholic convent and school. In the 1850s, these feelings were further inflamed by the great wave of impoverished Catholic immigrants escaping the Irish potato famine. The fiercely anti-Catholic and anti-immigrant Know-Nothing movement came to life, electing hundreds of legislators, governors, and other officials. (The name was born because when asked about their initially clandestine crusade, the group's members were supposed to say, "I know nothing.")

Know-Nothing-dominated Massachusetts expelled thousands of Irish Catholics from the state. Although we normally associate voter suppression with the Jim Crow South, Know-Nothings successfully pushed New York and most of the New England states to pass laws making it harder for recent immigrants to vote. At least 22 people died in a riot started by drunken Know-Nothings in Louisville, Kentucky, in 1855, and hundreds of Catholics fled the city. "As a nation we begin by declaring that 'all men are created equal,'" Abraham Lincoln wrote to a friend a few weeks later. "When the Know-Nothings get control, it will read 'all men are created equal, except negroes, and foreigners and catholics.'"

In the 1890s there appeared a fraudulent document, *Instructions to Catholics*, supposedly from the pope, which contained a secret plan for how Rome's faithful were to seize control. An anti-Catholic weekly, *The Menace*, would eventually have a circulation of more than 1.5 million.

Nativist feeling, expressed by cartoons of sinister invaders from the East, found a new target in Chinese immigrants arriving on the West Coast. The Chinese Exclusion Act of 1882 became the first significant law restricting immigration to the United States. In 1885, a white mob massacred 28 Chinese coal miners in Rock Springs, Wyoming, burning some of them alive.

Resentment soon flamed up again, stronger than ever, as immigrants began arriving from new sources. The United States, like the 13 colonies before it, had long been dominated by Protestants whose ancestors were from Great Britain and northwestern Europe. But by 1890, most of those coming ashore at Ellis Island and other ports of entry, the women in kerchiefs, the men in fur hats or workmen's brimmed caps, were now from Italy, eastern Europe, or the Russian Empire. And they were Catholic, Eastern Orthodox, or Jewish. More than four million arrived on American shores from Italy alone in the 35 years before the First World War. By 1900, the majority of men in Manhattan over the age of 21 were foreign-born.

Many in the country's Anglo-Saxon elite were appalled by these changes, including a young college professor who wrote in 1902:

> Throughout the [nineteenth] century men of the sturdy stocks of the north of Europe had made up the main stream of foreign blood which was every year added to the vital working force of the country . . . but now there came multitudes of men of the lowest class from the south of Italy and men of the meaner sort out of Hungary and Poland, men out of the ranks where there was neither skill nor energy nor

any initiative of quick intelligence; and they came in numbers which increased from year to year, as if the countries of the south of Europe were disburdening themselves of the more sordid and hapless elements of their population.

A decade later, the writer of these words became the nation's president.

Woodrow Wilson was not against all immigrants; after all, his own mother and all four of his grandparents had been born in the British Isles. Remarkably, however, that did not stop him from claiming that he was "bred, and . . . proud to have been bred, in the old revolutionary stock which set this government up." For him and millions of others, being of British and Protestant descent felt equivalent to having ancestral entitlement to America, no matter when your ancestors actually arrived. As president, Wilson no longer found it politic to speak about "the meaner sort" of immigrants, but, significantly, those he chose for his first cabinet—all white men, of course—were without exception Anglo-Saxon Protestants.

Senator Henry Cabot Lodge might be Wilson's worst political enemy, but on this question they completely agreed. Lodge, who proudly traced his ancestry to William the Conqueror, was a member of the Immigration Restriction League and spoke in the Senate about the need to keep out the "races" he found "most alien." To people who thought this way it seemed as if aliens had taken over the streets of big cities like New York, Boston, and Chicago. Not only could half a dozen languages be heard in a few minutes, but shop signs and newspapers serving immigrant Russians, Serbs, Syrians, Armenians, and Greeks were also in "alien" alphabets.

The early 1900s brought the new fad of eugenics, which categorized people into an elaborate racial hierarchy of Teutonic, Alpine, Celtic, Mediterranean, Semitic, and other types. To make these distinctions, enthusiasts of eugenics carefully measured ears, noses, and, above all, skulls. They advocated "race improvement" by encouraging the breeding of "superior" races and restricting that of "inferior" ones—whose numbers might otherwise overwhelm us all. Eugenics infused anti-immigration campaigning with the kind of overt racism that many whites had long directed at Blacks and Native Americans, and it enabled believers to cloak their prejudices with a statistical, scientific-sounding veneer. Just before the First World War, for example, a prominent eugenicist examined a cross-section of immigrants arriving at Ellis Island and classified 80 percent of Hungarians, 79 percent of Italians, and 76 percent of Jews as "morons."

Anti-immigrant feeling continued to boil up in more violent forms. Economic stress exacerbated it, for in such times it is always tempting to find scapegoats, whether newcomers "just off the boat" threatening to take your job and do it for lower pay, or people who seem to be prospering when you're not. During a severe depression in the 1890s, for instance, there were boycotts of Catholic merchants, and mobs set fire to Jewish-owned shops and houses in Louisiana and Mississippi and stoned Jews in northern cities. In 1902, a funeral procession for a prominent rabbi on New York's Lower East Side was bombarded with garbage, jets of water from fire hoses, and scrap metal when it passed beneath the windows of a plant that made printing presses. More than 100 people were injured, but the police who arrived on the scene began clubbing the mourners rather than those who had assaulted them. "You know what boys are," the factory owner said of his employees later. "Some of them have a dislike for the Jews." Some had a dislike for many other groups as well.

Many politicians made racism central to their careers—and this was true not only of segregationist southerners. Take, for instance, Representative Albert Johnson of Washington State. On the floor of Congress, he talked openly of "wops," "bohunks," "coolies," and "Oriental off-scourings," and was obsessively well informed about the percentage of the foreign-born in his colleagues' congressional districts. A surprisingly mild-looking man with wavy hair and blue eyes behind a pince-nez, Johnson defined his political life by his hatred of immigrants—at least those not from northern Europe. Born in Illinois, he had moved to the Northwest because of its reputation as "white man's country";

he thought it had the "best citizenry in the United States" in contrast to "the great cities of the East . . . overcrowded and filling with alien people from every land and clime."

A hard-drinking newspaperman popular as an after-dinner speaker, Johnson now owned a small daily in Washington's coastal timber country, as well as a monthly, the *Home Defender*, which crusaded against free love, radicals, immigrants, and conservationists "who tremble every time a tree is cut down." His was a voice not unlike that of those who flocked to the Tea Party a century later: the voice of a white, rural, or small-town America profoundly unsettled by change, and change that seemed embodied in people who looked or sounded different.

From the moment he campaigned by train and horseback to win his first race for Congress, Johnson sat on the House Committee on Immigration and Naturalization. Although there were only a minuscule number of Japanese immigrants in his district, he had long been obsessed by them. The Japanese, he warned in one speech, are "calling for the absolute equality of the Mongolian and Aryan races." He set up "a system of codes and wigwag signals" by which his newspaper "could receive the first information as to the number of Japanese coolies arriving on each Northern Pacific packet [ship]." He would then print the figure in bold type in the day's paper. "This was the beginning of my campaign for restricted immigration."

Resentment of immigrants had been simmering for decades, but the next few years would bring it to a full boil and thrust Johnson onto the national stage. The strife over this issue was only one conflict agitating a United States that had just gone to war. Others would be laid bare soon.

MOST AMERICANS ENTHUSIASTICALLY embraced preparations for war, but some who did not now found themselves watched closely. Managing some of that watching would be an army officer making use of skills he had learned some years earlier, on the other side of the world.

The 51-year-old Major Ralph Van Deman was far from the usual picture of a dashing soldier. Tall, gray-eyed, and almost cadaverously

thin, he had a long, hawklike face and ears that seemed to jut out from
his head at right angles. In 1901, he had been stationed in Manila, in
the American war against fighters for Philippine independence. There,
Van Deman found his métier: surveillance. The military occupation authorities, who considered Filipinos primitive and inferior people who
ought to be grateful for US rule, were deeply alarmed that so many of
them wanted the Americans gone. In an old Spanish army building in a
walled quarter of the city, Van Deman was put in charge of the Bureau
of Insurgent Records.

The army had set up this unit to collect information on the elusive
enemy in what was the first, but by no means the last, American counterguerrilla war in Asia. In instructions he sent to 450 US Army officers
throughout the archipelago, Van Deman demanded that data on all
mayors, priests, and suspected guerrilla leaders be "supplied from every possible source." To keep track of suspected Filipino independence
backers, he deployed the most sophisticated information management
system of his day: file cards. Each was printed at the top "Descriptive
Card of Inhabitants" and had subheadings with spaces for an American
officer to fill in details.

One Filipino suspected of killing an American, for example, was labeled, "very ignorant and depraved." Another was "very thick with former leading insurgent officers." A priest "has a mistress," the sister of
an "insurgent." Under the "Attitude toward U.S." section of the cards,
comments range from "Apparently friendly" to "Doubtful" to "Antag-
onistic to Americanism" and "Presumably treacherous." The movement for immediate Philippine independence eventually withered
not only because of American military might but because nationalists
suspected—correctly—that their organizations had been infiltrated
and that their plans were known.

Among the dusty boxes of Van Deman's Philippine War file cards
that can be found today in the National Archives there is an eerie absence. None of them mention that American soldiers obtained much
of this information about Filipino patriots by torture. "Now, this is the
way we give them the water cure," an infantryman named A. F. Miller

explained to a Nebraska newspaper. "Lay them on their backs, a man standing on each hand and each foot, then put a round stick in the mouth and pour a pail of water in the mouth and nose, and if they don't give up pour in another pail. They swell up like toads." Photographs show Filipinos pinned to the ground and enduring this slow drowning.

The "water cure" eventually sparked some protests back home and became, all too briefly, the subject of congressional hearings in Washington. No one then anticipated that less than two decades later US soldiers would use distinct echoes of this form of torture on their fellow Americans.

The country's declaration of war in 1917 found the gaunt, lanky figure of Van Deman stuck in a desk job at the War Department, frustrated that the army did not have a high-powered intelligence agency where he could practice the surveillance he so loved. He put the idea of such an agency to the army's chief of staff, who turned him down. The war had already been going on for nearly three years, the general said, and any American intelligence gathering would take a long time to catch up to what the British and French already knew about the Germans. Germany, however, was not the enemy Van Deman had in mind.

Lobbying for his plan, he then made a risky leap over his superiors' heads, to the secretary of war, Newton Baker. He picked his go-betweens carefully. One was a mutual friend, the Washington, DC, police chief, who had breakfast at the same club as Baker every morning. The other, Van Deman later wrote in a curious memoir that obfuscates more than it reveals, was "one of the best known and respected women novelists of the United States," whom he was escorting on a tour of military bases and who, he claimed, promised to raise the issue with Baker. Just who the novelist was or whether she existed at all remains unclear, but the maneuvering was successful. In short order Baker directed Van Deman to set up a new army intelligence branch.

On a scale never seen before, the American military would now be spying—on American civilians.

The Cardinal Goes to War

F OR A NATION that had just joined a world war, the United States was startlingly unprepared. Although it had by far the planet's largest economy, its army of just over 100,000 men was smaller than Portugal's. At the beginning of 1917, this force ranked in size only 17th in the world, and the lethargic War Department had no contingency plan for training a far-larger army, much less dispatching it across the Atlantic. In the words of one military historian, the US Army was "under a small, somnolent general staff. . . . Old, drunk and stagnant, forged in the doldrums of peace. . . . Company commanders were fifty years old, and some ran through one or two bottles of whiskey a day while reminiscing about their exploits in Montana or the Philippines."

In his speech to Congress, Wilson had not explicitly promised to send American troops to Europe, but the British and French wanted just that—and urgently. However, the conscription system necessary to supply those soldiers would have to be built from scratch, as would the array of camps to train them. And even once a draft was under way, the experienced soldiers in the small existing army, drunk or sober, would mostly have to be put to work training the draftees. It would clearly be as long as a year before large numbers of Americans were fully ready for combat. Well before then, however, the war would see the country fatefully transformed.

The vast conflict that the United States was now entering was taking place on several fronts, but the one that loomed largest in American eyes, where US troops would obviously be fighting, was the line of opposing trenches that snaked across northern France and a corner of Belgium. Here was where French, British, and a few Belgian troops had halted the German invasion. And despite millions of deaths and the explosions of hundreds of millions of artillery shells, that line had budged very little since the autumn of 1914. For both sides, the machine gun and massive amounts of barbed wire had proved to be two of the best defensive weapons of all time, and no one had yet figured out a way to overcome them. It is the fighting here that has given us the classic picture of the First World War: men sheltering from shellfire in deep, muddy trenches, then climbing "over the top" to attack into a hail of deadly bullets. Some of those trench parapets British soldiers climbed over, incidentally, were made of five million cotton sandbags purchased from the United States.

The year 1917 would see more rounds of this fruitless, lethal combat. Two weeks after Wilson spoke to Congress, for example, France launched a major attack that failed spectacularly: within a few days, 30,000 French soldiers were killed and 100,000 wounded, gaining a few miles in one spot and in some places nothing at all. French troops had had enough, and a rash of mutinies—the generals preferred the term "collective indiscipline"—swept the army. Soldiers resting in reserve areas refused orders to return to the front and flaunted the red flag, symbol of revolution. One group hijacked a train and tried to drive it to Paris. Several thousand men were convicted of mutiny and 49 were shot. Not a word about these events appeared in French, British, or American newspapers.

But the line of trenches through France and Belgium was not the war's only front. Another crucial one was on the opposite side of Europe, where millions of German and Austro-Hungarian troops had advanced far into Russia. The fur-hatted Russian soldiers, ill fed, often illiterate, and led by incompetent generals, were no match for the more efficient Germans. However, to Berlin's frustration, hundreds of thousands of German troops were tied down on this vast battle line, some of it still covered with snow, which stretched all the way from the Black Sea to the Baltic.

In April 1917, just as the United States was entering the war, Germany was trying to make Russia leave it. The key to Berlin's plans was a bald, middle-aged man with intense eyes, high cheekbones, and a trim mustache and goatee, who was now traveling north across Germany in a what would enter history books as the "sealed train." He and his several dozen comrades brewed tea on a portable kerosene burner but were not allowed to leave the train, and during the few stops it made, guards prevented anyone from boarding and talking to them.

The passengers, jubilantly singing left-wing songs, were Russian revolutionaries, and their leader was Vladimir Ilych Lenin. Rebellious Russians had overthrown the creaky and tottering regime of Tsar Nicholas II the previous month, but the new Provisional Government promising democracy was weak, divided, and still intent on continuing to fight the war on the Allied side. This sprawling country had seen millions of soldiers killed, wounded, or taken prisoner and had lost an enormous swath of its most fertile land to Germany and Austria-Hungary. Russia's people were weary, its factories hit by strikes, and its army was slowly draining away in mass desertions. The fractious nation's most radical political party, the Bolsheviks, was not part of the Provisional Government—and was opposed to the war entirely. If it gained power, party officials promised, they would make peace. Many leading Bolsheviks, however, including Lenin, the dominant figure, were in exile in Switzerland.

The German high command therefore made a high-risk gamble. It arranged for Lenin and a group of his comrades to travel to Russia, via the sealed train that sped them through Germany without giving them any chance to stop and preach revolution on the way. From a German Baltic port, the group would travel on, via Sweden and Finland, by ship, train, and sleigh, to the Russian capital, Petrograd. While Bolshevik revolutionary fervor might be dangerously contagious, the Germans calculated that if Lenin gained power it would be worth the risk, because he would pull his country out of the war. This, of course, would free up hundreds of thousands of German troops to attack the Allies in France and Belgium before enough Americans could be mobilized and trained to help them.

Meanwhile, American war preparations continued. As Lenin's train brought him closer to Russia, Congress weighed a bill sent by the president, the Selective Service Act.

Robert La Follette was the Senate's most outspoken opponent of conscription. It would enable the government "to enter at will every home in our country" to seize the young and "require them, under penalty of death if they refuse, to wound and kill other young boys just like themselves." The Civil War draft had come when the country's very existence was at stake, but, he asked, what was the threat now? Blockaded Germany had no way of transporting an invasion force across the ocean.

His protests were in vain. Conscription passed, setting in motion a huge bureaucracy that required all men between ages 21 and 30 to register for the draft on June 5, 1917. Wilson, continuing to paint everything in the loftiest terms, denied that the draft *was* a draft. "It is in no sense a conscription of the unwilling," he said as he signed the new law. "It is, rather, selection from a Nation which has volunteered in mass."

But had it? Although enthusiasm for war was palpable, La Follette was not alone. Germany might be militaristic and at fault for igniting the conflict, but many leftists and liberals knew the Allied nations had imperial goals of their own. Britain and France, for example, had enormous overseas empires, to which they clearly were eager to add Germany's colonies. To some conservatives in small towns and rural areas, especially in the South and Midwest, the conflict in Europe seemed merely a quarrel among foreigners. No matter how the carnage had started, many believed, the United States should not join. The authorities worried that young men might sympathize with an anonymous poet who wrote:

I love my flag, I do, I do,
   Which floats upon the breeze.

I also love my arms and legs,
    And neck, and nose and knees.
One little shell might spoil them all
    Or give them such a twist,
They would be of no use to me;
    I guess I won't enlist.

There were no opinion polls in those days, but compulsory registration for the draft was a good proxy for how Americans felt about the war. How many men, Wilson administration officials wondered, would actually show up on June 5?

FEAR THAT DISSENTERS might resist the draft, or otherwise thwart the war effort, provided the excuse for a relentless erosion of civil liberties that Americans had long taken for granted.

Someone whose role was strengthened by the nation's bellicose mood was Ralph Van Deman, now newly promoted to lieutenant colonel. He used his mastery of army bureaucracy to make sure his new Military Intelligence operation was lavishly funded. Based in a converted apartment building in downtown Washington, it would soon swell to 282 officers, 29 sergeants, and more than 1,000 civilians. Many of the latter were volunteers: businessmen, lawyers, or retired army officers. They were thrilled to have a role too hush-hush to talk about with outsiders, shuffling paperwork stamped SECRET or CONFIDENTIAL.

Van Deman found such recruits easily because his worldview, formed in the small Ohio town where he had grown up, reflected that of millions of Americans. He saw himself as virtuously defending the traditional social order against rebels of all sorts at home and revolutionary ideologies from abroad. Deeply suspicious of immigrants, he always demanded an ethnic breakdown of any group under his surveillance.

The army was largely segregated, and at Van Deman's headquarters a "Memorandum for Colored Women Employees"—most of them typists working on the building's sixth floor—ordered them to use only the ladies' room on the first floor and no others. A Black major (something rare in the army of 1917) investigating "Negro Subversion" for Van Deman was placed in a separate building, safely distant from embarrassing encounters with white officers he outranked, who would have to salute him if they met.

Alert to possible rivals, Van Deman skillfully blocked an attempt by the army's Signal Corps to start its own domestic counterespionage operation. Before long the network of people working for him far surpassed the size of competitors like the Justice Department's Bureau of Investigation. He recruited Military Intelligence agents from Pinkerton and other private detective agencies with experience spying on labor unions. Just as when tracking rebels in the Philippines, he compiled data about American people and organizations on file cards, whose number would grow to the hundreds of thousands by the war's end.

In cities around the country, Van Deman set up half a dozen branch offices. One agent in New York became an early expert in the art of telephone tapping. With odd clicks on their calls and strangers taking notes at meetings, it did not take long for people to realize that they were under watch. When a Socialist Party activist addressed a crowd on the Boston Common in June 1917, he began, "Mr. Chairman, friends, conscripts, and secret agents . . ."

The government's actions soon moved beyond surveillance. Wars are always an excuse to restrict freedom of speech—this had occurred during the Civil War, for instance—and it happened on an ominous scale in 1917. The most damaging blow came from a new law that, amended, is still in effect today, the Espionage Act, which Congress passed in mid-June. Despite its name, it had almost nothing to do with spies. Both opponents and supporters saw it for what it was: a club to smash left-wing forces of all kinds. Congressman Albert Johnson, who hated Wobblies as much as he did immigrants, told his fellow lawmakers that the bill would be a splendid way of getting rid of these "outlaw leaders." The IWW's "whole object is to breed hatred and treason." A North Carolina senator declared that the Espionage Act was needed to prevent propaganda "urging Negroes to rise up against white people."

The act defined opposition to the war of almost any sort as criminal.

The penalties were draconian: "a fine of not more than $10,000 or imprisonment for not more than twenty years, or both." And what actions could send you to jail for 20 years? The far-reaching list was a prosecutor's dream. At risk, for instance, was anyone who "shall willfully make or convey false reports or false statements with intent to interfere with the operation of the military or naval forces of the United States." Robert La Follette was horrified. "Treason <u>cannot</u> be committed by the <u>use of language</u>," he jotted down in a note to himself. "Treason must be committed by an <u>overt act</u>."

Dismaying liberal intellectuals who had previously admired him, Wilson wanted still more. "President Wilson today renewed his efforts to put an enforced newspaper censorship section into the espionage bill," reported the Washington *Evening Star* as the act was under debate in Congress. He wrote to the chair of the House Judiciary Committee, saying, "The great majority of the newspapers of the country will observe a patriotic reticence about everything whose publication could be of injury, but in every country there are some persons in a position to do mischief." This clause of the act would be defeated, and members of Congress would promptly congratulate themselves on having preserved free speech.

However, the new law allowed censorship; it just didn't use the word. For, at a time when there was no other way to distribute publications nationally, it gave to the postmaster general the authority to declare any newspaper or magazine "unmailable." That power could not have landed in more dangerous hands.

FORMER CONGRESSMAN ALBERT Sidney Burleson of Texas had landed in Wilson's cabinet thanks to his longtime patron, Colonel House. Burleson "has been called the worst postmaster general in American history," writes the historian G. J. Meyer, "but that is unfair; he introduced parcel post and airmail and improved rural service. It is fair to say, however, that he may have been the worst *human being* ever to serve as postmaster general."

So far two features had distinguished his time in that office: his opposition to postal workers' unions, which he felt were "a menace to our government," and his zeal to reimpose segregation. Burleson was eager to undo such lapses as having white and Black workers sorting letters in the same railway mail car, or using the same restrooms ("intolerable"), or having white and Black patrons line up at the same post office window. He segregated postal lunchrooms, and in work areas ordered screens erected so that white employees would not have their view sullied by Black workers.

The southern Democrats of Wilson's administration imposed some similar restrictions elsewhere, reducing the percentage of federal workers who were Black and requiring photographs with many job applications, so a manager wouldn't hire a Black person by mistake. For Burleson, such beliefs were rooted in his background. In the year of his birth, 1863, his father testified in a legal document that he owned "over twenty negroes and over five hundred sheep." Both his father and grandfather served in the Confederate army, and in 1917 the postmaster general was seen weeping at the sight of a parade of elderly Confederate veterans. Now this arch-segregationist had suddenly become America's chief censor, with powers seldom wielded by any single government official before or since.

One scholar describes Burleson as having "a round, almost chubby face, a hook nose, gray and rather cold eyes and short side whiskers. With his conservative black suit and eccentric round-brim hat, he closely resembled an English cleric." Wilson and other cabinet members nicknamed him "the Cardinal." This formal wear, however, was often in disarray. "Burleson acted the part of a homely, uncouth politician, which he was not," wrote Treasury Secretary McAdoo. "In reality he was a gentleman of education and ability. But he had a slovenly way of dressing. His clothes were frequently rumpled and rusty. I think he intended to create the effect that he was no better than the humblest citizen." However, despite playing the common-man role, the postmaster general could not conceal a taste for luxury, for he had a coachman who transported him and his wife around town in a two-horse barouche, or open carriage.

A Secret Service agent found the Cardinal "an extremely sly gentleman. He was so astute and secretive that his left hand never knew what his right was doing." Rain or shine, he carried a black umbrella that he tapped on the floor or sidewalk while walking, for he suffered from gout but was embarrassed to reveal it by using a cane. He combed his hair forward to cover a bald patch.

Like most who had occupied the job before him, Burleson, who normally dropped in at the White House three or four times a week, helped the president he served by artfully dispensing patronage, especially the country's 56,000 positions as postmaster. He gave one Kansas senator, for example, five postmasterships to distribute in return for voting the right way on a tariff bill. But to Burleson, exercising the virtually unprecedented power to censor the nation's press was far more exciting.

In his mind, some publications were automatically suspect, such as "those offensive negro papers which constantly appeal to class and race prejudice." Within a day after the Espionage Act became law, he instructed local postmasters throughout the country to immediately send him any newspapers or magazines that looked suspicious. His corner office was on the fifth floor of the Post Office Department headquarters in Washington, the building that a hundred years later would become a magnet for favor-seeking lobbyists as the Trump International Hotel.

Burleson was on the lookout, he said, for any publications "calculated to . . . cause insubordination, disloyalty, mutiny . . . or otherwise embarrass or hamper the Government in conducting the war." What did "embarrass" mean? The postmaster general listed a broad range of possibilities, from saying "that the Government is controlled by Wall Street or munition manufacturers, or any other special interests" to "attacking improperly our allies." Improperly? He knew that sweeping, vague threats can inspire more fear, and so, when questioned by a delegation of lawyers headed by the famous defense attorney Clarence Darrow, he refused to spell things out in more detail.

The first victim of Burleson's censorship powers went almost unnoticed. It was *The Rebel*, a socialist newspaper in Hallettsville, Texas. It opposed the war, but the postmaster general's swiftness in barring it from the mail was clearly due to something else. Calling him "a notorious exploiter of his peons," the paper had exposed how Burleson had managed a Texas cotton plantation his wife inherited. First, it declared, he evicted Mexican American tenant farmers, replacing them with whites; then he leased out the land to the state, which replaced the white farmers with prisoners in striped uniforms living in tents and working under armed guards. When they didn't work hard enough, the convicts were routinely whipped.

One reason Congress so willingly gave the Cardinal the power to declare something like *The Rebel* "unmailable" was that this authority clearly would not affect mainstream daily newspapers, whose publishers wielded great political influence. These were delivered to homes by carriers or sold at newsstands. When, for instance, the chain of dailies owned by the rich and politically powerful William Randolph Hearst criticized the British Empire, which he detested, or American participation in the war, which he opposed, they were left untouched. Most of the publications that depended on the mail were foreign-language papers, journals of opinion, and Burleson's prime target, the socialist press.

In English and other languages, there were well over 100 socialist dailies, weeklies, and monthlies; three-quarters of American states were home to at least one. American socialism, however, was not unified by a rigid ideology, other than the conviction that the people, not the powerful new class of robber barons, should own and control the nation's wealth. The Socialist Party contained both radicals and moderates, who differed in their vision of the world they wanted and exactly how to get there, but were united by a commitment to working within the electoral system, by their respect for their leader, Eugene V. Debs, and by a deep belief that the new society they were striving for would be the polar opposite of the yawning inequalities of the Gilded Age.

Another crucial conviction that united the great majority of socialists was their opposition to the war. Whatever the Allies claimed to be fighting for, they felt, American lives should not be added to the millions already lost. That was what gave Burleson the excuse to go after socialist newspapers and magazines, and he did so with a vengeance, banning 15 from the mail within the first month after the Espionage Act passed and before long stifling dozens more.

His best-known target was *The Masses*, a monthly published in New York. Named after the working class that socialists were convinced would triumphantly shape the world to come, it was never actually read by the masses—its average circulation hovered around 12,000. But it managed to be one of the liveliest journals the United States has ever seen, advertising itself on its masthead as "a Magazine with a Sense of Humor and No Respect for the Respectable." A precursor to *The New Yorker*, it published a mix of political commentary, fiction, poetry, and narrative reportage, also pioneering the sort of cartoons captioned by a single line of dialogue for which that later magazine would become famous.

Its star reporter was John Reed. In his far too short life, which would be ended by typhus when he was 32, his zest for being at the center of the action, whether in jail with striking silk workers in New Jersey or in the backcounty with revolutionaries in Mexico, made him one of the finest journalists in the English-speaking world. Unlike many left-wing publications, *The Masses* published women writers and articles about women's rights, even though it could never quite decide whether prostitutes were the exploited victims of capitalism or noble proletarian heroines. A "slapdash gathering of energy, youth, hope," the critic Irving Howe later wrote, *The Masses* was "the rallying center . . . for almost everything that was then alive and irreverent in American culture."

Masses editor Max Eastman had backed Woodrow Wilson in the 1916 election because he seemed likely to keep the country out of the war, and had visited him at the White House. But that was no protection now, for there was no doubt where the magazine stood. One cartoon, for example, showed a skeleton rising out of a dark body of liquid while clasping several screaming figures in its arms, with the caption,

"Come on in, America, the Blood's Fine!" Another item that reportedly infuriated Burleson was a *Masses* drawing that showed the Liberty Bell crumbling.

The postmaster general declared the magazine's August 1917 issue "unmailable" and soon afterward revoked its second-class mailing permit entirely. Eastman and several other editors were put on trial under the Espionage Act—twice, because the first trial resulted in a hung jury. At the second, John Reed testified about how, in covering the war for *The Masses*, he had witnessed the carnage at the front line in Flanders. In no-man's-land, he told the court, "the wounded had lain out there screaming and dying in the mud." This spectacle had made a soldier start shrieking so uncontrollably that his comrades gagged him, tied his arms, "and took him back to the base hospital." Then, Reed said, he returned to New York, where "the society columns were full about . . . knitting parties, knitting socks for the soldiers." The title of his article about his visit to the front was "Knit a Straight Jacket for Your Soldier Boy." His eloquence was powerful, and the jurors voted eight to four for acquittal. But the country's best magazine was halted for good. Many more would follow.

Another of Burleson's targets was the nation's large foreign-language press. After all, many people thought, how could you even tell what manner of subversion and disloyalty was being preached right under your nose by the roughly 2,000 newspapers and magazines in dozens of languages from Slovak to Japanese, which no proper American could read? A new law soon gave the postmaster general additional powers over such publications. For any article in another language "respecting the Government of the United States, or of any nation engaged in the present war," the editor had to file a complete translation with the local postmaster. In addition to being burdensome, this guaranteed delays, for a backlog of translations awaiting approval piled up on postmasters' desks. Before any direct censorship even took place, many of these periodicals were forced to close.

The author of more than a dozen books himself, Wilson knew many writers, and they besieged him with anguished letters. When Eastman,

Reed, and another *Masses* contributor wrote him protesting censorship "as friends of yours, and knowing how dear to you is the Anglo-Saxon tradition of intellectual freedom," Wilson forwarded the letter to Burleson with a note saying, "These are very sincere men and I should like to please them." This was the president's usual style with his cabinet. As when he had been a professor critiquing students' doctoral theses, he often gave suggestions rather than orders.

Burleson replied that "the publications involved have neither been suppressed nor suspended, but particular issues of them which were unlawful have been refused transmission in the mails, as the law requires." There were a few more mild complaints from Wilson when someone he knew protested to him about censorship, but only twice did Burleson bend to the president's suggestions. On the other occasions, the postmaster general's ax continued to fall. Not only did Wilson fail to restrain him, neither did the attorney general, Thomas Gregory, a zealous enforcer of the Espionage Act. When Burleson was not at home or the office or traversing Washington in his two-horse barouche, he and Gregory, another Confederate veteran's son and a fellow Texan, were often fishing companions, angling together for bass in the Potomac.

On at least one occasion, when he had no personal tie to the editor involved, the president urged an even harder crackdown on the press. In September 1917 Wilson sent Gregory a copy of an obscure Chicago antiwar newspaper that had provoked his ire, the *People's Counselor*, asking, "I would very much like you seriously to consider whether publications like the enclosed do not form a sufficient basis for a trial for treason. . . . One conviction would probably scotch a great many snakes." Gregory saw to it that the paper's publisher was arrested and indicted.

As chilling as the outright censorship was what emerges under all such regimes, self-censorship. The editor of New York's *Jewish Daily Forward*, the country's leading Yiddish newspaper, announced in the fall of 1917 that "the paper will henceforth publish war news without comment and will not criticize the allies, in order to avoid suspension of mailing privileges." Many other editors made similar decisions without openly saying so.

Moving beyond its control over the mail, the Post Office asked the "cooperation of librarians in the matter of destroying all copies in their libraries, of books that have been declared unmailable." And it was not the only arm of government that practiced censorship. After a novel called *Men in War* by a Hungarian pacifist, Andreas Latzko, was banned from the mail on the grounds that it called the ongoing conflict a "wholesale cripple-and-corpse factory," Military Intelligence began keeping its publisher, Boni & Liveright, under surveillance to see if it was preparing to publish anything similar. The National Security League, one of the many right-wing patriot groups that flourished in this period, pressured G. P. Putnam's Sons to cease printing *War, Peace, and the Future*, by the antiwar Swedish feminist Ellen Key, and wrote to all the country's public libraries saying that the book "contains sentiments which at present are dangerous" and urging them, "with the full consent and cooperation of the publisher," to remove it from their shelves. The War Department gave the American Library Association a list of additional books to be removed.

After Burleson killed off *The Masses*, Eastman and his sister Crystal, a journalist and feminist militant, started a new magazine, *The Liberator*, with many of the same writers. They steered a more careful course and managed to avoid being shut down. That didn't, however, deter the Bureau of Investigation from sometimes simply confiscating bulk copies of *The Liberator*. If Emma Little of 1430 Kern Street, Fresno, California, wondered what had happened to a package of *Liberator*s she evidently planned to sell or distribute, Justice Department files would have revealed that Special Agent George Hudson had seized them from the Wells Fargo Express company because they "contained seditious matter."

The Bureau controlled the press in other ways as well. In a report to his superiors, the bureau chief in Erie, Pennsylvania, Henry Lenon, described how he had asked the city's papers not to print "any news relating to labor trouble, the I. W. W., or Socialist activities without consulting this Office." When tensions erupted at two war industry plants in town, owned by General Electric and the American Brake and Shoe Foundry, a Labor Department official went to hear the workers' grievances. Then he spoke frankly and critically to local reporters, saying that the two factories should improve wages and working conditions. The editor of the *Erie Daily Times* called Lenon to read him a draft of the article the paper planned to run. Lenon told him "that this story would lend encouragement to the dissatisfied and might create trouble, and requested the *Times* to 'Kill' the story." He dispatched an agent to two other Erie newspapers with the same message and summoned the Labor Department man for a chewing out. "We have every reason to believe," Lenon said in concluding his report, that the errant official "will hesitate before breaking into print in the future."

THE ESPIONAGE ACT almost entirely silenced debate in Congress about the war. Fifty-six legislators had voted against the declaration of war, and 32 against the draft. But in the first several months following passage of the act, not a single one rose in either house to question whether the country had made the right decision in joining the conflict, for a time not even Robert La Follette.

Born in a log cabin, "Fighting Bob" had always been acutely conscious of his country's gap between rich and poor, and had pushed for years to regulate powerful industries. Now, along with a few colleagues, he fought a battle, only partially successful, to pass a strong excess-profits tax so that the vast flow of money financing the war would come mostly from the rich and not from ordinary citizens pressured to buy bonds. More nooses arrived in his mail. Nicholas Murray Butler, the president of Columbia University and a fierce war hawk, declared of La Follette, "You might just as well put poison in the food of every American boy" going to war "as to permit this man to make war upon the nation in the halls of Congress."

Finally La Follette spoke out again on the Senate floor, reminding his colleagues that Daniel Webster and Abraham Lincoln had forcefully criticized the Mexican War of 1846–48. This only increased the vituperation he faced. One senator after another rose to attack him, and the Committee on Privileges and Elections began hearings into whether he should be expelled from the Senate. He then learned through reading the newspapers that he had been expelled "on the ground of unpatriotic conduct," from a club he belonged to in Wisconsin's capital, Madison. Old friends stopped speaking to him.

La Follette was one of the first targets, although by no means the last, of the rage against dissenters that in the months ahead would come flooding up everywhere, like long-contained magma surging to the surface from the vents around a volcano.

4

Enchanted by Her Beauty

OPPONENTS OF THE war like La Follette were not the only people who raised the country's political temperature. Also denouncing the government were those who accused Wilson of not leading his nation into battle aggressively enough. Chief among them was the dynamic, well-known figure who sometimes still wore his khaki Spanish-American War uniform and who vibrated with an outdoorsman's impatience for action. When he lectured, his right hand went up and down like a piston; and, wrote one journalist, "he strode along the platform with the physical power of a landslide."

It was more than eight years after Theodore Roosevelt's presidency had ended, and nearly five since he had made a failed attempt to regain the White House, but he still yearned for center stage. He was a man, one of his sons once said, who wanted to be the bride at every wedding and the corpse at every funeral. Incensed that his country had waited so long to join the conflict in Europe, he had nothing but contempt for the "professional pacifists, poltroons, and college sissies" who preferred peace to war. They were, he raged, "a whole raft of sexless creatures."

He now wanted to be called "Colonel Roosevelt," his rank in the Rough Riders, not "Mr. President." In his grand house in Oyster Bay, Long Island, he was surrounded by mementos of what he proudly called "the strenuous life": elephant tusks and eland and Cape buffalo heads from hunting in Africa, spurs and branding irons from his days as a young man ranching in the West, binoculars and saber from his short but legendary time as a cavalry hero. Lion-, tiger-, and leopard-skin rugs covered the floors, and snowshoes hung on the walls. His enthusiasm for war was of a piece with his love of manly pursuits like boxing, harpooning manta rays, climbing high peaks, and slogging through the Amazon rain forest.

War was good for the country, Roosevelt felt—for its men, that is; a woman's job was to stay home and give birth to future soldiers. He called this one the "Great Adventure," trumpeting a plan, to which he hoped the Wilson administration would agree, to organize a volunteer division. Soon the proposed force was expanded to several divisions. Leading it would be his friend Major General Leonard Wood; Roosevelt would be one of Wood's subordinate commanders, as would descendants of Civil War generals both Union and Confederate, and of French noblemen—a bow to the memory of the Marquis de Lafayette coming to fight in George Washington's Continental army. Soon the former president was receiving 2,000 applications a day from eager volunteers.

"The bald fact," writes the historian George E. Mowry, "was that Roosevelt liked war—its noise, its smoke, its action were a part of his soul. War made heroes, and Roosevelt had to be a hero. Had he been a nobody in a country village he would certainly have been a member of the volunteer fire department." All four of Roosevelt's sons, who had been through a reserve officer training course organized by Wood, quickly joined the military. Despite being nearsighted—he memorized the eye chart to pass his army physical—Quentin, the youngest, dropped out of Harvard to train as an aviator on Long Island. Enthralled by flight ever since he watched an air show as a child, he now jubilantly zoomed above his parents' home to drop flowers on the lawn.

Meanwhile, Quentin's father, desperate that at 58 he would soon be too old to fight, barraged officials with letters citing officers he would recruit for the volunteer force he so hoped to create, a list heavy on Ivy League and prep school graduates. The aging warrior lobbied friends in Congress and went to Washington to put the idea personally to President Wilson.

The new and former presidents couldn't have appeared more different: the one tall, thin, and solemn; the other rotund, stocky, and bursting with an explosive energy that seemed barely contained by the watch chain always across his waist. Wilson had defeated Roosevelt's comeback try for the presidency in 1912, and the two men loathed each other. Roosevelt privately called Wilson the "infernal skunk in the White House," whose long face was that of an "apothecary's clerk." The president fully returned the antipathy. In the relaxed privacy of family evenings, when he revealed a humorous side hidden from the public, Wilson sometimes imitated Roosevelt on the 1912 campaign trail, gesticulating wildly and shouting, "We stand at Armageddon and we battle for the Lord!"

Not surprisingly, the last thing Wilson wanted was his charismatic predecessor seizing the spotlight with a new version of the Rough Riders. After diplomatically waiting some weeks, as if considering the idea carefully, the president told Roosevelt no. The draft gave him the perfect excuse: now there was no need to recruit volunteers.

"I asked not only to go over [to France]," Roosevelt complained a few months later to a cheering crowd in Madison Square Garden, "but I came with a hundred thousand more men in my hands to help. . . . I was blackballed by the committee on admissions, but . . . I have sent over my four sons."

Long joining Roosevelt in the call for additional military muscle had been his fellow Rough Rider General Wood. The two had known each other for 20 years, and as young men had hiked, swum, skied, and played impromptu football together. The tall, burly general remained a physical fitness buff with a 44-inch chest. He boxed, fenced, and, long before the sport became popular, was a long-distance runner. For several years before the United States entered the First World War, Wood had ignored an explicit directive from President Wilson ordering army officers not to speak publicly about "the military situation in the United States or abroad." In uniform, the general gave more than 200 speeches, calling for increased arms spending and compulsory training for all young American men.

Wilson was upset by Wood's lobbying and his ties to Roosevelt. He considered the ambitious general "full of intrigue and disloyal to his superiors." The president took revenge by inflicting the worst possible punishment: he refused to send Wood to Europe.

To command the American troops who would go into battle there he chose another general, John J. Pershing—who had once been Wood's subordinate. Wood was furious, even bad-mouthing Pershing to Wilson by bringing up an old accusation: that Pershing had supposedly fathered several illegitimate children when stationed in the Philippines. But his efforts were in vain. In a play on Wilson's 1916 campaign slogan, a cartoonist once showed Roosevelt and Wood, one man saying to the other, "He kept *us* out of war."

In uniform but chafing at not being in combat, Wood at one point traveled to Kansas City with Roosevelt, where they both spoke and enjoyed a banquet and parade in their honor. Roosevelt took the occasion to again slam the peace-minded La Follette, declaring that he would be "ashamed to sit" in the Senate with him. In another speech a few days later the former president referred to La Follette and others speaking up for peace as "old women of both sexes." Wood, still smarting from being passed over by Wilson, declared that the country was badly prepared for war. As the general continued to cross the nation making speeches, people noticed that he almost acted as if he were running for office, with an eye on key constituencies. When he saw a veteran in Charleston, South Carolina, holding a Confederate flag, he remarked, "That is an honorable flag. Men have died for it."

On June 5, 1917, any fears that lingering resistance meant the United States would have trouble putting together a large-enough army vanished. This was the day all eligible young men were required to register for the draft at county courthouses and city halls across the country. Nearly ten million of them appeared.

IF ANYONE IN American life was the polar opposite of Theodore Roosevelt, it was a woman with a fireplug figure and determined chin whose skillfully modulated voice could electrify a crowd whether she spoke from a college lecture hall platform, the dock of a courtroom, or the back of a truck. As for Roosevelt, New York City was her political base, but there the similarities ended.

The writer and activist Emma Goldman believed in anarchism, a creed that called for the abolition of the state, large corporations, and hierarchies of any kind. How society would be organized once these were overthrown was never completely clear, but somehow the people would rule. And, some anarchists believed, the new era would be ushered in by violence. In Goldman's youth, in the middle of one of his lectures, she once attacked—with a horsewhip—a fellow anarchist with whom she was having a dispute. She also took part in an attempt to assassinate Henry Clay Frick, an anti-labor steel baron.

The anarchist movement never attracted many American followers, especially after an anarchist assassinated President William McKinley in 1901. But Goldman claimed to have now put violence behind her, and had become a larger-than-life celebrity with a fierce gaze and fiery energy matched by no one. In the golden age of American oratory, before radio and TV, but when railroads could speed a popular speaker around the continent, she drew large crowds wherever she went. She appeared before audiences everywhere from Carnegie Hall to the Jewish Consumptive Sanitarium in Edgewater, Colorado. In 1915, she gave 321 lectures.

As an immigrant who had left tsarist Russia as a teenager, and who had also lived in Germany, she could give speeches in English, Yiddish, or German as the occasion required. She could talk to workers about revolution and her own experiences laboring in clothing factories, to the college educated about Verdi, Ibsen, Shaw, and Freud (whom she had heard lecture in Vienna), and she could shock or thrill everyone by insisting that they free themselves from the oppressive bonds of Christianity and monogamy. Conservatives hated her. "I have for the Goldman creature all the veneration due a snake," wrote one. "She is unfit to live in a civilized country. . . . She ought to be hanged by the neck until dead and considerably longer."

She dismayed many—and delighted some—with her open discus-

sion of homosexuality and the erotic lives of women. Untrammeled
sexual love was "the strongest and deepest element in all life, the har-
binger of hope, of joy, of ecstasy; love, the defier of all laws, of all conventions; the freest, the most powerful molder of human destiny; how
can such an all-compelling force be synonymous with that poor little
State- and Church-begotten weed, marriage?"

"If I can't dance," she supposedly once protested to a comrade, "I'm
not coming to your revolution." No scholar has been able to find her
actually saying that, but her followers repeated the story so often that
it shows how they saw her.

When younger, Goldman had spent a year in a New York penitentiary for "inciting to riot" at a demonstration where she urged workers to demand jobs or bread—and to take the bread if they weren't
given it. She proudly declared that prison made her stronger. In 1916,
she had spent two more weeks behind bars for defying the country's
Victorian-era laws against distributing information on birth control—
deliberately choosing jail rather than pay a fine. Having worked as a
midwife in the slums of the Lower East Side, she knew firsthand what
a lifesaver effective birth control could be. Women, she said, should be
free to open their minds and close their wombs.

Arguably, Goldman enraged the country's establishment more
than any other American of her time. And now not only was she
challenging the traditional subordination of women, but she was also
urging men to abandon their hallowed role as the fighters of wars.
Before Wilson had even signed the Selective Service Act, Goldman
and a group of supporters established the No-Conscription League.
Headquartered in New York with chapters around the country, it
circulated in short order 100,000 leaflets denouncing the draft. "I
for one," she wrote, "will speak against war as long as my voice will
last. . . . Except the one war of all the peoples against their despots
and exploiters."

The government was immediately apprehensive about her effect on
public opinion. "She is doing tremendous damage," reported a federal
agent monitoring her. "She is womanly, a remarkable orator, tremen-

dously sincere, and carries conviction. If she is allowed to continue here she cannot help but have great influence."

The day Wilson signed the draft bill, Goldman's No-Conscription League gathered 8,000 people for a rally in New York's Harlem. An even larger number, along with several hundred police, both uniformed and plainclothes, appeared at a meeting in the Bronx several weeks later, but the hall was smaller and most supporters had to remain on the street singing revolutionary songs. Inside, soldiers and sailors in the crowd whistled and jeered, and began pelting Goldman's sturdy figure with lightbulbs they had unscrewed from their fixtures.

She was undeterred, however, and a stream of anxious young men continued to come to the league's office asking for advice. Among them, she knew, were undercover police agents hoping to get her on record as advising them to break the law by not registering for the draft. On the very day the Espionage Act went into effect, a US marshal led a squad to arrest Goldman and her longtime collaborator and former lover Alexander Berkman. They ransacked her files and refused to let her see the arrest warrant.

The pair were charged with "conspiracy to interfere with the draft" and hustled off to the Manhattan prison nicknamed the Tombs, a spired, chateau-like building with stone walls, turrets, and a high passageway known as the "Bridge of Sighs" connecting it to the criminal courts building across the street. "The head matron was an old friend of mine," wrote Goldman. She was Irish, and "remarked that she saw no reason to be excited about what the Germans had done to the Belgians. England had treated Ireland no better during hundreds of years." The two of them also agreed on the need for birth control, campaigning for which had landed Goldman in the matron's custody the previous year.

When Goldman and Berkman appeared in court, he refused, as a matter of principle, to reveal any information and gave his age as 250. Goldman told friends she was perfectly happy in jail because she was reading a splendid new book by an author few people yet knew, James Joyce's *Portrait of the Artist as a Young Man*.

Beyond being in jail, Goldman was having a difficult time, for she was finding free love harder in practice than in principle. The man she called "the Great Grand Passion" of her life was the magnetically handsome anarchist Ben Reitman, who once proudly called himself a hobo, then became a physician. She had once written him, "You have opened up the prison gates of my womanhood." Reitman, however, had left town with a young Englishwoman pregnant with his child. Goldman's anguished letters to "my dear Hobo" full of erotic yearning were, of course, catnip for the Justice Department agents who opened his mail.

The trial began only two weeks after her arrest, on Goldman's 48th birthday, with extra police and US marshals on guard in a courtroom sweltering in the June heat and draped with patriotic bunting. Friends brought her a birthday bouquet of red roses. On the street below the courtroom was an army recruiting post, and the sounds of oratory and martial music wafted upward. When the military band played "The Star-Spangled Banner," wrote Goldman, "everyone in court was commanded to rise, the soldiers present standing at attention." But she and Berkman "remained seated throughout this display of patriotism by the mailed fist. What could the officials do? They could not very well order us removed."

Newspapers appreciated the trial as sport, the New York *Sun* headlining its story on the opening day, "'Reds' vs. U.S. Game Stands at a Draw." The writer explained: "When a small oblong parcel was sent to the Judge by mail it was decided that it was too risky for him to take any chances of opening it himself. Cautiously one of the officials carried the deadly possibility to the anteroom and there bravely ripped off the paper. A nice new volume of one of Emma's writings nestled innocently in all its purity." As if covering a football game, the article continued, "This swung the edge away from the [Federal] deputies and it looked pretty bad for them." But then the writer deducted points from Goldman's side when a supporter who refused to stand for the national anthem "was given the old coat collar and trousers method of ejection from the courtroom."

A parade of character witnesses, including *Masses* journalist John

Reed and the famous muckraker Lincoln Steffens, testified that the two
defendants were thoroughly nonviolent. This was not entirely convincing, for Berkman had once spent 14 years in prison for the bungled
attempt, with some advance help from Goldman, to assassinate Frick,
the union-busting steel magnate.

In the prosecutor's case against Goldman, there was an echo of the
Salem witchcraft trials when he declared that "her influence is so per-
nicious" because as a speaker she could hold "spellbound . . . the minds
of ignorant, weaker, and emotional people." Berkman, he suggested,
had been similarly spellbound and was acting "under Miss Goldman's
clever influence."

When the spellbinder herself addressed the court, gazing confidently at the room through her pince-nez, she spoke some of the most
eloquent words of this era, ones that still have resonance today: "Gentlemen of the jury, we respect your patriotism. . . . But may there not
be different kinds of patriotism. . . . Our patriotism is that of the man
who loves a woman with open eyes. He is enchanted by her beauty, yet
he sees her faults."

Goldman didn't know it, but a bold official had just saved her from
a fate worse than the prison sentence her prosecutor was asking for:
deportation. Even though she had lived in the United States most of
her life and spoke English with an American accent, she was not a US
citizen. She had become one three decades earlier, by marrying a naturalized immigrant. But years after this short-lived marriage ended in
divorce, the government revoked his citizenship because he had lied
about his age on his application. This meant Goldman, as well, was no
longer a citizen.

The Justice Department was eager to use her status as a noncitizen to expel her from the country. But deportations fell under the
Immigration Bureau, part of the Labor Department. A high official
there had to sign off on any deportation order, and the man whose desk
Goldman's paperwork landed on refused to do so. Assistant Secretary
of Labor Louis F. Post was a veteran progressive journalist who had
once had Goldman as a dinner guest in his home. To him, however,

that didn't matter; he simply didn't believe someone should be expelled from the United States merely for her political opinions. A man of strong conviction, he would turn out to be one of the most courageous figures of this grim time.

Neither he nor anyone else, however, could save her from something that was never really in doubt: the jury's verdict of guilty. The judge sentenced both defendants to two years in prison and a $10,000 fine. Within hours, they were on overnight trains, Berkman to the federal penitentiary in Atlanta, and Goldman to the women's side of the gray, stone, fortresslike state prison in Jefferson City, Missouri, which claimed to be the largest prison in the country. The US government housed some of its women inmates there, since there was as yet no federal penitentiary for them.

For the journey, Goldman was accompanied by a US marshal and his wife. She had been sworn in to give her authority and was instructed to keep the dangerous prisoner in sight at every moment, even leaving the door half open when Goldman used the train's bathroom. All three slept in the same compartment. "The watchful eyes of the law were closed in sleep," Goldman wrote, "but its mouth was wide open, emitting a rattle of snores."

Those Who Stand in Our Way

A S GOLDMAN WAS on her way to prison, General Pershing had already arrived in Paris. "Men, women, and children absolutely packed every foot of space, even to the windows and house-tops," he wrote of the delirious welcome he received on June 12, 1917. "Cheers and tears were mingled together. . . . Women climbed into our automobiles screaming, 'Vive l'Amérique,' and threw flowers until we were literally buried. . . . At several points the masses surged into the streets, entirely beyond control of the police."

Despite the lines of French soldiers flanking its pathway, crowds screaming "*Per-shang! Per-shang!*" surrounded the American motorcade, flowed among its cars, tried to jump onto their running boards, and stretched a 15-minute trip from the Gare du Nord to Pershing's hotel to over an hour. As the vehicles crept along in low gear, their engines began to overheat. Finally, from the safety of a balcony, Pershing could step out and acknowledge the cheers of the vast throng. The story is often told that he declared, "Lafayette, we are here!" But the taciturn, sometimes tongue-tied general later wrote that he had "no recollection of saying anything so splendid." It was said on another occasion by a colonel on his staff.

In the eyes of the Allies, there was no time to lose before the promised troops became the first men to fight under the American flag on European soil. The British and French armies continued to hemorrhage men by the tens of thousands every month. However, despite Wilson's eagerness to send large numbers of US soldiers to the front, it could not happen quickly.

The ghost of Lafayette might have appreciated the existence of the First Division of the American Expeditionary Forces, but not its military prowess. This token unit, which shortly followed Pershing to France, was cobbled together from four understrength army regiments, an artillery detachment, and some untrained recruits. The soldiers would, like their general, be wildly cheered by French crowds, who were especially thrilled that they included two sons of Theodore Roosevelt. This small advance guard was largely symbolic; it would require additional months of training in France before being of any significant help at the front. However, the rapturous welcome given Pershing and his men made some 100 million Americans feel that theirs was now a country at war.

While cheerful young women Red Cross volunteers handed out cigarettes and foil-wrapped chocolates in American railway carriages full of draftees, the war on dissenters was heating up. Woodrow Wilson, the most scholarly of American presidents, was rapidly turning into one of the most inflammatory. On Flag Day, June 14, 1917, two days after Pershing's arrival in Paris, thousands of people carrying small American flags gathered to hear the president talk before the Washington Monument.

The Marine Band warmed up the crowd, and as it played the national anthem a huge flag was hoisted to the monument's top. Crowd and president were undeterred by wind and rain. The applause was sometimes so loud, reported a wire service story, that it "drowned out the whistling of the gale." Looking out at a sea of umbrellas, Wilson condemned those against American participation in the war as "agents and dupes" of the kaiser. This set the harsh pattern for months to come: in the administration's eyes, such dissenters were not political opponents, they were traitors.

"Woe be to the man or group of men that seeks to stand in our way in this day of high resolution," the president continued, "when every principle we hold dearest is to be vindicated and made secure for the salvation of the nations." It was that distinctively Wilsonian note again, "the nations": The United States, as he saw it, had embarked on a sacred mission not just for itself, but for the entire world.

And who, exactly, sought to "stand in our way"? Millions of German Americans were desperate to show it was not them, and made few protests as a great spasm of name-changing swept the country. Berlin, Iowa, became Lincoln. Chicago's Bismarck Hotel became the Hotel Randolf. The hamburger was now the liberty sandwich, and German shepherds, Alsatian shepherds. Some transformations are still with us, such as from the frankfurter to the hot dog.

Even though the country would see cruelty against some German Americans in the months ahead, at much more risk were members of the Socialist Party. Not only was it openly against the war, but some supporters went further. The *Philadelphia Bulletin* regularly published the names and addresses of young men certified by their draft boards as ready for military service, inadvertently providing local Socialists with a ready-made mailing list. They printed 15,000 copies of a leaflet attacking the draft for destroying "the sacred and cherished rights of a free people," and began mailing it to the addresses the newspaper had so conveniently printed. Two Socialists were swiftly found guilty under the Espionage Act and sentenced to prison. Their lawyers appealed the verdict. They were hoping that if the case reached the Supreme Court, it might rule that the Espionage Act itself was unconstitutional. In the meantime, there would be a long, uneasy wait.

ANOTHER TARGET LOOMED still larger than the Socialists in the eyes of both the administration and business leaders, and the war provided the perfect excuse to rachet up their battle against it: the militant wing of the labor movement. Just as the war in Europe was being fought on several fronts, so was the war at home. If one of those fronts was the long-simmering conflict over immigration, another was over the rights of labor.

Shadowed by the violence of the frontier, the United States had long fought a bloody war on workers trying to unionize. No other country for instance, had anything comparable to Pennsylvania's Coal and Iron Police, a force essentially dedicated to battling unions and breaking strikes. Rare was the militant labor leader who had not spent a term in jail. American workers who tried to form unions had virtually no laws protecting their right to do so.

Strikes or attempts to unionize had long been met with armed force on a scale that seems today inconceivable. By the time troops suppressed an 1877 railway strike, roughly 100 workers were dead and more than 1,000 jailed. In the 20 years starting in 1890, 75 strikes saw workers killed, for a total toll of 308 deaths and thousands of injuries. In 1913 and 1914, more than 70 people, including women and children, died in battles between Colorado miners and National Guardsmen defending a Rockefeller-owned coal mine.

Fifteen years earlier, the Colorado National Guard had fought in the Philippine War, and many of the soldiers shooting down those miners were veterans. One, a notoriously ruthless officer named Karl Linderfelt, remarked, of ransacking miners' homes for arms, "In the Islands, we done exactly the same thing." At a later inquiry, a fellow officer testified that Linderfelt had tortured miner prisoners with the notorious "water cure" used on Filipino guerrillas.

Battling organized labor, in fact, had long been routine for the National Guard, which in the half century before 1917 had been mobilized more than 100 times to put down strikes. By the late 1800s, half of all National Guard actions involved labor disputes. Business groups funded many National Guard units outright. Chicago businessmen even purchased a grand home for a general who had put down a big railway strike.

Some of the fortresslike armories still found in American cities were built with direct contributions from business groups, at times when the country was not fighting any wars overseas. Although many of these handsome redbrick buildings are used for conventions, museum exhibits, theatrical performances, dances, or wedding receptions today, we forget that they embody an era when labor organizing was met with military force.

Not all the violence came from those in uniform. In 1899, hundreds of rebellious Idaho miners fighting police and corporate detectives hijacked a train that became known as the Dynamite Express, and then blew up a company mill. The governor who had declared martial law to suppress that uprising was later fatally injured by a bomb planted outside his home. In 1910, a labor militant placed another bomb at the office of the antiunion *Los Angeles Times*, killing 21 people and injuring more than 100. As with the violence against immigrants, in the sphere of labor, too, the United States was anything but a peaceful nation.

The organization corporate executives hated most was the Industrial Workers of the World, some of whose members would shortly be whipped, tarred, and feathered in Tulsa. The Wobblies were surprisingly few; they never composed more than 5 percent of all American labor unionists. At the group's peak of influence, in the summer of 1917, the IWW claimed only 150,000 members nationwide. But in the eyes of its often hysterical opponents it was gargantuan. "Plot for Revolt by 2,000,000 I. W. W. Men Exposed in Trial of Agitators," screamed one front-page newspaper headline that year. "Reign of Terror Was to Have Been Precipitated Last July from Maine to California." The always-fulminating Theodore Roosevelt called the IWW "unhung traitors."

For anti-labor politicians and businessmen, the Wobblies were a convenient bogeyman, and the war a welcome chance to crush them. Unfortunately, the IWW's incendiary rhetoric all too often made things easier for its enemies. Its newspapers, for example, sometimes advocated industrial sabotage, usually leaving vague exactly what that meant. So there were warnings from business and law enforcement officials about Wobblies setting forest fires, dumping ship cargoes overboard, tossing tools or sand into factory machinery, substituting dead rats for food in canneries, and driving spikes into logs heading for lumber mills. These provided the pretext that police, National Guardsmen, and corporate detectives used to kill dozens of Wobblies, and to injure or jail a far larger number. Although workers often did fight back, no prosecutor ever convicted any IWW member of actually committing industrial sabotage. As one historian put it, "Upon close investigation, it always seemed to be something that had happened to somebody else some other place."

The Wobblies believed in "One Big Union" that would encompass all occupations. They embraced all workers: skilled or unskilled, Black or white, male or female (several well-known activists were women), farmworkers or factory hands, native-born or immigrant. "Tell every slave you see along the line," ran one Wobbly song, "It makes no difference what your color, creed or sex or kind."

In one IWW strike by Philadelphia longshoremen, Black and Irish American workers walked off the job together—something extremely rare, and threatening to business, in an era when employers routinely played off different ethnic groups against each other. When Pennsylvania state troopers killed a Wobbly steelworker in 1909, the eulogies at his burial were in 15 languages. Many mainstream trade unions, by contrast, turned away women, Blacks, and the unskilled, and wanted to keep wages higher by curbing immigration. The IWW's openhearted welcome for all held one significant danger, however: the union was easy to infiltrate.

For both their friends and their enemies, the Wobblies loomed larger than their modest numbers. Their membership turnover was high, and they could point to no politicians they had elected, legislation they had passed, or contracts they had won. In fact, they felt that signing contracts violated revolutionary principles—a belief that was not a good recipe for successful labor organizing. However, the way they combined the class-conscious radicalism of Europe with the free-spirited independence of the American West seized the imagination of middle-class liberals and radicals, who loved the group as much as business interests hated it. "Wherever . . . there is an I. W. W. local," wrote *Masses* journalist John Reed, "you will find an intellectual center—a place where men read philosophy, economics, the latest plays, novels; where art and poetry are discussed." This was an enthusiast's exaggeration, but there was some truth to it: Wobbly offices did have libraries. At the same time, there was an appealing whiff of frontier spirit in such groups as the Wobbly-inspired Bronco Busters and Range Riders Union.

Many Wobblies were expert at riding boxcars, hopping them to travel to IWW conventions or to strikes that had called for supporters. And since so many laborers also rode the rails as they crisscrossed the country in search of work, boxcars became recruiting stations on wheels, places where activists could distribute red membership cards and Wobbly newspapers like the *Industrial Worker* and *Solidarity*. Sometimes a sympathetic "brakie," or brakeman, would look the other way if he found a boxcar full of Wobblies, but more often the riders had to battle or flee the railroad's armed guards. Romantic as all this may have seemed to the Wobblies' better-off admirers, however, migrants riding the rails were not necessarily the group best suited to be the tip of the revolutionary spear.

Wobbly posters were eye-catching, and their *Little Red Songbook* sold more copies than any other single piece of their literature. The writer of many of the songs in it was Joe Hill, an organizer executed by a Utah firing squad in 1915 after being convicted of murder on much-disputed evidence. Even his last will and testament was in verse, beginning:

> My will is easy to decide
> For there is nothing to divide.

Joe Hill's songs praised Wobbly heroes and heroines, mocked strike-breakers, denounced war, and scorned religion:

> *Long-haired preachers come out every night,*
> *Try to tell you what's wrong and what's right;*
> *But when asked how 'bout something to eat*
> *They will answer with voices so sweet:*
> *You will eat, bye and bye,*
> *In that glorious land above the sky;*
> *Work and pray, live on hay,*
> *You'll get pie in the sky when you die.*

The Wobblies were particularly strong among miners and loggers in the Pacific Northwest. It was as a small-town newspaper proprietor on the Washington State coast that the immigrant-loathing congressman Albert Johnson had cut his political teeth railing against the IWW. He joined a vigilante group whose members wore white badges and roughed up Wobblies in the streets. A local businessman described how, during a stormy 1912 strike, before Johnson went to Congress, "we got hundreds of heavy clubs of the weight and size of pick-handles, armed our vigilantes with them, and that night raided all the IWW headquarters, rounded up as many of them as we could find, and escorted them out of town."

What did "escorted" mean? A political enemy claimed that Johnson "had packed the strikers into box cars, closed the air vents, nailed the doors shut, and labeled the cars 'Cattle for Kansas City.'" Johnson denied this, but he proudly repeated the accusation in a newspaper article. And that seems mild compared with other acts he called for. When, for example, a militant unionist named Gohl was under arrest for murder in 1910, Johnson's newspaper virtually demanded his lynching: "Do you imagine that you hear the roar of the mob in pursuit of a human being? A mob swayed by passion! William Gohl, can you hear it? The yelp of the wolf, the horrid laugh of the hyena, the growl of the bear, the howl of the dog, all combining to make the wild cry of the mob, seeking . . . vengeance."

The Wobblies' flair for publicity added to their influence: they were responsible for one out of every six workdays lost to strikes in the half year following the US entry into the First World War. One of those 1917 IWW-led strikes shut down 75 percent of lumbering in western Washington, adding to Johnson's venom. This was tightly fused with his passion to shut off immigration, for many Wobblies were also immigrants. In his mind, his lifelong determination to close the country's doors was an effort to keep out the "immigrant with red in his heart and a bomb in his hand." Johnson epitomized something shared by many: more than ever, the long-standing American nativist hostility to immigrants was blended with hatred of any challenge to the power of business and industry. In the months ahead, each current of feeling would inflame the other.

A foretaste of what was in store for the Wobblies appeared that summer under the broiling skies of Arizona. Several mining companies, among them the behemoth Phelps, Dodge & Co., owned a massive copper lode that spread beneath a ring of hills in the desert scrubland around the town of Bisbee. The war sparked a surge in demand for the metal, a half ounce of which went into every rifle cartridge. The price of copper shot up and Bisbee's mines ran 24 hours a day. Corporate profits soared: that year, Phelps, Dodge's after-tax income would equal nearly 20 percent of its total capital investment. Some copper companies enjoyed still-higher profits.

As in many war industries, however, workers felt they were not sufficiently sharing in this bonanza. In late June 1917, two weeks after Wilson's menacing Flag Day speech, Bisbee-area miners organized by the IWW went on strike. Always eager to imagine foreign influence, Military Intelligence chief Ralph Van Deman reported to his superiors that "enemy agents" were "endeavoring to stir up trouble in the mining camps."

Also part of this combustible mix was the general manager of what was, after Phelps, Dodge, the other major mining company in the area. John Greenway was a close friend of Theodore Roosevelt and a swashbuckling veteran of Roosevelt's Rough Riders. He and the ex-president had been corresponding enthusiastically about the need for a new volunteer militia that could deal with troublemakers more aggressively than the Wilson administration was doing. "I know of some rattling good men" for such a force, Greenway wrote Roosevelt, and mentioned the county sheriff in Bisbee as one of them. Although the subversives they originally had in mind were revolutionaries across the nearby Mexican border, the striking Wobblies now suddenly offered Greenway an ideal target.

Greenway and Phelps, Dodge convinced the sheriff to assemble a vigilante posse of more than 2,000 company officials, hired gunmen, and armed local businessmen, all identified by white armbands. At dawn on July 12, led by a car mounted with a machine gun—one of five Phelps, Dodge owned—the group swept through Bisbee, broke down doors, and forced more than 2,000 strikers and their supporters from their beds at gunpoint. Much of the action was directed from a command center on Greenway's front porch. One member of the posse grabbed a baby out of its father's arms and tossed it to a bystander. When miners' families frantically tried to send messages pleading for help, they found that the posse had seized the town's telephone and telegraph offices.

The temperature reached 112 degrees Fahrenheit that day, as the vigilantes held the captured men for several hours on a baseball field. When threatened by Greenway, who was on horseback and brandishing a rifle, hundreds of miners agreed to go back to work. At bayonet point, the posse packed 1,186 men who refused to do so into a train of two dozen freight and cattle cars—the latter with several inches of manure on their floors—which hauled them 180 miles under the desert sun across the state line into New Mexico. Armed guards rode atop each car, and more armed men escorted the train in automobiles. After two days without food, the strikers were herded into an army stockade, from which they eventually were released. Any who tried to return to Bisbee were promptly arrested. For several months to come, no one could enter or leave the town without a special pass.

President Wilson privately voiced his disapproval, but bristled angrily when Arizona labor leaders asked him to allow the exiled men to return to their homes. "No human being in his senses," Theodore Roosevelt felt, "doubts that the men deported from Bisbee were bent on destruction and murder." Newspapers generally agreed, a *New York Times* editorial declaring "the Sheriff of Bisbee was on the right track."

GOVERNMENT AND BUSINESS officials worried about Wobbly influence everywhere, not just in the group's traditional stronghold of the Far West. Pittsburgh, for example, was a crucial industrial hub. Smoke poured from hundreds of the high, clustered stacks of its steel mills, from which an endless river of the critical metal flowed out to other parts of the country to be made into ships, gun barrels, artillery shells, and weapons and machinery of all kinds. The city had a strong labor movement. Many members of its largely Slavic and Italian working class had brought socialist or anarchist convictions with them when they emigrated from Europe. In 1912, some neighborhoods in the area had given more than 25 percent of the vote to Eugene Debs, the Socialist Party candidate for president. In 1916, 36,000 Pittsburgh workers had walked off the job in a May Day strike; in an ensuing battle with police, three were killed and several dozen injured.

One person drawn to Pittsburgh by the prospects for left-wing organizing there was a newcomer who arrived in July 1917, introducing himself as an auto mechanic named Louis Walsh. A sociable type, he went to left-wing gatherings and spent many evenings in working-class saloons like the Bismarck Café, drinking, talking about socialism and anarchism, and mocking the mainstream American Federation of Labor, which supported the war. He quickly came to know several activists determined to set up an IWW branch in the city.

The only known photograph of Walsh from this time, a mug shot taken after one of his several arrests for Wobbly activities, shows a man with dark hair, light-colored eyes, a mouth turned down at the corners, and a broad, impassive face. He described how he had previously worked with the Mexican revolutionaries Pancho Villa and Emiliano Zapata, a history that gave him stature in the eyes of his fellow Wobblies, who romanticized these rebels across the border. When they formed the IWW's Pittsburgh chapter a month after his arrival in the city, the members elected him recording and financial secretary.

In the next few years, he would be "shadowed for months by government agents," according to the *Pittsburgh Press*, denounced in another newspaper's headline as an "I. W. W. Plot Leader," and would give fiery speeches to rally his comrades. The *Press* called him "a nationally known radical." All evidence suggested that federal authorities considered him highly dangerous. The first time he was arrested, "Walsh was taken despite his own protests and those of his associates," another paper reported, "and was spirited away by the government agents, who declined to say where he had been incarcerated."

Walsh would be released from this period of detention, but it would not be his only arrest. The government was clearly sending a message: for left-wingers in wartime, normal civil liberties did not exist, especially for Wobblies.

6

Soldiers of Darkness

ROBERT GOLDSTEIN, A SAN FRANCISCO–BORN filmmaker, seemed the least likely person to provoke wartime hysteria. An actress who worked with him described him as a "gentle, soft-spoken man." Goldstein had great expectations when his silent movie, *The Spirit of '76*, made before the United States entered the war, had its Los Angeles opening in late 1917. Actors in the $200,000 production played various figures in this epic of the American Revolution: George Washington, Benjamin Franklin, Chief Brant of the Six Nations, and King George III. At the showing, a 40-piece orchestra provided the music, and the ushers were dressed in eighteenth-century costumes. The audience at Clune's Auditorium cheered as they watched the Minutemen gather at Concord, the Liberty Bell ring, and Paul Revere ride in what the city's *Evening Express* called "one of the longest film features" of the era. The two-and-a-half-hour movie, the paper said, narrated the story of "America's secession from British rule, and doesn't mince matters in telling what it thinks of the king business."

When his film had earlier premiered in Chicago, Goldstein tangled with censors who forced him to remove a few scenes, but he thought he had permission to show the full film in Los Angeles. He was gravely mistaken. A federal judge paused in the middle of his Thanksgiving dinner to sign a search warrant, and two Justice Department officials appeared at Clune's Auditorium to seize all reels of the film. Up went a

sign in front of the building: NO SHOW TONIGHT. The startled Goldstein was arrested and charged with violating the Espionage Act. In the
trial that followed, the jury viewed portions of the film. The director's
crime, it turned out, involved "the king business." The film showed a
mistress of King George hankering to become "Queen of America," a
mercenary in the British forces stabbing an elderly Quaker, and British
soldiers bayoneting a baby.

The filmmaker was found guilty and sentenced to a fine of $5,000
and ten years in prison. "He shook like an aspen," reported the *Los
Angeles Times*, "as Judge Bledsoe verbally excoriated him for his unpatriotic conduct." Whatever happened in 1776, the judge declared, "we
are engaged in a war in which Great Britain is an ally of the United
States," and this was no time for "sowing dissension among our people" or "creating animosity . . . between us and our allies." Goldstein's
sentence would not be commuted until long after the war ended. He
would serve nearly three years behind bars, most of it in the isolated
McNeil Island Penitentiary in Puget Sound.

Patriotic frenzy claimed many other victims as well. In Maine, a
schoolteacher was fired for taking driving lessons from a German citizen. An Iowa pastor and a friend were dragged through the streets with
ropes around their necks until one of them agreed to buy a $1,000 war
bond. Wilhelm Schumann, another Iowa preacher, first saw his church
mysteriously burn to the ground one night, and then was convicted of
spreading "disloyalty among his congregation" and sentenced to five
years, of which he would serve more than two. Theodore Roosevelt declared that "the clergyman who does not put the flag above the church
had better close his church and keep it closed."

A man in Texas went to prison for saying, "I wish Wilson was in
hell." The judge called this a murder threat because the president
"could not be in the state called hell until life was terminated." From
Oklahoma to New Jersey, crowds tarred and feathered people who refused to buy war bonds, calling them "bond slackers." A Pennsylvania
steelworker who failed to donate to the Red Cross had his head dunked
in a barrel of red paint by his fellow workers. When members of the

pacifist Hutterite sect in South Dakota did not buy bonds, the county's loan committee, with the support of the local sheriff, simply rounded up 100 steers and 1,000 sheep belonging to them, and auctioned them off. This was too much even for the federal war loan authorities, who refused to accept the money. So the local committee members simply bought themselves war bonds with the proceeds. Anyone who refused to buy a bond, Treasury Secretary McAdoo told one audience, "or who takes the attitude of let the other fellow do it, is a friend of Germany."

For every victim of actual violence, dozens of others had to undergo questioning by federal agents or hypervigilant neighbors, and hundreds more feared that the slightest "disloyal" remark might bring retribution. No one was safe: Richard F. Pettigrew, a former two-term United States senator from South Dakota, was indicted for having declared, "There is no excuse for this war." More than two years later prosecutors finally dropped the case against him, but not before vigilantes had painted his office yellow. In Berkeley, a mob of thousands, including many University of California students, attacked a pacifist church, setting fire to its tent tabernacle and several wooden cottages surrounding it, while tossing the pastor and two elders into the church's baptismal tank. In Seattle, a mob attacked a plant that printed socialist and Wobbly newspapers, jamming iron bars into running presses to cause $15,000 worth of damage. The ringleader was released from jail when a group of Elks paid his bail; the court then acquitted him after he claimed that he had a case of "mental irresponsibility" caused by the material published by the press.

When prosecutors now charged people under the Espionage Act, ever fewer lawyers were bold enough to defend them. At its annual meeting, the American Bar Association passed a resolution condemning "all attempts, in Congress and out of it, to hinder and embarrass the Government of the United States in carrying on the war. . . . We deem them to be pro-German, and in effect giving aid and comfort to the enemy."

About all this, Woodrow Wilson showed little concern. "I hear the voices of dissent; who does not?" he declared. "I hear the criticism and the clamor of the noisily thoughtless and troublesome. . . . But I know that none of these speaks for the nation. . . . They may safely be left to strut their uneasy hour and be forgotten."

AS WAR FEVER swept the land, millions of American men whose age denied them the archetypal masculine role of soldier were still eager for something similar. How could they, too, feel that they were heroically defending their country in its hour of need?

Early on, a heavyset, jowly Chicagoan named Albert Briggs heard this bugle's call. He ran his own advertising firm, handling accounts for clients ranging from Liggett & Myers tobacco and Aunt Jemima flour to Standard Oil of Indiana. Too old for the trenches of France at 43, he was determined to fight in a different way.

In February 1917, with war clearly on the horizon, Briggs paid a visit to the Chicago office of the Bureau of Investigation. "I am physically unable to join the active fighting forces, but I would like to help," he told the agent in charge. He made a proposal, and, soon after, a bureau official called Briggs and supposedly said, "There are thousands of men who are enemies of this country and ought to be behind bars, but it takes a spy to catch a spy, and I've got a dozen spies to catch a hundred thousand spies right here in Chicago. They have motor cars against my street cars. They're supplied with all the money they want; my own funds are limited."

Although this dialogue was almost certainly touched up by Briggs's skilled adman's pen, some exchange like it apparently did occur. For he would, in fact, mobilize a group of wealthy friends to loan or donate a substantial number of automobiles to bureau offices in Chicago, Washington, and New York. And on the eve of the declaration of war, he would make two trips to Washington to meet the national chief of the bureau, who gave him a go-ahead to form a force of civilian vigilantes—as an official auxiliary to the Department of Justice. Such a status was virtually unprecedented; the government even granted this group the "franking" privilege of sending mail for free. When the attorney general described the new organization at a cabinet meeting, neither President Wilson nor anyone else objected.

Briggs's creation was called the American Protective League, or APL. Significantly, given how that earlier conflict casts its shadow over this entire period, his key deputy in building the league was a veteran of the Philippine War. Thomas Crockett, a relative of the famous frontiersman, had impressed Briggs with his military bearing and record. In fighting on the island of Luzon 16 years earlier, he had commanded a unit that won repeated mentions in dispatches for capturing Filipino guerrillas.

A typical army report described how "Lieutenant Crockett, with Ilocano scouts, working in mountains north of Boso-Boso . . . captured one [guerrilla] with gun. On information received from prisoner, command marched all night and struck an outpost at daylight. Had skirmish, killing one and capturing one." The phrase "on information received from prisoner" probably means that the first captured guerrilla was subjected to the "water cure" torture. During his Philippine service, Crockett also recruited agents for the undercover network throughout the islands being built by the rising young intelligence officer Ralph Van Deman.

Now, from an office suite provided for free by Commonwealth Edison, Chicago's giant utility, Briggs and Crockett set out to found American Protective League chapters across the nation. It was a hierarchical, overwhelmingly male organization and in practice, if not officially, was all white: officers politely turned down a membership application from a 51-year-old self-described "Colored man" in San Francisco. Organized along military lines, each local branch had a chief who commanded captains, lieutenants, and mere operatives. Cities were divided into zones—New York, for example, had 12—and in turn districts, which multiplied the opportunity for positions of command. There was a cloak-and-dagger thrill as well, for APL members sometimes had code names, like A-372 or B-49. For men beyond military age seeking martial glory, it was a dream fulfilled.

The Bureau of Investigation provided Briggs a letter he could show to its field office directors around the country, asking them to "please assist Mr. Briggs in any way practicable and arrange to take advantage of the assistance and co-operation which he may offer." But, the letter added, the bureau's ties with the APL "must be kept . . . confidential."

Briggs and his burgeoning network, however, thrilled with their quasi-official status, had no intention of keeping that confidential. The membership card that each new APL recruit received proclaimed the league to be "Organized with Approval and Operating under Direction of United States Department of Justice Bureau of Investigation." And for 75 cents, each member received a silver shield, the size and shape of a police officer's, with his membership number and the organization's name encircling the words "Secret Service." When the US Secret Service eventually noticed this, the APL had to change the design, but by then tens of thousands of badges had been distributed to men who were loath to give them up. A later badge was gold-colored, surmounted by an American eagle, and included the bearer's rank, from "Operative" up to "Chief." "If there were no suspects handy," writes one scholar of the league, "the badge could always be used to obtain free admittance to theaters, subways, and parking lots."

Even before Americans were at the front lines in France, by joining the APL you could battle the enemy right here—and still go home for dinner every night. The organization offered its members both the thrill of being part of the war effort and a whiff of the traditions of the frontier, where sheriffs' posses chased down troublemakers. The league's members often joined Justice Department agents on raids; a supporter in Los Angeles, for example, accompanied the men who seized the reels of Robert Goldstein's ill-fated film.

Whipping up patriotic fervor, of course, is a classic way to obscure class differences and deflect demands for regulation or redistribution of wealth, demands increasingly insistent during the Progressive Era and stubbornly resisted by captains of industry. Everywhere, therefore, the APL had the enthusiastic backing of leading businessmen. Prominent supporters in Chicago—almost all of them, notably, Anglo-Saxon Protestants—included the CEOs of the First National Bank, the Chicago and North Western Railway, the Chicago Telephone Company, and Montgomery Ward. In Detroit, Henry Ford provided funding and a Ford executive supervised 400 APL operatives. The New York APL chief was the president of the Metropolitan Trust Company.

Convinced that there were subversives on all sides, APL members tapped phone lines and placed microphones near people under surveillance. They carried out black-bag jobs, surreptitiously picking locks to gather or copy letters and documents from suspects' homes and offices. "The League has done that thousands of times and has never been detected!" proudly claimed its official history. Members pitched in to help Post Office censors examine intercepted mail, and sometimes dressed up in army uniforms to ride trains full of draftees and listen for disloyal talk.

Some local police and sheriff's departments officially deputized APL members, giving them the authority to make arrests; in other places, no one bothered about such formalities. In an atmosphere of free-floating paranoia, almost anything could provide an excuse for action. In Philadelphia, the APL arrested a factory worker who, it claimed, was spelling out Morse code messages about troop movements with a machine-driven trip-hammer. In a six-month period, the APL chapter in Seattle claimed to have carried out more than 10,000 investigations, resulting in 1,008 arrests. The cases included 449 "Seditious Utterances," 677 "Disloyal Citizens," and 36 "Aliens and Citizens Living in Luxury without Visible Means of Support."

Reinforcing all this vigilance were stern warnings about enemy espionage that filled the speeches of public officials from Wilson on down. To most Americans the warnings sounded plausible, for a few years earlier Germany did have an underground network of saboteurs in the United States, who had succeeded in setting off several massive explosions of munitions. Almost all the spies, however, had fled the country or been identified before America entered the war. Many were found because their German paymaster had gotten off a New York City elevated train in 1915 and left behind a briefcase full of agents' names, which was promptly grabbed by the American counterspy tailing him. There were few real spies left. Of the more than 2,000 cases the government prosecuted under the Espionage Act, only ten would involve people accused of being actual German agents. The APL never uncovered a single such person.

BUSINESS ENTHUSIASM FOR the American Protective League had nothing to do with German spies. Moguls like Ford saw the organization as a powerful new tool for fighting organized labor, especially the Wobblies. In a Chicago APL unit whose commander affectionately called his men "soldiers of darkness," one member posed as a reporter for a Wobbly newspaper; others tapped Wobbly telephones. Even though they sometimes wore suits and ties, APL men were vigilantes. A group of them commanded by Philippine veteran Crockett, together with several hundred Chicago police—the police chief was an APL member—broke up an antiwar rally in Grant Park.

"Three of us worked our way to the speakers' stand," proudly wrote one league enthusiast. "When one particularly vicious orator began to incite the mob . . . I jumped on the platform and grabbed him. A few seconds later I landed on the heads of the people in front. My two companions rushed to me and, shoulder to shoulder, we battled for our lives. . . . Wagons full of police with riot clubs arrived, and we managed to arrest the leaders." Of breaking up another rally, he declared: "The anarchist men were tough to handle, but the women fought like wildcats, scratching, biting and kicking with feline ferocity."

APL members fought the IWW around the country, getting 50 Wobblies fired from military plants in Philadelphia and purging Wobbly farmworkers from wheat fields in South Dakota. A local Justice Department official approvingly called that state's APL branch "the Ku Klux Klan of the Prairies." APL members scoured libraries, demanding that they remove books deemed pro-German or left-wing. In the southern Illinois town of Staunton, APL men severely beat, tarred, and feathered a Wobbly leader and his attorney and left them on the outskirts of town.

"This work done," reported a newspaper, "members of the league proceeded to make a personal canvass of Staunton, asking each person to sign pledges of loyalty to the Government. . . . At least a hundred persons whose patriotism has been under suspicion were made to kiss the American flag in public." The mob tarred and feathered another Staunton resident when he refused to buy a Red Cross pin. As the frenzy spread to other towns nearby, a 21-year-old man was killed trying to defend his house from a mob attack. Ironically, he had just enlisted in the navy and was awaiting call-up.

Evidently forgetting that he had voiced no opposition when the plan for the APL was described at a cabinet meeting, Woodrow Wilson was disturbed when the group's activities began making news. "It seems to me that it would be very dangerous to have such an organization operating in the United States," he wrote to his attorney general, "and I wonder if there is any way in which we could stop it." But, as with so many similar matters in these years, his advisers reassured him, and he never showed much concern again.

The American Protective League was by far the largest group of its kind, but not the only one. In New York City 49 men—and, unusually, three women—signed up for the American Defense Vigilantes, whose aim was to hunt for "pro-German soap box orators." A man who tried to give an antiwar talk a few days later at the corner of Broadway and 37th Street found himself promptly arrested. Similar organizations sprang into being elsewhere, with names like the Home Defense League, the Anti–Yellow Dog League, and the Sedition Slammers.

But just what was sedition? The definition was loose. "The most dangerous type of propaganda . . . is religious pacifism, i.e., opposition to the war on the ground that it is opposed to the word of God," a high Justice Department official warned the House Judiciary Committee. In Iowa, a judge sentenced a man to a year in prison for *attending* a lecture "in which disloyal utterances were made" and "applauding some of the statements." In South Dakota, Fred Fairchild, a farmer and former Socialist Party candidate for governor, allegedly said, "If I were of conscription age . . . I would refuse to serve. They could shoot me, but they could not make me fight." He was fined $500 and sentenced to a year and a day in the federal penitentiary at Leavenworth, Kansas.

One of the largest outbreaks of violence in the early months of

America's war at home came on July 1, 1917, when left-wingers and labor unionists marched against the war on the Boston Common. The parade came under fierce attack by more numerous opponents, the *Boston Daily Globe* claiming that the total melee involved 20,000 people. The police did little, except to arrest and charge ten of the peace demonstrators. Vigilantes raided the nearby Socialist Party office, smashed doors and windows, and threw furniture, papers, and the suitcase of a traveling activist out the window and onto a bonfire. "A telephone in the Socialist room was torn from its moorings," said the *Globe*, "but some one advised that it was the property of the telephone company, and it was left with its wires cut."

Surveying everything that had happened in July, including the violence in Boston, the imprisonment of Emma Goldman and Alexander Berkman, and the expulsion of union activists from Bisbee, Arizona, John Reed called it "the blackest month for freemen our generation has known." But a worse act of repression was about to unfold in August.

THE RAW, GRITTY mining town of Butte, Montana, dotted with smokestacks and derricks, had six times as many saloons as churches. Its red-light district was a major source of municipal revenue, for hundreds of women paid a monthly license fee. Otherwise there was little cheer for miners. The town's air was so filled with arsenic-laden smoke from copper smelting that sometimes streetlamps burned during the day. Butte sat atop a gigantic labyrinth of several thousand miles of tunnels, branching out into copper-rich rock at dozens of levels, the lowest and hottest of which was more than 3,000 feet down. The men who worked in this underground metropolis—Serb, Croatian, Slovene, Italian, Mexican, Swedish, and more—mirrored the immigrant-rich working class of the country above. The "No Smoking" signs at mine-shaft entrances were in 16 languages.

On June 5, 1917, the day all those eligible had to register for the draft, some 2,500 men, led by Irish and Finnish miners, marched through Butte in protest. Both those groups wanted independence for their homelands from two of the countries—Britain and Russia—that were now America's allies.

Three days later, however, all thought of the fighting in Europe was replaced by an urgent series of short whistle blasts from a mine mouth, the signal for a major accident. An exposed flame of a miner's carbide lantern in one of the tunnels had ignited some oil-soaked jute insulation on a torn electrical cable. The fire rapidly spread through passageways and vertical shafts, feeding on timbers supporting tunnel roofs, and on supplies of oil. The mine's powerful ventilating system only fanned the blaze. Waves of smoke, flame, carbon monoxide, and other poisonous fumes quickly spread through the vast network. When miners desperately threw water on the flames, this produced scalding steam. Cables for the mine's elevator system melted. From the narrow tunnels there were few other ways out. Many of the cement or metal bulkheads meant to block the spread of such infernos did not have the required fire escape doors. In vain, trapped miners flailed at them frantically with sledgehammers. Aboveground, weeping, terrified family members waited at mine entrances.

Mining was dangerous to begin with: an average of one man was killed in Butte every week, and it was said that more young miners lay in the town's Mountain View Cemetery than worked in the mine itself. The fire was the deadliest hard-rock mining disaster in the United States, before or since. By the time the flames were out after several days, at least 163 men were dead. The true toll was probably higher, as some bodies were never found. Many died with agonizing slowness, trapped for days with little food or water, breathing ever less oxygen. In makeshift morgues, charred and mangled corpses lay by the score under white sheets. Small wonder that Butte miners walked off the job in a wildcat strike three days after the fire, other workers joining them in sympathy. It seemed a promising time to organize.

Six weeks later, 38-year-old Frank Little, a former miner and a veteran organizer for the Industrial Workers of the World with jail terms in at least three states under his belt, stepped off the train in Butte. A wiry man five feet, ten inches tall, he had survived a kidnapping by railway detectives during a strike, wore a Stetson hat tilted to one side, and was proud that one of his ancestors was Cherokee. With a broken ankle from an auto accident, Little was on crutches. From the moment he arrived, however, he lost no time in calling for revolution.

"We have no interest in the war," he told a crowd of thousands. Little called American soldiers "scabs in uniform," and promised to "make it so damned hot for the government that it won't be able to send any troops to France." Mining company detectives, now flooding Butte by the hundreds, attended union meetings and reported his words. Copper company officials pressed the US attorney, Burton K. Wheeler (later a senator), to use the Espionage Act to silence Little. But Wheeler, who had an unusually strong backbone, told them that Little had the legal right to voice his opinions. Meanwhile, several local unionists warned Little to go into hiding, for there were rumors of a death squad forming. One day he received a cryptic note at his boarding house: "This is the first warning, beware, 3-7-77."

There are various theories about what these digits meant, one being that they stood for the width and length (in feet) and depth (in inches) of a grave. Whatever their origin, Montana vigilantes had long used them as a threat. A man who found the numbers marked on his tent or cabin knew he should take the first stagecoach out of town. But Little refused to leave Butte.

Not all the town's miners were as militant as Frank Little, and some found his inflammatory rhetoric less than helpful. But there was almost no chance to see its effects. At 3:00 a.m. on August 1, only two weeks after his arrival, five armed, masked men entered his boardinghouse, next door to the IWW meeting hall, while two confederates stood guard outside. One aimed a pistol at the landlady and asked which room Little was in. They kicked in the door and seized him. He was wearing only his underwear and the cast on his leg. As they dragged him along the hall, he said, "Wait 'til I get my hat."

"Where you're going," replied one of his captors, "you won't need a hat."

The men threw him into a black Cadillac sedan and drove off. A few blocks away they stopped the car, took Little out, and tied him to the rear bumper, dragging him along and scraping the skin off his knee-caps. His body was found a few hours later, still warm, hanging from a railroad bridge. On his head and one leg, according to an autopsy, were the marks of blows from a blunt instrument, possibly a gun or pistol stock. A note in red crayon was pinned to his right thigh. Following the initials of half a dozen strike leaders, again came the numbers "3-7-77."

Butte's police chief was so enthusiastic a superpatriot that he demanded that all his officers spend a month's salary on war bonds, to prove they were "red-blooded American enough" to deserve their jobs. The police made little effort to solve the crime, perhaps because, hints suggested, one killer was the department's chief detective. A day after the killing he began a 20-day leave, to allow some scratches on his face to heal. The autopsy of Frank Little's body showed bits of someone else's skin under one of his fingernails.

No one ever followed up these and other clues, and witnesses who might have supplied more were too intimidated to talk. One unnamed person remarked, in earshot of a reporter, "Better start with a coroner's jury and have it reach a verdict of suicide." US Attorney Wheeler told a Justice Department colleague, "I think the Company had him hung."

Thousands of Butte miners joined Little's funeral procession, but the authorities lost no time in making sure that outrage over his killing would not strengthen the IWW's hand. Eleven days after his death, federal troops occupied the town, meeting an attempted strike some months later with loaded rifles and fixed bayonets. They would remain in place for more than three years.

No protests came from the Wilson administration about the lynching. Instead, Vice President Thomas Marshall cynically coined a pun on the victim's name. In solving labor problems, he quipped, "A Little hanging goes a long way."

Shoot My Brother Down

T HE LYNCHING OF FRANK LITTLE cast a shadow of fear over labor unionists throughout the United States. They had long endured violent attacks on picket lines, but it was far beyond that to seize a man from his bed in his underwear in the middle of the night, drag him behind a car, and hang him.

Millions of Americans, however, already were all too familiar with lynching. For decades, it was an unrelenting threat to Black lives. Many white southerners never really accepted the end of slavery and were determined to meet any hint of Black advancement—real or imagined—with terror. Throughout the former Confederate states, the gains made under Reconstruction, when Black children could go to school and Black men could vote for the first time, had been largely reversed. A blizzard of killings, terror, and legal barriers now made it impossible for the great majority of Black men in those states to cast a ballot. Jim Crow laws kept schools, housing, and the rest of southern life strictly segregated; Blacks were barred from hospital wards, hotels, restaurants, and even many public libraries used by whites, lived on dirt streets, and made do with textbooks discarded from white schools—if there were any available at all.

Despite all the other currents of violence in American life, nothing quite equaled the sadistic fury that met any hint of Black assertion. A man accused of something as mild as not yielding a sidewalk quickly

enough to a white person faced the risk of lynching—often preceded
by torture, mutilation, or castration. With their survivors living in fear,
few victims ever got the large funeral procession or national headlines
that followed the death of Frank Little. Mobs lynched thousands of
Black men over the decades, never less than several dozen per year and
often more than 100. Then in 1915 came the rebirth of the Ku Klux
Klan, its flaming torches and burning crosses once again lighting the
night sky.

All of this helped spur what came to be called the Great Migration,
the exodus of millions of rural and small-town Black Americans who
moved north and west in search of safety, justice, and better jobs. Those
who made this trek, which began in earnest around 1910, met hostility at both ends: white southern employers were furious to see their
lowest-paid laborers leave town, while the migrants often found white
northerners unwelcoming—sometimes violently so. Many whites in
the North were no more racially tolerant than their southern counterparts. They had been horrified, for instance, when the Black boxer
Jack Johnson became heavyweight champion of the world in 1908,
and when he defeated his challenger Jim Jeffries, "the Great White
Hope," two years later, angry whites attacked celebrating Blacks in two
dozen cities around the country, north and south, leaving many dead.
And then, just as Reconstruction had threatened the social order of the
South, so the Great Migration began to do so for that of the North.

As the First World War's manufacturing boom promised more jobs
in the industrial centers of the North, it speeded up that migration.
And it unleashed other events as well, which would make the next few
years some of the bloodiest for Black Americans since the end of slavery, forming a new front in the war at home.

Despite the soaring rhetoric and great hopes of the Progressive Era,
its modest reforms had had little effect on Black life. Liberal whites
might go to a jazz club in Harlem or even join the National Association
for the Advancement of Colored People, but this did not change the
discrimination on all fronts that Blacks faced daily. For all their promises of inclusiveness, the IWW and the Socialist Party attracted few

Black members, and many labor union locals barred them entirely. The Wilson administration was resegregating parts of the federal workforce, and almost the entire South was under the control of openly racist Democratic mayors, governors, and legislatures. In the Black community there were education-first followers of Booker T. Washington, Black nationalists like Marcus Garvey, and, sometimes facing death threats, civil rights activists like the bold anti-lynching activist Ida B. Wells. But to most Black Americans hoping for a better life, the most important single thing they could do was to get out of the South, where the vast majority of them still lived. As a poem in Chicago's Black newspaper, the *Defender*, put it:

Now, why should I remain longer south,
To be kicked and dogged around?
"Crackers" to knock me in the mouth
And shoot my brother down.

Black pilgrims leaving the South, often with nothing but the clothes they wore, headed for places like East St. Louis, Illinois. Across the Mississippi River from the much larger St. Louis, Missouri, the city was a smoky railway junction filled with stockyards, meatpacking plants, and glass-, iron-, and steelworks, its air pervaded by the smell of offal from slaughterhouses. East St. Louis factory lunchrooms and washrooms were segregated, while the jobs available were hard, ill paid, and often dangerous: killing frightened hogs or bulls on a blood-slicked floor, or manipulating red-hot ingots with tongs while trying to avoid getting splashed by molten metal. However, even if you had to sleep in a vacant lot until you got your first week's pay, such work promised more than spending a lifetime picking cotton as a sharecropper on a white farmer's land. A 1914 dip in cotton prices and several years of bad harvests spurred on the Black exodus, as migrants already in the North sent word that jobs were available.

To many white people in East St. Louis, however, these newcomers, most of them desperately poor, felt ominous. To the city's entrenched

Democratic political machine they were a huge threat, for the thousands of Blacks who now were free to vote when they moved north would most likely vote for the Republicans, still to them the party of Lincoln and emancipation. In East St. Louis, a white political boss typically declared, "Something has got to be done, or the damned niggers will take the town." At the national level, too, leading Democrats portrayed the Great Migration as a plot to import Republican voters to traditionally Democratic cities. "Approximately 60,000 Negroes have been transported from certain southern states to northern and western states," charged the attorney general, the Texan Thomas Gregory. "A number of these Negroes have registered [to vote] in violation of the laws." He sent Justice Department agents to interrogate Blacks in a vain attempt to prove this accusation.

For East St. Louis employers, Blacks might be useful as low-paid labor, but they certainly didn't want them living and voting there. Their aim was to make the city a "sundown town," one of the thousands of such spots across the country where Blacks knew they had to get out of town at the end of the workday. A sensationalist local newspaper, which supported the Democrats, magnified the friction by printing lurid stories of Black crime. Many were untrue, for the county jail's population had actually dropped in 1916. Truth, however, has often counted for little when it comes to race in America, and white resentment continued to smolder.

In this city, as in others across the country, workers continued to feel the sharp pinch of wartime inflation. White labor unions had been pressing hard for higher wages—and had thought they now had a chance of success because the war had dried up the stream of new immigrants from overseas willing to work for low pay. But suddenly here were Blacks glad to do so, for whom the meager existing wages might be double what they had earned as southern farmworkers. In the eyes of white workers, fearful of losing ground, this threatened to depress their own wages—or lose them their jobs entirely. These Black competitors became just what immigrants had been: someone to blame. And their skin color made them dangerously conspicuous.

Some East St. Louis plants even sent recruiters south to sign up Black workers and pay their train fare. Often they hired Blacks at lower wages to undercut demands for better pay by white workers. An East St. Louis aluminum plant did exactly that in the spring of 1917. Whites were angry, and focused their rage on Blacks, rather than management—just as management hoped. A few skirmishes put the city on edge, and some local Black men started arming themselves in self-defense.

On the night of July 1, 1917, a crowd of angry whites, some of them drinking, invaded a Black neighborhood. From a Model T Ford, several white men opened fire. When a similar car soon arrived, Black men shot at it, killing two occupants—who turned out to be plainclothes policemen.

Life in a grimy industrial city was tough for many reasons, most of them having nothing to do with Black people. But the policemen's deaths became the pretext to make Blacks the target for a generation of accumulated grievances. A bell in a Black church began ringing an urgent warning.

The next evening a *St. Louis Post-Dispatch* reporter, Carlos F. Hurd, was on the scene:

"I saw man after man, with hands raised, pleading for his life, surrounded by groups of men" who "knew nothing about him except that he was black—and saw them administer . . . death by stoning. I saw one of these men, almost dead from a savage shower of stones, hanged with a clothesline, and when it broke, hanged with a rope which held. Within a few paces of the pole from which he was suspended, four other negroes lay dead or dying." Authorities called out the National Guard but, Hurd wrote, "most of the men in uniform were frankly fraternizing with the [white] men in the street."

There was no limit to what the enraged white crowd did. When they could find no living targets, mobs kicked and stoned Black corpses. White women attacked Black women and children with fists, shoes, stones, and pieces of pipe, and poked at their victims' eyes with hatpins. Although Hurd spared no category—police, soldiers, workers, the well dressed—in describing the bloodshed wrought by the city's white men, he was awkwardly at pains to stress that the female attackers were not "representative of the womanhood of East St. Louis." Rather, he hinted, their painted faces "showed, all too plainly, exactly who and what they were." But even if no other classes of "womanhood" joined them, which seems highly unlikely, they proved just as ferocious as the men, at one point ripping a Black baby away from its mother—who fled for her life, the baby's fate unknown.

As the carnage grew, the crowds set fire to more than a dozen blocks of a Black neighborhood and then used guns to prevent residents from fleeing the inferno. The mob blocked fire engines trying to get through, ensuring the destruction of 245 buildings, almost all of them Black homes, shops, and businesses or flimsy shanties where penniless new migrants had lived. It was as if the flames, which were visible for miles, unleashed all inhibitions and spurred the crowds on. White rioters tossed a Black child into the fire. When the crowd discovered a Black man who had tried to hide in a large wooden box, they nailed it shut and threw it, too, into the flames.

As thick, dark smoke filled the sky, more than 7,000 Black residents fled, by streetcar or on foot, across the Mississippi River to Missouri. Some never returned. It was the most severe outburst of American racial violence in decades. No one knows the exact death toll, which a later grand jury investigation estimated at close to 100. Counting and identifying the Black dead was difficult, for many of those recently arrived from the South left no paper trail as homeowners, tenants, or employees, while some bodies were burned to ashes, and others tossed into the Mississippi River and swept downstream.

Two of the nation's leading Black crusaders for justice, Ida B. Wells and W. E. B. Du Bois, went to East St. Louis to write exposés of what had happened. Wells followed up by bringing a delegation to the state's governor to demand courts-martial for the soldiers who had failed to protect Black citizens, and, in at least one case she described, fired on them. Du Bois's account, published in the NAACP's widely circulated magazine, *The Crisis*, which he edited, was particularly influential.

The country's foremost Black intellectual—he had already published a pathbreaking array of articles and books of history, sociology and biography—was also a formidable reporter who had honed his skills by writing for publication since he was in high school. In East St. Louis he grilled the mayor and other city officials closely, and the article he wrote included photographs, eyewitness testimony, an interview by a white coauthor with soldiers boasting about the Blacks they had killed, and (Du Bois always had a keen eye for incriminating documents) a facsimile of a letter from local trade union officers asking the mayor and city council to rid the town of the "growing menace" of "undesirable negroes."

Horror at this carnage produced the twentieth century's first major American civil rights demonstration: a march of more than 8,000 Black men and women down New York's Fifth Avenue, to the beat of muffled drums. The women and children wore long white dresses, the men dark suits. Du Bois, his coat unbuttoned in the summer heat, can be seen in photographs just behind the drummers, his goateed figure as unassuming in stature as he was towering in intellect. The marchers carried placards such as "Mr. President, Why Not Make America Safe for Democracy?"

Wilson showed no signs of trying to do so. The Bureau of Investigation sent an agent to East St. Louis to look into whether the violence had been caused by German influence. When he found none, the federal government dropped any further inquiry. Despite the pleas of a delegation of Black leaders who visited him, the president—who several weeks earlier had warmly welcomed a reunion of Confederate veterans to Washington—made no public statement about the events in East St. Louis.

This was the first eruption, but by no means the worst, of similar mob violence that would shake American cities over the next several years. Encyclopedias and history books often refer to it as the East St. Louis Race Riot. But Oscar Leonard, superintendent of the Jewish Educational and Charitable Association of St. Louis, used a different word after he crossed the river and walked through the charred remains of Black neighborhoods.

He called it a "pogrom."

RACIAL TENSIONS SOARED in another way as well. The draft law applied to all young men, and many white southerners were appalled that therefore those in uniform would include hundreds of thousands of Blacks. Even worse, they would be mobilized in the name of fighting for democracy.

"Inflate his untutored soul with military airs," warned Senator James K. Vardaman of Mississippi about the Black soldier, and "it is but a short step to the conclusion that his political rights must be respected . . . a problem far-reaching and momentous." An ardent defender of lynching, Vardaman wanted to prevent the drafting of Blacks. When he couldn't, the following year he would call for Black veterans to be banned from returning to the South. Their contacts with Frenchwomen, he said, had raised their expectations to dangerous heights.

The US Army was not one where equality reigned. When a man signed up for the draft, a note on the bottom left-hand corner of the registration form instructed the clerk, "If person is of African descent, tear off this corner." Officers would then quickly shunt the draftee into a segregated unit, usually a labor battalion doing work like digging ditches or loading and unloading trains. These units were last in line for everything. At one base in Virginia, Black soldiers had to sleep through the whole winter of 1917–18 in tents. Throughout the South, troops in the labor battalions were often just issued workmen's blue denim, for officers feared local whites would be enraged at seeing Black men in uniform. It was also not unknown for white officers, taking advantage of soldiers who were sometimes illiterate, to pocket their troops' wages.

Even though the number of Black officers was small, another Mississippi senator, John Sharp Williams, was horrified to hear that a white constituent of his had come under the command of one of them, Lieutenant Colonel Charles Young, a West Point graduate, a veteran cavalryman, and the army's highest-ranking Black soldier. Williams complained to the president, who asked his secretary of war, Newton Baker, to do something. A mere four days later, Wilson reassured Senator Williams that Young "will not in fact have command because he is in ill health." This news startled Young, who rode from his post in Ohio to Washington, DC, on horseback to show that his health was fine. Despite a storm of protest organized by his longtime friend Du Bois, the army forced Young to retire.

The military made sure that, even in uniform, Blacks lived in fear. At Camp Dodge, Iowa, for example, all men stationed there were ordered to witness the hanging of three Black soldiers who had allegedly raped a young white woman, a telephone operator at the base. The 3,000 troops of the all-Black 92nd Division in training at the camp were deliberately placed in the front ranks before the specially constructed gallows. "All were unarmed," reported one eyewitness, "while the white soldiers and officers were armed with rifles and revolvers." Horror-stricken, Black men who had hoped that serving in the military might lead to a better life found themselves forced to watch what looked all too much like a lynching.

It was obviously a shattering experience for them. "'God save my soul,' rent the death like silence," said one newspaper, "'Have mercy,' and 'Oh, Lord save me.' The cries of the condemned men echoed and re-echoed. Soon the shrieks of Negro soldiers, unwilling and terrified spectators, driven into a hysterical state, added to the sickening scene." One of the victims continually shouted to the crowd that he was innocent. "Three negro soldiers among the spectators fainted when the men dropped to their death and another ran amuck," reported another paper. "He started on a dead run directly toward the scaffold, but guards overpowered him." The troops were then marched away from the site to the tunes of a military band.

Despite such shocking episodes, most Black organizations did not oppose the war, and encouraged young men to serve. Even the militant Du Bois urged his readers to "close ranks" with white Americans in the fight against Germany. With a doctorate from Harvard and more study and travel in Europe, Du Bois had a sophisticated grasp of world politics and no illusions about the sacredness of the Allied cause. A champion of the Irish battle for freedom against Britain, he was also keenly aware of the rivalry of all the major European powers over colonies in Africa. Above all, however, he was an activist whose prime loyalty was to his fellow Black Americans. He fervently hoped, like millions of them, that if Black soldiers fought bravely, the country would treat them more fairly once the war was over.

For the domestic Military Intelligence chief, Lieutenant Colonel Ralph Van Deman, however, any threat of Black advancement only deepened his paranoia. "In the fall of 1917," he wrote later, "it became evident that agents of the Central Powers [Germany and its allies] were circulating among the Negro people of the United States." This was nonsense, for no such people needed German or Austro-Hungarian agitators to make them angry. But to Van Deman and the millions who thought like him, Blacks defending their rights in any way were cause for immediate suspicion, and he redoubled his orders for surveillance of them.

Van Deman was ready to believe the wildest of rumors. He asked an agent to investigate word that "fortune tellers, supposed to be gypsies, [are] visiting various colored women in this city [Washington], even entering the kitchens of well-to-do residents and telling the fortunes of the servants. These fortunes . . . all point out that unless Germany wins the war the colored race will be made slaves again." He gave credence to another claim that Germans stirring up Blacks were going door to door posing as sewing machine salesmen. One report to his office related "several incidents of where [*sic*] colored men had attempted to make appointments with white women." From an agent in New York came a report that "German money in large sums is being used in the Harlem district among the negro population" to purchase $600,000 worth of property.

Just as in the Philippines years before, surveillance was not just about gathering information; it was about control. When a dean at the all-Black Howard University wrote a pamphlet that was "a protest against lynchings," Van Deman sent an agent to have a stern talk with him. He urged that Du Bois's monthly, *The Crisis*, which despite its support of the war remained a powerful voice against racial injustice, be kept out of YMCA reading rooms on military bases, where it might be read by Black soldiers.

He threatened Black newspapers. The most influential of these, the *Chicago Defender*, known for its exposés of lynching and Black disenfranchisement, contained, Van Deman asserted, "repeated attacks on the Government, and will tend to create . . . a feeling of disloyalty among the negroes." A Military Intelligence agent visited the *Defender* and told the editor "that he would be held strictly responsible and accountable for any article. . . . I have . . . informed him that the eye of the government is centered upon his paper." That eye seems to have accomplished its aim, for the *Defender*, although continuing its protests against lynching and discrimination, now filled many columns with expressions of patriotism. The editor presented a flag to a Black infantry regiment and pledged to buy Liberty Bonds with money that he had put aside toward a new press and building.

Writing to the Justice Department, Van Deman warned of weekly meetings at the home of the principal of the Colored High School in Baltimore, "presided over by a white man" of "loose habits" who declared that "the atrocities committed by Germany are no worse than the lynchings and burnings which have taken place in the South." Another object of his suspicions in 1917 was the Reverend A. D. Williams, pastor of the Ebenezer Baptist Church in Atlanta. A forceful organizer, Williams helped found an Equal Rights League and a branch of the NAACP to register Black voters. Intelligence officers were ordered "to find out all we possibly can about this colored preacher." The preacher's grandson would eventually become pastor of the same church, and the subject of a later generation of government surveillance: Dr. Martin Luther King Jr.

A Wily Con Man; A Dangerous Woman

I N PITTSBURGH, THE small group of Wobblies around Louis
Walsh continued their activities. To be a left-wing activist in this
highly repressive era was not just a matter of belonging to one organization; you were part of an entire subculture. Walsh raised money
for the IWW by selling "Industrial Freedom Certificates" to better-
off supporters, he was active in Pittsburgh's Radical Library, and he
went to Socialist Party picnics and meetings at the Labor Temple and
the Jewish Labor Lyceum. It was a predominantly male world of fast
friendships, one where people danced, drank, and went swimming together on hot summer days. When a Wobbly comrade made a trip to
New York, he wrote to Walsh about a dance hall in Greenwich Village,
regretting that Walsh hadn't been along on the trip: "Together I am
sure we could be savages for one night." The constant harassment from
business and government forged tight bonds among the Wobblies,
and those in trouble knew they could turn to Walsh for help. When a
veteran Scottish-born organizer named Sam Scarlett lost his job as a
machinist, he moved into Walsh's room at Gibson's Hotel on the city's
Grant Street.

Walsh attended rallies, distributed IWW literature, and was invited
to give a speech about unionism to a new group of Hungarian American Wobblies. The authorities considered Walsh so dangerous, according to a news story after one arrest, that he was "confined in a secret

cell, the location of which is known only to government officials. . . . Several attorneys working in the interests of the I. W. W. made every possible effort within the last few days to ascertain where Walsh is detained. So far they have been unsuccessful."

Curiously, none of Walsh's trusting IWW friends seemed to wonder why, if he was really so dangerous, after each arrest he was always released and back in action a few days later. There was no secret cell. "Walsh" was really Agent 836 of the Justice Department's Bureau of Investigation, and his real name was Leo M. Wendell.

Months earlier, the bureau had heard rumors that the IWW was planning to organize in Pittsburgh and an official reported to his superiors that it could be "an easy matter for a clever person to rope in with this outfit," but that it ought to be someone unknown, from out of town.

"Roper" was detective slang for an undercover informer, and the 32-year-old Wendell was the roper chosen. Hundreds of thousands of pages of reports by undercover operatives are now available in archives, but nearly all of them are signed only with code numbers, and we do not know who their authors were. Leo Wendell is a rare exception, for, as the historian Charles H. McCormick discovered some years ago, at the beginning of his Bureau of Investigation career, he signed his reports with his real name before switching to "836." Like many bureau undercover men, he had previously been a private detective and was one of many who took those same skills into government service during this period.

The bureau came to consider his intelligence about the IWW and other groups on the left so valuable that, several times in the years ahead, while still posing as a Wobbly and working undercover, he would be secretly summoned to Washington or New York to give briefings to a fast-rising young official who had begun his career in the Justice Department the same month Wendell arrived in Pittsburgh and who would rapidly gain great power: J. Edgar Hoover.

From Pittsburgh, Wendell sent a continuing blizzard of reports to his Bureau of Investigation superiors about the Wobblies and other labor organizers among the city's working class. Since he left few written traces beyond these reports, we can only guess at what motivated him, leading him not just to infiltrate the IWW, but to play that role with zest, organizing demonstrations and giving speeches. (One of these, praising the Wobblies, scoffing at traditional trade unions, and defending political prisoners, he boasted was "well received.") Did he proudly believe he was defending his country against dangerous threats? Unlikely, for there are no statements of fervent patriotism in the thousands of pages he wrote for the bureau. Was it money? Also unlikely, for there were surely more lucrative and less risky ways of earning a living than as an undercover agent making four or five dollars a day. As with many other spies throughout history, he was more likely motivated by the enjoyment of successfully playing a role, with a secret no one around him knew. The adulterer or the con man sometimes seeks the same thrill, not merely sex or money, but the very pleasure of deception.

There is a hint of a con man's satisfaction in one of Wendell's reports, in which he relays scraps of news he picked up during an evening with Wobbly comrades; the report ends, "We loafed together until 11:00 P.M. then separated." The "loafed" is almost a reveling in his role-playing. He used the word again in another report: "Loafed around the Radical Library until 11:00 P.M." (As the local IWW secretary, incidentally, Wendell had a key to the Radical Library, of which he made a copy for his bureau supervisor.) Another evening he stayed up talking "science and anarchy" in a bar until 5:00 a.m. He proudly records many other late evenings of drinking, sometimes ending the night asleep on the couch or floor of another Wobbly's room. Sometimes, as if playfully flaunting the role he was playing, he writes a report from "836" describing a meeting at which "Walsh" was one of the speakers.

Like a con man, Wendell took a professional's pride in how much his IWW friends trusted him. The letter from the comrade about the dance hall in Greenwich Village, for instance, Wendell transcribed for his superiors. The comrade who lost his job and moved into Wendell's room didn't know, as the historian McCormick puts it, that "he owed his firing to his new roommate."

Wendell attended gatherings of every conceivable left-wing organization, from labor unions to the local branch of a national antiwar coalition, the People's Council of America for Democracy and Peace. He proudly reported to his superiors starting a "factional fight" with the aim "to break up the *Peoples Council*."

This was not the only group he tried to disrupt. When there was a move to bring the local tailors' union into the IWW fold, Wendell told the bureau, "I have discouraged [this] as much as possible without creating suspicion" because "practically all of these Tailors are foreigners and over fifty per cent Italian . . . and could do great harm" if their numbers augmented the Wobblies. He evidently succeeded, for a few days later the group dropped the plan to include the tailors. "Attended a meeting of the Socialist Party," he also boasted, "and started another fight within the party by having an Anarchist elected to membership."

NATIONALLY, THE IWW's membership was surging; more than 30,000 new recruits joined between April and September 1917. Even though other unions organized far more strikes, this year saw a cascade of those led by Wobblies, with, it seemed, workers in a new industry walking out every month: sawmill hands in Minnesota, construction laborers in Utah, button makers in New York, railway track crews in Washington State, fruit pickers in California, silk weavers in New Jersey, teamsters in Iowa.

Hundreds of letters and telegrams from governors, corporate executives, and trade associations flooded Washington demanding a crackdown on the IWW. Senator Henry Ashurst of Arizona, referring to the German kaiser, declared that the organization's initials stood for "Imperial Wilhelm's Warriors." He urged President Wilson to take "prompt and courageous action." Others agreed. "Fear is the only force," said Assistant Attorney General William Fitts, "that will keep the wretches in order."

On September 5, 1917, hundreds of men raided all 48 Wobbly offices across the country to make arrests. Wilson had personally approved the raids. A Bureau of Investigation man led each party, but other agencies eagerly got in on the act: US marshals, the Secret Service, county sheriffs' deputies, and the "Red squads" that city police forces had started forming to watch and harass leftists. In Pennsylvania, men from the Internal Revenue Service and the Immigration Bureau took part, and in Arizona, a US cavalry officer. The raid on the Wobblies' Chicago headquarters was joined by American Protective League vigilantes.

The raiders altogether seized five tons of material, mostly documents. In Butte, Montana, they also took several thousand prints of a photograph of the martyred Frank Little; in Omaha, two copies of Victor Hugo's novel *Les Misérables*, and one each of Shakespeare's *Julius Caesar* and Frederic W. Farrar's *The Life of Christ*, plus a box of cigars. Targets also included homes; from Wobbly editor and poet Ralph Chaplin agents took three bundles of love letters he had written to his wife years earlier. In Detroit, raiders seized so much from the home of a single Wobbly that the district attorney complained to the US attorney general that it "became necessary to procure wagons to haul the stuff." One of the senior Wobblies the Chicago raiders arrested was, unknown to them, an operative of the Burns Detective Agency. It would take his frustrated employers months to secure his release.

The unprecedented raids were accompanied by government leaks to the dependably gullible daily press. The *New York Times* breathlessly reported learning "from a source of undoubted authority" that the IWW was planning "the destruction . . . of the wheat and corn crops" by setting "the great fields of the West ablaze," "the wrecking of farming machinery" by cleverly inserting rocks and metal scraps, and "a multitude of crimes, all intended to hamper the successful prosecution of the war." The paper assured readers that "German spies" had infiltrated the organization.

In Pittsburgh, to maintain Leo Wendell's credibility, government agents conspicuously ransacked his room in Gibson's Hotel. Thanks to information from Wendell, bureau operatives could quickly seize his former roommate Sam Scarlett in Ohio, where he was organizing under another name.

"With financial records, membership records, cash, plates for printing presses, and all correspondence gone," writes one historian, "the entire union was disabled." This was the point. "Our purpose being," the US attorney in Philadelphia wrote to the attorney general, "as I understand it, very largely to put the I. W. W. out of business."

The government slapped 166 Wobblies with identical charges under the Espionage Act: vague and sweeping counts of conspiracy to obstruct the draft, cause insubordination in the armed forces, block the flow of war goods, obstruct the rights of employers, and urge sabotage and other illegal action.

The 166 would be tried in Chicago, but similar mass indictments were issued in Omaha, Wichita, and Sacramento, covering some 300 Wobblies in all. Meanwhile, raids continued, and included attacks on the defense committees set up to help those arrested. Agents barged into the office of the defense committee for the Sacramento group seven times in six months. When one of its members, Theodora Pollak, produced bail for some Wobbly defendants, the police took the money, arrested her, forced her through the medical exam usually performed on prostitutes, and jailed her. The government would arrest nearly 400 more IWW members over the next two years.

The war against the Wobblies emboldened those who wanted to go even farther. "I want to see Congress take action to take away the citizenship of every disloyal American—every American who is not heartily in support of his Government in its crisis," declared the feckless Vice President Marshall. "I would annul the citizenship of every such individual and confiscate his property."

EMPLOYERS HAD THEIR own motives for weakening the labor movement, but the war on the IWW drew much support from the public. Why were so many Americans in 1917, especially men, so passionate about going on the attack—not just against the Germans but also against imagined domestic enemies?

Their fervor partly came from yet another front in the war at home: a long-growing tension over the changing positions of men and women. This was magnifying anxieties among American men. Fifty years before the First World War, most of them worked on farms, doing the strenuous field labor that had defined manhood for millennia. Farm wives and widows sometimes had to do such tasks as well, but men still traditionally preferred to imagine women as doing only women's work, such as cooking, cleaning, sewing, and fetching water from the well. The census did not even count such farm women as workers.

By 1910, however, only a third of American men still worked on farms, for motor-driven tractors and harvesters had swept millions off the land. Meanwhile, in the preceding 40 years the percentage of women in the paid workforce had nearly doubled. Military production brought yet an additional million women into the labor force during the war, some of them even doing—and doing well, employers' studies showed—classically male labor like welding or operating cranes or machine tools. An automobile industry trade journal reported in 1917 that "the Link Belt Co., Indianapolis, finds women more efficient and productive" than men in certain factory jobs. Other women became streetcar drivers or conductors, replacing drafted men. Many earned more than their husbands or brothers did as soldiers.

These changes left many men unsettled. The newspaper of a streetcar workers' union, for instance, published a poem that began:

We wonder where we are drifting, where is the freedom of
     the stripes and stars
If for the sake of greed and profit we put women conductors
     on the cars.
Woman is God's most tender flower, made to blossom and to
     bear
To keep our homes, raise our children, and our joys and sor-
     rows share.
She was made by God the weaker, like a vine on man to lean;
She was meant to work like her nature, tender, sweet and
     clean . . .

A worried psychologist bemoaned the disturbing new times when "spinsters can support themselves with more physical comforts and larger leisure than they would have as wives; when married women may prefer the money they can earn and the excitement they can find in outside employment . . . when they can conveniently leave their husbands should it so suit their fancy" and, worst of all, when "men . . . must compete in the market with women."

In white-collar work, especially, women sometimes successfully competed with men, and in a few occupations, such as secretary and telephone operator, employers preferred them. Another sign of changing roles was the vocal, ever more popular movement for women's suffrage. By 1917, it was clearly on its way to victory. Once women got the vote, many men feared, what might they want next? To abolish marriage, as Emma Goldman urged? Or to rob men of their jobs?

The clearest sign of the slowly changing balance of power between the sexes was that the overall American divorce rate, though low by today's standards, more than tripled between 1890 and 1920. Many women were no longer including the word "obey" in their wedding vows, and the spread of information about birth control—even though illegal—was giving them more control over their reproductive lives. In the eyes of millions of American men, ambitious women were as much of a threat to the traditional order as immigrants, socialists, and Blacks.

"Women are successfully invading all the professions," one alarmed author wrote. "The doors of the leading colleges have been thrown open to them, and thousands have been graduated. . . . Yet with all these privileges, 'the shrieking sisterhood' still cries for more."

In the face of these threats, however, war remained an exclusively male occupation. It's no accident, as well, that other movements many American men beyond draft age now plunged into, such as the APL with its badges, ranks, and commanders, or the Ku Klux Klan with its robes and titles like Kleagles and Klaliffs, echoed the military's elaborate hierarchy—and its promise of violence.

Significantly, many of the antiwar dissidents who provoked the most male rage were women. Among them was a feisty, popular Socialist Party activist with a mass of red hair. Known as "Red Kate" to both friends and enemies, Kate Richards O'Hare sometimes played the part by dressing in bright red.

During her Kansas childhood, her parents' thriving corn and wheat farm went bankrupt in a severe drought and recession, and the family had to move to the slums of Kansas City. "The bitterness of it all was seared upon my memory and I never see a strong man vainly seeking and begging for work that my whole soul does not revolt." As a young woman, she worked as a machinist, where she learned to deal with men who thought no woman should be allowed near a forge or lathe. "There is nothing else that brings the exultation, the consciousness of power," she wrote, "like taking hard, unyielding steel, and conquering it, shaping and forming it. . . . And watching it grow under your hand to a beautiful polished thing of use and beauty."

She also taught briefly in a sod-walled schoolhouse, and then became a journalist, working undercover in jobs ranging from garment maker to waitress, and reporting on the violence that so often met labor struggles. "I heard heads crack and bones snap," she wrote after visiting striking copper miners in Michigan's Upper Peninsula who battled company detectives and the National Guard. "I walked over bloodstained snow. I heard bullets whistle."

Kate and her husband, Frank O'Hare, an organizer for the Socialist Party, spent their honeymoon on the lecture circuit. She took her first baby to a national convention of the party. They had four children in all, naming their twin boys Eugene and Victor after the party's revered leader, Eugene Victor Debs. While Kate was on the road on marathon one-city-per-day speaking tours, Frank was the manager who organized them, and, most unusually, stayed home with the children, helped by his sister and older children from a Socialist youth group. Together, the couple published a monthly, the *National Rip-Saw*. Kate was the party's most popular woman speaker; to book an appearance by her, a local Socialist group had to sell 500 *Rip-Saw* subscriptions.

A tall, thin woman of formidable energy, she gave 300 speeches while running as a Socialist Party candidate for Congress from Kansas in 1910 (in an election in which, as a woman, she could not vote).

Someone orating three or four times a day in the era before public address systems needed a powerful voice, and O'Hare was convinced that hers came from a regimen of chest-expansion exercises that she performed daily for weeks before going on tour. She ended each talk sweating profusely. Especially in the states of the Great Plains, where she had known rural hardship and debt firsthand, she could attract crowds of thousands, as she put it, while traveling "up and down this earth preaching the gospel of Socialism."

Like most socialists, O'Hare depicted a promised land as beautiful and as hazy in its details as that envisioned by Christians. She never lost the fervor of her Disciples of Christ upbringing (she had once hoped to become a minister) and was a perennial speaker at the Socialist Party's summer encampments, which were festivals of oratory and song not unlike revival meetings. The Bible threaded through her talks. "This is a bloody, brutal war," she declared of the conflict in Europe. "We [socialists] had no part in bringing it, but it has performed a mighty service for us. . . . We are branded now. Like Cain, we wear a brand upon our brow: the brand of being the followers of the Prince of Peace."

In 1913 O'Hare defeated several prominent men, to their shock, in an election among party members to represent the United States at a meeting in Europe of socialist parties from across the world. Seven months before the war began, she was the only woman delegate at the London gathering, where she found some of the European leaders intrigued by her success at rousing enthusiasm for their cause among farmers. This was still a time when socialists were confident that their movement was on the rise everywhere and that workers from different countries would never fight each other. The high point of her trip was when she addressed a mass meeting of 10,000 striking workers in Dublin:

"Never to me again perhaps will there come so great a moment as when the crowd recognized in my speech the voice of brotherhood from across the sea and accepted me as of the clan. Never again will I be so deeply moved as when two hundred Irish policemen stood with lifted helmets to make a path through the seething mass of people through which two stalwart Irishmen carried me on their shoulders."

By less than a year later, however, all of Europe had turned, in O'Hare's words, to "blood-stained mire." Like most American socialists, she found the outbreak of war a shattering blow, and as a Christian she was outraged that both sides claimed God's support. She felt, however, "that the real religion of Jesus must come as the result of this war. . . . A new world will be born of our travail, a United States of the World."

O'Hare was the Socialist Party candidate for the US Senate from Missouri in 1916. After the country entered the war the following spring, she began noticing government agents at her talks. "No Queen of royal blood has been so carefully cared for as I have been by the United States Department of Justice," she joked to an audience. "They are, always, on the job. When I lie down at night they are there. When I get up in the morning they are at the other side of the breakfast table. . . . They carefully look over my mail. . . . Every once in a while they go through my baggage and inspect my corset covers and underwear." Sometimes she went up to one, looked at his transcription of a speech, and suggested corrections.

It took little time for her to become the first prominent Socialist Party figure indicted under the Espionage Act. The offense was a talk she had given in Bowman, North Dakota, "a little, sordid, wind-blown, sun-blistered, frost-scarred town," she recalled, where she was accused of encouraging men to resist the draft. Once she came to trial, O'Hare denied the charges, saying that instead she had declared that "if any young man feels that it is his duty to enlist, then with all my heart I say—'Go and God bless you. Your blood may enrich the battlefields of France.'" The prosecutor left no doubt about his own enthusiasm for the war; he was a combat veteran of the Philippine campaign and the judge addressed him in court as "Colonel."

The indictment charged that O'Hare had said that American women had become "brood sows to raise children to get into the army and be made into fertilizer." This, the judge declared, impeded the war effort because "the only way to win a war [is] to have soldiers." The prosecutor called O'Hare "a dangerous woman" because she was "shrewd and brainy." Her assertiveness as a woman was clearly as infuriating to judge and prosecutor as her opposition to the war. Yet, doubtless to their frustration, they couldn't denounce her in the same way they might have condemned Emma Goldman, for O'Hare was the mother of four and said she hated capitalism because it destroyed the family.

After a mere 30 minutes of deliberation, the all-male jury found her guilty. The judge sentenced her to five years, delivering a fierce 26-page speech. He was especially riled by her remarks about motherhood: "American sons are not going to allow their mothers to be likened unto brood sows, and American fathers and mothers are not going to submit to having their sons assigned to no more glorious destiny than that of fertilizer."

O'Hare remained out on bail and still vocally denounced the war while appealing the verdict, but with other antiwar activists all over the country now being jailed, there seemed little chance of her escaping those five years in prison.

WITH PROSECUTIONS OF dissidents like Goldman and O'Hare, the sweeping raids on the IWW, and help from vigilantes like the American Protective League, the government was in full combat against its enemies at home. But as the end of 1917 approached, few American troops were anywhere near the enemy in Europe.

The training of millions of draftees was going slowly. Fully a quarter of them, it turned out, were illiterate. General Pershing was also worried about "the large number of men of alien birth who had no knowledge of English." Army officers would have to be found who could censor soldiers' mail in 49 languages. Presiding over all of this was Wilson's secretary of war, Newton Baker. He had no military training and little administrative experience other than a term as mayor of Cleveland. Wilson, one historian comments, "never selected advisers who might overshadow him."

The Allies were eager to do anything to bring US troops to the front lines. At one point French prime minister Georges Clemenceau proposed setting up brothels for them. When Baker saw the letter making this offer, he said, "For God's sake . . . don't show this to the president or he'll stop the war!"

The British and French urgently wanted American reinforcements because their own men continued to die in huge numbers. In Belgium, the second half of 1917 saw the Battle of Passchendaele launched by the British, a monthslong slaughter in heavy rain in which, besides being felled by shrapnel and machine-gun bullets, some soldiers drowned in deep mud. The Allies gained a few miles of ground, but, as in many battles of this war, the attackers suffered even more than the defenders: British, Canadian, Australian, and New Zealand troops lost 275,000 men killed and wounded; the Germans, 220,000.

On another front, Italy suffered a humiliating loss of territory and men in the Battle of Caporetto, with hundreds of thousands of its soldiers killed or captured. This epic defeat would later be the background to a novel by a Red Cross ambulance driver with the Italian troops, Ernest Hemingway's *A Farewell to Arms*. The British and French rushed divisions to reinforce Italy, but that weakened their forces in France and Belgium. "We shall be hard pressed to hold our own and keep Italy standing," British prime minister David Lloyd George told his ambassador in Washington. "Our manpower is pretty well exhausted."

Just as this battle was unfolding so disastrously, the Wilson administration and the Allied governments were further dismayed by events in Russia. Although it was by far the largest of the Allies, that country's army was ragged and undisciplined, and the immense nation was drained and half-starved by more than three years of brutal war. The British military attaché estimated that over the course of 1917, a million Russian soldiers deserted their units and started walking back to their villages. Hungry workers demanding a change of government staged demonstrations that shook the capital, Petrograd.

Now, finally, the German gamble of sending Lenin and his revolutionary comrades back to their homeland in the sealed train paid off—spectacularly. On November 7, 1917, came what the Allied governments had dreaded for months: the Bolsheviks seized power. In Petrograd, they occupied the symbol of government, the Winter Palace. The city's army garrison supported them, and sympathetic sailors took over naval ships in the harbor.

Newspapers across the United States filled with photographs of these fierce-looking rebels with their long winter coats carrying rifles with bayonets and occupying the Russian capital. At the front, troops listened eagerly to appeals from Bolshevik agitators, who urged them to band together and take control from their officers. Left-wingers in the West were thrilled: the Wobblies awaiting trial in Chicago's Cook County Jail sang revolutionary songs, beating tin cups and wooden stools against their cell bars in time with the music. The startled sailors on a Russian freighter that stopped to refuel at Seattle, a Wobbly stronghold, found themselves cheered as heroes.

Most people in the United States, however, were not believers in violent revolution, and the Bolsheviks frightened them—all the more so because they were holding as prisoners (and would soon execute) the Russian tsar and tsarina and their entire photogenic family: the girls in lacy white dresses, the boy in a sailor suit. That this ruthless, relatively small party had seized power in such a vast country reignited an ancient American fear of secret conspiracies, something always stronger in unsettled times, when people fear that their own positions in life are threatened or eroding and need someone to blame.

That fear has found different targets over the centuries: the witches of Salem, Freemasons, the Illuminati, the Rothschilds, the pope. But never previously had it flourished on such an extravagant scale. Over the next few years people would blame Bolshevism for everything from strikes to anti-lynching protests to loosening sexual mores to untrimmed beards. In the words of the historian David Brion Davis, "The years from 1917 to 1921 are probably unmatched in American history for popular hysteria, xenophobia, and paranoid suspicion."

The Bolshevik seizure of power only intensified the crackdown on American dissent. Vigilante organizations found the number of their followers increasing dramatically. Albert Briggs moved the headquarters of his American Protective League from Chicago to Washington, DC, to be at the center of power. As 1917 ended, the

APL claimed 1,200 branches around the country, with a total of 250,000 members. In the year to come, the organization would be more aggressive than ever.

In Washington, London, Paris, and Rome, officials were uniformly horrified by the Bolshevik coup, for Lenin and his new government were determined to make a separate peace with Germany and its allies. Meeting in the captured Russian city of Brest-Litovsk, envoys from the two sides quickly agreed on an armistice. British, French, and American generals were appalled to see news photographs of fur-hatted Russian soldiers, from a huge army once their ally, fraternizing with German troops at the front.

Now, with its war against Russia ending, Germany could withdraw soldiers from the eastern side of Europe and redeploy them in France and Belgium. The German high command began transporting some half-million men across the continent. Within weeks, Allied intelligence detected signs of plans for a major new German offensive in France. Once it came, however, there would still not yet be enough trained US troops at the front to be of help in turning it back. "The war," one worried American general wrote in his diary, "is practically lost. . . . Alas, I think we came too late."

The Water Cure

O NCE AGAIN, WOODROW Wilson appeared before Congress, this time with less than an hour's notice. "Practically every taxi-cab in town was commandeered by members" of both houses to rush them to hear the president's speech, reported the *Washington Times*. The British ambassador managed to reach the House of Representatives chamber in time, but few other diplomats did. The doorkeeper announced, "The president of the United States," and Wilson made his way to the podium. His wife and Colonel House, quiet rivals, watched from the gallery.

It was January 8, 1918, and the president was worried. Morale among the Allies was shaky: Italy remained deeply demoralized from its disastrous defeat at Caporetto, and the French army had not dared launch any major attacks after the previous year's mutinies. Strikes over food shortages were sweeping through Britain.

Both Wilson and the Allied prime ministers in Europe feared the offensive certain to come from more than 40 divisions of troops Berlin was moving from Russia to France and Belgium. A year earlier there had been three Allied soldiers for every two Germans on that front; now, with most American draftees still in training camps, there were four German soldiers for every three Allied men. A German attack, it was clear, could produce a disaster for the Allies.

Although the United States brimmed with martial enthusiasm, the president was apprehensive about the appeal to war-weary Europe of the armistice just concluded, between Germany and its allies and the new revolutionary government of Russia, in a great redbrick fortress at Brest-Litovsk. Wilson wanted to stave off calls for a negotiated peace by claiming the most altruistic possible goals for the months of bloodshed ahead.

As the assembled lawmakers fell silent, he began what became known as his "Fourteen Points" speech. These were the aims, he said, that the United States was fighting for. Some were goals already taken for granted, such as Germany's withdrawal from territory it occupied in Belgium, France, and Russia. Alsace and Lorraine, seized by Germany decades earlier, would of course be restored to France; the senators and representatives rose to their feet cheering at the mention of that. Another war aim—"open covenants of peace, openly arrived at"—reflected the impact of the Russian Revolution, for the Bolsheviks had just opened the archives of tsarist Russia's foreign ministry and revealed to the world treaties the Allied powers had agreed to in secret. They had decided, for example, that after the war they would parcel out among themselves great swaths of the Ottoman Empire, a German ally, either as territory controlled directly or as zones of influence.

Another of the Fourteen Points was not quite as noble as it sounded: "a free, open-minded, and absolutely impartial adjustment of all colonial claims." Surely that would not include the claim of any African colonies to independence from their European masters, or of the Philippines from the United States, or of Ireland from Britain. (Indeed, authorities in New York had recently used the Espionage Act to shut down meetings of an organization called the Friends of Irish Freedom.) But for other territory, it was self-determination all the way: the peoples of the sprawling, multiethnic Austro-Hungarian Empire should have the right to autonomy, and a new "independent Polish state" should be carved out of the territory where Poles now lived, in Austria-Hungary, Germany, and Russia.

The fourteenth point was the president's call for what would become known as the League of Nations. People had talked about such an idea for years, but Wilson now made this vision his own. The league would be a permanent forum of all the world's countries, where they would peacefully negotiate and resolve the tensions that in previous times had led to war.

Even though none were genuinely new, the Fourteen Points were vague enough so that many could see in them their own goals, and they proved a great political success in the United States. Most Americans, like the president, ignored the fact that socialists and peace activists had long voiced many of these same aims, such as opposing secret treaties and winning freedom for subject peoples. But even Robert La Follette was deeply impressed and now moderated the critical tone of his speeches.

W. E. B. Du Bois, his eye always on Black freedom, took a different tack, using the Fourteen Points as a step toward the more radical transformations he sought: "Out of this war will rise, soon or late . . . a self-governing India . . . an Africa for the Africans. . . . Out of this war will rise, too, an American Negro with the right to vote and the right to work and the right to live without insult. These things . . . are written in the stars, and the first step toward them is victory for the armies of the Allies."

Among Europeans, at least privately, there was a touch of cynicism. Of Wilson's Fourteen Points, French prime minister Georges Clemenceau remarked, "*Le bon Dieu n'avait que dix.*" The good Lord had only ten.

ONE GOAL THAT the Fourteen Points did not include was the right to dissent at home. The postmaster general, Albert Burleson, continued his war on newspapers and magazines that offended him. "He is in a belligerent mood against the Germans, against labor, against pacifists etc.," Colonel House wrote in his diary. "He is now the most belligerent member of the Cabinet." Within less than a year after the passage of the Espionage Act, "the Cardinal" had deemed 44 American periodicals entirely "unmailable," a total that would soon include some 30 more. He also banned, or singled out for warnings to publishers, specific issues of many more. *The Nation* earned his wrath for criticizing a labor leader who was a key Wilson ally; *The Public*, a progressive Chicago weekly, for urging that the government raise money by taxes instead of loans, to put more of the burden on the wealthy; and the Black *Amsterdam News* when it complained that Black soldiers were dying for the rights of Serbs and Poles in Europe while they risked being lynched at home.

Burleson banned various issues of the *Gaelic American* for backing independence for Ireland and of the *Freeman's Journal and Catholic Register* for reminding readers that Thomas Jefferson had supported that cause. Taking their lead from Burleson, when local postmasters around the country saw newspapers and magazines they didn't like, they sometimes simply removed them from the mail. Southern postmasters were particularly likely to do this when widely read Black periodicals like the *Chicago Defender* or Du Bois's *The Crisis* published exposés of lynching.

Before long, Burleson would ban from the mail virtually the entire socialist press, with a prewar combined circulation of some two million. Particularly devastated by this were the many rural socialist papers, which had no way to reach their subscribers except through the post office. Only one in ten kept publishing.

Sometimes, after banning an issue or two of a periodical, the postmaster general would then declare that, because it had not been publishing regularly, it was no longer entitled to second-class mailing privileges. Losing such a permit, which charged printed matter only a penny a pound for postage, multiplied a publication's mailing costs eight times over—an expense few could afford.

For one journalist, censorship was the least of the penalties. When the *San Antonio Inquirer*, a Black newspaper in Texas, published a letter that the Justice Department thought too sympathetic to some Black soldiers who had mutinied, the paper's editor was sentenced to two years in the Leavenworth penitentiary.

Burleson maintained that he was not out to suppress free speech and that he would interfere with no publication unless he found it treasonous or seditious. But then he added, "Most Socialist papers do contain this matter." He also seized and banned 600 copies of a pamphlet, *Why Freedom Matters*, not because it criticized the war—it didn't—but because it attacked censorship. He found "unmailable" no less than 14 pamphlets published by the National Civil Liberties Bureau, soon to become the American Civil Liberties Union.

From such a ban, there was no appeal. The prohibited newspaper or magazine could only file a lawsuit—none of which, during Burleson's tenure, succeeded. Sometimes, as if anticipating the protagonist of Kafka's *The Trial*, a journalist could not even learn what he or she was accused of. When the publisher of one banned pamphlet asked for an explanation, a Post Office official told him, "If the reasons are not obvious to you or anyone else having the welfare of this country at heart, it will be useless . . . to present them." According to the editor Oswald Garrison Villard, William H. Lamar, the Post Office's chief legal officer, declared, "You know I am not working in the dark on this censorship thing. I know exactly what I am after. I am after three things and only three things—pro-Germanism, pacifism, and 'high-browism.'"

THE FIERY KANSAS-BORN Kate Richards O'Hare, no high-brow, was still out on bail while appealing her five-year sentence. Traveling the country, her slender, red-haired figure standing on one platform after another, she made her case itself the topic of her speeches: "Shall the Sentence Stand? Which Shall It Be? A Criminal or Joan of Arc?" Her supporters published photos of O'Hare and her four children captioned "Shall this family be broken up?" Already they were having a tough time financially; to scrape by, her husband, Frank, had taken a job selling vacuum cleaners. O'Hare's persecutors had seen her, she said, like a witch of old prepared "to cast the evil eye on the younger generation." Meanwhile, the judge and prosecutor from her trial barraged Washington with demands to jail her immediately. Ignoring legal ethics, the judge even suggested to the Justice Department arguments it could make to the US court of appeals.

Meanwhile, the country's other most prominent woman troublemaker, Emma Goldman, remained ensconced in the four-story women's cellblock of the state penitentiary in Jefferson City, Missouri. Her home for many months to come would be a seven-by-eight-foot cell with a cement floor and steel ceiling and a bunk fastened to the wall, with bags of straw for both mattress and pillow.

For six nine-hour days a week, Goldman earned 28 cents a day sew-

ing denim jackets and overalls in stuffy air. She caustically observed
that the prison had contracts with various clothing companies who
"bought our labor for a song and they were therefore in a position to
undersell those employing union labor." Her gift for befriending people was repaid when a group of Black women prisoners sewed her daily
quota of 54 jackets, to give her a day off for her birthday.

However, not all war opponents were yet behind bars. One of the
most colorful was still at liberty, and, like O'Hare and Goldman, was
a woman. Marie Equi never won the national renown that they had,
but she was easily their match in feistiness. And, despite her five-foot,
three-inch frame, she outdid any woman of her time in her willingness
to battle for what she believed in with her fists.

Equi's mother had emigrated from Ireland, her stonemason father
from Italy, and they raised their 11 children in New Bedford, Massachusetts. Three siblings and several young cousins died during her
childhood, and Equi herself survived tuberculosis before the age of
ten. She had to drop out of high school to go to work in a textile mill.
After two years, a young woman friend from a better-off family paid
her tuition for a year at a private girls' school. Finally, in 1892, the
two women went west and settled together on a rugged patch of land
near the Columbia River in Oregon. It was apparently the first in a
succession of relationships Equi would have, in an era when same-sex
romances between women did not draw quite the public ire of those
between men.

Equi's partner worked as a teacher in a nearby town. The school superintendent, however, was a notorious con man, selling tracts of real
estate depicted alluringly in illustrated brochures—which turned out to
be barren wasteland when the purchasers finally arrived. He also failed
to pay Equi's partner the full salary she was due. Outside his office one
sweltering summer day, Equi attacked him with a rawhide horsewhip,
cheered on by a sympathetic crowd. Note the crowd: however much
Equi departed from traditional womanly behavior, she always had the
knack of doing so in a way that drew public support.

In her twenties, Equi went to medical school and then opened a practice in Portland, where she then became a state leader in the battle for women's suffrage. By now she had a new partner. This time, however, there was a public scandal, because Equi's love interest, 23-year-old Harriet Speckart, was the heiress to part of an Oregon brewery and real estate fortune. Speckart's mother tried to get herself appointed guardian, said one newspaper, because "her daughter was under the influence of Dr. Marie Equi." Then Speckart's brother got involved and had a "violent quarrel" with his sister.

When Equi appeared on the scene, according to another paper, she "is said to have grasped the youth by the throat and to have shaken him violently." He fled via a fire escape. Despite a wave of publicity that would have ended many another person's career, or at least forced someone to leave town, Equi had a remarkable ability to survive such fracases. Although there would be more romances in her life, she and Speckart remained close for years and adopted a child together. When Equi later took their daughter to street rallies, she told her beforehand, "If the police come, you run."

Equi ignored the law that outlawed distributing birth control devices and information, and defied both the government and the American Medical Association by performing abortions. If her poorer patients couldn't afford to pay, "Doc," as she became known, treated them for free. When trigger-happy vigilantes and sheriff's deputies in Everett, Washington, killed five Wobblies and wounded many more, Equi dropped everything and rushed to treat the victims.

In 1913, she appeared at a rally to support striking women at a Portland fruit cannery where several of her patients worked. A pregnant Native American striker was speaking when mounted police leapt from their horses to arrest her. Enraged, Equi followed the police to the courthouse and marched in after them, typically rallying a crowd behind her. "Deputy Sheriff Downey tried to restrain the infuriated woman," a newspaper reported. Undeterred by her short stature, "she gave him a right arm swing in the jaw. Night Watchman Fifer . . . tried to remonstrate with Dr. Equi, but her ready fist caught him below the left eye." Equi seems to have accomplished what she intended, for the police did not book the speaker they had seized, and allowed her to leave the jail in Equi's company.

When the birth control crusader Margaret Sanger came to Portland, she asked Equi's help in adding more medical information to her widely distributed booklet *Family Limitation*, and Equi eagerly obliged. When Sanger gave a speech on a return visit, the police promptly arrested them both. More than a hundred shouting women followed them to the jail.

Sanger later wrote about how women prisoners "scampered around talking over their troubles and complaints with Dr. Equi, and receiving condolence and wholesome advice in return." Equi wrote extravagant love notes to Sanger—"My arms are around you. I kiss your sweet mouth in absolute surrender." Sanger apparently returned some of these feelings for years, writing (in a letter carefully copied by the Justice Department): "Your picture is on my dresser always [and] as I look into those blue, blue eyes, I remember our dinner, our ride, everything—*everything.*"

As pressure for war rose in 1916, Portland staged a big "preparedness" parade, complete with Civil War veterans and 15 brass bands. Equi, however, put a white banner on the side of her car covered with antiwar slogans such as "Thou Shalt Not Kill." Adroitly, she slipped the car into the parade, right behind the Knights of Columbus. Once again, she found herself under arrest.

When agents raided Wobbly branches all over the country in September 1917, they also targeted Equi, carrying away armfuls of her correspondence and medical records. When she and a new lover discovered a Dictaphone planted in their hotel room, they threw it over the transom with a note fastened to it: "Here you poor fish you might need this again."

Knowing that the authorities were quick to arrest antiwar speakers, she came up with a maneuver to foil them. In downtown Portland, Equi borrowed the crampons of a telephone company lineman, and used them to climb high up a pole. From there, she unfurled a banner reading DOWN WITH THE IMPERIALIST WAR. When a crowd appeared, she addressed them, safely out of reach. "The police tried to enlist the fire department to get her down," says one account of this exploit, "but firemen were in no rush to harass the Doc who cared for their families. Only when she was ready did she climb down."

After this, a case against her was only a matter of time. Indicting her for violating four different provisions of the Espionage Act and preparing to put her on trial, the US attorney in Portland called Equi "the most dangerous person at large in Oregon."

ON THE OTHER side of the Atlantic, the long-feared new German offensive burst upon the Allies on March 21, 1918, with an artillery barrage of unprecedented ferocity: more than one million explosive, smoke, and poison gas shells were fired in a mere five hours at a 40-mile stretch of British trenches in northern France. The reverberations could be heard across the English Channel in England.

The attack that followed was far more deadly than anyone had expected, for the Germans had made a shrewd change in tactics. Instead of repeating the frontal assaults both sides had launched during the first three and a half years of war, in which long lines of men plodded abreast toward the enemy only to be mowed down by machine-gun fire, German officers had rigorously retrained tens of thousands of infantrymen to form groups of seven to ten "storm troopers" who would dart forward half-hidden in ditches or gullies. Helped by a fortuitous dense fog that covered the battlefield, storm trooper teams tossed hand grenades into British trenches and machine-gun posts from the side or even the rear. The result was devastating: in a single day the Germans captured nearly 100 square miles of territory, while the British, fearing being surrounded, evacuated another 40.

Day after day American newspapers ran headlines in thick black type: "Teutons Are Still Gaining Ground"; "French Are Completely Surrounded by Enemy"; "How Germans May Shoot into London If They Capture Calais and Boulogne"; "Allies Are Forced Back!" Church bells rang in Berlin. The kaiser declared a national holiday for schoolchildren. Germans took some 100,000 Allied soldiers prisoner, and before long their forces had advanced far enough that they could begin firing a new long-range artillery gun that shot enormous shells more than 80 miles, striking Paris. Millions were horrified at the thought that the Germans might capture the French capital.

The Wilson administration tried to speed up the training of millions of American soldiers, to respond to the Allies' urgent pleas. But it was also faced with men who refused to be drafted. The vast majority did so not for reasons of belief but because they had families to support or small farms to keep going, or simply did not want to be killed. All told, 338,000 men who registered for the draft failed to show up when called, and an estimated three million who should have registered never did so.

In those pre-electronic days, of course, it was easy to drop from sight. A common trick was to register for the draft, but to give a vacant lot as your address. Although Vietnam is the conflict we associate with draft refusal, "a higher percentage of American men," writes the historian Michael Kazin, "successfully resisted conscription during World War I." Several men and women, among them the Socialist Party luminary Norman Thomas, the Black labor leader A. Philip Randolph, and Congresswoman Jeannette Rankin, lived long enough to speak out against both wars.

The draft law granted conscientious objector, or CO, status to members of pacifist churches like the Quakers or the Mennonites, provided they wore uniforms and performed noncombatant war service such as working in hospitals. There remained, however, a determined core of "absolutists," some motivated by socialist politics, some by religion, who refused to make that compromise. Legally they were considered drafted troops refusing to obey orders, and some 450 of them served time—in many cases several years—in harsh military prisons.

On them fell the army's full fury, driving several to suicide. After being sentenced to 90 days of solitary confinement, for instance, 23-year-old Ernest Gellert was housed through the winter of 1917–18 in an unheated cell and forced to stand outside during a blizzard. "I feel that only by my death will I be able to save others from the mental tortures

I have gone through," he wrote before killing himself with an army rifle at a base in New Jersey. "If I succeed, I will give my life willingly." At least 16 other conscientious objectors died behind bars, by their own hand or otherwise.

One notorious torment for the COs who refused to work was to shackle their wrists to cell bars and so force them to stand on tiptoe for the eight hours a day they were supposed to be working. Maurice Becker, a former illustrator and cartoonist for the shuttered *Masses*, endured this and left a dark charcoal drawing: the bodies of three men are suspended from shackles, their muscles stretched taut, the head of one bent down in despair. The tableau is a haunting echo of the crucifixion of Jesus and the two thieves. Known as "high cuffing," the practice could cut off blood flow and leave a prisoner's wrists and hands injured.

That was far from the only punishment. "Men were forcibly clad in uniform, beaten, pricked or stabbed with bayonets, jerked about with ropes round their necks, threatened with summary execution," wrote Norman Thomas, whose brother endured such torments. "In at least two cases men were immersed in the filth of latrines, one of them head downward." When such reports began emerging, a disturbed Secretary of War Baker ordered these punishments stopped.

Newton Baker was a more decent man than many of the fire-breathing commanders nominally under his control, but, mild, bookish, and gentle voiced, he had little effect on an army officer corps that considered conscientious objectors despicable. In other ways as well, the army went out of its way to impress upon them its culture of violence. When the three Black soldiers were hanged before thousands of troops at Camp Dodge, Iowa, officers forced 161 COs in custody at the base to watch, deliberately placing them close to the gallows.

The social work pioneer Jane Addams received an appeal for help from the "frightened little widow" of one resister, a religious pacifist at an army base in Kansas. "Finally, after a prolonged ducking under a faucet in the prison yard on a freezing day, [he] had contracted pneumonia and died." In his diary, another CO, again in Kansas, reported what happened to three comrades confined to a cage in a basement. Guards beat them, then hoisted them off their feet by ropes tied to their arms while "a garden hose was played on their faces with the nozzle about six inches from them, until they collapsed completely, when they were carried and dumped screaming and moaning into the cage." A fellow prisoner told of how "noncommissioned officers took me to the bath house which was soon well occupied with spectators or would-be assistants. . . . They had me on my back with [my] face under a faucet and held my mouth open." Another prisoner described guards immersing a CO in a vat of water: "This corporal had a couple of guys . . . hold him down under the water just about as long as he could take it, and then they let him up. . . . Then they put him down again about as long as he could stand it. . . . He had a pretty hard time to come to. If it had been much longer, he'd have been a goner."

Why were these men treated so ruthlessly? We can only speculate. The role of prison guard—dealing with shunned people you have total control over—sometimes attracts sadists. And perhaps treating these pacifists so harshly was proof, for a guard in the United States, that he was just as tough, manly, and patriotic as an infantryman shooting Germans in France.

Another explanation has to do with this army's recent past. It is significant how often the torture inflicted on these resisters involved water. So, of course, did the notorious "water cure" American soldiers had used on captured Filipino guerrillas. In that war it was so common that troops used to sing a boastful ballad, to the tune of a Civil War song:

> *Get the good old syringe boys and fill it to the brim*
> *We've caught another nigger and we'll operate on him*
> *Let someone take the handle who can work it with a vim*
> *Shouting the battle cry of freedom*

A later verse vowed to teach a captive that liberty was "a precious boon" and to pump him full of water until he "swells like a toy bal[l] oon."

The largest single group of imprisoned COs was at the newly con-

structed Camp Funston, Kansas. We do not know the names of most of
their tormentors, but local newspapers from 1917 and 1918 are filled
with mentions of soldiers at the base who were veterans of the Philippine War.

THROUGH THE FRANTIC efforts of their friends, supporters, and
families, some details of the brutalities against COs reached legislators
and the pages of those liberal periodicals that still managed to publish.
President Wilson, however, said nothing on the subject.

One of the most searing of all conscientious objector cases was that
of Joseph, Michael, and David Hofer, three brothers from the pacifist Hutterite sect in South Dakota. They and another Hutterite found
themselves on Alcatraz, the rocky, notoriously escape-proof island in
San Francisco Bay that was then a military prison. The four Hutterites
refused to don uniforms, because to them these symbolized submission
to the army. Guards then led them down a narrow flight of stairs to
basement punishment cells, known collectively as "the hole." In each, a
pail served as a toilet.

Meals were bread and water. Jailors chained the prisoners to the cell
bars, standing, arms crossed, eight or nine hours a day. On at least one
occasion, guards whipped the men when they were in this position.
There were no blankets, beds, or other furniture. Still refusing the uniforms, they slept on the floor in their underwear. Rats roamed the cells,
and moisture from a cistern seeped through the walls. The cells had no
lights, and the two dim bulbs in the hallway were turned on only when
guards came. "The air in the cell was stagnant," wrote a CO who was in
the Alcatraz hole six months after the Hutterites, "the walls were wet
and slimy, the bars of the cell door were rusty with the dampness, and
the darkness was so complete that I could not make out my hand a few
inches before my face."

By law, the authorities could not keep convicts in "the hole" for more
than 14 days at a stretch, so the four Hutterites rotated between two
weeks there and two aboveground. After four months, the army moved
them, severely weakened, to the main military prison at Fort Leaven-

worth, Kansas, a few miles from the federal penitentiary housing many civilian dissidents. Joseph Hofer felt some foreboding. "My dear wife," he wrote while chained and guarded on the train to Kansas, "since we will no longer see each other in this troubled world, then we will see each other yonder."

After reaching their destination, the Hutterites were marched uphill to the prison. "When we arrived," recalled David Hofer, "we were worn out and very sweaty and warm. We were told to undress. We did so, and were required to stand in the chilly night air in our sweated underwear for two hours." The next morning, "Michael and Joseph complained of sharp pains in their chest, and were taken to the hospital."

Still refusing to work, David found himself in solitary confinement, again on bread and water. His brothers Joseph, 24, and Michael, 25, both died several days later. When Joseph's wife, Maria, arrived and asked for his coffin to be opened so she could see his body, she was dismayed to find it dressed in the military uniform he had refused to wear while alive. David Hofer, who survived, wept after his brothers' deaths. But he could not wipe away his tears, for he was on his feet, his hands chained to the cell bars above him.

Nobody Can Say We Aren't Loyal Now!

T HE BAD NEWS from the front in Europe further inflamed the search for scapegoats at home. One result was the Sedition Act of 1918, in effect a set of amendments toughening the Espionage Act. In May of that year, Congressman Albert Johnson, an enthusiast for any measure that could be used against labor, called for a "bill strong enough to curb treasonable doings of antigovernment people all the way from the red-handed Industrial Workers of the World, the dynamiters, the poison[ous] dark spreaders of revolution, and so on up to the white-livered rabbits who try to tear down the Army and the Nation under the guise of free speech."

Sweeping and vague, the new law made it criminal to provide "disloyal advice" about buying war bonds, or to "utter, print, write or publish any disloyal, profane, scurrilous, or abusive language about the form of government of the United States." Once again, as with Van Deman's file cards and the "water cure," there was a curious echo of the Philippine War. As the US Army was crushing the resistance in that archipelago, the new American colonial government imposed a harsh sedition act, which defined as a criminal "every person who shall utter seditious words or speeches, [or] write, publish, or circulate scurrilous libels against the Government of the United States." Nearly two decades later, having subdued Filipino rebels, Washington was now using some of the same tools to subdue American ones.

The Sedition Act also made legal something Albert Burleson had already been doing with great zest: refusing to deliver mail. A committee preparing the defense of the hundreds of arrested Wobblies, as well as trying to support their wives and children, found that checks mailed to it never arrived. The staff of a socialist paper in Milwaukee noticed they were failing to receive business correspondence and even their mail subscriptions to the *New York Times* and the *Chicago Tribune*. Letters were returned to senders stamped UNDELIVERABLE UNDER THE ESPIONAGE ACT.

That Milwaukee newspaper was harassed in other ways as well. Soon its advertising income began to dry up. When the editor went to call on a longtime supporter, a baker who had suddenly stopped buying ads, the man "slumped down in a chair, covered his eyes and, with tears streaming through his fingers, sobbed, 'My God, I can't help it. . . . They told me if I didn't take my advertising out they would refuse me . . . flour, sugar and coal.'"

During 1917 and 1918, prosecutors convicted more than 1,000 men and women under the Espionage and Sedition Acts for voicing criticisms of the war effort or the government. Although some were able to overturn verdicts on appeal, most went to prison. Many additional people were sentenced under the raft of similar state and municipal sedition laws passed during this period. Even the university town of Berkeley, California, for instance, had an ordinance "Prohibiting the Utterance or Use of Seditious Language, or of Words Tending to Disturb the Peace." Fearful of seeming unpatriotic, legislators often passed such bills without a single dissent. The Bureau of Investigation pushed hard for state laws of this sort, and a bureau agent who was a lawyer actually drafted the New Hampshire bill, which the state legislature swiftly approved.

Virtually no one inside the federal government spoke up for civil liberties. One rare exception, however, was the author of a letter that landed on President Wilson's desk in February 1918. It came from Assistant Secretary of Labor Louis F. Post, the man who, some months earlier, had refused to sign off on an order to deport Emma Goldman.

Post was among the many left-leaning idealists who had hopes for Wilson when he was elected president in 1912. When offered a job in the new Department of Labor, with its mission of promoting the welfare of working people, an agency long advocated by unions, he was happy to take it.

Although Post himself did not oppose the war, he was disturbed to see people jailed for exercising what he saw as "their assumed Constitutional rights of free speech," as he later wrote. "My dear Mr. President," his letter began. "May I offer a personal suggestion?" He suggested "a blanket pardon" for all those convicted of opposing the draft, since that law "seemed inconsistent with their notions of American democracy" and they had no "treasonable motives."

Wilson's reply ignored the fact that the best-known people convicted for interfering with conscription were women: Emma Goldman, already in prison, and Kate Richards O'Hare, still free for the moment while appealing her sentence. "Your suggestion," the president wrote, gracious as always, "about pardoning the men who at first resisted the conscription interests me very much and appeals to me not a little, but I think perhaps it is unwise to show such clemency until we have got . . . a grip on the whole conduct of the War. . . . I don't feel that I can follow my heart just now."

WITH SO MANY war opponents indicted or already behind bars and no real German spies to be found, the American Protective League needed targets. Draft-dodging "slackers" provided one. Nothing aroused the rage of middle-aged APL members more than young men who might be failing to fight. In addition, the government offered a $50 bonus to anybody who caught such a man. Worth more than $1,000 today, such a reward was tempting because you could seize a suspected "slacker" without a warrant. APL members leapt at the chance.

The organization's first "slacker raid" took place in Minneapolis on the chilly night of March 26, 1918, in an atmosphere of heightened tension over the ominous German offensive launched a few days earlier. A convoy of trucks pulled up in front of a row of boardinghouses and cheap residential hotels that housed single men who worked for the area's factories, meatpacking plants, and farms. Out leapt 120 APL men with their police-like badges, plus 65 Minnesota National Guardsmen with combat boots and long Krag-Jørgensen rifles left over from the Spanish-American War. The Guardsmen stationed themselves at each building's entrance, while APL members banged on the doors of every room, demanding that each man show his draft card.

The soldiers also surrounded a performance of the Ringling Brothers circus, while the APL searched for slackers in wagons and tents. The raiders trucked off about 100 men for further questioning, and then took 21 to the county jail.

The organization staged additional raids over the months ahead, rounding up 1,000 men in Des Moines; 250 in New Orleans; 1,000 in Cleveland; and 600 in Atlantic City, where league members stood at the exit of each oceanside pier and would not let men leave unless they could show their draft cards.

When summer came, Chicago, the APL's birthplace, saw the biggest raid to date, with more than 10,000 league members participating. At movie theaters, vaudeville shows, and a Cubs doubleheader, the raiders made everyone file out of designated exits, where each draft-age man had to show his card. Badge-wearing vigilantes checked every arriving train or steamboat, and combed parks, bars, restaurants, elevated train stations, and nightclubs. They stopped cars to question drivers and passengers and even appeared at the beaches in bathing suits, wading into Lake Michigan to interrogate suspects. Of the more than 150,000 men grilled, the APL took one in ten into custody to investigate their draft status. When jail cells and the Bureau of Investigation office overflowed, those seized were housed in warehouses and on the Municipal Pier, where they had to spend the night on a concrete floor. Altogether, more than 1,400 Chicagoans were found to be draft evaders or deserters and were shipped off to the army.

Soon after, the APL found more to do in Chicago. To keep patriotic enthusiasm high, the government had created an "Allied War Exposition" that traveled the country. During its two-week stop in Chicago's

Grant Park, the APL claimed to have 250 operatives monitoring the crowds for anyone suspicious. More than 100,000 people came daily to be thrilled at the sight of captured German artillery, mortars, helmets, and pieces of downed aircraft; at trenches dug in the park's lawn; and at a tank showing how it could crash through tangles of barbed wire. Children posed for photographs atop cannon barrels. Fighter planes swooped overhead, machine guns rattled, bands and bagpipes played, and the British ambassador led a delegation of dignitaries. At scheduled times, bugles rang out as soldiers charged a trench, and other soldiers playing the role of Germans dutifully raised a white flag of surrender.

SOMEONE WHO WOULD have loved to lead a charge on an enemy trench, Theodore Roosevelt, still raged at not being at the front himself. But all four of his sons were in uniform in Europe, and one of his two daughters was a nurse there, caring for wounded soldiers, as was her doctor husband. "You and your brothers . . . have seized the great chance," the ex-president wrote to one of his boys, "as was seized by those who fought at Gettysburg, and Waterloo, and Agincourt."

Away from public view, the Roosevelt sons were not all poster boys. Kermit became an alcoholic; Archibald would later take up extreme right-wing conspiracy theories; and Quentin had an odd obsession with witchcraft. But they played the role of heroes that the American public wanted. Archibald was wounded when German shrapnel mutilated his arm and knee. Theodore Jr. was gassed and hit by a German bullet in his leg. Kermit, who had won the Military Cross from Britain while attached to its army in Mesopotamia, now transferred to an American unit in France. Only Quentin, the youngest, in France and still training as a fighter pilot, had not yet seen action. It was so cold at 15,000 feet, he wrote, that "I don't see how the angels stand it." To his fiancée, who, like his parents, waited anxiously on Long Island, he described his joy at feeling "part of the machine" when flying a new French fighter.

News of Americans at the front like the young Roosevelts, not to mention a continuing stream of invective from people like their father, only increased the national ferocity against all things German. Since most beer brewers were of German descent, rage against Germans fueled the decades-long drive for Prohibition that was now approaching victory: Germans were accused of trying to kill Americans with drink as well as bullets. Frightened families changed their names: Feilchenfeld became Field, Koenig became King, Koch became Cook. The Cincinnati city government ordered that the words "Made in Germany" be chipped or filed off public health department medical equipment.

Just across the Ohio River from Cincinnati, Covington, Kentucky, was home to many German Americans. In the late nineteenth century the state was one of several that recruited German immigrants, who had a reputation for being literate and hardworking. Now a local vigilante group, the Citizens Patriotic League, packed a school board session with an angry crowd and forced all teaching of German to stop. Nearby communities followed suit, and German books began disappearing from public library shelves. Covington's Bremen Street became Pershing Avenue, a choice that won out over Liberty Avenue and Wilson Street.

Sixty-six-year-old Charles Schoberg, with close-cropped dark hair and a bristly mustache, was a Covington cobbler. In March 1918, he apparently thought nothing was out of the ordinary when several workmen came into his shop and busied themselves, they explained, checking the voltage level in his electric meter. Nor did he pay much attention when they twice returned, saying that the meter needed to be serviced. Although born in Germany, Schoberg had come to the United States at the age of five and over the course of his life had served as a police officer, town marshal, and magistrate.

He was astonished when, on July 4, 1918, a date that seems to have been carefully chosen, he was arrested and charged with treason. Seized at the same time were two friends who had frequently dropped in to chat with Schoberg at the shoemaker's shop, J. Henry Kruse, 56, a real estate developer and brewery executive, and Henry Feltman, 65, a well-to-do tobacco merchant. In a courtroom specially opened on the holiday, 400 people quickly assembled to see the three indicted.

The men who had said they were checking Schoberg's meter were planting a bug. Microphones were larger in those days, and they had trouble concealing it. The only place big enough was the base of Schoberg's grandfather clock. The men then hid the wires behind the wallpaper and ran them into the building's basement. For more than three months, private detectives had sat there in shifts taking notes, exasperated by the ticktock and hourly tolling of the clock.

Prompting the surveillance were some customers of Schoberg's, who had told the Citizens' Patriotic League that they overheard "pro-German" remarks when getting their shoes repaired. The league then hired a Cincinnati detective agency for the eavesdropping operation. Although the three men would be tried in federal court for violating the Espionage and Sedition Acts, they were actually arrested and indicted by the county prosecutor—who, as it happens, was president of the Citizens' Patriotic League.

The bewildered trio were charged with attempting to "favor the cause" of Germany and its allies, by bringing American military forces into "contempt, scorn, contumely and disrespect." Detectives and shop visitors testified about conversations in which Schoberg was accused of saying, "This is a damn war for money. . . . Somebody is getting rich. Not me, that is a cinch." Witnesses also declared that they heard him claim that Abraham Lincoln was of German origin and "that his father's name was not Lincoln, but was Lunkham." Schoberg had also been heard singing in a language that was not English.

Defendant Kruse acknowledged that he had called the two top German commanders, Field Marshal Paul von Hindenburg and General Erich Ludendorff, "great generals"—a reasonable-enough observation to make in the spring of 1918, when their innovative storm trooper offensive had sent the Allied armies reeling. Kruse was also accused of saying that the war "will be over in three or four months because the United States soldiers cannot get over there in time"—which was, of course, exactly what the country's military brass feared.

It made no difference that these statements were all made in private conversations, for, as the judge instructed the jury, "by disloyalty we mean a state of mind or heart" and if the jury believed a person's "mind and heart is with the country's enemy," they should find him guilty. They did. Schoberg received a sentence of ten years, Kruse five, and the wealthy Feltman seven and a $40,000 fine. The shocked defendants, temporarily free on bail, desperately hoped the verdict would be overturned on appeal.

WAR FEVER KNEW no boundaries. In New Jersey, a Women's Revolver League was formed, and in New York City a women's gun club set up a rifle range on the roof of the Hotel Majestic on Central Park West. In New Haven, Connecticut, volunteers manned an antiaircraft gun around the clock.

Montana, too, was swept by rumors of sinister German airplanes and dirigibles cruising the night skies. Exactly how they would have gotten there was not clear, for neither type of craft had yet succeeded in crossing the Atlantic. Nonetheless, frightened citizens of Helena fired a fusillade of shots into the heavens. "Airship with Two Men in It Distinctly Seen above the State Capital Building—Searchlight Played upon State Arsenal," reported the city's *Independent-Record*. "Notify me at once, next time . . . and I will pursue it in my auto," declared Montana's governor. "This thing must be run down." He told the newspaper that "he would take an expert rifleman with him." A Northern Pacific freight train crew said they had seen the plane fall to earth and heard an explosion. Soldiers and a police posse combed local farmland, but they could not find the mysterious craft or its pilots.

Vigilante patriots also turned their attention to German music. Marriages now had to take place without Mendelssohn's "Wedding March." When a San Francisco orchestra hired a German-born conductor, vigilantes barraged the Justice Department with accusations that he had done everything from flying the German flag from his car to buying German, not American, butter at a local grocery.

Purges began. The Boston Symphony Orchestra hired two detectives to keep an eye on its musicians who were "enemy aliens." Even though he was a Swiss citizen, suspicion fell on the orchestra's conductor, the German-born Karl Muck. People claimed that he had radioed information to German U-boats from his vacation home on the Maine coast.

The Boston police finally arrested him in the middle of a rehearsal of Bach's *Saint Matthew Passion*, poring over his annotations on the score and suggesting that they might be a means of sending messages to Germany in code. A raid on Muck's home uncovered a cache of fervent love letters from a 19-year-old Boston heiress; now he could be accused of corrupting innocent young womanhood as well being a spy. Along with more than 4,000 Germans and Austro-Hungarians, including many other musicians, he was sent to an internment camp at Fort Oglethorpe, Georgia, surrounded by searchlights and barbed wire.

Muck got off easily compared with Robert Prager. In the coal town of Collinsville, Illinois, a row erupted between this 30-year-old miner and local mineworkers' union officials—by some accounts because he was preaching socialism, by others because he was a company spy. Prager had tried to enlist in the US Navy, but he was turned away because he had a glass eye. He also had the bad luck to be born in Germany.

That was enough to inflame a mob of several dozen, some of them drinking, who seized him from his home on April 4, 1918, stripped him to his underwear, and forced him to walk barefoot down the street draped in an American flag. A policeman rescued him and took him to jail. But when the mob swarmed into that building, the police stood aside. The crowd now swelled to more than 200. Just after midnight, they took Prager to a hackberry tree on a hill outside the city limits, put a rope around his neck, tossed the other end over a branch, and yanked him ten feet off the ground. The killing drew little outrage. "In spite of such excesses as lynchings," commented the *Washington Post* a week later, "it is a healthful and wholesome awakening in the interior part of the country."

The eleven men who were put on trial for Prager's death posed proudly at the courthouse in coats and ties, holding small American flags, with red, white, and blue rosettes in their lapels. One acknowledged to reporters and a coroner's jury that he had taken part in lynching Prager. The defense lawyer claimed that the lynching was justified by an unwritten law allowing "patriotic murder" in time of danger. During a recess just before the case went to the jury, a 25-piece navy band, in town on a recruiting mission, played "The Star-Spangled Banner" in the courthouse rotunda. After deliberating 45 minutes, the jury found all 11 men not guilty.

It is, of course, not easy to parse the motives of a drunken lynch mob or of the members of the jury who acquitted them. But statistics offer at least one clue. Like many mining centers, Collinsville had a high proportion of immigrants, more so than any town nearby. Slightly more than half its population was foreign-born or had at least one foreign-born parent. A significant percentage of these came from Germany or Austria-Hungary; two of the indicted 11 men, for instance, had German surnames. In a country aflame with war fever, killing a "pro-German," or finding his killers not guilty, could be one way to prove your patriotic bona fides. Something revealing happened just after the judge released the defendants. From the jury box, one juror waved to them and shouted, "Well, I guess nobody can say we aren't loyal now!"

Cut, Shuffle, and Deal

N
O NEED TO prove their loyalty bothered the editors of *The Can Opener*, one of the country's more unusual newspapers. It suffered no harassment by Albert Burleson's vigilant censorship, because its writers were already behind bars. Listing its place of publication as "Cook Co. Can—Chicago," the handwritten paper served up stories, advice, and cartoons of top-hatted plutocrats to the dozens of Wobblies awaiting trial in the Cook County Jail.

Most of the men were in the "big tank," as the jail's main wing was known. Their cells were full of lice, dust, and cobwebs, and the food was uninspiring: one day they found a large cockroach baked into a loaf of bread. To keep their spirits up, the inmates did gymnastics, held political discussions, and, when there was enough daylight to read, enjoyed a large library of books donated by supporters. A handwritten program for a "Grand Entertainment Given by Class War Prisoners" shows 14 items, including songs by the "I. W. W. Chorus," one by the "Swedish Chorus," a "Stunt," several individual singers, and five "Recitations." On Sundays, a pianist accompanied the hymns of a church service, which took place in a corner of the building that doubled, when required, as an execution chamber. The wall had a socket for the beam of a gallows.

The Wobblies' trial, which began in April 1918, was—and as of this writing remains—the largest civilian criminal trial in American history. The defendants were accused of conspiring to violate the Espionage Act and the Selective Service Act—laws that had not even been passed when the conspiracy supposedly started. Notably, none of them were charged with acts of theft, sabotage, or violence. The indictments rested solely on words they had spoken or written. However, they were, as Woodrow Wilson wrote to his attorney general, still "worthy of being suppressed."

Despite the defense attorneys and the right to cross-examination, this was a show trial. With more than 100 men sharing four overworked lawyers, justice would obviously not be carefully meted out to each individual defendant. Yet in their way the accused sometimes put on as forceful a show as the prosecution.

The dominant figure on trial was the longtime Wobbly leader William D. "Big Bill" Haywood. Imposing, stern looking, and with what the journalist John Reed called "a face like a scarred battlefield," he was a man acutely aware of crafting his image. He earned his nickname more through his charisma—the high-crowned hat he was always careful to wear, and his commanding posture—than through his size, for he was actually just under six feet tall. But he always stood erect, chest out, and, except for police mug shots, was rarely photographed in anything other than a three-piece suit, its long, unbuttoned coat accentuating his bulk. He always turned the left side of his head toward a camera, to hide his right eye, sightless from a childhood accident.

Haywood had a way with words and was skilled at talking to journalists, even when now they could interview him only through the slats in his steel cell door. John Dos Passos described him in one of the prose-poem biographical portraits in his novel *U.S.A.*:

Big Bill Haywood was born in sixty nine in a boardinghouse
    in Salt Lake City.
He was raised in Utah, got his schooling in Ophir a min-
      ing camp with shooting scrapes, faro Saturday nights,
      whisky spilled on pokertables piled with new silver
      dollars.

When he was eleven his mother bound him out to a farmer,
   he ran away because the farmer lashed him with a whip.
That was his first strike.

As a boy, he explored abandoned mine shafts and watched a combative miner named Slippery Dick shoot another man dead. At 12 he saw
a mob lynch a Black man. As a young man on the frontier, he worked as
a saloon card dealer, a cowboy, a surveyor, and a homesteader on virgin
farmland, where, with no doctor or midwife nearby when his wife gave
birth, he delivered the baby himself. He was born into a violent world,
and used his fists freely, especially if anyone made fun of his ruined eye.
Once, when attacked by a Colorado sheriff's deputy, he pulled out a
revolver and wounded the man. (Amazingly, a court ruled that he had
acted in self-defense.) While a teenager, he had worked as a theater
usher in Salt Lake City and acquired a lifelong love of Shakespeare,
long passages of whose plays he could recite by heart.

He spent 16 years underground as a miner, badly mangling his right
hand when a pile of rocks fell on it. "I've never read Marx's *Capital*,"
he once said, "but I have the marks of capital all over my body." He
could talk to western miners, inspire immigrant Wobblies who barely
spoke English, dazzle New York's Greenwich Village intelligentsia, and
charm some of its women into bed.

"Fellow workers," Haywood had declared as he banged a piece of
two-by-four on the podium for a makeshift gavel at the founding convention of the Wobblies in 1905, in a Chicago meeting hall thick with
cigar smoke, "this is the Continental Congress of the working class!"
He fought many battles in the labor wars before and after, earning a
beating from mining company detectives and dealing out blows in return. His rhetoric was pithy: "The capitalist has no heart, but harpoon
him in the pocketbook and you will draw blood." He lived modestly,
earning $22.50 a week from the IWW, only $4.50 more than his secretary and bookkeeper. Few other labor union staffs, or organizations of
any kind, had salaries so egalitarian.

Once the trial began, each morning Chicago police and US marshals escorted the Wobblies, two by two in handcuffs, a dozen blocks from the Cook County Jail to the city's domed, colonnaded federal building. The windows of the courtroom looked out, wrote Reed, "upon the heights of towering office buildings, which dominate that courtroom as money power dominates our civilization." The room was elegantly decorated in mahogany, white marble, and brass, with a mural on one wall of King John and his barons agreeing to the Magna Carta, and one on another showing Moses standing amid clouds and flame, receiving the Ten Commandments from God.

The space was packed. To accommodate all the defendants, the court had to erect bleachers. Supporters, onlookers, and newspaper reporters squeezed in wherever they could, sometimes finding only standing room. The Wobblies arrived each day in coats, ties, and fedoras, except for Haywood in his trademark black Stetson hat. On the first anniversary of the death of the martyred Frank Little, they all came to court wearing small black-and-red ribbons beneath a button with his picture.

Proceedings were surprisingly haphazard. Although 112 defendants were in court when the trial began, the government had put little effort into rounding up several dozen other Wobblies indicted as part of the same conspiracy. In making his opening statement, even the chief prosecutor seemed hazy about the exact number of people on trial. The defendants lounged casually on the bleachers, chatted, chewed tobacco, read newspapers, or dozed off.

Prosecutors tried to tarnish the Wobblies in the jurors' eyes by asking each man his "racial stock," particularly looking for those who were German or Jewish. They also were careful to point out when a defendant was not an American citizen, or was unmarried or divorced. One prosecutor, over defense objections, asked a defendant, "Do you believe in the ceremony of marriage?" The defense, meanwhile, was working under major handicaps, for Burleson's Post Office failed to deliver lawyers' letters seeking witnesses.

The judge the Wobblies faced was one of the country's more curious, and curiously named. Kenesaw Mountain Landis was christened after a Civil War battle in Georgia in which his Union Army father had been severely wounded. Justice Department officials were delighted to have him on the case—and in fact had secretly, and unethically, met with him at a Chicago hotel before the trial began. They knew he would be tough on the Wobblies, because the previous year he had sentenced a large group of draft evaders to a year and a day at hard labor, calling them "whining and belly-aching puppies."

Landis's feelings toward the Wobblies lounging in the bleachers before him were undoubtedly worsened by the fact that half of them were from a category of people he had no use for—immigrants. When he graduated from law school, he had given a speech warning his classmates against "the danger that threatens from the wholesale importation of the ignorant and vicious Hun and the cowardly and revengeful Sicilian."

A man of slight stature with a gnomish face and an unruly mop of gray hair, he was startlingly informal in court. He wore a business suit instead of a robe, and when a defendant was late returning from lunch break, Landis asked him, "Don't you know what time we begin this matinee?"

Occasionally, as if he were a movie director, the judge stood up and walked to different parts of the courtroom, sometimes sitting on the steps to the jury box, to get a better view of a person or exhibit. As if welcoming visitors to his movie set, Landis periodically invited a celebrity guest to sit beside him and watch the proceedings. One was the country's most famous evangelist, Billy Sunday, a strident superpatriot who had called for pacifists to be lynched, "and then let the coroner do the rest." Another was an actor, Louis Mann, currently appearing on the Chicago stage in a patriotic drama, *Friendly Enemies*. Mann played the role of an immigrant whose renounces his pro-German feelings when the Germans torpedo a ship carrying his son.

The Wobblies had their own sense of theater and used every possible opportunity as the trial proceeded, occasionally scoring points against the humorless prosecution team. One defendant was Sam Scarlett, the veteran organizer captured thanks to information supplied by his former Pittsburgh roommate, undercover man Leo Wendell.

"Where is your home?" a prosecutor asked him.

"Cook County Jail."

"Before that?"

"County Jail, Cleveland, Ohio."

"And before that?"

"City Jail, Akron, Ohio."

As the lawyer-historian Dean Strang describes those on trial, "They had cut the forests' thickest trees, harvested the prairies' wheat, loaded eastern ships, unloaded western ore at the mouths of mine shafts, shoved tons of orange-glowing steel under showers of cinders, and spent months or years in bars, rooming houses, freight cars, hobo jungles, sweltering army bullpens, jails, and now courtrooms. . . . But only a few had seen the span of a formal primary education." Trying to show how uneducated the defendants were, the chief prosecutor asked one if the group's library had any books written by Wobblies themselves. "I don't know whether Victor Hugo was an IWW or not," the man replied dryly. "I have never seen him around the hall."

Haywood was one of the last to testify before the case went to the jury. Beneath the murals of King John and Moses, he spoke of his hope for a day when there would be "no rich and no poor; no millionaires, and no paupers no palaces and no hovels . . . and where no man will have to work 13 hours in a smelter." If working for that dream "is a conspiracy, then we are conspiring."

EVEN AFTER HAMSTRINGING the IWW with mass arrests and indictments, the Justice Department kept the surviving chapters of the group under close observation. In Pittsburgh, its grimy mills turning out more steel than ever for war industries, Leo Wendell continued to serve as secretary of the local Wobbly branch. Bureau of Investigation officials kept his identity a tightly held secret, for at least three other undercover operatives filed reports on the activities of "Walsh," his cover name, apparently convinced they were providing information about a dangerous IWW leader. Another possibility, however, is that this was a deliberate effort by the bureau to maintain Wendell's cover, since it shared these reports with other agencies and didn't want word leaking out that the notorious "Walsh" was really its own man.

Wendell kept an eye on a range of figures on the city's left. Many of his reports in 1918 concerned Jacob Margolis, a left-wing attorney he had befriended. Margolis knew leading radicals all over the country, including Emma Goldman, who corresponded with him from her prison cell. After the attorney went to Chicago to testify as a character witness at the Wobbly trial, Wendell told the bureau, "I asked him about the morale of the defendants." It was low, Margolis told him; "practically all" were sure they were going to prison. Wendell was dismayed, however, when Margolis, a foe of autocracy of all kinds, began denouncing the Russian Bolsheviks, thereby alienating sympathizers of theirs in Pittsburgh whom Wendell was eager to monitor. The life of an undercover agent can be difficult when someone you're spying on is not as subversive as you want him to be.

Wendell's hundreds of reports to the bureau—sometimes several pages long and often produced at the rate of three or four a week—are all neatly typed on special forms with his code number, "836," filling in a box in the upper left-hand corner. Where did he type them? He would not have risked doing so in his room at Gibson's Hotel, or taken the chance of being noticed entering the local Bureau of Investigation office. Most likely the bureau maintained an inconspicuous safe house in some neighborhood where Wendell would not be suspected by his comrades if he were seen.

To burnish Wendell's bona fides in the eyes of Pittsburgh's leftists, at least twice the bureau had him arrested. In 1918, it did so in a way no one could miss: three federal agents seized him in front of 50 people attending a Socialist Party meeting at the New Era Hall. The daily press reported his jailing, as always dutifully repeating whatever the bureau told it. "With the arrest," Pittsburgh's *Gazette Times* said, "agents of the Department of Justice believe they have broken the backbone of a conspiracy, with headquarters in Pittsburgh and extending across the country. . . . According to the Federal operatives, Walsh is one of the big men of the I. W. W. . . . . He has been traced from coast to coast, always leaving a trail of sedition and labor unrest behind him."

In fact, he wasn't incarcerated at all, but was quietly put on a train to Ohio, where—doubtless unknown to the Pittsburgh Wobblies—he had a pregnant girlfriend. Several days later, after supposedly releasing him from a prison cell, the authorities publicly forced him to sign up for the draft, even though, according to a third newspaper, "he objected strenuously." What better way to enhance a spy's radical credentials?

Many of Wendell's reports were shared with Lieutenant Colonel Ralph Van Deman's Military Intelligence operation. Van Deman, too, remained obsessed with the IWW. From reading his correspondence, you would never guess that the organization was drastically hobbled—its offices vandalized by raids, hundreds of members indicted or on trial, and local branches infiltrated by the likes of Wendell. Across Van Deman's desk came reports about a "suspicious" Wobbly seized from a United Fruit Company ship in New Orleans, and another IWW member working for the US Weather Bureau in South Dakota. Van Deman asked for a federal investigation of deposits made in Wobbly bank accounts in Arizona and referred to reports "that the recent I. W. W. activities are supported by funds from German sources."

Military Intelligence was also watching a wide range of other activists, including the Conference of Christian Pacifists, a California organization that Van Deman judged "watery and neutral as far as its war loyalty is concerned." In a letter to the secretary of war's office, he boasted of threatening this group: "Ample warning . . . has been given to all concerned." He felt all troublemakers anywhere to be within his domain, even those behind bars. Writing to the warden of the federal penitentiary in Atlanta, where he thought—incorrectly—that Emma Goldman was imprisoned, Van Deman claimed she was still wielding influence and suggested "that it might be well to place greater restrictions upon her."

His huge stock of intelligence data, however unreliable, allowed him to deal with officials who far outranked him. He corresponded with Theodore Roosevelt, as well as the governor of Montana, whom he

told about a possible mining strike. The situation "is a seething volcano," the governor replied. "I sincerely appreciate your kindness in
sending me the information."

Van Deman's tall, thin figure, always smartly dressed in his army
uniform, was now familiar to many influential people in Washington.
Knowing that a free meal has long been a useful tool in that city, he invited cabinet members and newspaper correspondents to a weekly luncheon he hosted, known as the General Hindquarters, bringing them
up to date on just how he was preserving the country's security against
subversive threats on all sides.

However, riding high with his nationwide army of agents, Van Deman fatally overreached when he showed his ambitions too nakedly. In
April 1918, he testified before the Senate Military Affairs Committee
that because civilian courts were "tied up with form and red tape and
law"—note the last word—the country needed to impose "summary
justice" on the unpatriotic by using military tribunals. Ever since the
American Revolution, these had sporadically meted out death sentences and other punishments to spies and enemy combatants during
wartime. We can easily guess whom he imagined running a new round
of such tribunals.

Despite his own draconian crackdown on dissent, the following day
President Wilson declared himself "wholly and unalterably opposed"
to military tribunals, saying that the Espionage Act and other legislation already were sufficient. By now, senior War and Justice Department officials were feeling their authority threatened by Van Deman's
growing empire and began planning to oust him. Although their ma-
neuvers were cloaked by a grand farewell party and a promotion to full
colonel, his rivals soon dispatched Van Deman, with only the vaguest
of assignments, to Europe. Military Intelligence, however, remained
in place and would continue monitoring left-of-center Americans for
decades.

Van Deman did not leave a record of his own feelings, but he must
have been disappointed to lose control of the surveillance network he
had built with such remarkable speed. He remained, however, a mas-

terful bureaucratic strategist, and the commander in chief of American forces in France, General Pershing, was an old friend, an Army War College classmate. Surely, promising new possibilities for him lay ahead.

AS AMERICAN TROOPS finally began crossing the ocean in large numbers, Europeans greeted them rapturously. "They looked larger than ordinary men," remembered the English writer Vera Brittain, who was nursing British wounded. "Their tall, straight figures were in vivid contrast to the under-sized armies of pale recruits to which we had grown accustomed." The exhausted Allies had great hopes for the Americans and felt there was no time to lose, for the still-advancing Germans had captured Cantigny, less than 60 miles north of Paris, and fearful citizens of the French capital could see the flash of artillery fire against the night sky.

In late May, US troops, fully trained at last, scored their first major victory. Supported by French artillery, tanks, and planes, Americans recaptured Cantigny from the gray-clad Germans, and held it against seven counterattacks in the days that followed. Among the officers involved—great fodder for newspapers back home—was Theodore Roosevelt Jr.

The Roosevelt family was again in the news when young Quentin, in action at last, shot down a German plane. Thrilled, the victorious pilot rode his motorcycle from his air base to Paris for a celebratory dinner at the fashionable restaurant Ciro's. "Whatever now befalls Quentin," his father proudly told his younger daughter, back home on Long Island, "he has now had his crowded hour, and his day of honor and triumph."

Two grueling battles east of Paris, at the town of Château-Thierry and in the forested hunting preserve the Americans called Belleau Wood, were the bloodiest that US soldiers had fought since the Civil War. After three weeks of combat at Belleau Wood, some of it hand to hand, a single US division suffered more than 8,200 men killed, wounded, or missing. The forest floor was strewn with bloodied uniforms, abandoned equipment, and putrefying corpses, American and German. But when a group of newly arrived marines encountered some French troops who were retreating and who urged the Americans to do the same, an officer famously replied, "Retreat, hell! We just got here!"

By midsummer, more than a million American troops were in Europe, and tens of thousands more landed each week. Mixed in with the celebration of their triumphs, however, was one very public loss. Just three days after Quentin Roosevelt shot down his first German plane, he was again aloft over the front when three German fighters caught him by surprise, several of their machine-gun bullets piercing his skull. He died instantly.

Quentin's father, who had preached the restorative virtues of combat all his life, was devastated. One day his coachman found him in the stable of his house at Oyster Bay, sobbing, his face pressed against the mane of Quentin's pony.

IT WAS A month after Quentin's death when the voice of a US marshal rang out, "Hear ye, hear ye. The United States District Court for the Northern District of Illinois is in session, the Honorable Kenesaw Mountain Landis, presiding. . . . God save this honorable court and these United States." The fate of the Wobblies on trial was finally placed in the hands of the jury.

The defendants naturally expected some differences in the verdicts on them. Through illness, dismissals, or severance of cases, the 112 who had gone to trial four months earlier had been reduced to 97 men, all of whom faced four counts. They had, however, played very different roles in the IWW. Some were national leaders, others foot soldiers, and one was a 19-year-old Harvard dropout. Mathematically, the jury had to render 388 separate verdicts of guilt or innocence.

In such a long and complex trial, a jury normally would take time to reexamine exhibits entered in evidence, reread the 43-page indictment, and review the months of testimony. Knowing this, the chief defense lawyer went to his hotel for what he must have hoped would be some rest. In less than an hour, though, the jury sent word that it had reached verdicts. The deliberations, if they can even be called that, were so swift that only a single lawyer from the defense's legal team had made it back to the courtroom when Judge Landis assembled the defendants, plus an extra contingent of police, to hear from the jury. It found all the Wobblies guilty on all counts. As they filed away in handcuffs, one of the defense attorneys, Caroline Lowe, broke into tears.

In the days ahead, the most poignant statement came from 51-year-old Anson Soper of Oregon, who asked Landis, "if it would be possible that you can find a place in any of those laws that will permit me, in addition to the sentence you are going to impose upon me, to serve that of . . . N. G. Marlatt, my fellow-worker, and allow him to go back to his family, to his wife and babies . . . I am willing to serve his time." Surprisingly, Landis seemed to have listened, for Marlatt, a locomotive engineer for the Chesapeake and Ohio Railway, was among the only three men (one of whom was dying), whom he set free.

The sentences the judge handed down on the rest varied. All but two men received at least a year in prison, some got five, some ten, and one group, including Big Bill Haywood, twenty. All told, Landis passed out 807 years of prison time, plus fines totaling more than $2 million. Ralph Chaplin, the poet and songwriter whose love letters had been seized in the raids, and who got twenty years, told the judge, "I am proud that I have climbed high enough for the lightning to strike me."

Almost without exception, daily newspapers across the country applauded the verdict and sentences. After dark, guards shepherded the Wobblies out of the Cook County Jail for the last time, and put them aboard a special train to their new home, the federal maximum-security penitentiary in Leavenworth, Kansas. The IWW would never again be a significant force in American life. "The big game is over," the former saloon card dealer Haywood wrote to John Reed, "and we never won a hand. The other fellow had the cut, shuffle and deal."

Cheerleaders

I N AUGUST 1918, the same month the Chicago Wobblies were found guilty, 33-year-old Grace Hammer said goodbye to her bricklayer husband and three small children in New York City and boarded a train. Like other trips she had made—to a collar factory in Troy, New York, as well as plants in Jersey City and Birmingham, Alabama—she was headed for a clothing works: the Fulton Bag and Cotton Mills in Atlanta, a city where she had lived as a child. "In this line of business," she later wrote in a letter, "one has to travel and I have seen a good deal of the United States."

Her line of business was with the Sherman Service, the new, sanitized name for what had previously been the Sherman Detective Agency. In the long-simmering war between American business and labor, this was a booming profession: the three largest detective firms alone employed 135,000 agents while smaller ones, like Sherman, which had eight offices around the United States and Canada, had tens of thousands more. Most were men, but sometimes a client needed a woman.

That was the case with Fulton Bag, whose president, Oscar Elsas, was fretting about restiveness and lack of patriotism among the female workers at his Atlanta plant. Elsas hired a lot of undercover detectives, which we know from a cache of his papers discovered in a factory basement 60 years after his death: 47 operatives at his main plant alone over the course of a decade, including one crew that was discovered bugging a union meeting hall during a strike. At the moment, he needed someone who knew clothing work and who was a woman, white, and southern. Grace Hammer was that detective.

It was an uneasy time in the American workplace. Although jobs were plentiful and company profits soared from orders for war matériel, workers were angry that inflation often undermined their earnings. Food prices, for example, had been rising faster than real wages ever since 1914.

To business owners like Elsas, the people he hired seemed harder to control. The threat of firing was no longer enough to keep a rebellious factory hand in line, for in the wartime period of full employment he or she could easily find a job elsewhere. In addition, there were still murmurings against the war, and Elsas, it appears, was always eager to demonstrate his patriotism, perhaps because he was Jewish in a part of the country known for its anti-Semitism. Fulton Bag gave interest-free loans to help workers buy Liberty Bonds, and during a round of bond sales in 1918 the company itself bought $100,000 worth—the most of any Atlanta business.

But Elsas worried that his employees didn't share his enthusiasm. "The workers are careless and indifferent," he wrote to the Sherman Service. He wanted Grace Hammer to put her "entire efforts to overcome this by using such arguments as will show the employees that it is a duty they owe to themselves as well as their employers and the country to work steady and do their best." And so, rather than playing the traditional labor spy's role of disrupting unions, Hammer's job was to whip up patriotic enthusiasm. She was to be an undercover cheerleader.

The Sherman Service prided itself on offering businesses a higher class of operatives than the private detectives notorious for cracking workers' skulls. In the instructions it gave to agents like Hammer, it asked them to find fellow laborers who were "dissatisfied" and "cultivate their friendship . . . after which you can proceed to present facts and arguments to them . . . by spending your spare or unemployed time with them, in the mornings around the plant before work begins, at noon time, or in the evenings about town."

Elsas usually first met privately at his home with the detectives he hired before sending them into his factories. When Hammer finally arrived at the giant redbrick Atlanta mill, tall smokestacks towering over it, she jumped into her new assignment energetically, filing reports as "Operating Representative No. 52 (Fem.)." "This morning I reported at the plant and mingled with various of the workers to further cultivate their friendship and gain their confidence," she wrote on August 24. "In this I am becoming very successful.

"I spoke to a number of the workers today," she continued, "showing them that the Government at this time needed every bit of production . . . and that we should stand solidly behind our Government in this war." By doing so "we would be doing our bit to assist those who are sacrificing their lives for us." She also suggested to Elsas that the factory should not pause all operations while "the operators . . . clean their machines." Abolishing this practice could "eliminate this unnecessary waste of time."

A few days later she reported chatting with fellow workers as they waited to enter the plant, telling them that the sugar and flour bags they made "were no doubt for the soldiers, so that they would be properly fed, and be in a position at all times to successfully combat with the barbarious [sic] Huns, and protect us women from the atrocities which have been practiced on the women of Belgium and France." At the day's end, she "advanced patriotic arguments" while employees were walking to streetcars. The only clue we have to workers' reactions is that she reported several of them asking "why was I so interested."

She continued trying to perform her mission after hours: "During the evening I walked about town endeavoring to come into contact with some of my co-workers, but I did not meet any of them." Could it be that they slipped out of sight when they saw approaching this woman who talked like a nonstop Fourth of July orator?

Whatever the case, Fulton Bag and Cotton Mills was far from the only employer to hire detectives for covert propaganda work. Telling a coworker that quitting her job would be "benefitting the Kaiser," as

Hammer did, was a way employers could try to keep dissatisfied workers in line. Once the war stopped, that would prove much harder.

IT WAS NOT merely undercover detectives who spouted war propaganda. In normal times a family going to the movies in this era might expect to see slides from local merchants advertising anything from sausages to women's hats during the four minutes or so that a projectionist needed to change the reels of a silent film. Now, however, a slide would appear onscreen: "Please remain seated. A representative of the government is to deliver an important message." Then a man would walk onstage and give a short, punchy oration, about the need for vigilance, planting victory gardens, or the latest successes of brave American troops at the front.

These were the Four Minute Men, and they were indeed almost all men. There were 75,000 of them, all volunteers. Besides movie theaters, the Four Minute Men held forth at Rotary and Kiwanis luncheons, county fairs, Indian reservations, women's clubs, churches, synagogues, labor union meetings, band concerts, between innings at the World Series, revival tents, and some 500 logging camps. Junior Four Minute Men spoke in schools, and College Four Minute Men on campuses. A corps of Colored Four Minute Men spoke in Black churches. More Four Minute Men gave speeches in Yiddish, Italian, Polish, Lithuanian, Armenian, and other languages. A group of speakers who gave longer talks were informally dubbed Four Hour Men.

The Four Minute Men were carefully trained and drilled by a team of historians and teachers of rhetoric. The closely monitored speakers received more than 40 instructional bulletins over the course of the war, laying out topics for their talks, "appropriate quotations and catch phrases," and entire sample speeches. Seldom if ever has an American president had so powerful a megaphone, for roughly half the material spoken by the Four Minute Men quoted or paraphrased Woodrow Wilson.

By the end of the First World War, the Four Minute Men had given more than seven million speeches on topics ranging from "Why We

Are Fighting" to "Onward to Victory." In Chicago some were joined by a "Liberty Chorus" singing patriotic songs. "It became difficult for half a dozen persons to come together," wrote the columnist Mark Sullivan, "without having a Four Minute Man descend upon them."

Even before the evening Wilson asked Congress to declare war, he and Colonel House had strategized about how to mobilize martial zeal for the conflict they were so eager to join. The result of their discussion was the Committee on Public Information, or CPI, an agency Wilson created by executive order a week after the country went to war. The Four Minute Men were the CPI's best-known project, but it oversaw a larger propaganda offensive of unprecedented scope and power. The organization was dominated by its ebullient chief, a 40-year-old former newspaperman and ardent Wilson supporter named George Creel. The committee's aim, as Creel put it in distinctly Wilsonian language, was to convince the country and the world of "the absolute selflessness of America's aims." On occasion he was more direct: "If ads could sell face cream and soap," he said, "why not a war?"

The CPI was headquartered in several town houses on Lafayette Square, just steps from the White House. Creel sometimes strolled over at the end of the workday to chat with Wilson. The agency quickly mushroomed, employing or commissioning artists, journalists, film-makers, and novelists, everyone from the actress Mary Pickford to the author William Dean Howells to eminent professors who turned out pamphlets on the historical roots of German perfidy. Its ten foreign-language bureaus produced a torrent of words for immigrants not yet comfortable in English. Overseas outposts trumpeted America's war aims to other countries—including Germany and Austria-Hungary, where aviators dropped leaflets printed on weatherproof paper and Al-lied artillerymen shot them across the front lines in hollow shells.

The committee paraded circus elephants through the streets, their sides covered with banners urging people to buy war savings stamps (25 cents each; buy enough and you could trade them in for a bond). It pro-duced small posters for living room windows and larger ones for walls, including four million copies of the famous image of a stern Uncle Sam pointing at the viewer and saying "I Want YOU for U.S. Army." From its offices poured forth 75 million pieces of literature ranging from short pamphlets to a 321-page encyclopedia of the war. The *Bulletin for Cartoonists* suggested themes for drawings. The agency produced films with titles like *Pershing's Crusaders*, *Our Colored Fighters*, and *America's Answer*, plus a cascade of 6,000 press releases and upbeat feature stories that received lavish space in newspapers, for this was often the only war news available. When Wilson gave his Fourteen Points speech, the CPI distributed four million copies.

Creel left no outlet ignored. Black newspapers, for instance, had a combined circulation of more than a million, but government officials fretted to see them devote space to matters such as lynching or discrimination in the armed forces. And so, jointly with Military Intelligence, the CPI called a "Conference of Colored Editors" in Washington aimed at "stimulating negro morale throughout the country by a modification of the bitter tone of the colored press," according to a report to the army chief of staff.

In an all-out charm offensive, 31 Black editors were addressed by the secretary of war; by the assistant secretary of the navy, Franklin D. Roosevelt; and by a French general, who told them how well African colonial troops were treated in the French army. CPI officials took the editors to the theater, a film showing, a luncheon at the YMCA, and on "a tour of the city in sight-seeing automobiles." Despite the effort, an army officer reported that "heated argument was not infrequent." The editors presented a list of demands, at the top of which was "National legislation on lynching." There was no chance of that, but officials monitoring the Black press after the conference congratulated themselves when they began finding more enthusiasm for the war effort.

Thousands of CPI advertisements appeared in newspapers and magazines. "German agents are everywhere," warned one, "eager to gather scraps of news about our men, our ships, our munitions. . . . Do not wait until you catch someone putting a bomb under a factory. Report the man who spreads pessimistic stories. . . . Send the names of such persons, even if they are in uniform, to the Department of Justice. . . . You are in contact with the enemy *today* just as truly as if you faced him across No Man's Land." The attorney general confirmed that "complaints of even the most informal or confidential nature are always welcome." A CPI pamphlet, *Friendly Words to the Foreign Born*, did not sound so friendly: for hyphenated Americans, as recent immigrants were often called, the issue is "whether the man's heart is at the American end of the hyphen."

Commercial moviemakers followed the CPI's lead, churning out silent films like *The Slacker*, in which a cowardly draft dodger realizes the evil of his ways and enlists, and demonizing the enemy in movies like *The Kaiser, The Beast of Berlin* and *The Claws of the Hun*. The sinister-looking little spikes atop German helmets were God's gift to cartoonists and filmmakers; audiences could depend on such villains throwing crying children aside and carrying away screaming women to a vile fate offscreen.

Significantly, many films also glorified the war at home. In *The Secret Game*, a ring of German agents scheming to steal top-secret military documents includes a sneaky-looking Dr. Smith, whose real name is Schmidt, and a beautiful young woman, the screen text informs us, "with a deeply concealed hyphen in her name." Moviegoers could also watch *An Alien Enemy, The Hun Within*, and *The Prussian Cur*, which showed German spies wrecking American trains and factories. At its climax, a crowd of "pro-Germans" in a Far West town is foiled by a mob of hooded and robed Ku Klux Klansmen on horseback—described as "loyal Americans" in a title card. They surround the evildoers, force them to kiss the American flag, and throw them in jail.

Hollywood films like these, plus the CPI's torrent of propaganda, only heightened the hysteria. The Justice Department received up to 1,500 letters a day accusing people or groups of disloyalty and demanding investigations. When the young Eugene O'Neill took his typewriter to the beach on Cape Cod, the sun reflecting off the metal made someone think the playwright was sending coded signals to German ships or submarines. He was arrested at gunpoint.

Honesty was not high on the CPI's agenda. One of its architects, the journalist Arthur Bullard, had written, with revealing candor, "Truth and Falsehood are arbitrary terms. . . . There is nothing in experience to tell us that one is always preferable to the other. . . . The force of an idea lies in its inspirational value. It matters very little whether it is true or false."

The most notorious CPI falsehood built upon a kernel of fact, namely that Germany had transported the exiled Bolshevik leaders back to Russia in the famous sealed train. But the CPI went much farther, publishing and distributing a set of documents entitled *The German-Bolshevik Conspiracy*, supposedly proving that Vladimir Lenin and Leon Trotsky were German-financed agents, and that through secret outposts on Russian soil the German general staff was controlling revolutionary Russia. After a con man in Russia sold these papers to a credulous CPI official, British intelligence concluded that the documents were all forgeries, many of them written on a single typewriter. The CPI ignored this finding, and barraged the American press with them. Newspapers dutifully treated the revelations as authentic, providing the perfect bridge to translate the anti-German frenzy of the war years into the Red Scare that would follow.

When CPI chief Creel twisted arms, he did his best to hide it. He quietly sent the Bureau of Investigation lists of books, magazines, and organizations he thought suspicious. He wrote to one supporter in Minneapolis about the People's Council of America for Democracy and Peace, the pacifist coalition whose Pittsburgh chapter Leo Wendell had infiltrated. The group included so many prominent citizens that it was difficult for the government to attack it head-on, as it had the Wobblies. "Have patriotic societies and civic organizations pass resolutions condemning the People's Council as pro-German and disloyal," Creel asked, "and see all the newspapers and see to it that they get the point of view." At the end, he added, "Tear this letter up."

Fanning the flames this way often had brutal consequences. Two months after Creel sent that letter, Herbert S. Bigelow, a prominent Protestant minister, was seized and handcuffed as he was about to make a speech for the People's Council in Newport, Kentucky. In a convoy of

22 cars, vigilantes dressed in white Klan-like robes took him to a forest, gagged him, tied him to a tree, cut off his hair, covered him with crude oil, and a masked man gave him a dozen lashes with a metal-weighted leather whip.

THE PROPAGANDA WAR unfolded on another front as well. As with wartime administrations since that time, Wilson's underlings knew the power of giving influential people an exclusive chance to meet troops and commanders and be photographed at the front. And so the government took groups of VIPs across the Atlantic and gave them tours of an artillery factory in England, shipyards in Scotland, and various headquarters of the Allied armies in France. A Grenadier Guards officer escorted one such group around Britain, and British and French officials always effusively thanked the Americans for their country's contribution to the war effort.

One of these trips included nine members of Congress, among them Washington State's Albert Johnson. In England, they visited hospitals, went to a service in the chapel of Windsor Castle, and listened to a debate in the House of Commons. In France, they laid a wreath on Lafayette's tomb and were received by General Pershing. Johnson's pince-nez, wavy hair, and pleasant face, so unexpectedly benign-looking for someone full of venom toward immigrants and radicals, appeared in a newsreel that showed the congressmen, in helmets, looking toward German lines. They were wined and dined in a grand, moated, multiturreted seventeenth-century chateau in Radinghem, France, taken over by the British and used specifically for housing visiting dignitaries.

When Johnson and three of his colleagues were being shown through a Belgian trench, nearby Germans opened machine-gun fire, forcing the party to shelter in a dugout. No one was hurt, but it made for the kind of headlines that warm a politician's heart. "Albert Johnson under Hun Fire," said the *Tacoma Times* in his home state; "Congressmen Face Death in Trenches," reported another newspaper. Johnson told a journalist—who, conveniently, was not on hand to verify the claim—that they had been only 50 yards away from the Germans and that a shell had exploded a mere 20 yards from them.

Death-defying as this appeared, it was not, to Johnson, the climax of the trip. That came when King Albert I of Belgium, commanding his country's troops at the front, invited the congressmen for tea. Europeans, after all, know how much Americans love royalty. Some weeks later, Johnson regaled crowds back home with tales of his experiences and predicted, oddly, that after the war Belgium would become a republic, but that "the people will elect Albert president."

In late September 1918, hankering for more of the attention that had come his way from being under fire in Europe, the 49-year-old Johnson made a new bid for glory. Having waited until the war was almost over, he joined the army. "My colleagues," he told his fellow representatives, "I can not resist that call." Johnson heeded the call to arms without giving up his seat, however, for it would be as "Captain Johnson," still safely in the United States, that he would win reelection seven weeks later. His entire military career would last only 91 days.

The House gave him a rousing send-off as he prepared to leave for a training base in Virginia. He replied by evoking some of his favorite enemies:

> Americanism is what America stands for. . . . We want no Bolshevism and do not propose to reach it by any steps toward "internationalism," which has been the cry of the red-flaggers, the anarchists and the firebrands. . . . We will be watchful now when we see mice of a gentler breed gnawing at the very foundations of our Republic. When we were at peace most of us paid little heed. But they shall not nibble and gnaw while we are at war.

Peace?

WHO DID JOHNSON and people like him consider the "mice" who were nibbling and gnawing at the country's foundations? Opponents of the established order came in many varieties, but with the IWW now crippled, the domestic enemy that loomed largest in the government's eyes was the Socialist Party. Its leader was America's most beloved leftist.

Born to Alsatian immigrants in Terre Haute, Indiana, Eugene V. Debs left school at 14 to take a job cleaning grease from the wheel assemblies of freight locomotives. Then he worked on board such engines as a fireman, shoveling coal. After many years as a railway union organizer, he eventually decided that socialism was the solution to the brutal inequalities of the age. He presided over the Socialist Party's growth while managing, by the force of his personality, to keep its disparate factions under one roof. Debs gave generously to those in need: money, when he had any, clothes from the suitcase he carried on his endless travels. He charmed even his enemies, on one speaking tour stopping to visit the sheriff who had been his jailer during a railroad strike.

Saintly, gentle, and charismatic, Debs was a faithful Christian, and the fervor he inspired in his followers was almost religious. A socialist writer described how "children used to flock to him as they must have flocked to the Carpenter. I remember gray-bearded farmers, who as American Railway Union strikers had followed him to defeat, rushing up to their Gene, crying 'Gene, Gene, don't you remember me anymore?' And Gene remembered them always, threw his long arms around them, pressed them to his heart until their eyes moistened in love and gratitude."

The Wobblies might be more colorful, and groups like La Follette's Wisconsin progressives more influential in a particular state, but the Socialists were a national political force. Theodore Roosevelt, alert to any movement that threatened his own martial vision of America, once called the party's growth "far more ominous than any populist or similar movement in times past." The Socialists seemed "ominous" to him because they commanded considerable support and could not be condemned as violent revolutionaries, for they competed at the polls. As a young man, Debs, for example, had been elected city clerk of Terre Haute, and later an Indiana state senator.

Barnstorming across the country in the Red Special, a campaign train flying red flags, carrying a brass band, and greeted by enthusiastic whistle blasts from passing locomotive engineers, Debs had won 6 percent of the popular vote for president in 1912, running ahead of the Republican candidate in several states. Over the years more than a thousand Socialists were voted into state legislatures, city councils, and other elective offices—more than 175 merely in Oklahoma, a stronghold. Socialists became mayors in cities as disparate as Milwaukee, Schenectady, Toledo, and Pasadena, many of them gaining a reputation for more honest governance than was typical of the era's big-city Democratic machines. The longtime Socialist administration in Milwaukee not only expanded the park system but actually raised the city's credit rating.

Twenty-three Socialist mayors were in office in 1917. That year, both Republicans and Democrats were horrified to see the Socialists make impressive gains in the November municipal elections, in which they won an average of more than 20 percent of the vote in 14 of the country's larger cities, and well over 30 percent in several.

In New York, the biggest, the party's candidate for mayor was Morris Hillquit, a lawyer who had defended half a dozen of the publications Albert Burleson had banned from the mail. Hillquit was from the moderate wing of his party, but spoke in favor of peace and infuriated Woodrow Wilson by refusing to buy Liberty Bonds. During the campaign, the president wrote to his attorney general, Thomas Gregory, asking what could be done about Hillquit's "outrageous utterances." Gregory replied that Hillquit had indeed "been very close to the line a number of times, but, in my judgment, any proceedings against him would enable him to pose as a martyr and would be likely to increase his voting strength. I am having my representatives in New York City watch the situation rather carefully, and if a point is reached where he can be proceeded against it will give me a great deal of pleasure." To the administration's dismay, Hillquit won nearly 22 percent of the vote.

In half a dozen cities in 1917, including Chicago, worried Republicans and Democrats had agreed to support a single "fusion" candidate for various posts to keep the Socialists from winning a plurality. Socialists increased their representation from two to ten seats in the New York State Assembly. Jubilant party members knew that if they did equally well in the 1918 midterm national elections, their vote total could for the first time be in the millions.

For Wilson, however, whose Democrats controlled the House of Representatives by only the narrowest of margins, it would be unthinkable to allow an antiwar party to gain the balance of power in the next Congress. The president was determined to crush the Socialists. If the administration's attack on the Wobblies had been all-out frontal assault, its offensive against the Socialists was a more sophisticated air, land, and sea operation, with strikes on several flanks.

Already the party's most popular woman, Kate Richards O'Hare, had been sentenced under the Espionage Act. In short order, the government used the same tool to indict, in various states, officials of the party and candidates it had run for office. It also tried, though eventually failed, to jail Victor Berger of Wisconsin, the first Socialist elected to Congress. To boot, Burleson's Post Office, which had already barred most Socialist Party newspapers from the mail, now stopped delivering letters to and from the party's Chicago headquarters and some state and local offices as well. This was a damaging blow in an era when the only other means of communication between cities were costly tele-grams or long-distance telephone calls.

Also joining the assault were vigilante groups and the police, who attacked Socialist speakers or denied them meeting halls. In January 1918, for example, the mayor of Mitchell, South Dakota ordered the party's state convention broken up and all delegates expelled from town. One party leader was seized "on the streets by five unknown men and hustled into an automobile in which he was driven five miles from town," a local newspaper reported. "There he was set out upon the prairie and . . . told to proceed afoot to his home in Parkston [an 18-mile walk] and warned not to return."

Finally, there was the question of what to do about Debs. The Wilson administration was at first leery of prosecuting someone so widely respected, even by non-Socialists. For a time it hoped that Debs might abandon his opposition to the war, for, like some other Socialists, he had declared himself impressed by the president's Fourteen Points speech—which, after all, had echoed some longtime left-wing goals. When it gradually became clear, however, that Debs was not changing his basic stand, someone—it is not clear who—began a campaign of what today we would call disinformation. The historian Eric Chester believes this operation may have been carried out by a dirty-tricks unit of Military Intelligence.

Misleading news stories mysteriously started appearing. "Socialists Led by Debs Come Out for War," declared the *New York Tribune* on May 14, 1918, adding that Debs had called Lenin and Trotsky "virtually the agents of German imperialism." "Debs to Reform," declared the *Topeka State Journal* two days later: "Under His Leadership Socialists Will Change Attitude." The next month, a headline in the *Indianapolis News* claimed, "Debs Asserts He Is with Government in the War"—a few days after he had given a ringing speech saying the opposite.

Debs had made that speech, in part, because he was exasperated at the string of blatantly false stories and at the fact that no nonsocialist newspapers had reported a statement he issued denying that he had changed his position. Despite frail health that made it hard for him to even get out of bed on some days, he wanted to make his feelings completely clear, and so in June 1918 he traveled to Canton, Ohio, for a state convention of his party, which climaxed with an open-air rally in a downtown park. Bureau of Investigation agents were listening, and a stenographer transcribing his words, as Debs spoke from a bandstand. No fewer than 34 American Protective League members mingled with the crowd, arresting men, 55 in all, who did not produce a draft card.

Always a riveting speaker, Debs would pace back and forth across a stage, his piercing eyes fixing on one person after another in the audience. He would lean far forward and throw his arms wide as if to embrace them all, while his long face seemed to carry all the cares of the world. On that day, he had plenty of cares, for he had just visited several Socialist Party draft resisters in the local jail, where two of them had been hung by their wrists from a rafter.

Sweating in his three-piece suit in the summer heat, he talked of their courage: "Those prison bars separate their bodies from ours, but their souls are here this afternoon. . . . They are there for us; and we are here for them." He spoke about socialists in jail in Germany for defying the war fever in that country and declared, "I would rather a thousand times be a free soul in jail than to be a sycophant and coward in the streets." He spoke of Kate Richards O'Hare, still out on bail as she appealed her case, in a "country that would send a woman to the penitentiary . . . for exercising the right of free speech."

Those who condemned her and other war opponents, he said, were speaking just as "the same usurers, the same money changers, the same Pharisees" spoke "of the Judean carpenter twenty centuries ago." Well aware of the law, Debs did not directly advocate defying the draft. The closest he came was to say, "They have always taught you that it is your patriotic duty to go to war and to have yourselves slaughtered at their command. But in all the history of the world you, the people, never had a voice in declaring war."

That was enough. Two weeks later he was indicted under the Espionage Act.

The 62-year-old Debs went on trial before a judge who was the former law partner of Wilson's secretary of war. The Socialist leader's legendary grace and dignity did not desert him. "I have often wondered," he told a hushed courtroom, "if I could take the life of my fellow man, even to save my own. Men talk about holy wars. There are none."

He went on:

> Much has been made of a statement that I declared that men were fit for something better than slavery and cannon fodder. . . . Men *are* fit for something better than slavery and cannon fodder. . . . I can hear the shrieks of the soldiers of Europe in my dreams. I have imagination enough to see a battlefield. I can see it strewn with the legs of human beings, who but yesterday were in the flush and glory of their young manhood. I can see them at eventide, scattered about in remnants, their limbs torn from their bodies.

The jury swiftly found him guilty. The judge sentenced him to ten years.

IN EUROPE, THE tide of war decisively turned in the Allies' favor. The German offensive to capture Paris had failed. British, French, and a rapidly growing number of American troops were slowly pushing the Germans back. Long hemmed in by the British naval blockade, Germany was running out of food. Civilians were desperately short of meat, milk, and eggs; troops at the front were eating horsemeat and nettles; and there were few new men of military age left to be drafted. Behind the lines, German soldiers started to desert. And in Germany itself, metal was so scarce that more than 10,000 church bells were melted down to make arms and ammunition.

In the United States, with the scent of victory in the air, militaristic fervor only grew. This weighed heavily on Robert La Follette, who was having a difficult year. One of his sons was gravely ill, and La Follette stayed home for months to help care for him; the other son, against his parents' wishes, had enlisted in the army, and was being trained to fight in the war that so dismayed the senator. Although La Follette had virtually ceased criticizing the war effort since Wilson's Fourteen Points speech, a committee was still charged with investigating whether to expel him from the Senate. On the rare occasions when a fellow senator made a friendly remark he reported it to his wife and children. He had long had spells of what today we would call depression, and the threat of expulsion from the Senate did not help. "Sometimes I wonder," La Follette wrote his family, "if I will ever be just the same again."

Someone who hated La Follette, Theodore Roosevelt, was still grieving the death of his son Quentin. Although overweight and showing his age, his mustache now white, the former Rough Rider had lost none of his desire to see his country fight the war to the very end. "In my youth . . . I used to be quite fond of glove fighting," he told a war bond rally in Columbus, Ohio, in September 1918, "and . . . was taught that when you've got a man groggy, put him out." As he was leaving the rally, he passed a group of "Gold Star Mothers," who had each lost a son at the front. They were sobbing, but he told them, "We must not weep. Though I too have lost a dear one, I think only of victory. We must carry on no matter what the cost."

"But," added his longtime valet-bodyguard, who accompanied him, "he had to swallow in order to talk."

Wearing a black mourning band on one arm, Roosevelt made no secret of his hope to run again for president in 1920, despite serious health problems that several times landed him in the hospital. He had already published his own plan for the postwar world, complete with a redrawn map of Europe. If for any reason he could not run, he often told his admirers, the best candidate would be his friend General Leonard Wood.

Still angry at being denied a role of command in Europe, Wood lost no chance to say that he thought the government was conducting the war ineptly, making headlines when he testified to that effect before Congress. In private, he was even more excoriating: it leaked into the press that at one dinner party, Wood had referred to his commander in chief, President Wilson, as "that rabbit."

More than 200,000 additional US troops in their broad-brimmed hats were now pouring into France each month, and many were delighted that they had gotten there in time to fight. Unlike their bloodied, exhausted British and French allies, the newcomers were so impatient for action that the US Army's rear-area support units suffered an epidemic of men "deserting to the front." More than 3,000 of these combat-hungry "deserters" would die in battle.

By September 1918, American soldiers made up nearly one-third of the troops fighting the Germans in France and Belgium. And now the press had homegrown heroes to celebrate: Sergeant Alvin York of Tennessee, using his backwoods sharpshooter's skills to kill 28 Germans and then bluff 132 others into surrendering; or the "Lost Battalion" from New York, which got trapped so far in front of its flanking units that it was completely surrounded by Germans for nearly five days. Most of its men were killed or wounded, but the battalion still refused to surrender.

Back in the United States, the Lost Battalion's home city was engaged in a different kind of war. New York was the scene of an intensified hunt for dissidents, especially in education. Columbia University's war enthusiast president, Nicholas Murray Butler, engineered the firing of two pacifist faculty members. Meanwhile, the state passed a series of laws affecting schoolteachers: they could now lose their jobs for "treasonable or seditious statements," they had to be American citizens, and all schools had to give a course in patriotism and citizenship. New York City's Board of Education went further, requiring all teachers to sign loyalty oaths, and holding hearings at which students testified about what their teachers said in class. Across the country, educators lost their jobs. E. A. Schimmel, a professor of modern languages at Northland College in Ashland, Wisconsin, antagonized a local vigilante group, the Knights of Liberty, which tarred and feathered him.

In September 1918, New York saw the largest of all the "slacker raids" by the American Protective League, with more than 20,000 APL members combing streets, railway stations, ferry terminals, hotels, and theaters, and moving from table to table in restaurants. Some 650 cars and trucks transported thousands of young men who couldn't produce a draft card to two armories in the city and two more in New Jersey. When one group was seized in Manhattan, the raiders commandeered a passing truck to take them to an armory, but its driver couldn't show a draft card, so they arrested him as well. George Miller, a 23-year-old flagman in the subway system, was so frightened of being caught that he hid out for three days in a shelter in a subway tunnel at 145th Street, until a fellow worker turned him in. Attorney General Thomas Gregory boasted that, with the "invaluable" help of the APL, "it is safe to say that never in its history has this country been so thoroughly policed."

The zeal of the APL and its Bureau of Investigation sponsors prevailed over the protests of draft officials, who complained that they hadn't yet completed registering and classifying all eligible men. Estimates of the number arrested in the New York raids range up to 50,000; at least 300,000 were stopped and interrogated. The authorities held many of them for several days. Anxious relatives thronged streets outside the armories, waving birth certificates and other identification documents for the men inside. A group of women who stormed the gates of one armory were pushed back by the police. The chaos, and an inadvertent admission to the press by a bureau agent that only one out of every one hundred men arrested was actually a draft evader, produced some of the first real pushback the APL received: disapproving editorials and a flood of protests from representatives and senators. But the raids continued for the rest of the war.

On the other side of the country, in Portland, Oregon, more than four months after her arrest under the Espionage Act, the bold, diminutive Dr. Marie Equi finally went on trial. Her prospects did not look promising. All the jurors were men, mostly farmers or small businessmen who were not likely to be merciful to a woman who had spoken out against the war from atop a telephone pole.

Prosecutors appealed strongly to homophobia and pointed to Equi's defiance of traditional femininity, one referring to her as "an unsexed woman." Another spoke of her and her "kind" as "long-haired men and short-haired women" and appealed to the fear of revolution now increasingly in the air: "The red flag is floating over Russia. . . . Unless you put this woman in jail, I tell you it will float over the world." He ended by reciting "The Star-Spangled Banner," looking each juror in the eye.

The jury found her guilty, and, some weeks later, the judge sentenced her to a $500 fine and three years in prison.

IN THE EYES of the government, even more despicable than women war opponents like Equi were men who had been drafted but would not fight. Hundreds of "absolutist" conscientious objectors, who refused to do even noncombatant military duties, remained imprisoned, many of them in a jail within the large army training base at Camp Funston, Kansas. In September 1918, following a hunger strike in which guards pushed rubber tubes down prisoners' throats to force-feed them, 18 COs signed a statement:

> The "officer of the day". . . . proceeded to abuse and insult us, referring to those of Jewish birth as "damn kikes," etc. He then had our beds and blankets taken from us, and ordered that we be given raw rations—pork and beans—which we were to cook in the toilet, if we wanted to eat. . . . We had no supper and slept on the bare floor in our clothes.

For a week, the group was put on bread and water. Soon after came a day when

> the sergeant of the guards issued some military commands to us. When we did not obey promptly, he shoved us about violently. . . . Bayonets were pressed against the bodies of Larsen, Silver and others, to obtain compliance, but no one ran. The guards now insisted that we walk in strict military posture, and cuffs, kicks and blows were rained upon those who failed to do so. . . . Steiner ceased walking. He was seized by the ears and dragged around the building. Another guard . . . seized him by the throat and choked him so forcibly that he sank breathless to the ground.

Guards forced the men to run outside, shoeless, while following them and stepping on their bare feet. A colonel administered a beating to one CO with a riding crop. When packages of food for the prisoners arrived from home, guards dumped them into the garbage.

> At 8 P.M. the "Officer of the Day," a captain, and the sergeant of the guards ordered all to undress . . . and prepare for a cold shower, the third that day. . . . The Captain himself brought forth scrub-brushes, used ordinarily for cleaning toilet seats and brooms used for sweeping, and ordered that we scrub each other with them. Franklin refused to use the filthy brush. He was seized and roughly thrown to the cement floor. . . . He was then placed under the cold spray and left there until he collapsed. Eichel and Shotkin helped him back to his bed. When he recovered he became hysterical. . . . The captain . . . told Eichel he was carrying out the instructions of the Post Commander in treating us so.

The post commander was Major General Leonard Wood.

In charge of Camp Funston and the larger army base of which it was a part, Wood and his wife lived in a house on a small rise above the camp. Still passionate about physical fitness, he could defeat all challengers at arm wrestling, his admirers claimed, including even the captain of the Harvard football team. To the exasperated general, Camp Funston was a place of exile. Instead of leading a vast and battle-hardened army across the fields of northern France, winning victories that could be stepping-stones to high political office, he was training raw recruits on a muddy floodplain in Kansas, where the temperature soared above 100 degrees Fahrenheit in summer. And he had the COs on his hands as well.

In the Philippines a dozen years earlier, the short-tempered general had waged a campaign in Moro Province against rebels fighting American rule. The Moros, he told his friend Roosevelt, "require one severe lesson. . . . We will attempt to make it such a one as not to require repetition." An imperialist to the core, Wood believed that Moro law and customs were "for the greater part rubbish." He personally led several expeditions into tropical swamps and wilderness, burning Moro villages. One scorched-earth foray alone claimed 1,500 Moros killed, including women and children.

A decade and a half later, Wood was now waging something of a scorched-earth campaign against conscientious objectors, for whom he made no secret of his contempt. "They are," he wrote to the father of one CO who had protested the abuse, "as shown by their words and acts, avowed enemies of this Government. . . . Fortunately for the Nation . . . men of the type of your son and his associates are rare." When six COs were court-martialed at Camp Funston and sentenced to life imprisonment at hard labor "for disobedience of orders and other offences," reported a Kansas newspaper, Wood "exercised clemency." He reduced the sentence to 25 years.

AT CAMP FUNSTON, without fully realizing it, General Wood had presided over the beginnings of a worldwide cataclysm that before long would take even more lives than the First World War. The base was one of the first places on earth where, in the spring of 1918, doctors noticed the appearance of a particularly virulent strain of influenza. The disease then traveled to Europe with the US Army, spreading outward from Brest and other debarkation ports in France.

As the year progressed, the virus seemed to mutate. A second, more severe wave struck both hemispheres in the fall of 1918. Most shocking, people between 16 and 40 made up more than half the death toll, dying in agony, often with blood pouring from their nostrils, mouths, ears, or eyes. Sometimes they perished within 24 hours of falling ill. At Camp Funston, where hundreds died, Wood eliminated mass meetings and ordered dining tables separated by cotton screens.

A third wave of the pandemic would sweep around the world the following year. Estimates today are that the virus killed some 675,000 people in the United States, and at least 50 million worldwide. Influenza spread with particular speed wherever people were in close quarters, which meant not just army barracks but prisons. Four Wobblies awaiting trial died in a Sacramento jail. In the women's penitentiary in Missouri 35 inmates fell ill, and the short, sturdy figure of Emma Goldman, who had experience working as a nurse, moved from cell to cell doing what she could for them.

Most of Europe had already had four years to become accustomed to young men dying on a large scale. American civilians, however, thought of themselves as safe, an ocean away from enemy shells or bombs. To see hundreds of thousands die, suddenly and painfully, half of them men and women in the prime of life, was a bewildering shock. The white gauze masks people wore on the streets, the warning posters, the vast temporary hospitals with long rows of white-sheeted beds, the masked workers everywhere loading bodies into hearses or trucks, all put a note of menace in the air. And people knew worse was happening where they couldn't see it: from army bases across the country came urgent pleas for civilian doctors, nurses, bedsheets—and coffins.

What made the pandemic even more eerie was the lack of honest news. While the war raged, none of the nations fighting it wanted to reveal to their enemies the disease's immense toll. One of the few major countries not to muzzle its press was neutral Spain. Especially when its king fell ill, the nation's journalists published abundant reports on the mysterious scourge; such material could be safely reprinted elsewhere. Hence the pandemic was informally misnamed "the Spanish Flu."

American newspapers had already learned the wartime habit of keeping stories upbeat. "As terrifying as the disease was," writes the historian John Barry, "the press made it more so. They terrified by making little of it, for what officials and the press said bore no relationship to what people saw and touched and smelled and endured." The chief of health and sanitation for the American wartime shipbuilding program, for example, blithely declared that the virus was "nothing more or less than old-fashioned grippe." Even more absurdly, he claimed the disease "was brought to the United States by members of the crews of German submarines" who "have been ashore at New York and other places."

Influenza killed some 195,000 Americans in October 1918 alone, up to that point the greatest death toll of any month in American history. In particularly hard-hit Philadelphia, priests drove horse-drawn carts collecting corpses, bodies overflowed from the city morgue into the street, and on October 10, 1918, the virus killed 759 Philadelphians, more than ten times the average daily deaths from all causes. But the front page of the next morning's *Philadelphia Inquirer* carried not a single mention of the disease.

IN THE DEEP FURROWS of sandbagged trenches that ran across northern France and Belgium, soldiers had experienced every kind of terror imaginable over more than four years of warfare. They had been the target of attacks by human waves, by pulverizing artillery bombardments, by poison gas, by tanks, by flamethrowers. And in recent weeks they had seen comrades suddenly succumb to the deadly virus. But shortly after 8:00 p.m. on November 7, 1918, French troops in positions near the town of La Capelle saw something completely different.

From the north, three large automobiles with the black eagle of Imperial Germany on their sides approached the front, headlights on. Two soldiers stood on the running boards of the lead car, one waving a white flag, the other blowing an unusually long silver bugle with the call for cease-fire—a single high tone repeated in rapid succession four times, then four times again, with the last note lingering.

This spot had been chosen because here the remains of a road crossed the scarred and cratered no-man's-land between the opposing armies. By prior arrangement, the three German cars slowly made their way along it. When they reached the French trenches, a French bugler replaced the German one and the peace envoys continued their journey. At La Capelle, flashes lit up the night as waiting press and newsreel cameramen photographed the group.

Transferred to French cars, the German envoys traveled onward past houses, factories, barns, and churches reduced to charred rubble by the years of fighting. Then a train carried them to a clearing in the forest of Compiègne, near another train occupied by the staff of Marshal Ferdinand Foch, the Allied commander in chief, a short Frenchman with an immense, shaggy mustache. The two groups met in Foch's train, in what had formerly been a dining car of the luxury sleeping car service Compagnie Internationale des Wagons-Lits.

A month earlier, Germany had formally approached President Wilson to ask for peace talks based on his Fourteen Points. The German high command, fast losing the war, was desperate. Its major ally, the Austro-Hungarian Empire, was fragmenting as one ethnic group after another declared its independence. Ottoman Turkey, another ally, was also collapsing. The most powerful German commander, the stern-faced General Erich Ludendorff, suffered a nervous breakdown, resigned, and would shortly flee Germany in disguise.

In rear areas, desertions mounted. Many German civilians were scraping by on only 1,000 calories a day, eating bread with sawdust in it and sausages made of horse and rabbit meat. Mutinous crews in the German navy, ordered to sea for a suicidal last-ditch foray against the British, seized their own ships, ran up the red flag of revolution, arrested their officers, and made common cause with rebellious workers and soldiers ashore.

The Allied powers yielded to the French, so much of whose territory the fighting had ravaged, the role of voicing the peace terms. As the German envoys entered Foch's railway carriage, no one in the Allied delegation shook their hands. Although what resulted has gone down in history as the Armistice, the Allies really demanded, and would receive, a German surrender.

German troops, Marshal Foch told the envoys, must swiftly evacuate the territory they still occupied in France and Belgium. France would regain Alsace and Lorraine, and Allied forces would occupy the west bank of the Rhine—Germany's industrial heartland—at German expense. Foch also demanded that the Germans turn over to the Allies not merely immense numbers of artillery pieces, machine guns, aircraft, and warships, but also 5,000 trucks, 5,000 railway locomotives, and 150,000 freight cars. Further reparations would come later, as part of a comprehensive peace treaty.

The German delegation, anticipating much more generous peace terms in the spirit of Wilson's Fourteen Points, was stunned. The major general representing the high command could not suppress a sob. He and his colleagues pleaded for an immediate cease-fire while the two sides discussed these stringent demands. Foch refused. Instead, he ordered Allied commanders to step up attacks: "It is urgent to hasten and intensify our efforts."

Meanwhile, Germany continued to collapse from within. Inspired by the Russian Revolution, workers and soldiers were forming soviets, or councils. A soviet took over the city of Cologne. At German military headquarters in the Belgian resort town of Spa, soldiers formed a soviet and refused to salute their officers. Kaiser Wilhelm II abdicated his throne and fled to neutral Holland.

Given these events, it was no longer even clear what government the German delegates in the railway carriage were representing. All that concerned the Allies, however, was that the German army accept Foch's terms. Ferocious combat continued as a courier traveled back through the front lines, again with a white flag and bugle calls, carrying the text of the Allied demands to Spa. At last the German high command radioed its approval, and, in the railway train before dawn on the morning of November 11, 1918, delegates from both sides signed the Armistice, to take effect at 11:00 a.m.

At that point the fighting was finally to stop, but its last spasm was particularly cruel, even by the mad logic of this conflict. Because the Allies had rejected German pleas for a cease-fire while the Armistice was being negotiated, an additional 6,750 men died and an additional nearly 15,000 soldiers were wounded. Worse yet, British, French, and American commanders all issued orders that the bloodshed should continue at full pitch for six hours *after* the two delegations signed the Armistice. As General Pershing put it, there should be "absolutely no let-up in carrying out the original plans until 11 o'clock."

The delegates in Foch's railway carriage put their signatures to the agreement just after 5:00 a.m. on November 11, and the key terms were immediately radioed and telephoned to commanders up and down the front on both sides. After the news reached New York, where it was still the middle of the night, floodlights lit up the Statue of Liberty. But in France, Allied soldiers continued attacking until the last minute.

Since the armies tabulated their casualty statistics by the day and not the hour, we know only the total toll for November 11, 1918: 2,738 men from both sides were killed, and 8,206 left wounded or missing. But it was still dark at 5:00 a.m. and attacks almost always took place in daylight, so the great majority of these casualties clearly happened after the Armistice had been signed. And they were incurred to gain ground that Allied generals knew the Germans would be vacating within days, or even hours after the cease-fire.

Lieutenant General Robert Bullard, the commander of the US Second Army, was openly disappointed to see the fighting end. On November 11, he wrote, he went "near the front line, to see the last of it, to hear the crack of the last guns in the greatest war of all ages. . . . I stayed until 11 a.m., when all being over, I returned to my headquarters, thoughtful and feeling lost."

A few generals had held their troops back when they heard that the Armistice had been signed, but they were in the minority. And so thousands of men were killed or maimed during these last six hours of war for no political or military reason whatsoever. Among the victims were troops of the American 92nd Division, part of Bullard's Second Army.

The US military was rigidly segregated, and the men of the 92nd were Black. All their higher-ranking officers, however, were white, often southerners resentful of being given such commands. "Poor Negroes!" wrote Bullard, an Alabaman. "They are hopelessly inferior." Like Leonard Wood, Bullard was a veteran of the campaign against the Moro rebels in the Philippines, whom he, too, had considered inferior, or, as he put it at the time, "low in the scale of civilization . . . the most primitive and remote of American subjects."

The troops of the 92nd had already known terror at home. Mobs would lynch 60 Black Americans in 1918 alone—one of them, William Bird of Sheffield, Alabama, on the very day that the Armistice stopped the war. When the 92nd Division was in training at Camp Dodge, Iowa, four months earlier, its troops had been forced to watch the hanging of the three Black soldiers accused of rape. The division's men shared the hope of hundreds of thousands of other Black soldiers that their service would earn them some protection from such atrocities in postwar life.

In the army itself, however, they were treated as second-class citizens. One Black soldier—decades later posthumously awarded the Congressional Medal of Honor—heard a white officer remark, "Send the niggers to the front and there won't be so many around New York." And a lieutenant in the 92nd reported that, in combat, "the negroes were hit more from behind than they were in front"—meaning that they were fired upon by white American soldiers.

These Black troops did not yet know it, but the friendliness and respect shown them by French soldiers and civilians had alarmed top American generals so much that they tried to put a stop to it. W. E. B. Du Bois would later score an investigative coup, obtaining a memo that a French liaison officer at American headquarters circulated to French commanders. It said that the "Americans"—meaning white Americans, of course—"are afraid that contact with the French will inspire in black Americans aspirations which to them appear intolerable. . . . We must not eat with them, must not shake hands or seek to talk or meet with them outside of the requirements of military service. . . . We must not commend too highly the black American troops, particularly in the presence of [white] Americans."

On November 11, these Black soldiers found themselves advancing into German machine-gun fire and mustard gas, ordered to make their last attack at 10:30 a.m., a mere half hour before the cease-fire. The 92nd Division officially recorded 17 deaths and 302 wounded or missing on this day; one general declared that the real toll was even higher. The First World War ended as senselessly as it had begun.

At home, the worst was yet to come.

PART II

14

Another Savior Come to Earth

O N NOVEMBER 11 . . . the electric power in our shop was switched off, the machines stopped, and we were informed that there would be no further work that day," wrote Emma Goldman. "It was an unheard-of event in the prison. . . . The men were banging on bars, whistling, and shouting." She asked the matron, "You mean that . . . the war has come to an end and the prisons will be opened for those who refused to take part in the slaughter? Tell me, Tell me!"

Like Goldman, the Wobblies in prison at Leavenworth, the COs at Camp Funston, and the thousands of people sentenced under the Espionage Act and state sedition laws all gained hope as cheering and church bells sounded throughout the country. "The coming of peace should bring with it the pardon both of [conscientious] objectors and of political prisoners," said the liberal *Nation*.

Goldman was still optimistic at Christmas, six weeks after the Armistice, when "members of my family, comrades, and friends fairly deluged me with presents. Soon my cell began to look like a department store." She recruited three inmates to help her, and "on Christmas Eve, while our fellow-prisoners were attending the movies, a matron accompanied us to unlock the doors, our aprons piled high with gifts. With gleeful secrecy we flitted along the tiers, visiting each cell in turn. When the women returned from the cinema, the cell-block re-

sounded . . . 'Santa Claus's been here! He's brung me something grand!'
'Me, too!' 'Me, too!'. . . . My Christmas in the Missouri penitentiary
brought me greater joy than many previous ones outside."

Also feeling joy at the war's end was Woodrow Wilson. His certainty
that he was carrying out the Lord's work reached a new high. "The
eyes of the people have been opened and they see," he declared in a
statement issued on the day of the Armistice. "The hand of God is laid
upon the nations. He will show them favour, I devoutly believe, only if
they rise to the clear heights of His own justice and mercy." God would
be getting some assistance from Wilson himself, for he revealed that he
was going to Europe to help negotiate a comprehensive peace treaty.
He would be the first American president to cross the ocean while in
office.

Less than a month after the fighting stopped, a locomotive with flags
fluttering pulled his train from the capital directly to the pier at Hobo-
ken, New Jersey, where the USS *George Washington* awaited him, his
wife, and a large entourage. It was a twin-funneled luxury German passenger liner seized and renamed during the war. As a navy band played
"Hail to the Chief," soldiers and Secret Service men patrolled the
decks. Aircraft and dirigibles escorted the ship past the Statue of Liberty and out of New York Harbor, along with 17 navy vessels headed by
the battleship *Pennsylvania*.

The sky echoed with the sound of 21-gun salutes and of ships of all
sizes blowing their whistles and sirens. Crews and passengers rushed
to the rails to get a glimpse of the president, who smiled, waved, and
raised his black top hat as he stood on the *George Washington*'s bridge.
Carrier pigeons flew up from the ship, to carry messages about peace
back to land. As the vessel skirted Staten Island, hundreds of schoolchildren gathered outdoors to sing, "My Country, 'Tis of Thee." Heading
toward the Atlantic, the *George Washington* passed another ship coming
in to dock, its decks packed with cheering troops. A novelist could not
have written a more dramatic scene: soldiers returning from the war
crossing paths with their leader heading off to craft the peace.

Before leaving, Wilson said to his secretary, "Well, Tumulty, this trip will either be the greatest success or the supremist tragedy in all history; but I believe in a Divine Providence." He was so eager to carry out the will of Providence that he headed for Europe weeks before the Allied powers were ready to talk in earnest, for the British needed to wait until after a national election. Wilson, observed one diplomat, was drawn to Paris, where the peace negotiations would be taking place, "as a debutante is entranced by the prospect of her first ball."

Some of his eagerness surely came from knowing how rapturously Europeans would receive him, for the United States was the fount of much of the food that had kept the Allied nations alive, and the source of the two million strapping soldiers who had helped win the war. And to millions of the continent's peoples, Wilson's Fourteen Points promised a new and more democratic world.

After he landed, even during the night, people in small villages knelt in the snow beside the railroad track as his train thundered past. An ecstatic crowd estimated at two million greeted him in Paris, where brass-helmeted Republican Guards on horseback escorted the presidential carriage down the Champs-Élysées and through the Arc de Triomphe, an honor the French government had not given to anyone else for decades. Photographers with heavy boxlike cameras raced alongside, and even the trees and roofs were filled with cheering onlookers.

In the weeks before the peace talks began, the presidential couple enjoyed Europe's welcome. The delighted Edith Wilson bubbled over with enthusiasm at the luxurious quarters they were given, the kings and queens they met, the gifts they received, and the chance to show off the elaborate wardrobe she had brought along. Everywhere one red-carpet celebration followed upon another: an honorary degree here, the keys to the city there; streets renamed Rue Wilson, Via Wilson, Wilsonstraat. All of this was far better than having to deal with strikers, Wobblies, socialists, and Republicans at home.

The king of Italy sent his personal train to bring the couple to Rome, where showers of white roses cascaded down on their motorcade. After uniformed guards heralded the president's arrival with bugles, the white-robed Pope Benedict XV welcomed him to the Vatican's throne room. There were state dinners, a speech to the Belgian parliament, a stay at Buckingham Palace while 200,000 people cheered outside, opera at La Scala in Milan, and an address to a thousand mayors in Turin. The Italians in particular, observed one aide, seemed "to consider him as another Savior come to earth." Everywhere he was escorted: by coachmen in top hats driving him through delirious crowds, by warships when crossing the English Channel, by plumed cavalrymen with glittering breastplates when parading through capital after capital.

It was temptingly easy for the president to imagine that he was representing the people of Europe as well as his own. In fact, he was more popular in Europe than in America, where the still-influential Theodore Roosevelt loudly denounced "Mr. Wilson and his Fourteen Points and his four supplementary points and his five complementary points." Furthermore, Wilson's Democrats had just lost control of both houses of Congress in the 1918 midterm elections, only weeks before his departure.

Moreover, the president had done nothing to prepare Congress for whatever peace treaty he might now negotiate. Nor, with his usual lofty disregard for everyday politics, had he empowered his largely invisible vice president, Thomas Marshall, to mind the store while he was gone. "I was in favor of his going," wrote the humorist Will Rogers, "because I thought it would give us a chance to find out who was Vice President. But it Dident [*sic*]."

Wilson could not escape pressures for more democracy at home, and for farther-reaching changes than he had ever pictured abroad. In Paris, for example, the determined W. E. B. Du Bois helped bring together 57 "representatives of the Negro race" from 15 nations in a Pan African Congress. They petitioned delegates to the peace talks and won press coverage with their demands for freedom for people of African descent across the world.

Inspired by the president's talk of self-determination, emissaries from every corner of the earth vied for his attention: Jews wanting a homeland in Palestine, Polish peasants in black fur caps with a priest translating their pleas into French, Mohandas Gandhi arguing for

Indian independence, Lawrence of Arabia and sheiks in keffiyehs reminding him that the Allies had promised freedom to the Arabs, and a young Vietnamese patriot and kitchen worker in Paris who would later adopt the name Ho Chi Minh. "About every second man of this type one meets," wrote the journalist Ray Stannard Baker, "fishes out of his pocket a copy of a cablegram that he or his committee has just sent to President Wilson."

The very presence of Baker, a famous muckraker, as Wilson's press aide was evidence that the president could still attract idealistic intellectuals to work for him. Officials, however, saw to it that Wilson would not be besieged by too many people "of this type" who might be carrying the idea of democracy a step too far. The State Department denied passports to more than a dozen leading Black Americans, including the anti-lynching activist Ida B. Wells, as well as to two women's suffrage campaigners who had demonstrated on the White House lawn. No one in the presidential party wanted such protests in Paris.

Wilson settled into quarters at the Palais Murat, an elegant eighteenth-century mansion filled with mirrors, gold-embroidered damask draperies, and portraits of Napoléon. Sometimes he walked over to Colonel House's large suite of rooms at the Hotel Crillon to confer with the slight, soft-voiced man who was still his closest adviser. The peace conference finally began on January 18, 1919. For this occasion, the president wore striped trousers, a high collar, and a cravat with a pink pin. Limousines flying national flags bore him and the other leaders to the French Foreign Ministry at the Quai d'Orsay. The conference would take place in its grand reception rooms, one of them now renamed Le Salon de la Paix: a thick red carpet, glittering chandeliers, high ceilings with gilded trim, and tall windows framed by cream and crimson curtains overlooking gardens and the Seine. Cupids danced on frescoes and stern-faced liveried chamberlains stood against the walls.

The Old World had its glories like these, but in Wilson's mind he represented a country that was a superior moral force and, with his League of Nations, would help Europe put an end forever to its centuries of bloodshed. "He does not seem to have the slightest conception," remarked a French diplomat, "that he can ever be wrong."

The economist John Maynard Keynes was in the British delegation. "It was commonly believed at the commencement of the Paris Conference," he wrote, "that the President had thought out, with the aid of a large body of advisers, a comprehensive scheme not only for the League of Nations but for the embodiment of the Fourteen Points in an actual Treaty of Peace. But in fact the President had thought out nothing. . . . He had no plan, no scheme, no constructive ideas whatever for clothing with the flesh of life the commandments which he had thundered from the White House. He could have preached a sermon on any of them or have addressed a stately prayer to the Almighty for their fulfillment; but he could not frame their concrete application to the actual state of Europe."

On a continent that had seen many political assassinations, one of which had ignited the war, the dignitaries were closely guarded. And who was in charge of protecting the Americans? His rivals may have ousted him from Military Intelligence in Washington, but thanks to his friendship with General Pershing, the lanky, jug-eared figure of Colonel Ralph Van Deman had landed on its feet in Paris. With a staff of 56, he was in charge of security and counterintelligence for the 1,300-member American delegation. His letters home to his wife are a curious mixture of dire warnings ("There is a widespread attempt to start a world revolution along Bolshevic [*sic*] lines") and bureaucratic triumphs ("Gen. Pershing had personally told the Adjutant General . . . that I was to perform my duties in connection with the Peace Commission in addition to my other duties and that I was not to be detached from G-2, G.H.Q., A. E. F.").

Van Deman far exceeded his brief, sending one agent, for example, on an investigative trip to Germany and Russia, hunting for an American leftist the colonel was spying on. His post in Paris, close to so many powerful men, was a social climber's dream. When he retired from the army a decade later, it would be as a major general. Even after that, his career in surveillance would have a remarkable final act.

The American dignitaries Van Deman was guarding, and their counterparts from other countries, faced an immense agenda. It included everything from the reparations Germany would have to pay to the drawing of new national borders on several continents and the recognition of nations that had just declared themselves independent. Europe alone, not to mention the rest of the world, festered with disputes: between Italians and Austrians over the South Tyrol, Italians and Croats over the Adriatic port of Fiume, French and Germans over the coal-rich Saar basin, and many more. Leaders appointed sixty separate commissions to study specific problems and come back with recommendations. And then there was the ominous shadow of Soviet Russia, now engulfed in a massive civil war, with a disparate collection of forces, mostly supplied by the Allies and commanded by former tsarist generals, trying desperately to overthrow the Bolsheviks.

The prime ministers of Britain, France, and Italy, the president's principal negotiating partners, were intent on extracting reparations, territory, and colonies from Germany; David Lloyd George of Britain had just won an election by promising to make the Germans pay "to the last farthing" in revenge for the more than 700,000 British war dead. Wilson, however, felt differently. Before entering the war he had spoken of a "peace without victory," and was still wary of imposing punishing terms on Germany that could fan resentment and lead to another war.

Although the crowds in the snowy streets were thrilled to welcome him, national leaders were less enthusiastic, for at the top of the president's to-do list was his vision for the League of Nations. It was not, however, high on anyone else's agenda. Wilson, it was said, was someone who had brought a Bible to a poker game. Lloyd George and his fellow prime ministers would have privately agreed with Theodore Roosevelt had they been able to read a letter he had recently written to his friend Rudyard Kipling, in which he dismissed the idea of the league as "mush."

However, they had no chance to make common cause with the old Rough Rider. Ill with a variety of maladies, still shaken by the death

of his son Quentin, but firing off strident statements to the last minute, the 60-year-old Roosevelt suffered a fatal heart attack in his sleep
just before the peace conference began. Wilson ordered government
flags to fly at half-staff for 30 days, sent a telegram of sympathy to
Mrs. Roosevelt, and issued a lavish tribute. He could barely conceal his
satisfaction, however, at seeing his nemesis and possible rival for the
presidency in 1920 gone from the scene. When Lloyd George offered
his condolences, he was, he wrote later, "aghast at the outburst of acrid
detestation that flowed from Wilson's lips."

SOMEONE WHO SURELY felt more mixed emotions at Roosevelt's
death was Leonard Wood. He had lost a longtime friend and patron,
but with the ex-president dead, nothing now stood in the way of Wood
making his own run for the White House. He was one of a select group
the Roosevelts invited to a simple funeral service, and wore his army
greatcoat with the two stars of a major general on its shoulders as he
mingled with the other mourners on the snow-dusted sidewalk outside the small Christ Church in Oyster Bay and followed the coffin
up a steep, muddy hill to the cemetery. During his visit, the Roosevelt
family urged him to campaign for the Republican nomination for president. He needed no persuading.

Even while remaining in command at Camp Funston, Wood met
with potential financial backers like Clarence Rockefeller and the steel,
coal, and whiskey tycoon Henry Clay Frick (once the target of the assassination attempt by Emma Goldman's friend and former partner
Alexander Berkman). Ramrod erect, with his war ribbons on his khaki
uniform and the traditional diagonal leather strap across his chest,
Wood posed for photographs with his wife, daughter, and two sons,
who were both also army officers. He gave frequent speeches in uniform, taking advantage of Wilson being out of the country to travel the
United States and implicitly criticize his commander in chief. In Kansas
City, for instance, he turned a memorial gathering for Roosevelt into
a scornful put-down of the proposed League of Nations. Roosevelt, he
assured the enthusiastic audience of 15,000, "never believed nor for a

moment tolerated the idea that we should enter into any league which would . . . render us unable to defend our own interests."

By March 1919, a "Leonard Wood Republican Club" had formed in Colorado, and counterparts began to appear elsewhere. The mustachioed general's embodiment of the military virtues had great appeal in a nation facing labor turmoil at home and revolutions abroad. When he spoke, it was in a forceful, even voice that rose and fell little, pumping forth platitudes with the steady, relentless determination of the steel rod driving the wheels of a steam locomotive.

One newspaper described a Wood speech as "twelve minutes of detached granite. . . . He tramped in, he stood up and clasped his hands behind his stocky body. . . . Grizzled, ruddy, stalwart, he stood square and talked square. No flowing periods. No gestures. . . . The level voice hammered out grim sentences. Not a flicker of emotion crossed the oak-hewn face. . . . He puts the fear of the Lord into your heart."

Wood saw the world in stark terms: on one side were Americans, especially "old stock" Americans—he let audiences know that he was a *Mayflower* descendant—while on the other were Bolsheviks, socialists, anarchists, labor agitators, and a menacing tidal wave of immigrants. All of them, he hinted, he could vanquish as decisively as he had put down Apache and Filipino rebels.

ALSO ENJOYING THE president's absence from the United States was Postmaster General Albert Burleson. Even though the war was over, he continued to despise left-wing newspapers and magazines and to shut them down—a power granted him, supposedly, because the country was at war. Even the mainstream New York *World* was critical. The postmaster general, it commented, "appears to think that the war is either just beginning or is still going on."

Wilson continued to prefer suggestions to orders, and just before he left for Paris he had written to Burleson saying that censorship was "no longer performing a necessary function" and that "I hope that you agree with me." He did not follow up. "The President does not know what is going on in any of the departments," Colonel House once observed in his diary.

The postmaster general completely ignored Wilson's message. The president wrote Burleson again three months later, and again less than decisively, saying, "I cannot believe it would be wise to do any more suppressing." But the wily Texan, knowing that Wilson was totally consumed by the peace conference and his battle for the league, simply ignored this letter, too. In his files, he scrawled across it, in evident satisfaction, "Continued to suppress and Courts sustained me every time."

Until he left office more than two years later, Burleson would keep on refusing second-class mailing privileges to many periodicals. The president soon forgot his occasional earlier questioning of Burleson's heavy hand and backed him up. Nor did Congress have much interest in ending censorship. A proposal by a few senators to do so was quickly doomed. Robert La Follette declared that its failure "ought to make the framers of the Constitution open their eyes in their coffins."

Another realm where people like La Follette hoped the war's end might bring a change had to do with the many dissidents in prison. Surely the end of the fighting might mean pardons for most of them, and the government's dropping of charges against those like Marie Equi and Kate Richards O'Hare, who were both still free on appeal. That seemed not unreasonable to expect: Britain, which had suffered a vastly greater toll of war deaths than the United States and had also had a significant antiwar movement, was already releasing jailed COs and other peace activists. That country's prisons would be virtually empty of such dissenters by mid-1919. But so far there were no signs of anything like this happening in America. In January, 46 Wobblies on trial in Sacramento were found guilty and almost all were shipped off to join their comrades from the Chicago case in prison at Leavenworth.

As she awaited an appeals court's decision, O'Hare had no regrets that she had opposed the war. In it, she said, "death has come in most frightful forms to men whom I knew and loved. . . . On the bloody fields of France and Belgium . . . are the bodies of the boys with whom

I worked in Dublin; there are the miners who sang for me in Wales." In April 1919, her appeal was denied and she passed inside the gray stone walls of the Missouri penitentiary. "I entered quite as calmly as I have registered at hundreds of hotels," O'Hare said, "and the clang of the cell door did not disturb me more than the slamming of my room door by a careless bell boy."

A guest at this particular hotel, of course, was Emma Goldman, who turned out to occupy the very next cell. She and O'Hare were as different in politics as they were in appearance: the one anarchist, the other socialist; the one short, rotund, and heedless of her appearance, the other tall, willowy, and conscious of the allure of her famous head of red hair. "Had we met on the outside," Goldman wrote, "we should probably have argued furiously." But "in prison we soon found common ground. . . . I also discovered a very warm heart . . . and found her a woman of simplicity and tender feeling. We quickly became friends. . . . Kate O'Hare had been taken away from her four children . . . an ordeal that would have taxed the strength of many a woman."

"Emma is very fine and sweet and intellectually companionable," O'Hare wrote her husband. "All of our time and energy is consumed in feeding hungry stomachs and supporting faltering spirits. . . . Instead of hurling anarchist texts at me Emma raps on the wall of the cell and says, 'Get busy Kate.'" Goldman had a large supply of extra food sent by her admirers and, wrote O'Hare, "I am waiter and pass the 'eats' up and down the line. You have no idea how expert I have become in serving a meal through the bars." They traded jokes about Jewish and Irish cooking, and about O'Hare's snoring. When prison authorities finally allowed O'Hare to have a typewriter, she typed some of Goldman's letters for her.

They also bantered about their looks, a subject to which Goldman claimed to be indifferent, while, according to her, "not for anything would [O'Hare] appear . . . without an elaborate coiffure." One day Goldman heard O'Hare swearing because she had stuck herself with a hairpin.

"You will be vain," Goldman teased.

"Sure, how else am I to show off my beauty? Nothing in this world can be had without a price, as you well know yourself."

"Well, I would not pay for such foolishness as curled hair."

"Why, E. G., how you talk. Just ask your male friends, and you'll find out that a fine coiffure is more important than the best speech."

Their friendship helped Goldman deal with some painful news that had reached her in prison: less than a month before the war's end, her beloved nephew, with a promising career as a violinist ahead of him, was killed in France in the fierce battle for the Argonne Forest. His body was never found.

O'Hare read aloud to other prisoners, many of whom were illiterate, and created a considerable ruckus by smuggling out a letter about how inmates were forced to bathe in the same tubs as women who had tuberculosis or who had pus dripping from syphilis sores. "Kate was bringing about changes," wrote Goldman, "which I had in vain been trying for fourteen months to accomplish. . . . After the library and the hot food came an influx of convict plumbers, carpenters, and mechanics to install showerbaths."

Supporters of the two women and others like them felt they had some grounds for hope in early 1919, for an important case had at last come before the Supreme Court. Lawyers had long felt that it would test the constitutionality of the Espionage Act. And the court, after all, included such distinguished progressives as Justices Louis Brandeis and Oliver Wendell Holmes Jr., a Civil War veteran with a magnificent white handlebar mustache.

Schenck v. United States involved the Socialist Party leaders in Philadelphia sentenced in 1917 under the Espionage Act for mailing antidraft leaflets to young men whose names had appeared in the newspaper. Their lawyer argued that the act violated the First Amendment. Wasn't the distribution of this leaflet a matter of freedom of speech? To widespread liberal dismay, however, the court upheld the conviction of the Socialists and the constitutionality of the act. Even more disturbing, it did so unanimously. Worst of all, the ruling was written by one of the justices in whom the defendants had placed hope, Holmes. "The most stringent protection of free speech," goes a famous passage in his decision, "would not protect a man in falsely shouting fire in a theater and causing a panic."

For anyone who cared about civil liberties the decision was a major blow, for the ruling set an ominous precedent. Before long, the federal court of appeals heard the case of Charles Schoberg and the two other Kentuckians sentenced to long prison terms because of their private conversations in his cobbler's shop. Citing the *Schenck* decision, the judges upheld the verdict and sentence, speaking darkly of the trio's "extremity and recklessness in opposition to the war"—a war that had ended months earlier.

ACROSS THE ATLANTIC, Woodrow Wilson was making little headway with his fellow leaders in rousing enthusiasm for the League of Nations. Nor, when he made a quick trip back to the United States in early 1919, did he find great support for the idea in Congress. Many legislators dismissed it as a "League of Notions," and felt a deep suspicion of the idea that the United States might be in any way beholden to an international body. "If the Saviour of mankind should revisit the earth," commented one of them, Republican senator William Borah of Idaho, "and declare for a League of Nations, I would be opposed to it."

It never seems to have occurred to Wilson that the censorship, political imprisonments, and harsh crackdown on antiwar dissidents he had presided over for nearly two years had not nurtured a climate of enthusiasm for a peace-oriented, internationalist idea like the league. His plan was for the league to be embedded in the peace treaty, but according to the Constitution, the Senate would have to approve any treaty America signed by a two-thirds margin. With his usual tin ear for political bargaining, Wilson had ignored suggestions that he include in the massive American delegation to the peace talks influential senators from both parties. Returning to Paris confident as ever, the president resumed negotiating. But the talks progressed slowly, in part because, as Lloyd George said, "He was not accustomed to confer with equals."

The French were delighted that the shape of the world to come was being negotiated in their capital, and signs of triumph filled the city. Children played on the captured German artillery pieces that lined the Champs-Élysées; military bands gave concerts; flags hung from windows and lampposts; and elegant women took out of their closets the jewelry, pearls, and ostrich-feathered hats that had been considered an extravagance in wartime.

At the British embassy, young staff members put on amateur theatricals. Famous restaurants like La Tour d'Argent and Maxim's once again boasted of the continent's best cuisine. The prime ministers, diplomats, and generals spent their evenings in a whirl of receptions, banquets, and balls. Thousands of Allied military and civilian officials, almost all male, enjoyed the attention of Frenchwomen who had lost nearly 1.4 million of their own country's men in the war.

Outside Paris, however, lay a more somber panorama. Barely an hour's drive north began a wide swath of land dotted with thousands of graveyards, marked and unmarked, and scarred by trenches, steel and concrete pillboxes, barbed wire, and unexploded artillery shells and land mines. Shell craters, shattered tanks, and discarded or broken weaponry dotted ravaged fields. And, beyond the debris of combat, the retreating Germans had left devastation in their wake, blowing up tens of thousands of buildings, flooding mines, cutting down fruit trees, poisoning wells.

More ominously, future tragedies were clearly in the making, for tens of millions of Germans did not believe their country had actually lost the war. For more than four years of fighting, the German military had imposed tight censorship, and even in the last months of combat, the country's press remained relentlessly upbeat. The apparent German retreat? Merely a temporary setback. As late as a few weeks before the Armistice, Germany's newspapers were still running stories about an imminent final victory. This illusion was all the easier to believe because, to the very end, almost all the combat took place on foreign soil.

What's more, in the Peace of Brest-Litovsk, in early 1918, Russia had yielded to victorious German and Austro-Hungarian troops more than a million square miles of fertile land. Who ever heard of a country surrendering after gaining so much? Finally, once the Armistice took effect, the Allies did not take German soldiers prisoner. Instead, they marched home, welcomed by crowds throwing flowers. At Berlin's Brandenburg Gate the country's new chancellor congratulated one large contingent for having returned "unconquered from the field of battle." As far as most civilians could see, this was true.

Small wonder, then, that Germans were outraged to learn just how harsh the Armistice terms actually were, and to see British, French, and American troops occupy the Rhineland. If their army was "unconquered," who was responsible for such humiliation? Who had betrayed the 1.8 million German soldiers killed in the war? In the last months of combat, even before the Nazi Party was born, powerful right-wingers were already crafting the legend of the *Dolchstoss*, or "stab in the back."

A few years hence, Adolf Hitler would have an easy time convincing millions that the sinister plotting of socialists, pacifists, and Jews had robbed the German military of victory. The hapless German delegation that had signed the Armistice in Marshal Foch's railway carriage were branded the "November Traitors." Its chief would shortly be assassinated by a right-wing death squad.

Such developments were beyond the control of the Allied leaders negotiating in Paris, but something else was well within it. Ever since Britain's Royal Navy had thrown its blockade around Germany and its allies in 1914, these countries had been severely short of food. By 1918, each German consumed less than half the calories per day he or she had enjoyed in peacetime. Starvation and malnutrition claimed the lives of an estimated 478,500 German civilians, and millions more suffered hunger and lasting aftereffects. The average German boy or girl in 1918 was more than an inch shorter than in 1914. On top of these privations, Germany, like all of Europe, had been swept by the influenza epidemic. Desperately hoping that the Armistice would relieve their ordeals, Germans were dismayed to learn that the blockade would remain in place until their country signed a final peace treaty, which was clearly many months away. And that treaty was being shaped by negotiations in which Germany had no part.

"I have seen infants in Berlin and Dresden hospitals with the shrunken limbs and swollen stomachs characteristic of famine sufferers," the American journalist Oswald Garrison Villard reported in March 1919, "and I have seen that the midday meal for all patients in one hospital is simply a carrot soup—nothing else—for all ages and all conditions. . . . The week I was in Dresden not one pound of meat was distributed." He found that "a bitter hatred" was rising, and that "there is now talk of revenge which was not heard before."

If Wilson was even aware of such conditions, he gave little sign. But Robert La Follette saw them for what they were. The fortunes of the Republican senator had been much improved by the previous November's elections, when his party had won control of the Senate, but by such a narrow margin that it was no longer politic to have him under threat of expulsion. The Senate Committee on Privileges and Elections dropped its investigation of him.

From the moment the Paris Peace Conference started, La Follette remained a dissenter. Here were the four top Allied leaders deciding the fate of the world "in secret behind locked doors," he pointed out, even though Wilson's Fourteen Points had included "open covenants openly arrived at." The agreement likely to emerge would be "a cold-blooded, sordid peace dressed up in a maze of flimflam."

La Follette also attacked the continuing blockade of Germany: The fighting was over, so why were half-starving German civilians not allowed to import food? Furthermore, the Wilson who had spoken so nobly of the right of every people to determine its own fate was now silent about a cause dear to La Follette, the independence of Ireland. And finally, the senator was angry that Wilson had sent some 13,000 American troops to Russia—including several hundred draftees from La Follette's own Wisconsin—who were now supporting one side in Russia's all-engulfing civil war. If the United States assumed a right to jump into such a complex and distant conflict, waging undeclared war, where would such interventions end? La Follette's question has contin-ued to echo for more than a century.

UNLIKE GERMANY, THE nations that had won the war were not suf-fering hunger, but they were still ravaged by influenza. Three US con-gressmen died in the pandemic. Kate Richards O'Hare survived the disease in prison. In Paris, Colonel House, Edith Wilson, the presi-dent's physician, Dr. Cary Grayson, and the chief White House usher, Ike Hoover (the head of the presidential housekeeping staff), all fell ill but survived. The same was true of Wilson's two most powerful—and most stubborn—negotiating partners, David Lloyd George of Britain and France's corpulent Georges Clemenceau, with his white walrus mustache.

Those around him worried about Wilson, whose health was never strong and who had long suffered high blood pressure. He was clearly tired, and also discouraged by the territorial ambitions of Britain and France and their lack of interest in his league. By the end of March he seemed increasingly volatile in the negotiating sessions. As his press aide Ray Stannard Baker described it, he had "a 600 horsepower motor in a frail, light, delicate chassis."

Finally, on April 3, 1919, the virus struck the 62-year-old president. Newspapers, however, were told it was just a cold and fever. "Is Not Stricken with Influenza Says Dr. Grayson," read the *Washington Post* headline. But the president's temperature soared above 103 degrees Fahrenheit. Shaken by paroxysms of coughing and diarrhea, he began wheezing. He lay in bed for several days, unable to move. A 25-year-old staff member of the American delegation, who had fallen sick the same day, died. So did several other delegation members. Aides found Wilson haggard and pale, his eyes sunken. He began showing curious obsessions, insisting that unauthorized people were using American vehicles and that French servants were spying on him. "One thing was certain," wrote Ike Hoover. "He was never the same after this little spell of sickness."

The negotiations continued, but now Lloyd George and Clemenceau came to Wilson's bedroom to talk. These two canny politicians knew how attached he was to his beloved league, and they used it to bargain for what they wanted. They had another advantage over him as well: the French prime minister was in his own capital and Lloyd George only a half day's journey from his, while their American counterpart was an ocean away from Washington and incapable of easily rousing political support in the Senate, which would have to approve any treaty.

They also knew he was receiving disturbing news about strikes and inflation at home. At one point an almost desperate telegram arrived from Tumulty that ended, YOU CANNOT UNDERSTAND HOW ACUTE SITUATION IS BROUGHT ABOUT BY RISING PRICES OF EVERY NECESSITY OF LIFE.

With surprising suddenness, Wilson abandoned his resistance to a vindictive treaty and gave in to British and French demands for the harsh peace these two much-bloodied nations were eager to impose on Germany. There would be severe reparations; Germans would have to accept full responsibility for starting the war; France would be able to mine the Saar coalfields; Italy would win part of the Austrian Tyrol; and Germany would lose territory containing about 10 percent of its population and a larger proportion of its coal and iron ore. A portion of Germany, East Prussia, would be separated from the rest of the country because the new nation of Poland needed a corridor to the Baltic Sea. Germany's overseas possessions, stretching from Togoland in West Africa to New Guinea in the Pacific, would be parceled out among no less than eight Allied nations. Officially, they would be called "mandates," although colonies they remained. Wilson's League of Nations would still be in the treaty, but there were few remnants of the president's call for a "peace without victory." The negotiations inched toward their conclusion, the treaty still unsigned, the blockade still in place, and Germans still daily dying of starvation.

World on Fire

N O LONGER WERE immense crowds cheering President Wilson in Europe. "We are running a race with Bolshevism," he said to Dr. Grayson in Paris, "and the world is on fire." For months to come, the US government would be battling to contain that fire at home, and fearing its spread abroad.

Appeals to patriotism had helped restrain labor militance on both sides during the war. But now that the conflict was over, old discontents reemerged, exacerbated by the privations and shortages the war had left and the example, or so it appeared, of workers in Russia who had seized power for themselves. It now sometimes seemed to the statesmen under the frescoes and chandeliers at the Quai d'Orsay that revolutionary upheaval might sweep away all the lines they were drawing on maps. Since the war's end, general strikes had erupted everywhere from Zurich to Winnipeg. On May Day 1919 a one-day strike hit Paris itself, and cavalry broke up a march of workers, leaving hundreds wounded and streets stained with blood. Sailors on a Royal Navy ship briefly hoisted the red flag. Workers seized factories in France and Italy. Others in Glasgow mounted a red flag over the city hall, and in response the British government sent in six tanks and 8,000 troops.

Protests against British colonial rule flamed up in India, Egypt, and close to home in Ireland, where before long the government would rush extra police and thousands of soldiers. Radical uprisings continued to erupt in Germany, one briefly producing a soviet republic in Bavaria that took over factories and houses of the wealthy.

Most ominously to the tailcoated leaders negotiating at the French Foreign Ministry, their support for anti-Bolshevik forces in the Russian Civil War was failing. French navy sailors in the Black Sea, sent to support this effort, staged a mutiny. The Bolsheviks, dedicated to overthrowing capitalism everywhere, seemed destined to remain in power—and to inspire similar uprisings outside Russia itself. Winston Churchill, part of the British delegation to Paris, out for a walk in the Bois de Boulogne, pointed to some dark storm clouds on the eastern horizon and said to a companion, "Russia! Russia! That's where the weather is coming from!"

While Wilson labored on, the treaty still not completed, across the Atlantic the United States was suffering its stormiest year since the aftermath of the Civil War. Behind much of the discontent was a soaring rate of inflation. From 1917 to 1920, the Consumer Price Index rose more than 40 percent. For food, the increase was over 50 percent, and for household furnishings almost 100 percent. Doctors raised their fees, and many grocery stores and small businesses stopped giving credit. Although workers had shared some of the prosperity of the war manufacturing boom, wages in many industries still lagged behind.

Then the war's end added a new shock. When the fighting stopped, more than four million Americans were in uniform, including some two million in France. Among the graffiti scrawled on walls there by impatient soldiers was, "Lafayette, we are still here." But as the army demobilized this vast force over the course of 1919, the hundreds of parades before cheering crowds in American cities disguised a grim fact. These men were pouring into an economy without sufficient work for them. "If your home is NOT in one of the big industrial cities," the YMCA newspaper for soldiers warned, "DON'T GO THERE after you are discharged. . . . There aren't enough jobs."

No longer were factories hiring workers to turn out rifles, tanks, and artillery pieces. After the war ended, the government canceled nearly

$3 billion worth of outstanding orders for such products. Industrial output dropped. Job hunters flooded the streets. From Pittsburgh, undercover agent Leo Wendell told his superiors that local radicals were planning to "advise the unemployed . . . to arm themselves for the battle which they feel will come in the very near future."

Signs of upheaval appeared everywhere. One of the first came at 10:00 a.m. on February 6, 1919, when Seattle, a city known for its powerful labor unions, turned eerily quiet. No buses or trolleys ran. No cranes unloaded ships. No smoke came from foundry chimneys, and factory whistles were silent. Downtown streets were deserted. Streetcars stopped and elevator operators stayed home. Public schools closed their doors. It was the country's first major general strike.

From local shipyards, 35,000 employees walked off the job, and in solidarity, 25,000 workers from other industries joined them. Shocking Seattle's establishment, unions on strike included some belonging to the moderate American Federation of Labor. Gun shops ran out of supplies. Some well-to-do families fled the state for hotels in Portland, Oregon; others rushed to buy extra groceries and stayed fearfully inside locked homes. Businesses quickly took out extra insurance.

The strike remained peaceful, won little, and lasted only four days, but it showed an impressive coordination among workers from different fields—and highlighted their ability to temporarily run a city. Cooks from culinary unions provided meals at temporary food depots (25 cents for strikers, 35 cents for others); teamsters made sure supplies reached hospitals; unarmed guards patrolled the streets.

Using the strike as an excuse, federal and city authorities, aided by local vigilantes, once again raided the local offices of the Socialist Party and the IWW. As the Wobblies watched their desks and files ransacked, little did they imagine that in this same city, months later, some of them would have an unprecedented face-to-face meeting with President Wilson himself.

Despite the lack of violence, Seattle mayor Ole Hanson accused the strikers of wanting "to duplicate the anarchy of Russia." He played the role of defender against that peril for all it was worth: escorting federal troops into the city with an American flag draped atop his car and swearing in 3,000 extra police. Everything about his law-and-order stance emphasized masculinity. He posed for a photograph with his wife and eight of their nine children that appeared on the front page of a local newspaper with the caption "Mayor Hanson and Nine Reasons Why He Insisted That Seattle Remain an American City." Press accounts played up Hanson's male toughness as a "two-fisted, square-jawed man" who "stood firmly," "set his face with unswerving determination," and had "a backbone that would serve as a girder in a railroad bridge." The mayor had given his sons names like William Howard Taft Hanson and Theodore Roosevelt Hanson. None of his daughters, however, bore the names of notable women.

The general strike did not ignite a revolution—nor had that been the strikers' intent—but it was a flexing of labor muscle that helped inspire more strikes throughout the year. It frightened both the Wilson administration and big business, and launched Hanson as perhaps the first member of an occupation that would prove lucrative for other twentieth-century Americans: professional anti-Communist.

Hanson took advantage of his newfound fame by setting off on the lecture circuit, warning everyone about the dangers ahead. "You've got to grab it when it comes along," he said cheerfully of this opportunity to reach a wider public. In a mere seven months, charging $500 per appearance, he earned $38,000—the equivalent of well over half a million dollars today—after making only $7,500 a year as mayor of Seattle.

Headlines recorded his progress around the country: "Ole Hanson Urges Proper Upbringing of Children as Antidote for Bolshevikism" (Montclair, New Jersey); "'Make It a Felony to Belong to I.W.W.' Urges Ole Hanson" (Asheville, North Carolina); "Fighting Mayor May Speak Here" (Grand Forks, North Dakota). In a book, *Americanism versus Bolshevism*, he denounced "bearded aliens whose faces had never known a razor," and held up the traditional family as the cure for the disorder of the times. "Americanism," he wrote, "stands for one wife and one country." Like quite a few others, he had his eye on the Republican nomination for president the following year.

OVER THE COURSE of 1919, four million people, one out of every five American workers, would go on strike. They would include telephone operators in New England, blacksmiths in Ohio, streetcar drivers in Indiana, cigar makers in Baltimore, and even several thousand inmates in the army prison at Fort Leavenworth, Kansas. In Portland, Oregon, and Tacoma, Washington, socialists, radical labor unionists, and discharged soldiers borrowed a word from the Russians and formed groups they called soviets. A thousand people came to the first meeting of the Portland soviet.

It was indeed a world on fire, and American business fought back. In the ensuing witch-hunt, comments the writer Eliot Asinof, the witch's broom had a union label. The Ford Motor Company produced a cartoon short for movie houses showing an Uncle Sam–like farmer guarding bags of grain and calling out "Hark! I'll fix that varmint!" as he grabs a shovel to kill a huge rat labeled "Bolsheviki (I.W.W.)" and toss it out a window.

In a day when popular magazines published thousands of pieces of fiction each year, several business groups began putting out the *Open Shop Review* for management to give to employees. It was filled with uplifting short stories about virtuous workers, evil unions— and, once again, the sacredness of the traditional family. In "How the Union Slugger Broke Up the Family," the big, gentle Jacob Laboski crosses a picket line so that his children will have enough to eat— and is beaten to death. In "Ma Becomes a Socialist," women show their striking husbands the error of their ways by going on strike themselves and refusing to do any housework. (The men then call off their strike.) In another story, a young worker goes to a socialist meeting where he finds a pamphlet that is, in ways too shocking to specify, "an insult to all womankind." As the historian Kim Nielsen sums it up, this "Red Scare praise of male heroes underscored the notion that the nation needed patriarchal power . . . to withstand domestic subversion."

The turmoil further inflamed those Americans who had long believed that if there was trouble, it must be caused by foreigners or immigrants. A graphic illustration of this was an unusual map produced in early 1919 by Military Intelligence. It divided portions of New York City into zones of 11 different colors, highlighting which dangerous ethnic group lived where: red for "Russian Jews," orange for Italians, green for Irish, black for "Negro." The map was also sprinkled with numbered blue stars and white circles. The 86 circles marked the locations of union headquarters, IWW halls, and other places "where radical meetings are held," while the 44 blue stars identified offices of "radical and liberal" publications, from the *Inter-Collegiate Socialist* to the literary and political journal *The Dial* and the NAACP's *The Crisis*.

The map was the brainchild of the Military Intelligence chief for the city, 40-year-old Captain John B. Trevor. Of Trevor, a critical journalist once wrote, "If a man's love for his country is measurable by his detestation of all who had the bad taste to be born elsewhere, there probably is no greater patriot in America to-day."

Nativist feeling in the United States had long simmered at opposite ends of the class spectrum, from brawling street fighters to those wanting to keep the doors of the country club shut. There is no doubt to which group Trevor belonged. Among his ancestors were a signer of the Declaration of Independence and a member of George Washington's staff. He had two degrees from Harvard and one from Columbia. Since childhood, he had been close to John D. Rockefeller Jr., whose wallet repeatedly came to the aid of Trevor's causes.

Not that Trevor needed money himself. He had grown up in the grand 26-room Victorian stone home of his banker father, staffed by 11 servants, on an estate perched on a bluff overlooking the Hudson River in Yonkers, just north of New York. The family's greenhouses and stable of trotting horses were nearby. He now lived in a limestone mansion on Manhattan's Upper East Side. At his summer home, on one of the most fashionable lakes in the Adirondack Mountains, he was commodore of the Saint Regis Yacht Club. The cause dearest to him was that of slamming the door on immigration.

In his role as New York chief of Military Intelligence, Trevor was focused on the dangers he imagined from the immigrants already here. Besides designing the color-coded map, he drafted "Plans for the Protection of New York in Case of Local Disturbances," which divided the city into eight battle zones. In case of "an organized uprising," he believed, the army would need 10,000 soldiers to defend Manhattan, and 4,000 for Brooklyn.

He told his superiors in Washington what weaponry would be required, including equipment for a mobile machine-gun battalion that could be sent "to the points where the emergency demands." These, he said, would likely include "the congested district chiefly inhabited by Russian Jews," the Lower East Side—the largest Jewish neighborhood in the world. Trevor proudly shared his map with the Chamber of Commerce, National Guard officials, and New York's police commissioner, who found it of much help "in view of the existing restlessness." As if to prove Trevor's suspicions right, in March 1919, days after he started distributing his map, a Bolshevik-style regime with a heavily Jewish leadership temporarily seized power in Hungary.

Meanwhile, a Senate subcommittee had been holding hearings about the radical menace. Chairing it was Lee Overman of North Carolina, a plump, courtly Democrat, who, later in his career, would help filibuster an anti-lynching bill to death. His hearings would become the first, but far from the last, congressional investigation into the loyalties and political opinions of American citizens.

Not only did the new Soviet regime in Russia portend danger for the world, declared one committee witness, the Reverend George Simons, a Methodist missionary who had worked in that country, but, he revealed, it was controlled from top to bottom by Jews who had "come over from the lower East Side" who orated from "benches and soap boxes, and what not, talking until their mouths frothed." Even though Simons maintained that some "men of Jewish blood" were "among my best friends," he swore that of the 388 members of the Petrograd

Soviet—the key body in staging the Bolshevik coup—372 were Jews, and 265 had come to Russia directly from New York. And not only that, also in the Petrograd Soviet was "a Negro from America, who calls himself Prof. Gordon," a boxer who had been a doorkeeper at the American embassy. (The slight wisp of fact in these claims is that many early Bolsheviks were indeed Jewish, a few of whom had lived in the United States; Leon Trotsky himself had spent several months in exile in the Bronx in early 1917. Prof. Gordon seems to be a product of Simons's imagination.)

Simons further buttressed his testimony before the Overman committee with data from *The Protocols of the Elders of Zion*, now notorious as a forgery, copies of which a Military Intelligence officer had given him and the committee. A far-right group in which Trevor was active published an American edition of the book, even though Trevor himself was sophisticated enough to inform his Military Intelligence superiors that this supposed blueprint for Jewish world domination was an elaborate fake.

In case such an appeal to prejudice was not enough, the Overman committee once again stoked the fear that revolutionary ferment was undermining the age-old roles of men and women. Another witness recently returned from Russia, a Commerce Department official, told the committee that women there were now "nationalized." Even more alarming, he declared that the Soviets granted women power *over men*. He read aloud from what he claimed to be an official decree from the city of Vladimir declaring that all women over 18 were "the property of the State" and required "to register at the Bureau of Free Love of the Commissariat of Surveillance. Having registered at the Bureau of Free Love, she has the right to choose from among the men between the ages of 19 and 50 a cohabitant husband. . . . The consent of the man in the said choice is unnecessary."

Unnecessary? For a United States in which millions of men—and some women—had long resisted the idea that women should even have the right to vote, such a specter was terrifying. It was even more so just then, when millions of men no longer had the traditionally male role of soldier, and hundreds of thousands of women had just shown that they could perform previously male jobs in industry. The myth of a "Bureau of Free Love" in Russia spoke to deep American fears.

Hollywood also stoked these fears. Released within weeks of the Overman committee hearings was a feature film, *Bolshevism on Trial*, centering on a scheming Russian agitator with black eyebrows as thick as the bristles of two push brooms. He induces naive Americans to join him in setting up a Communist colony on an island and electing him Chief Comrade. As the film approaches its climax, he announces: "The marriage laws will no longer bind us. Divorce will be on application. The state will raise the children." He then tells his wife, "Tonight I declare my divorce" and makes a grab for the heroine—an innocent young beauty who now has second thoughts. A shipload of US Navy sailors in white uniforms arrives just in time to preserve her virtue.

Anticipating Senator Joseph McCarthy more than 30 years later, a Military Intelligence agent working with Trevor gave Overman and his fellow senators a list of some 200 dangerous subversives, whom he claimed had campaigned against the war and were now backing the Bolsheviks. The clergymen and college professors among them, he asserted, could have a sinister influence on young people. The committee publicly released many of the names, which were splashed all over front pages. For some people on the list, like Eugene Debs and Kate Richards O'Hare, such an accusation was all in a day's work, but others were startled: the social worker Jane Addams, for instance, or former Stanford University president David Starr Jordan, or the eminent historian Charles Beard, who fired off a furious letter to Overman.

Just then, the Seattle general strike erupted, launching Overman on a fresh round of investigations and giving Military Intelligence a new lease on life. It helped do the same for the American Protective League. After the war ended, and with it the need to hunt down draft dodgers and imaginary German spies, the Justice Department had ordered the league it once chartered closed down. But its members were reluctant to give up their derring-do. The threat of Bolshevism gave them the perfect excuse to stay in business under different names. APL chapters reorganized as the Committee of Thirteen in Minneapolis, the Loyal American League in Cleveland, the Patriotic American League in Chicago, and under other names elsewhere.

With so many organizations hunting subversives, and undercover operatives both military and civilian spying on left-wing gatherings, people with the right skills could make money. In New York, for instance, one William F. Smart, "certified shorthand reporter," advertised to all interested intelligence agencies that he could produce two copies of a typed transcript of any meeting for 60 cents a page.

As the national paranoia simmered, Trevor continued to fuel it. Jews were by no means his only target. He also wrote a memorandum on "Negro Agitation," warning that it went "far beyond" any "alleged grievances," and "aims at Pan-Negroism and a combination of the other colored races of the world. . . . It naturally sympathizes with and has relations with the Irish, the Jews, and Hindus." He warned of a Black activist who "speaks at both radical and Irish meetings." He also passed up the chain of command a rumor that "wealthy women" were financing a "Soviet for Negroes," and noted with suspicion a National Conference on Lynching.

Zeroing in on just the sort of groups identified on the color-coded map, a new attack on subversives of all kinds began. In March 1919, the New York State Legislature established a joint committee to investigate radicals under an ambitious state senator, Clayton Lusk, who hoped to run for governor. A key committee staff member—newly appointed to the position of special deputy state attorney general—was John B. Trevor.

Trevor gave each member of the legislature's lower house a copy of *Throttled!*, a sensationalist "as told to" memoir by the head of the New York City bomb squad about catching anarchists and German spies. The book just happened to feature a full-page photograph of Trevor in his army uniform.

The Lusk committee's massive report, published in four volumes the following year, is a monument of alarmist pseudoscholarship. Besides reproducing Trevor's ethnic map of New York, its more than four thousand pages of text and documents tied together the various dangers supposedly facing the country: Bolshevism, anarchism, the American Civil Liberties Union, "hyphenated Americans" of every stripe, and liberals duped by them.

Operating out of headquarters in New York's Prince George Hotel, the Lusk committee employed two dozen agents and a similar number of clerks and secretaries. It held hearings, infiltrated operatives into various Black and left-wing organizations, bugged offices, sent stenographers to political meetings, intercepted mail and telegrams, and, with the help of American Protective League veterans, staged more than 70 raids with search warrants prepared by Trevor, bringing along friendly journalists as witnesses.

His work with the committee, however, was only a way station for Trevor. Several years later he would leave his mark on the country in a manner that lasted for decades.

WHILE THE PRESIDENT remained in Paris, the nation's tensions exploded into more violence. In May, vigilantes attacked Socialist Party headquarters in Boston and a reception at a left-wing newspaper in New York, where they smashed furniture and beat guests with clubs. In Cleveland, 30,000 people marched on May Day protesting the jailing of Eugene Debs and American intervention in Russia. Fighting broke out when a spectator tried to seize a red flag carried by a veteran marching in uniform. That gave the police an excuse to attack, mobilizing officers on horseback and even two army tanks manned by soldiers. Two people were killed, many injured, and 124 arrested, including a man who had recently won nearly 30 percent of the vote as the Socialist Party candidate for mayor.

Battles like this were both political and ethnic. Nearly a third of Cleveland's population was foreign born, and the percentage was far higher among those who marched, May Day being the international workers' holiday long celebrated in Europe. Their attackers saw themselves as true Americans fighting off foreigners. As more such clashes rippled across the country, attacks on radicals became closely tied to calls for an end to immigration—and for deporting immigrants already here.

General Leonard Wood, planning his run for the White House, called on the country to "deport these so-called Americans who preach treason openly." The newly formed American Legion demanded the expulsion not only of noncitizens who had evaded wartime military service, but of all men who had done so. Furthermore, why should merely being born in the United States confer citizenship? The Anti-Alien League called for this right to be denied to "peoples of Asiatic races," and a senator from Washington State announced that he would introduce such a bill.

Another facet of growing anti-immigrant fervor was a deep suspicion of foreign languages. After all, if you couldn't understand what people were saying, it might be something un-American. An Iowa senator called for "a one-language nation." The *American Legion Weekly* demanded that this one language be called "American."

In New York, the most multilingual city on earth, an alderman introduced a bill banning meetings held in "alien tongues." In Oregon, a member of the board of the Portland Public Library urged it to get rid of all foreign-language newspapers. In Kentucky, the Citizens Patriotic League, the vigilantes whose hidden microphone had brought prison sentences for the men in Charles Schoberg's cobbler's shop, called for a ban on the teaching of any modern foreign language in American elementary schools.

Even the august and sober *New York Times* was swept along by this linguistic crusade. On June 8, 1919, it devoted almost an entire page to a story headlined "Official Translations of Our Bolshevist Papers." This contained thousands of words of calls for revolution and attacks on "bankers and merchants" from the country's foreign-language press. All this "hatred of the American Government" was being quoted by agitators "in hidden and secret halls." In New York City, the breathless reporter told readers, "half of a floor in one of the important Federal buildings has been set aside for the work of the official Government translators."

The agency involved was situated on the mezzanine of the main post office across from Pennsylvania Station. This joint effort of the Justice and Post Office Departments employed more than 30 translators and made recommendations about what to censor under the Espionage Act. A publication could come under suspicion by reflecting something as subversive, in the words of one functionary, as "tendencies looking toward social equality." Officials there prided themselves on being able to catch sedition in almost any tongue, but they were once flummoxed when they could not find anyone who knew Ladino, the language of Sephardic Jews. Finally they discovered a Ladino speaker at another government agency, who examined the newspaper under suspicion and reported that it "was not an offensive publication."

Despite this atmosphere of paranoia, those who hoped for the easing of the Wilson administration's war on dissent felt some cause for optimism. In early 1919, Thomas Gregory stepped down as attorney general, to the great relief of progressives like Robert La Follette. It was Gregory's Justice Department that had drafted the Espionage and Sedition Acts, and that had wielded a harsh hand in jailing war critics and smashing the IWW. It was Gregory who had boasted of the American Protective League's work as an official auxiliary of his department, "keeping an eye on disloyal individuals and making reports of disloyal utterances." Gregory had swept aside anyone who questioned his charging more than 2,000 people under the Espionage Act, claiming, absurdly, that not a single one had been convicted for "mere expression of opinion."

Choosing as his successor someone who appeared more tolerant, Wilson nominated former Pennsylvania congressman A. Mitchell Palmer. Not only was the president replacing a conservative southerner with a liberal northerner, but the genial, broad-shouldered, 46-year-old Palmer, known for his friendly smile and backslapping manner, seemed to have gentler politics. He recommended that Wilson grant clemency to more than 100 of several hundred who were serving Espionage Act sentences, and the president did so. He favored repealing parts of the act itself and called the American Protective League "a grave menace."

Palmer was a Quaker who, like many in that denomination, sometimes used the old forms of speech, "thee" and "thou." When first elected president in 1912, Wilson had asked him to be secretary of war. Palmer had reluctantly replied that it would be against his pacifist principles and instead remained in Congress for another term, where he introduced a far-reaching child labor bill and enthusiastically backed women's suffrage. By any measure, he was now the most progressive member of Wilson's cabinet. With such a man in a key role, many hoped, the harsh repression of the war years might at last be on its way out.

Sly and Crafty Eyes

I N THE FINAL months of the Paris peace talks, President Wilson, already weakened by his bout with influenza, seemed to suffer a minor stroke. His aides said nothing to the press but quietly brought in several doctors to examine him. During one negotiating session he had trouble reading a text aloud, and for the first time his graceful handwriting turned jagged, forcing him to write awkwardly with his left hand. Again he was beset by obsessions, now about rearranging the furniture in his Paris living quarters. Dr. Grayson tried to relax his patient by suggesting a day at the horse races. Wilson began increasingly leaning on the doctor for help beyond medical matters, suddenly distancing himself from Colonel House. It was now sometimes Grayson whom the president dispatched to talk to people involved in the negotiations, and to brief journalists on their progress.

As the peace conference delegates sketched in the final details of the severe terms to be imposed on Germany, they carved new nations out of dismembered empires, among them Yugoslavia on the Adriatic; Estonia, Latvia, and Lithuania on the Baltic; and Syria and Iraq in the Middle East. At one point Wilson took a break from the talks to dedicate a hillside cemetery for 1,500 American war dead near an ancient fortress on the outskirts of Paris. As he removed his hat before the long rows of white crosses and spoke in the bright sun for half an hour, people noticed that his hair had grown white.

It was one of the most heartfelt speeches of his life, and one that left many weeping. He took personal responsibility for the bodies beneath the soil, saying, "I sent these lads over here to die." Despite his love for his native American South, he connected these latest dead with "the dust of the men who fought for the preservation of the Union, and that as those men gave their lives in order that America might be united, these men have given their lives in order that the world might be united." This, of course, referred to his great hopes for the League of Nations. After a bugler played "Taps," the Wilsons, drained, returned to Paris for the final grueling weeks of meetings.

Germany, it first appeared, would refuse to agree to the peace treaty, which shrank its territory and required huge reparation payments, and which had been essentially dictated by the Allies rather than negotiated. German citizens across the political spectrum felt humiliated and angry. But the naval blockade, though somewhat porous, was still in force, and, as Senator La Follette put it in the title of a magazine article he wrote, the Germans now faced the choice of "Sign or Starve." They signed.

On June 28, 1919, at a velvet-covered, horseshoe-shaped table in the Hall of Mirrors at the Palace of Versailles, beneath portraits of King Louis XIV and a white marble statue of the goddess Minerva, Wilson and the other leaders assembled for the ceremony. It was five years to the day since a Serbian nationalist had assassinated the Austro-Hungarian archduke Franz Ferdinand and his wife at Sarajevo, igniting the fuse that led to war.

A tightly packed crowd of diplomats, journalists, and VIP guests, including Edith Wilson, filled benches upholstered in red. Her husband's hand trembled as he signed the vellum page. It was more than half a year since the president had left the United States to come to Paris for what he thought might be a month or two. The next day, the Wilsons once again embarked on the *George Washington* as a military band played on the wharf, and, escorted out of a French harbor by warships, they headed home.

After a devastating war that left more than 9 million dead and 21 million wounded—not even counting millions more civilian casualties—perhaps no conceivable treaty could have left Europe permanently at peace. In the face of deep German bitterness, this one certainly did not look as if it would do so, despite the establishment of the League of Nations. After the delegates signed, the fountains at Versailles were turned on for the first time since 1914, and in France, Britain, and on US Navy ships at sea, artillery boomed out triumphant salutes. Fireworks lit the Paris sky. In Germany, however, flags were lowered to half-staff.

A popular song of the time was in the voice of a British soldier saying goodbye to a French girlfriend:

Blow your nose and dry your tears
We'll all be back in a few short years.

THE *GEORGE WASHINGTON* had a calm passage across the Atlantic, and Dr. Grayson was pleased that his patient walked on deck, sunbathed, and relaxed enough to watch movies with the other passengers. While at sea, Wilson changed his formal top hat for a sporty-looking tweed cap with a small brim. But as the ship steamed closer to the United States, the president began to worry about what lay ahead. Would the Senate ratify the treaty? The body was now controlled by the Republicans and, by the count of Joe Tumulty's experienced hand, the votes were not yet there—even from some Democrats.

The League of Nations was now officially in existence, so far mostly on paper, but unless the Senate ratified the peace treaty including it, the United States would not become a member. People from both ends of the American political spectrum objected to the peculiar combination of the treaty's terms. Conservatives were suspicious of entangling the United States in an international body like the league, and moreover one in which nonwhite nations could vote, while liberals, although more favorable to the league, feared that the punitive provisions imposed on Germany might ignite another war.

An additional frustration for the thin-skinned Wilson was that he had had a bitter parting of the ways with his closest friend, Colonel House. Months earlier, he had left House in Paris as his representative when he made a short trip back to the United States, but the president thought the colonel had exceeded his brief by negotiating with Clemenceau and Lloyd George almost as if he were a head of state, giving way on issues Wilson cared about.

Edith Wilson, whose spirited manner concealed a wily side, was always quietly jealous of House, considering him "a perfect jellyfish" for his alleged spinelessness, and she did all she could to reinforce her husband's suspicions. House denied Wilson's accusation, and the evidence seems to support him. For the Texan, the president's sudden antipathy remained "a tragic mystery." After Wilson boarded the *George Washington*, the two men would never see each other again. An inner fragility left Wilson prone to feeling suddenly betrayed by those close to him; several years later, retired from the presidency, he would have a similar falling-out with the faithful Tumulty.

Two days after his return, the president appeared before the Senate with a copy of the book-length peace treaty under his arm. His speech in its defense, however, proved weak and hesitant, for he sensed how hostile many of his listeners were. "His audience wanted raw meat, he fed them cold turnips," wrote one senator in his diary. A different man now from the one who had so forcefully asked Congress to declare war more than two years earlier, Wilson also seemed to stumble over words and had to repeat several passages.

He faced opposition on all sides. Even some members of the American delegation to Paris had resigned in protest, feeling that their leader had given way to British and French desire for revenge on Germany. And Irish Americans were angry that nearly half a year of talk in Paris had not brought freedom for their homeland. At a rally in Madison Square Garden, 17,000 of them booed for three minutes at the mere mention of the president's name.

In the Senate, where the treaty's fate rested, most Republicans, led by Wilson's archenemy, Henry Cabot Lodge of Massachusetts, disliked both the League of Nations and the prospect of handing a diplomatic success to a Democrat. Lodge found the president pretentious and sanctimonious. "I never expected to hate anyone in politics with the hatred I feel toward Wilson," he had once told Theodore Roosevelt. The senator announced that he would hold hearings on the treaty before the Foreign Relations Committee, which he chaired and which was full of league opponents.

Wilson was further handicapped because he was no natural politician. "There can seldom have been a statesman of the first rank more incompetent than the President in the agilities of the council chamber," wrote John Maynard Keynes, who had observed him closely in Paris. "A moment often arrives when substantial victory is yours if by some slight appearance of a concession you can save the face of the opposition." But Wilson could never manage this—in Paris or in Washington. Bargaining felt beneath him.

Moreover, his six months in Europe had left him out of touch with the turmoil sweeping his country: the soaring cost of living, growing unemployment, and the repressiveness of his own government. Wilson seemed unconcerned about the latter. When Clarence Darrow and the novelist Upton Sinclair suggested to him that it was time to consider pardoning jailed antiwar dissidents like Debs, the president replied that he would "deal with the matter as early and in as liberal a spirit as possible." Debs remained behind bars.

There were signs as well that Wilson may have suffered another minor stroke, for he had visible trouble remembering dates and details. Meanwhile, as Washington sweltered in the summer heat, Lodge's hearings began. Before they were over, he would call some 60 witnesses and Wilson himself would testify, inviting committee members to the White House and serving them a lunch of melon and cold Virginia ham. But he succeeded in changing no minds—especially when he made clear that he was firmly opposed to any changes to the treaty, however minor. The mysterious rupture with Colonel House had deprived him of the Texan's skill at behind-the-scenes persuasion, and the president preferred to lecture rather than to negotiate. Still, clumsy but unyielding, like a preacher determined to make his congregation see the path of virtue, he pushed on. But matters other than the peace treaty loomed much larger in the nation's eyes.

LATE ON THE evening of June 2, 1919, a month before Wilson returned from France, the unusually hot night air of eight cities in the Northeast was torn by almost simultaneous bomb blasts. One, in New York City, missed the judge who was apparently its object, but killed a night watchman. None of the other victims targeted were hurt, but the bombs severely damaged several homes, and the country was shocked by the evidence of a coordinated conspiracy. At most of the bomb sites investigators found leaflets on pink paper proclaiming that "class war is on and can not cease but with a complete victory for the international proletariat." The manifesto was entitled *Plain Words*. "You jailed us, you clubbed us, you deported us, you murdered us," declared the strange pink leaflet.

Pittsburgh was the only city to see two explosions, which came within five minutes of each other from pipe bombs filled with dynamite and shrapnel. Both were aimed at men—a federal judge and an immigration official—involved in deportation cases against radicals.

The bombings took the authorities everywhere by surprise, but provided the perfect excuse to once again crack down on the usual suspects. Jailing Wobblies was always a dependable way for police to show that they were on the job. "Wholesale Arrests after Blasts Wreck Homes," read the headline in the *Pittsburgh Press*. It also reported the arrest of "L.M. Walsh," Leo Wendell's alias, along with more than a dozen other local men, and quoted the city's police chief promising that "every hangout of the I. W. W. and Bolsheviki will be cleaned out."

The next day mug shots of Wendell and two comrades were on the newspaper's front page, along with photos of bomb fragments. "Walsh," another paper declared, was "regarded by government officials as one of the most dangerous labor propagandists in the country." Arresting him again gave Wendell a boost in prestige in the eyes of Pittsburgh radicals—and also, the police hoped, might let him overhear from his cellmates clues to who had planted the bombs. After three days of listening to jailhouse talk, however, Wendell told his superiors that none of the men seemed to have had anything to do with them.

The June 2 bombings were not the first such attack. A month earlier, a mail bomb had exploded in the home of a former US senator from Georgia, blowing off the hands of his maid. Another bomb failed to detonate, and thanks to an alert New York City postal clerk who noticed a group of identical brown paper packages addressed to prominent people, officials intercepted some three dozen additional mail bombs before they reached their targets. These included John D. Rockefeller, J. P. Morgan Jr., Senator Lee Overman, Judge Kenesaw Mountain Landis, and Postmaster General Albert Burleson.

Of the bombs that exploded on June 2, the one that had the biggest effect on the country was a blinding flash that shattered the night at 2132 R Street Northwest, in a fashionable Washington, DC, neighborhood filled with lilac and dogwood trees and elegant redbrick town houses. The former president William Howard Taft, Wilson's immediate predecessor and the largest man ever to occupy the White House, as well as Senator Warren Harding of Ohio and a rising young army officer named Dwight Eisenhower, all lived nearby.

The blast shattered the entire facade of one house. Its double front door hung in pieces; all 11 front windows were blown in. The explosion tore pictures and a stuffed elk's head from the walls, blew over furniture, smashed the staircase banister, and left the floor scarred and covered with broken glass. The sidewalk outside was awash in tree branches; cars knocked askew; fragments of wood, plaster, and brick; pulped, bloody pieces of human flesh; and, scattered far apart, two legs. The air was acrid with the smell of explosives. Police cars and fire engines raced to the spot, their sirens filling the almost moonless night.

The bomb had gone off at the home of Wilson's new attorney general, A. Mitchell Palmer.

Palmer, his wife, and their 10-year-old daughter were badly shaken, but survived unharmed because they were upstairs. Had the blast occurred a little earlier, when the two adults were in their downstairs library, they would probably have been killed, for there was nothing left of the chair in which Palmer usually sat. After the explosion, a neighbor, Assistant Secretary of the Navy Franklin D. Roosevelt, rushed across the street to see if the Palmers were all right, and helped the stunned attorney general search through the wreckage. The human remains outside the house were those of the bomber, who had apparently tripped on Palmer's front steps and accidentally blown himself up.

Some of Roosevelt's own windows were shattered. He invited the Palmers to his house for the night, but Mrs. Palmer wanted to leave the neighborhood, so Roosevelt drove her and her daughter to a friend's home several miles away. Her traumatized husband thanked him profusely. "I never knew before that Mitchell Palmer was a Quaker," Roosevelt told his wife, Eleanor, later. "He was 'theeing' and 'thouing' me all over the place—'thank thee, Franklin!'"

Palmer's Quaker convictions might have made him an opponent of war, but the attempt to murder him and his family three months after he had taken office left him profoundly transformed. It marked the beginning, largely under his leadership, of a domestic war the likes of which the United States had never seen. Its climactic episodes, half a year later, would go down in history with Palmer's name attached.

The war to come, however, would not be waged on the planners of these bombings, because the government never found them. Various clues suggested the bombers belonged to a tiny, shadowy sect of Italian American anarchists, who believed that bold acts of violence would trigger a widespread popular revolt. Police, poring through the body parts and other debris outside Palmer's house, first under searchlights and then in daylight, found a small Italian-English dictionary. The next day, a Roosevelt son found on their lawn part of the bomber's collarbone. But no one discovered enough conclusive evidence to identify the perpetrators and prosecute them.

Good detective work is difficult, but finding scapegoats is always easy—especially when you already know whom you want them to be. The sect that most likely planted the bombs, known as the Galleanists, had no more than 50 members in the entire nation. But Wobblies numbered in the tens of thousands, active Socialists in the hundreds of thousands, and participants in the many strikes that were shaking the country in the millions. These were the people whom Palmer now saw great political advantage in attacking—regardless of the lack of evidence connecting them to the bombings.

After the first set of mail bombs had been discovered weeks earlier, the ambitious Mayor Ole Hanson of Seattle, one of the targets, promptly blamed the Wobblies. He attacked the Wilson administration's "skim milk, weak, vacillating and changeable" policy toward leftists. "These men must be ruled by a rod of iron." Newspaper editorials demanded action. "Free speech has been outraged long enough," declared the *Washington Post*. "Let there be a few free treatments in the electric chair." Palmer was eager to show that he was a decisive, aggressive prosecutor.

As the news of the latest bombings spread, "I stood in the middle of the wreckage of my library with Congressmen and Senators," recalled Palmer, "and without a dissenting voice they called upon me in strong terms . . . to run to earth the criminals who were behind that kind of outrage." One told him, "Palmer, ask for what you want and you will get it."

What did Palmer want? Understandably, he wanted to catch the people who had tried to kill him, and he also wanted to defend himself against right-wing critics like Hanson, but for some time he had clearly had a higher goal. An imposing-looking man with a dignified shock of prematurely gray hair who wore three-piece suits crossed by a watch chain, he had long had his eye on higher office. Wilson was in his second term and no American president so far had ever served a third. An election was coming up the next year. As the chief law enforcement officer in a strife-filled country, Palmer was a strong potential candidate for the Democratic nomination. With his confident manner, dark eyebrows, and determinedly jutting jaw, he looked suited for the role. His years in Congress had honed his campaigning skills. He knew whose hand to shake and which women to tip his hat to. And now he suddenly had an additional boost: great sympathy from the public for having been the target of the bombing.

As he drove from his ruined home to the Justice Department the morning after the explosion, Washington appeared like a city at war. Police checkpoints dotted the streets, and 300 plainclothesmen protected the entrances to public buildings. Extra guards were on duty at the White House.

One of the first things on the attorney general's agenda was to find a new chief for the Bureau of Investigation, a position currently vacant. The bureau's 54 field offices would be crucial outposts in the war Palmer had decided to wage against leftists, the war he hoped would carry him into the nation's highest office. He needed a tough-looking figure who would telegraph his resolve, and he found one in William J. "Big Bill" Flynn, former chief of both the Secret Service and New York City's detectives, who was fond of joining his men on raids or in shadowing suspects. Headlines and front-page photos told of Flynn's exploits capturing bank robbers, gangsters, counterfeiters—and, during the war, German spies, whose numbers he wildly inflated.

Already media bait with his broad chest, dapper suits, derby hat, cigar, and history as a semipro baseball player, Flynn polished his aura by churning out a series of silent-film scenarios and melodramatic crime novels with Wobbly or Italian villains. Some of his output glorified his own work, such as *The Eagle's Eye: A True Story of the Imperial German Government's Spies and Intrigues in America*. Although better at promoting himself than actually catching criminals, Flynn made great copy. Headlines about Red-hunters and bombings sold papers when the press could no longer offer readers suspenseful daily reports from Europe's battlefields.

Testifying before Congress the following year, Palmer would invite its members to study the Justice Department's collection of mug shots of radicals. "Out of the sly and crafty eyes of many of them leap cupidity, cruelty, insanity, and crime; from their lopsided faces, sloping brows, and misshapen features may be recognized the unmistakable criminal type."

On the hunt for such villains, Palmer and Flynn kept up a drumbeat of arrests. In the days after the June bombings, agents seized 61 men. They wasted no time on obtaining warrants. Flynn raced among cities, spurring on his underlings, questioning suspects, boasting to reporters, and warning police chiefs to beef up security—for more bombings might be coming, very soon. The ones in June were "connected with Russian Bolshevism, aided by Hun money," he declared. Palmer warned a Senate committee that "on a certain day in the future, which we have been advised of, there will be another serious and probably much larger effort . . . which the wild fellows of this movement describe as a revolution" in which the miscreants planned to "destroy the Government at one fell swoop." An alarmed Congress appropriated additional money for both the Justice Department and Military Intelligence.

Palmer, Flynn, and other top officials soon gathered at the Justice Department to discuss a new strategy. The most important aim, after all, was not merely to solve these crimes, but to halt the threat of revolution. Why not simply rid the country of any sly and crafty-eyed types likely to cause trouble? Such a campaign would also distract attention from the government's embarrassing failure to catch and prosecute the June bombers.

In the United States at this time there were more than seven million foreign-born men and women who had not become naturalized as citizens. Some had never done so because the bureaucracy involved seemed intimidating for those who spoke little English. To others, formal citizenship hadn't felt important when the country seemed to welcome newcomers.

The presence of all these people was, for Palmer and Flynn, highly convenient, for a newly toughened immigration law allowed the government to expel noncitizens whom it judged to be political radicals. Everybody knew that places like Italy, Russia, and eastern Europe were the source of a large proportion of the nation's anarchists and socialists. If "we can round up those men and upon proper proof rush them back to Europe, you will find this agitation will subside very rapidly," one of Palmer's aides told the press.

We do not know what details of this strategy Palmer shared with Wilson. The two would have had plenty of chances to talk before, during, and after cabinet meetings, and they met on at least three other occasions in the summer and fall of 1919 as well. "It is hard to conceive," writes the historian Kenneth Ackerman, "that Palmer would have hid [his plan] from the president."

One more piece of the strategy had to be put in place, something that, in Palmer's mind, would help ensure success and thus pave his path to the presidential nomination. To find those who could be deported, Palmer and his aides decided, they would need a new Radical Division of the Justice Department—to compile lists of subversives, track them, and build the legal cases that would expel them to whatever benighted lands they had come from, once and for all.

The Radical Division would have a staff of 30 in Washington, and 60 agents in the field devoted exclusively to its work. Its chief was to report directly to Palmer, so that on the campaign trail he could take credit for its achievements. The attorney general was convinced that he had the right man for the job—someone who was already working as a senior aide, just down the hall from his own corner office.

The candidate was unusually young—as an 18-year-old, he had led his high school drill team in the inaugural parade for Wilson in 1913—but he was bright, energetic, and well organized. While completing both college and law school in a four-year marathon, he had also worked cataloging books at the Library of Congress and had grown intrigued by the way the library kept track of millions of items by using file cards. Although only 24, he had entered the Justice Department right out of law school. A skillful young man could rise quickly in wartime Washington, and this one had done so. Living an apparently monastic life with no visible interests beyond his job, the intense, talented youngster had shown himself to be a ferociously hard worker, known for being in the office nights and weekends. Palmer was sure he was the perfect person to head the new Radical Division and on August 1, 1919, appointed him. Everyone called him Edgar; his full name was John Edgar Hoover.

THE COUNTRY SHOWED no letup in its repression of dissidents. In Oregon, Dr. Marie Equi's case was still on appeal, but this didn't stop her activism. She did nothing as dramatic as orating again from atop a telephone pole, but she was arrested once more, this time "for spreading I. W. W. propaganda." Hundreds of conscientious objectors remained in prison at Camp Funston and elsewhere. Emma Goldman, Kate Richards O'Hare, and other radicals were also still behind bars.

In a stream of letters to her husband and children, the 42-year-old O'Hare poured out details about prison life. Frank O'Hare published a regular bulletin about his wife's case and a small book of the letters, some of them smuggled out of the prison, uncensored, by a friendly chaplain. High in prestige among her fellow inmates, she found, were "women who had disposed of undesirable husbands . . . I want to expound for all of my male friends a bit of wisdom. If you chance to have one of those meek, patient, quiet, long-suffering wives, beware that you do not try them too far."

Among the worst things for her at the prison was the lack of sanitation. "The dining room was not screened, and fifteen years' accumulation of well preserved fly-specks was an astonishing thing to behold. . . . We ate with one hand and picked roaches out of our food with the other. . . . The rats were perhaps worst of all. They overran the place in swarms, scampered over the dining tables, nibbled our bread, played in our dishes, crept into bed with us, chewed up our shoes." Flies feasted on the open sores of a woman dying in a "cell directly below me . . . and then awakened us in the morning by crawling over our faces."

Her friendship with Emma Goldman helped take her mind off such matters. O'Hare learned from other inmates how to fasten photographs and pictures to her cell's concrete walls with chewing gum. Gifts flowed in from comrades across the United States and Europe, and she shared them—soap, perfume, letter paper, and food of all kinds, including things novel to her fellow prisoners, like gefilte fish and matzos from Jewish socialists in New York. As much the organizer inside prison as she had been outside, she wrote that "I have volunteered to start a night school to send the inmates out a little less ignorant than when they entered." She tutored in English a 20-year-old "dear little Italian girl" whom she and Goldman had befriended. When fellow prisoners were released, Kate's husband, Frank, sometimes helped them find jobs.

She recalled the excitement of her trip to Europe a few months before the First World War began, representing the United States among socialists from across the world and meeting people like Jean Jaurès, leader of the French party, who would soon be assassinated for his antiwar beliefs. "With the memory of great souls like these to keep me company, my prison cell is a palace."

When her 14-year-old son visited, O'Hare was upset that warders denied him permission to play his trumpet for her. But they had no control over what happened outside the prison's walls. "Last night we were locked in our cells waiting for the lights to be turned out when suddenly I heard a sweet but wavering note that I instantly recognized as Dick's cornet. . . . Nothing ever sounded sweeter than the noble strains of 'Lead Kindly Light.' Before the first bar was ended a dead silence reigned. . . . From cell to cell a whisper ran 'Be still and listen—it is Mrs. O'Hare's son!' No artist ever held an audience more breathless. . . . When he played 'Silver Threads among the Gold' I could hear the women sobbing."

Above: Woodrow Wilson with his chief adviser, Colonel Edward House (*right*) and his second wife, Edith, who was fiercely jealous of House. *Below:* Wilson with the other key members of his inner circle, his secretary, Joseph Tumulty (*left*), and Navy physician Dr. Cary Grayson (*right*).

War fever: Boy Scouts run down New York's Fifth Avenue, in a "Wake Up, America!" parade two weeks after the declaration of war; a sign in a Chicago park.

Above: Indicted members of the Illinois mob that lynched the German-born Robert Prager; all were found not guilty after the jury deliberated for 45 minutes. *Below:* John Meints, a Minnesota farmer tarred and feathered for refusing to buy a war bond.

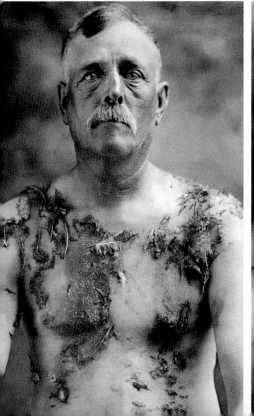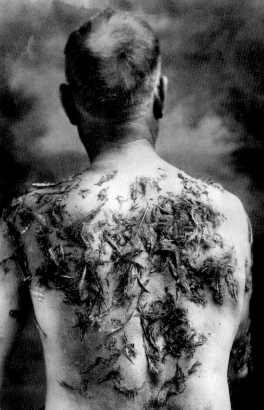

Voices against war: Robert "Fighting Bob" La Follette, the strongest progressive in the US Senate; conscientious objectors imprisoned at Camp Funston, Kansas.

Postmaster General Albert Burleson, the nation's chief press censor; a cartoon of the Liberty Bell in the magazine *The Masses* that reportedly enraged him.

Leo Wendell on page 1 of the *Pittsburgh Press* as "L. M. Walsh"—an IWW kingpin under arrest, and (*right*) in his later years as a lieutenant colonel in the Michigan State Troops. *Below:* A dispatch from Wendell, undercover, to the Bureau of Investigation reporting a speech by himself as "Walsh."

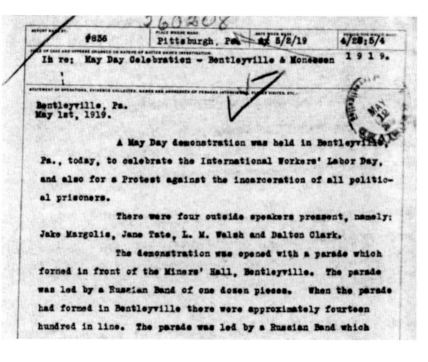

Above: Striking Pittsburgh streetcar workers in 1919 who had no idea that Wendell was an agent provocateur. *Below:* In the "Red Summer" racial attacks of that year, two white Chicago men stone to death John Mills, 34, a military veteran and stockyard worker.

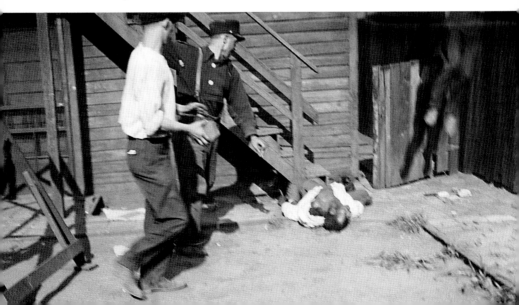

Above: The "Harlem Hellfighters" return to New York after suffering 40 percent casualties and 191 days under enemy fire, more than any other American unit. *Right:* The America that awaited them included this Omaha mob burning the body of a Black man, Will Brown, accused—on highly suspect evidence—of raping a white woman.

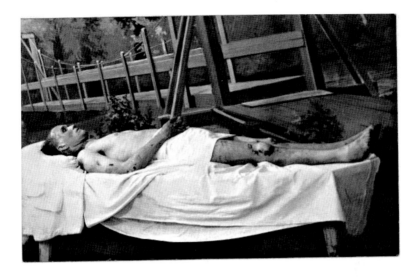

The high price of being a Wobbly: The corpse of organizer Frank Little, who was seized from his bed in the middle of the night, dragged behind a car, and hanged; Big Bill Haywood (*lower left*), and his IWW comrade George Speed, under arrest by Chicago police.

President Wilson in Paris with the two negotiating partners who outsmarted him, Prime Ministers David Lloyd George of Britain (*seated, left*) and Georges Clemenceau of France (*seated, center*). *Right:* Wilson after his stroke.

Presidential aspirant Major General Leonard Wood (*right*), with his close friend and patron, former president Theodore Roosevelt. *Below:* Soldiers under Wood's command on the streets of Omaha after he declared martial law there.

Above left: Louis F. Post, who saved thousands from being deported. *Above right:* Dr. Marie Equi, the radical feminist who orated against the war from atop a telephone pole. *Below:* Close prison friends Emma Goldman (*left, from a police mug shot*) and Socialist Kate Richards O'Hare (*right*).

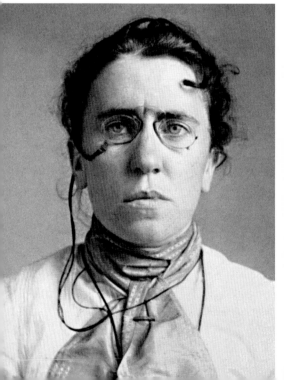

Above: Eugene V. Debs, walking free at last after more than three years in prison. *Below:* A still from an animated film made by the Ford Motor Company and shown in theaters across the country.

Facets of repression: Lieutenant Colonel Ralph Van Deman, surveillance enthusiast whose Military Intelligence operation spied on thousands of civilians; badge worn by vigilantes of the American Protective League; police with machine gun at the site of a 1919 Massachusetts textile workers' strike.

The remains of the office of a left-wing book bindery in Cambridge, Massachusetts, after a raid in November 1919. *Below:* Instigators of the raids, Attorney General A. Mitchell Palmer (*left*), with his eye on the presidency, and his fast-rising deputy, J. Edgar Hoover (*right*).

Above: Key allies in slamming the door on immigrants, Congressman Albert Johnson (*left*), and John B. Trevor, former Military Intelligence chief for New York City. *Below:* Foreign-born IWW members awaiting deportation from Ellis Island in 1919, after eighteen months of imprisonment there.

On the Great Deep

FEDERAL PRISONERS WERE held not only in penitentiaries like
the one in Missouri that housed O'Hare and Goldman. Some
were also now incarcerated at a place that had long symbolized
freedom.

For more than a quarter century, a 27-acre patch of land in New
York Harbor had been the biggest gateway to the country. With the
nearby Statue of Liberty looming above it, Ellis Island was where most
immigrants formally entered the United States. Its Beaux-Arts main
building, with a redbrick and limestone facade and four towers topped
with gingerbread cupolas, contained the Great Hall, whose high,
arched windows, vaulted roof, and interior balcony almost gave it the
feeling of a cathedral. That was a fitting image for the hopes of the
millions of people with suitcases, trunks, and bundles moving through
the room toward what they hoped would be a better life.

Starting in 1892, more than 12 million people passed through that
building. Nearly 40 percent of Americans today have at least one an-
cestor who entered the country through Ellis Island. By mid-1919,
however, rising hostility to immigrants had largely turned the island
into a place of detention—for people denied entry, or for those the
government was trying to deport.

Paradoxically, the man in charge of the island, officially the immigration commissioner for the port of New York, was a well-known

reformer, Frederic C. Howe. The author of a string of books with titles like *The City: The Hope of Democracy* and *Privilege and Democracy in
America*, he had joined the Wilson administration with great hopes for
the president who had promised that he would be "more concerned
about human rights than about property rights." Wilson had been a
professor of Howe's in graduate school, inspiring the young student
with his "moral passion" for what government could achieve. Howe
was a friend of outspoken progressives like Supreme Court justice
Louis Brandeis, Senator Robert La Follette (whose picture Howe kept
in his office), and Assistant Secretary of Labor Louis F. Post, the man
who had unsuccessfully urged Wilson to pardon draft refusers and who
had intervened to stop Emma Goldman from being deported.

When Wilson offered him the Ellis Island job in 1914, Howe felt,
"I wanted to do this work for the sake of the immigrants." He hoped
to make the island "a kindly place." To improve conditions for those
whom war or bureaucracy had stranded there, he opened a children's
school, built playgrounds, and approved a handwritten newspaper,
Gazeta, whose pages contained articles in Russian, German, Yiddish,
Lithuanian, and other languages. He brought in musicians to give concerts, including the famous tenor Enrico Caruso. On occasion, Howe
was able to intervene to prevent someone from being deported. He
was dismayed to find in his custody many who were being expelled
because of personal vendettas: "A stenographer from Knoxville, Tenn.,
had been seduced by her employer. He had grown tired of her and had
advised the immigration authorities. . . . My telephone rang constantly
with inquiries from persons seeking news of husbands and fathers who
had been arrested." Increasingly, Howe felt anguished that he had become "a jailer" in charge of a "dumping-ground under the successive
waves of hysteria which swept the country."

He continued to write and speak, but both the Bureau of Investigation and Military Intelligence began monitoring his public appearances, and the Senate's Overman committee included him on the list
of suspicious people it released to the public. Howe's 1916 book *Why
War?*, which was actually dedicated to Woodrow Wilson, was on the

list of volumes banned from army camp libraries. He found the president's attitude toward political repression "incomprehensible." Howe was prominent enough so that when he took his protests to the White House, Wilson received him "attentively, apparently interested in my statement. He was scrupulously attired, trim and erect, even debonair— every inch the gentlemanly President. . . . He would listen for a moment, then take up the matter, state it in a few phrases better than I had done—and treat the interview as ended. . . . He wrote me letters breathing his old belief in freedom." But then it was back to Ellis Island, where Howe found himself once again in charge of a prison. He began wondering if he should resign.

The president, meanwhile, seemed not to be thinking about immigrants, his attorney general's plan to deport radicals, or the nation's increasing turmoil. Instead, he was appalled that he had just spent an exhausting half year in Paris negotiating a peace treaty that the Senate might now refuse to ratify. He could not imagine a compromise, and saw only one course of action. Deterred by neither his shaky health nor the country's turbulence, he decided to take his case directly to the American people. And he would concentrate on those states whose senators most fiercely opposed the League of Nations.

Dr. Grayson, friends, and staff members argued that he was too weak to make such a trip, but Wilson was determined, despite the risk of being stranded en route by a threatened railroad strike. He began planning a four-week journey of 10,000 miles, with nearly a hundred speeches in 29 cities.

HUNDREDS OF THOUSANDS of cheering New Yorkers lined the parade route as the ranks of returned soldiers marched up Fifth Avenue, led by a famous jazz band, passing people throwing flowers, passing the state's governor and other dignitaries on a reviewing stand. This unit had suffered 40 percent casualties and repeatedly endured poison gas attacks while serving an extraordinary 191 days under enemy fire, more than any other American troops. Officially, the men were the 369th Infantry Regiment (Colored), but everyone called them the "Harlem Hellfighters."

Newspapers praised the "dusky fighters" and told of their successes in battle. In civilian life they may have been construction laborers, waiters, doormen, and elevator operators, but in combat they had done themselves proud. They were among the 380,000 Black American war veterans who had braved mud and influenza, and had often risked their lives and seen comrades lose theirs. Surely, they hoped, the country they returned to would show them more fairness than the one they had left, something ensured by the very uniforms they proudly wore.

A reminder of the stark contrast between these men's heroism in battle and what could await them back home had appeared some months earlier in the *New York Tribune*. On May 20, 1918, the newspaper ran two stories next to each other on page 2. One was headlined, "Two N.Y. Negroes Whip 24 Germans; Win War Crosses." A pair of Harlem Hellfighter privates, Henry Johnson, 25, a diminutive "redcap" railway station porter, and Needham Roberts, a 17-year-old bellhop, had fought off two dozen Germans who'd raided their trench in the middle of the night, Roberts hurling grenades and Johnson clubbing one raider with his rifle butt and disemboweling another with a bolo knife. Both suffered wounds, and "these chocolate soldiers," in the words of the newspaper, became the first Americans awarded the Croix de Guerre by the French military.

The adjoining article was topped by the headline "Georgia Mob Lynches Negro and His Wife." It was one of the most horrific episodes in the long, grisly history of American lynching. A white man who used Black prison labor on his farm in Brooks County, Georgia, had a longstanding reputation for treating those workers brutally. After one of them, working off a sentence for gambling, was severely beaten several times and watched others endure the same, he stole the farmer's gun, shot him dead, and wounded his wife. There were rumors—later proved untrue—that he had also raped her, something always guaranteed to inflame a lynch mob. This one swelled to some 300 white men.

Over several days, looking for victims wherever they could find them, the mob killed at least 13 Blacks, one of them a farmworker named Hayes Turner. The next day, his wife, Mary, eight months pregnant, made what a Georgia newspaper called "unwise remarks . . . about the execution of her husband." The mob strung her up to a tree by her ankles, doused her with gasoline, and set her on fire. As she screamed in pain, a member of the mob knifed open her belly, and when her unborn child fell to the ground and gave a cry, men stomped it to death. When her remains and those of her child were buried, the grave was marked, triumphantly, by a whisky bottle stoppered with a cigar. The mob included the foreman of the county's grand jury. No one was ever prosecuted.

Once again, it was Black defiance or desire for equality that provoked white Americans to the most savage acts of violence. Someone acutely outraged by horrors like this was W. E. B. Du Bois, now returned from the Pan African Congress he had helped organize in Paris. "It was right for us to fight," he wrote in *The Crisis* six months after the war's end. "But by the God of Heaven, we are cowards and jackasses if now that that war is over, we do not marshal every ounce of our brain and brawn to fight a sterner, longer, more unbending battle against the forces of hell in our own land."

The article deeply alarmed Albert Burleson's Post Office, which for the past two years had been warily monitoring Black publications. Officially the journal of the NAACP, *The Crisis* was no mere house organ; Du Bois's powerful mind and skilled pen had given it a larger circulation than any other liberal or left-wing opinion magazine in the country, and the NAACP was a biracial organization that included many influential whites. The postmaster general ordered 100,000 copies of this issue impounded in a back room of the main New York City post office. Finally, after a storm of lobbying from Du Bois's allies, Black and white, Burleson relented and released the magazines.

Du Bois was right to anticipate "the forces of hell." Demobilized soldiers were permitted to wear their uniforms after being mustered out, but instead of that being a form of protection, Blacks quickly discovered it was *more* dangerous to be a veteran. More than 70 Black Americans would be hanged by mobs—or, in 11 cases, burned alive—in 1919, the highest total in over a decade. Seventeen of them were veterans, at least three of whom were in uniform when murdered.

One of the first was Private Charles Lewis of Tyler Station, Kentucky. He fought back against a sheriff's deputy who had accused him of robbery and demanded that he empty his pockets. When word of his arrest got out, a mob of masked men broke into the jail with sledgehammers, seized Lewis, and hanged him from a nearby tree—in his army khaki. "The incident is a portent of what may be expected in the future as more of the negro soldiery return," warned a Louisiana newspaper editorial. Their army service had "given these men more exalted ideas of their station in life than really exists. . . . This is the right time to show them what will and will not be permitted."

Most commonly, the pretext for a lynching was the charge that a Black man had raped a white woman. Such accusations were seldom true, but to ardent white supremacists, that did not matter. Sometimes they even *said* it didn't matter. "The news . . . of the lynching of a negro charged with attempted rape thrills the electric wires," wrote James Vardaman, the former senator from Mississippi, about one case in 1919. "It is said that the young woman assaulted was not able to definitely and surely identify the man who was killed as the man who had made the attempted assault on her. But negroes have been guilty of a series of crimes of this character."

Something else that aroused whites was that those 380,000 Black veterans were competing with them for scarce jobs, threatening to depress wages. And the same fuel that had fed the attacks on Blacks in East St. Louis two years earlier remained, for the Great Migration continued unabated, enraging white northerners who found these newcomers moving into previously all-white neighborhoods. More battles exploded in the hot summer months of 1919, north and south. The United States had seen plenty of murderous violence against immigrants, Wobblies, and other militant labor unionists. But that was surpassed by the fury the country mustered against Black people.

Despite books, articles, and museum exhibits that continue to use the phrase "race riots of 1919," the events that now unfolded almost all began as *white* riots. Take, for example, Chicago, a place already precarious with tension, for its steel and meatpacking plants had long used Blacks as strikebreakers. Looking for work, Black migrants carrying their belongings in bundles or flimsy suitcases continued to pour into the city, their numbers more than doubling over the course of the decade. In addition, hundreds of southern Black servicemen were released from the army in Chicago but not given train fare home. Nor did some of them want to return to homes in the South, when week after week newspapers reported lynchings in garish detail, including the way white crowds cheered as they cut off and flourished body parts from a Black corpse. Not surprisingly, the counties with the most lynchings often produced the greatest number of Blacks fleeing north.

Chicago's Black population was mostly packed into a run-down neighborhood on the city's South Side, but as its numbers expanded, unscrupulous real estate agents began frightening whites elsewhere into selling their homes at low prices. The newcomers' "presence here is intolerable," declared the newsletter of a white homeowners' association in March 1919. "Every colored man who moves into Hyde Park knows that he is damaging his white neighbor's property." In the preceding two years, bombs had damaged more than two dozen Black homes in Chicago—often those of families who had just moved into white areas. One of the explosions killed a six-year-old girl. No culprits were ever prosecuted.

Sunday, July 27, 1919, fell on the hottest weekend of the summer, and as the temperature reached 96 degrees Fahrenheit, tens of thousands of people headed for the city's beaches. These, too, were unofficially divided by skin color, an imaginary line extending into Lake Michigan. But when two Black couples appeared at a traditionally all-white beach at 29th Street, whites began throwing rocks at them and at several Black teenagers floating toward the beach on a homemade raft. One of the boys on the raft, struck on the forehead, was apparently the first person to die that day. The police refused to arrest the white man who had thrown the rock and seized a Black man instead.

Rocks escalated to knives and guns. Cars full of white gang members sped through Black neighborhoods, firing at random. Even a hospital came under assault, with white and Black gangs each attacking patients from the other group. But when the police opened fire, it was almost always at Black crowds.

One Black veteran was coming home from work when he saw a gang of twenty white youths, one of whom yelled, "There's a nigger! Let's get him!" As he jumped aboard a streetcar, they pulled its pole off the overhead power line. The veteran ran for his life, at one point slipping into a drugstore in hopes of safety, but a white woman there forced him out. The mob followed, yelling, "There he goes! Stop him! Stop him!" Two people fired guns at him. Finally he outran his pursuers, then hid for several hours in terror before warily making his way home. He asked a Black journalist, "Had the ten months I spent in France been all in vain?" Later, when he saw a lone white man, he said, "My first impulse was to jump on him and beat him up." Another man, a wounded Black veteran of the Canadian army, in uniform, was beaten so badly he had to be hospitalized.

Transit workers were on strike. Blacks who depended on streetcars to get to work were terrified to walk through white neighborhoods and stayed home. Whites made up more than 95 percent of the city's population and mobs roamed the streets, pulling Blacks out of restaurants, shops, and railway stations to beat them. In the middle of the fighting, the Black activist Ada McKinley linked arms with Jane Addams and two other white social workers, and together they walked through the angry crowds in a silent but fruitless demonstration of friendship.

The mayor called in 6,000 troops from the state militia. After it was all over, 38 people lay dead and at least 537 had suffered serious injuries, ranging from gouged-out eyes to gunshot and stab wounds. The great majority of both dead and wounded were Black, at least five of whom had been killed by the police.

Similar and often fatal warfare erupted in two dozen other cities and towns during what came to be called the "Red Summer" of 1919, from Connecticut to South Carolina, and from Texas to Washington, DC, where 2,000 soldiers were called out. Vigilantes burned more than a dozen Black churches in Georgia alone.

The deadliest violence of all was in Phillips County, Arkansas. The killers included American Legion members who joined a sheriff's posse, other vigilantes from outside the county, and 550 federal troops. There were at least 103 known Black deaths, but some estimates put the total number at double that or higher. One reason no one could completely pin down the toll, in an echo of what had happened at East St. Louis two years earlier, is that many dead bodies were thrown in the Mississippi River.

In exposés they each wrote, both Ida B. Wells and W. E. B. Du Bois pointed out the real reason behind the violence in Phillips County, which much of the press had ignored: white property owners were infuriated that Black sharecroppers were organizing a union. Confronted with scenes of death and destruction like this all her life, it is small wonder that Wells once wrote, "If it were possible, [I] would gather my race in my arms and fly away with them." But she did not give up hope, and by ceaseless writing, fund-raising, and organizing was able to save the lives of 12 Black survivors of this particular massacre who were on death row. The commander of the federal troops who carried out most of the Arkansas killings was a veteran of the Indian Wars who ordered his soldiers to "kill any negro who refuses to surrender immediately." Many were machine-gunned before they had a chance to do so.

More Black Americans died violently at the hands of their white countrymen in 1919 than had in decades. In public, President Wilson said only a single, reluctant, vague sentence about the bloodshed, regretting "the race riots that have occurred in some places" where "men . . . have run amuck." Liberals like Robert La Follette spoke out, but in vain. The Justice Department made no move to investigate the leaders of the white mobs that instigated almost all the killings, instead looking for signs of IWW or Bolshevik influence among Black protestors.

Although the nation had seen earlier outbreaks of such violence and would see many more, one thing was new about the racial upheavals of 1919, shocking the country's establishment: Black Americans fought back. In Chicago, some Black war veterans took weapons from their regiment's armory; in Washington, DC, others mounted rooftops with rifles; in Knoxville, armed veterans built street barricades. "Brothers we are on the Great Deep," Du Bois wrote in September. "We have cast off on the vast voyage which will lead to Freedom or Death. For three centuries we have suffered and cowered. . . . When the armed lynchers gather, we too must gather armed. When the mob moves, we propose to meet it with bricks and clubs and guns."

On top of all the other tensions, the specter of "bricks and clubs and guns" raised the country's level of anxiety still further. J. Edgar Hoover, newly empowered as chief of the Justice Department's Radical Division, leapt at the chance to include "Negro Activities" as a subheading in the weekly intelligence bulletins he began circulating to officials in Washington and to American diplomatic missions overseas. Hoover's agents searched for ties between the racial violence and radicals. They found nothing, but he was skillful at persuading sympathetic journalists to imply otherwise. It is not unlikely that he was the unnamed "Federal official" quoted in a *New York Times* story headlined "Reds Try to Stir Negroes to Revolt."

ONE OF THE last upheavals of "Red Summer" broke out in Omaha. The target of white rage this time was a jailed Black laborer named Will Brown; once again the charge was raping a white woman. A white mob went wild, chasing and beating any Black men they saw. They slashed fire hoses that were turned on them, broke into two gun stores to steal weapons and ammunition, and used gasoline to set the courthouse, containing the jail, on fire. Smoke poured from the windows as bricks and bullets hit the building.

When Omaha's unusually enlightened mayor, Edward Smith, bravely tried to intervene at the burning courthouse, the crowd seized him, put a noose around his neck, and started to hang him from a streetcar signal pole. The police managed to rescue the bloodied and unconscious Smith just in time. As the mob prevented firefighters from putting out the flames, sheriff's deputies and prisoners inside the jail fled to the courthouse roof. Desperate to save themselves, the deputies yielded Brown to the crowd, which quickly beat him senseless, stripped him, riddled him with bullets, and strung up his body to a pole. Finally they dragged his corpse through town behind a car and set it on fire.

The outline of what happened in Omaha was gruesomely similar to hundreds of other lynchings in this era. But the story has another layer. Like other American cities, Omaha was not without racism to begin with, but, as so often happens, an ambitious politician deliberately inflamed it. The story of what he did, however, would not fully emerge for years.

As with many Black men accused of raping white women, the accusations against Will Brown were somewhat hazy and changed over time. The alleged victim identified her Black rapist as hunchbacked, but when Brown was arrested and turned out not to be hunchbacked, she still said, "Yes, he is the man!" She accused Brown of assaulting her when she was strolling with her boyfriend, and of keeping one hand over her mouth while with the other he kept a pistol trained on the boyfriend 50 feet away. There were no other witnesses. Several days later, the boyfriend was seen leading the lynch mob. Conveniently, neither the accused, the woman who claimed to be the victim, nor the boyfriend ever had to testify in court, because Brown was killed before he could come to trial. And police and journalists could not question the boyfriend about the rape or his role in the lynch mob, because, they discovered, he had disappeared from town—and would remain gone for years.

The boyfriend was in fact an operative for Omaha's longtime political boss, Tom Dennison, a tall, burly man fond of elegant suits and diamond pins, with a lucrative web of connections to corrupt police, gambling saloons, and brothels. To his dismay, however, he had lost control of city hall the previous year, when voters had elected as mayor the reform-minded Edward Smith. The best way to get rid of Smith and regain power, Dennison decided, was to create the impression that Black crime was soaring out of the mayor's control. One of the city's newspapers, run by a Dennison ally, was quick to call Will Brown the "Black Beast" and published a long string of sensational headlines about more than 20 other Black men assaulting, raping, or binding and gagging white women, after which the police always quickly arrested a Black suspect. These cases, however, often completely fell apart in court. Most of the attackers, a talkative Dennison insider revealed years later, were Dennison operatives—in blackface.

Someone else who worked hard to turn the summer's racial turmoil to his advantage was General Leonard Wood. For him the outbreak of violence in Omaha was a great boon. He was now chief of the army's Central Department, essentially commanding all troops in the Midwest. It was a good perch from which to continue to travel the country making rousing speeches against Bolshevism and enjoying receptions by mayors, governors, and businessmen in his undeclared campaign for the presidency.

When Omaha erupted, the general commandeered a freight train to take him to the city in its caboose, and immediately called in troops. Without waiting for orders from Washington, he declared martial law. He reinforced his men by adding 200 armed, white American Legion vigilantes to his forces. He asked newspapers to censor what they reported, declaring that he "was strong for the freedom of the press," but in favor of "the suppression of a rotten press where there is one." He set up machine-gun nests in front of public buildings and on street corners. He deployed 1,300 soldiers throughout Omaha, and sent up an army observation balloon to look for any suspicious crowds forming.

By the time Wood actually did all of this, the violence had already subsided. However, he claimed in a Chicago speech a few days later, "the troops and the American Legion were all that stood between the local authorities and the destruction of the city. It is now known that plans had been laid for widespread destruction. . . . Just one agency was to blame for this—that was the I. W. W. and its red flag." Wood knew better, having personally interrogated arrested members of the Omaha mob, who had nothing to do with the much-weakened Wobblies. But they remained a convenient scapegoat, and this kind of accusation, it was clear, would be the foundation of his presidential campaign.

I Am Not in Condition to Go On

O N THE EVENING of September 3, 1919, a tall, gaunt figure in a blue blazer, straw "boater" hat, and white pants and shoes walked down the platform at Washington's Union Station to board the Mayflower, a private railroad car. Against the pleadings of his staff, a frail President Wilson was beginning a long journey across a deeply troubled country to campaign for the peace treaty he had helped negotiate in Paris, driven by what he saw as its centerpiece: the League of Nations. This would be the great forum where countries large and small would settle their differences peacefully and forever end the scourge of war. If he lost the fight for the league, he declared, it would "break the heart of the world."

"He was obviously a sick man," remembered a British diplomat who had lunch with him just before his departure. "His face was drawn and of a grey color, and frequently twitching in a pitiful effort to control nerves." The league was to be his crowning achievement, and he was determined to take his case for it over the heads of those obstinate senators, directly to the voters. Confident of the power of his professorial silver tongue, he knew that the more than 20 journalists aboard the presidential train, and additional reporters at each stop, would carry his words still further. "I promised our soldiers . . . that it was a war to end wars," he told his wife, Edith, "and if I do not do all in my power to put the Treaty in effect, I will be a slacker and never able to look those boys in the eye."

It was one of those statements that at first sounds too eloquent to have been said in conversation, but, as far as we can tell from many accounts, the president actually did talk in the same elevated tones in which he wrote. When Dr. Grayson argued that weeks aboard a rattling train and so many speeches to huge audiences would be too much, he said that Wilson responded, with tears in his eyes, "I cannot put my personal safety, my health, in the balance against my duty—I must go."

"Never have I seen the President look so weary as the night we left Washington," wrote Joe Tumulty, always at his right hand. Wilson cannot have felt any better about the grueling trip that lay ahead when he learned that several senators determined to kill the treaty were planning their own nationwide tour.

At the first stop, in Columbus, Ohio, Wilson had a headache and found that streetcar workers were on strike—not the last strike he would encounter on this journey. But he spoke anyway, and continued to do so as the train stopped in Indiana and Missouri. Asthma began bothering him. In Iowa, he was at last able to spend a night in a hotel. Dr. Grayson showed him how to sleep with his head and chest raised on pillows, to make it easier to breathe. The doctor also took him for walks whenever there was a break in his schedule.

Most crowds were friendly, but more than one governor or mayor who turned out to greet him made clear that he was not a fan of the league. The president had little appetite. "With each revolution of the wheels my anxieties for my husband's health increased," Edith Wilson later wrote. "He grew thinner and the headaches increased in duration and in intensity until he was almost blind during the attacks."

There was little comfort in the news: more labor battles, more racial violence, and more Senate hearings conducted by Henry Cabot Lodge. The Massachusetts senator was now inviting testimony from an official who had resigned in protest from the Paris delegation and who quoted Wilson's own secretary of state as feeling the league was "useless." When this report reached the president's train, he grew pale and his lips trembled with rage. He was, remembered Tumulty, "incensed and distressed beyond measure."

AS HE FOLLOWED the newspaper headlines about Wilson's departure on his cross-country journey, the reformer Frederic Howe was still in charge of Ellis Island. But to him, the majestic vista of the Manhattan skyline across the harbor seemed to mock the hundreds of fearful, unhappy people around him awaiting deportation. With little actual power, Howe was facing the kind of painful cases that would confront American immigration officials a century later. A young Armenian woman who had arrived as a stowaway was being deported—to Turkey, which had just carried out a notorious genocide against her people. Three Indian nationalists were ordered expelled—although at risk, their attorney warned, of being executed by the British.

Howe also found his island's prison filling with radicals whom A. Mitchell Palmer and J. Edgar Hoover were sending there to await deportation. "The Red hysteria was at its height. . . . There was talk of chartering a vessel and sending a boat-load of deportees back to Russia," Howe wrote. "Many of them I had personally examined and found held on the most trivial charges."

Several days after Wilson embarked on his speaking tour, Howe sat down and wrote the president a letter resigning from his job. "I had entered whole-heartedly into my principality of Ellis Island, hoping to make it a playhouse for immigrants," he later said in his autobiography. "I left a prison. I recalled what [the abolitionist] Wendell Phillips said about negro slavery, that it 'made a slave of the master no less than the slave.'"

LESS THAN A week into the president's travels came the year's most shocking strike. Shortly before dusk, at evening roll call, more than 70 percent of the Boston police force turned in their revolvers, badges, and helmets, and walked out. The night shift appeared at the city's station houses, handed over their equipment, and also headed home.

For police officers to go on strike was virtually unheard of. After all, for decades one of their prime jobs had been to *suppress* strikes. The Bureau of Investigation telegraphed its Boston field office asking "whether radical elements or I. W. W. are in any way responsible." Agents dutifully relayed to Washington scraps of overheard talk, but even the bureau seemed to know it would have a hard time convincing the public that revolutionaries had infiltrated the city's overwhelmingly Irish Catholic police force.

However, that didn't stop the press from sounding those very alarm bells. "Has Bolshevik Russia presented any more alarming spectacle than this?" asked an editorial in the *Los Angeles Times*. "Lenin and Trotsky are on their way," declared the *Wall Street Journal*. The police officers had reasonable grievances, from low pay to 12-hour shifts, and their main demand was to be able to unionize under the American Federation of Labor. Police in 37 other American cities, they pointed out, belonged to unions, as did Boston's firefighters. But the city's police commissioner and the governor of Massachusetts, who had authority over him, refused. The governor was the hitherto inconspicuous Calvin Coolidge, who now gained so much national attention from defying the strikers that the following year he would win nomination as the Republican candidate for vice president.

For two days, looters took advantage of the strike to grab food and clothing from smashed storefronts and snatch women's handbags. Veteran criminals from other cities hopped trains to ply their trade in unpoliced Boston. Wilson, who had now reached Montana on his cross-country odyssey, described the city as "at the mercy of an army of thugs," and called the strike "a crime against civilization."

Boston authorities recruited volunteers to replace the police. Those chosen were overwhelmingly middle- and upper-class Protestants of the sort who had flocked to the American Protective League. For them it was a thrill, one akin to flashing an APL badge, to be outfitted with pistols or nightsticks and sent out into the streets. Among them were more than 200 Harvard students, including virtually the entire football team. "To hell with football, if the men are needed," declared its coach.

This was an opportunity for students eager to prove their manliness, something it was nearly a year too late to do on the battlefield in Europe. Popular magazines had often made a glamorous figure of the professional strikebreaker, portraying him as a sort of latter-day frontiersman risking bullets and blows to keep order. Now students could play that role and feel that they were protecting others, especially women. The university's president and dean toured the city visiting students on patrol, like generals inspecting troops in frontline trenches.

The governor also called out the state militia, including machine-gun crews and cavalrymen armed with swords. When rioters threw bricks and bottles, the soldiers opened fire. Eight people were killed by the militia, which would continue to patrol the city's streets for months, while striking police officers were fired and a new force, many of them job-hungry war veterans, was trained.

Strikes rippled across the nation in other lines of work that had seldom known them before. At the Cohan and Harris Theatre on New York's Broadway, where spectators were awaiting a performance of a three-act musical, *The Royal Vagabond*, the curtain rose to disclose the cast in their street clothes. More than 100 actors in 12 shows walked off the job. "Several of the musical shows attempted to give performances with the chorus alone, but the audiences did not take kindly to the innovation," reported the *Illustrated Daily News*. Masses of would-be theatergoers surged up and down Broadway looking for other amusements. Actors in eight cities joined the strike, halting 37 plays and postponing the opening of 16 more. They demanded payment for rehearsals that ran longer than four weeks, extra pay for matinees and road trips, and recognition of their union, Actors Equity. The public was generally supportive, sometimes cheering the performers outside their theaters. "All the world's a stage; and all the men and women merely strikers," commented the *New York Tribune*.

SOMETIMES IT DID seem as if all the world's men and women were on strike as the Mayflower rolled westward, the rest of the train carrying its load of reporters, stenographers, Secret Service agents, and White House servants. More than 300,000 American workers were off the job in a variety of industries, in 20 different states. Upheavals continued to shake Europe, and the Bolsheviks were on their way to winning the Russian Civil War. Many executives feared that the Russian Revolution would spread to the United States. Big business heavily funded organizations with names like the National Security League and the American Defense Society, which produced millions of anti-Bolshevik pamphlets to be included in workers' pay envelopes. And unknown to the president, thousands of Wobblies in the Pacific Northwest, their stronghold, were preparing to confront Wilson when his train reached Seattle.

On his journey across the country, the president twisted the turmoil into an argument for the League of Nations. The world needed this organization, he said, to provide stability in an era filled with "the poison of disorder, the poison of revolt, the poison of chaos." It was a sinister world he evoked in his speeches, one in which that poison could get "in the veins of this free people," spreading "quietly upon steamships, silently under the cover of the postal service, with the tongue of the wireless and the tongue of the telegraph, all the suggestions of disorder are spread through the world." His claims for the league soared into an almost magical realm. It would be the "incomparable consummation of the hopes of mankind," he told one audience, and to another he called it an "enterprise of divine mercy and peace."

As upsetting as was the Boston police walkout, the strike that most shook the economy occurred in the country's largest heavy industry. By the end of September 1919, well over 300,000 steelworkers had stopped working. This was the largest strike the United States had yet seen, and it included both skilled and unskilled workers and immigrants from some four dozen countries.

Many had regularly been required to work 7-day weeks and 12-hour days, and sometimes even 24-hour shifts. The average workweek for steelworkers, a careful study showed, was 68.7 hours. And, of course, dealing with heavy machinery, big blocks of steel in motion, blast furnaces showering cinders and sparks, and molten metal is dangerous. Safety precautions were primitive and many workers were killed each year. Improving such conditions was one of the prime goals of Progressive Era reformers, but it now seemed to many in these mills that they had accomplished very little, for the average unskilled steelworker earned less than what the government's own calculations showed as the minimum necessary to support a family of five.

A prime target was the US Steel Corporation. A behemoth that produced roughly half the entire country's supply of the metal, it had earned a surplus the previous year of nearly half a billion dollars (a sum worth more than 17 times as much today) *after* paying 14 percent of its stock price in dividends. Its chief was Elbert H. Gary, known as Judge Gary, because he had been a county magistrate in his youth. A well-spoken, teetotaling, devout Methodist, he projected an image of rectitude and determination. But he hated unions and had long seen racial rivalry as a tool to break them, leading the industry in recruiting Black strikebreakers—more than 30,000 in all.

This was easy for management to do, because some steelworkers' union locals banned Black members. Sometimes, to protect them from angry white workers, Black strikebreakers were given cots to sleep on inside the steel mills. In Gary, Indiana—named after Judge Gary—they were brought in on ships carrying ore from Minnesota's iron mines, to evade the workers picketing the mills' front gates.

In that city's giant complex of steelworks, where 35,000 men were on strike, the conflict grew more intense when strikers tried to force their way into the US Steel plant, fighting a battle with state militia that left many casualties. Indiana's governor then called in federal troops. They would stay for months, housed in a local YMCA, at a businessman's club whose president was a US Steel official, and on US Steel property. Their commander, looking every inch ready for war with his stern, no-nonsense face, trim mustache, and well-tailored uniform, was General Leonard Wood.

As in Omaha just days earlier, Wood again had a God-given chance to show his toughness to potential voters and to his business backers, one of whom was Judge Gary. Taking over city hall for his command post and setting up machine guns on the city's streets, he promptly banned all public meetings and declared martial law. Eager to tie the strike to leftists, he ordered his soldiers to ransack the home of a union lawyer, raid the city's Socialist Party office, and arrest and interrogate 120 Gary radicals, setting up a barbed-wire stockade near city hall to hold them all. Inmates of this impromptu concentration camp the general put to work sweeping the city's streets.

One of several vigilante groups that turned out to help Wood was known as the Loyal Legion. A member of the organization described an attack by his "posse" on striking steelworkers: "Every one of us had a deputy's star in his pocket, a heavy gun under his left shoulder and a blackjack in his right hand. A bunch of these foreigners . . . met us this side of the tracks, and we went into them. . . . Our method of work was to grab a man's right arm with the operator's own left hand, then bring down the blackjack across the hand bones or wrist of the man thus caught. . . . We have a nice hospital in Gary. There were thirty-five people in there the next day with broken wrists and hands."

Wood lost no time in capitalizing on his crackdown, going to New York only a few days later to give a speech blaming unspecified foreigners and "Red agitators" for the strike. "At Gary the trouble was wholly the alien, unassimilated group among the strikers," he declared, referring to many "hundred pounds of Red literature in four or five South European languages" seized in his raids. Once again, he argued for mass deportations. "The great need is keeping this kind of cattle out of the country and getting those who are here out of it. . . . Every man of this type ought to be summarily deported." It was these agitators who were the problem; "the strikers themselves generally behaved particularly well, the Americans especially"—meaning those of Anglo-Saxon descent.

The day after his New York speech, Wood met with a group of Republican leaders in the Hudson Valley north of the city, then boarded a New York Central express train—hailed by a signal to make a special VIP stop for him—to return to the Midwestern battlefields. His still-undeclared presidential campaign looked promising.

The vast majority of steelworkers, however, cared not about revolution, but about the more mundane issues of hours and wages. Even J. Edgar Hoover knew this, privately referring to General Wood's warnings as "more fiction than truth." This did not stop newspapers—almost certainly with encouragement from Hoover—from running headlines like "Reds and I. W. W.'s Active in Strike, Worker Charges" (New York's *Evening World*) or "Reds Fomenting a Revolt among Strikers in U. S." (the *Topeka State Journal*). These were also the terms in which the Bureau of Investigation reported its findings to Congress.

In Pittsburgh, three-quarters of steel plants had come to a halt, and the companies rushed to surround their mills with rifle-carrying guards and to press sheriffs' departments to swear in thousands of new deputies. By one estimate, in the city and its vicinity 25,000 men were under arms—in some areas matching the number of striking workers. Bitter clashes here and elsewhere left a mounting number of deaths and injuries. Still posing as Wobbly activist Louis Walsh, Leo Wendell apparently got himself elected to the steelworkers' strike committee in the city, for he filed blow-by-blow accounts of its meetings. One noted happily of the strike organizers that "there is a great deal of dissention among them."

Impressed with Wendell's sleuthing, Hoover summoned him to Washington and "examined him at great length and had him remain over," according to Hoover's record of the conversation. It was apparently the first meeting between the two men; there would be more to come. "I believe there is no better confidential informant in the service," Hoover wrote the following year.

Wendell was far from the only clandestine agent watching the steel strikers. Private detectives hired by the companies were out in force. Labor unionists in Chicago intercepted a letter a Sherman Service executive sent on October 2, 1919, to one of the agency's men, "No. 300." It said:

> We want you to stir up as much bad feeling as you possibly can between the Serbians and the Italians. Spread data among the Serbians that the Italians are going back to work. Call up every question you can in reference to racial ha-

tred. . . . Urge them to go back to work or the Italians will
get their jobs.

Union-breakers always liked to make use of ethnic rivalries, and this
one was now especially easy to take advantage of, for Italy and Yugoslavia were squabbling over the port city of Fiume, and just a few weeks
earlier armed Italian nationalists had occupied it.

Other industries wracked by strikes this year included textile mills.
An outspoken, militant unionist in Massachusetts who said his name
was John Mach argued for a tough stance against the companies and
was elected financial secretary of a strike committee. He was actually a
detective. When his handlers ordered him to sow discord by announc-
ing that more than $100,000 in the union's relief fund had been stolen,
this was too much for him. Shame stricken, he came clean, revealing to
union activists his role and his real name. Bureau of Investigation records show that his exploits undercover include once leading an IWW
parade astride a white horse.

AS WILSON'S TRAIN continued westward, an extra locomotive was
coupled on to help pull it across the Rocky Mountains. Telegrams and
headlines at every stop made clear that the tumult roiling the country was growing worse. And several thousand IWW members from
throughout Washington and Oregon were now gathering in Seattle, to
be there when he arrived. The president approached the city from the
east, his train pausing for the night on a secluded railway siding so he
could get an undisturbed sleep. When he talked in Spokane the next
day, a newspaper found "a man very much fatigued in his delivery."

After his train finally pulled into Seattle, a motorcade carried him
to his hotel. There was no escaping the Wobblies, who were joined
by other trade unionists: men dressed in workers' blue denim, shirt-
sleeves rolled up, wearing suspenders. They had large white badges
tucked in their hatbands lettered, "Release Political Prisoners!" "The
men with badges for the most part remained silent," reported the *New
York Tribune*. "Block after block the sidewalks were packed." Another

newspaper recorded, "They stood in swarms along the curbings, some with arms folded defiantly, some looking sullenly at the president as he passed."

Wilson, unaccustomed to hostile demonstrations, "looked flabbergasted," remembered one Wobbly, a miner and dockworker named Jack Kipps. The president had been standing up in an open car, waving his hat, but "at the third block Wilson sat down beside his wife. . . . He seemed to be crumpling up. He put on his tall hat, a little to one side. . . . He didn't expect anything like this. He was white as a sheet."

The IWW members had signed a petition to the president and, surprisingly, he agreed to receive it from a Wobbly delegation at his Seattle hotel suite the next morning. At last he would come face-to-face with members of the union, hundreds of whose comrades his administration had sent to prison, and whose offices his Justice Department had pillaged. At the city's IWW headquarters, the Wobblies quickly assembled a delegation of Kipps and four other men, two of them war veterans, one of whom had been wounded. "Each one of us was supposed to make a little speech, and we rehearsed half the night."

When the five got to the hotel the next morning, Kipps recalled, a presidential aide "led us into a great big room. Right near the door was a tremendous basket of flowers. . . . Wilson stood by a long heavy table, his left hand holding the edge of the table top." Wearing a cutaway coat and striped pants, he "looked small. I had an idea he was taller. His face was long and his head seemed to be heavy on his neck. And he looked old—just *old*. . . . He shook hands with us. His hand felt dry and shaky in mine."

Somehow the double shock of actually getting in to see the president and then finding him a visibly sick man rendered the Wobblies, for all their militance, almost mute. The wounded veteran who was supposed to give the first short speech couldn't get the words out and finally "just handed Wilson the petition. Wilson took it. His hand shook pretty badly."

Kipps, by his account, was the only one who managed to say anything. The president replied but, Kipps remembered later, "I barely heard what he said. . . . Wilson looked pretty bad, but perhaps he was the least flustered man in the room." After a few minutes, he shook the men's hands again and aides ushered them out. The Wobblies were stunned and embarrassed at being so tongue-tied. "We couldn't talk about it for an hour or more," remembered Kipps. "We had been before the President of the United States—and what a mess he was! A pale old man standing in the middle of a big room, under a high ceiling, with a bowed head."

SEEING THE WOBBLIES and the constant drumbeat of headlines about strikes around the country made clear to Wilson that he had urgent worries beyond the peace treaty. He planned to turn to them—but only after finishing his cross-country tour. As his train arrived in California, large audiences awaited him: 10,000 outdoors in Berkeley and 12,000 in nearby Oakland. And he had to reach them all with his voice, in an age when to speak in public meant shouting. Only at a stadium in San Diego did he have the help of a new device his aides referred to as a "voice phone"—an early public address system. And everywhere, there were hundreds of people who wanted to shake his hand, or who called for him to come out and say a few words from the Mayflower's rear platform when the locomotive paused to take on coal and water. By this point, wrote Tumulty, "the fatigue of the trip began to write itself in the President's face."

As his train finally turned eastward, it passed a forest fire in the Sierra Nevada mountains. Through the Mayflower's windows the presidential party could see blazing trees, and the dense smoke worsened Wilson's asthma. After he spoke for an hour and a half to 15,000 people packing the Mormon Tabernacle in Salt Lake City, his wife noticed patches of sweat soaking through his coat.

In Pueblo, Colorado, signs of the country's turmoil awaited him: more than 6,000 workers had just walked off the job at a local steel mill. As he approached that city on September 25, Wilson was feeling so tired that he canceled a speech to some 10,000 people waiting at a fairground. Later in the day, walking to the speaker's platform in an auditorium, his Secret Service guard recalled, "there was a single step. He stumbled on it, and I caught him. I kept my hand on his arm, and almost lifted him up the steps to the platform."

Wilson's Pueblo speech was the most eloquent of all his addresses pleading for the league; none hearing him realized that it would be his last. Some combination of his great passion for his goal and his physical weakness seems to have stirred the crowd. "A great wave of emotion, such as I have never witnessed at a public meeting," remembered Tumulty, "swept through the whole amphitheater." As he spoke, said the *Boston Globe*, "men and women were seen to weep. The President's fervent prayer that America join the world in preventing another such war as the last touched the heart of his wife and she, too, was seen to wipe the tears from her eyes." Another newspaper reported a "workingman" without a necktie in the front row breaking down completely.

The speech in Pueblo was a bravura performance that has found its way into books on oratory. Yet it also revealed this man at his most contradictory: the inspirational idealist abroad, determined to end war forever—who can deny that it is better for nations to talk than fight?—and the nativist autocrat at home.

That first side of Wilson was there when he spoke of "mothers who lost their sons in France. . . . I consented to their sons being put in the most difficult parts of the battle line, where death was certain. . . . There seems to me to stand between us and the rejection or qualification of this treaty the serried ranks of those boys in khaki, not only those boys who came home, but those dear ghosts that still deploy upon the fields of France." This was the passage that produced tears among his listeners.

Yet Wilson also made it clear that the America he cared about, *his* America, was that of people like himself, with no foreign birthplace or foreign accent. "I want to say—I cannot say it too often—any man who carries a hyphen about with him carries a dagger that he is ready to plunge into the vitals of this Republic." It was almost a throwaway line, but implicitly it pointed to scapegoats—and was a nod of approval to the massive deportations that Palmer and Hoover were setting in motion. In modern parlance, it was a dog whistle.

As the Mayflower pulled away from Pueblo, the headache the president had suffered all day grew worse. Dr. Grayson ordered the train stopped so that he and the Wilsons could take a half hour's walk on a nearby highway. An elderly farmer, wrote Grayson, "asked to have the honor of shaking hands with the President, and after doing this presented him with a head of cabbage and some apples." Wilson got back on board, feeling much better as the train headed east, scheduled to make stops in Kansas, Oklahoma, Arkansas, Kentucky, and Tennessee. He was moved that crowds were collecting at every station en route. Even in tiny Rocky Ford, Colorado, some 5,000 people had gathered, and he came out to shake a few hands when the train stopped briefly.

The league seemed to be gaining support, for almost all the auditoriums where the president had spoken were filled to capacity, and an impressive 200,000 people had crowded into the streets of Los Angeles hoping for a glimpse of him. Wilson and his staff were so buoyed, according to Tumulty, that they planned, "upon the completion of the Western trip, to invade the enemy's country, Senator Lodge's own territory, the New England States, particularly Massachusetts. This was our plan . . . when about four o'clock in the morning of September 26, 1919"—the day after the Pueblo speech—"Doctor Grayson knocked at the door of my sleeping compartment and told me to dress quickly." The president was nauseated, his skin twitched, and he was barely able to speak. "His face was pale and wan. One side of it had fallen. . . . His left arm and leg refused to function. I then realized that the President's whole left side was paralyzed." For a time Wilson haltingly tried to argue his wife, Tumulty, and Grayson into merely suspending the speaking tour for a 24-hour rest, but finally he acknowledged, weeping, "I am not in condition to go on."

In a Tugboat Kitchen

A s wilson's train was making its circuit of the Far West, yet another strike had erupted on the other side of the country, this one in Pittsburgh. The large streetcar barn on the city's Craft Avenue was full of bedding and mattresses, sleeping quarters for strikebreakers brought in from Philadelphia and New York after Pittsburgh's drivers and ticket-takers walked off the job in a demand for higher wages. Cars that set off down the tracks from the barn carried armed guards. Protestors halted one streetcar by yanking its pole from the power line overhead and throwing bricks, stones, bottles, and horseshoes at the strikebreakers. Mounted police had to push through the crowd to rescue the out-of-town crew. At least four of the imported strikebreakers were injured, as well as three police officers, and several streetcars were wrecked.

In the thick of the fighting was Leo Wendell, thoroughly enjoying himself. In a three-page report to the Bureau of Investigation, he named the "prominent Reds of Pittsburgh" who had joined him in battle. He zestfully described how he had "assisted" a Wobbly companion in breaking into one car with a switch iron, the metal bar used to adjust track switches. The two of them "knocked the motorman and another strike breaker unconscious" while other leftists he named "were busily engaged breaking windows, beating strike breakers and finally in taking the oily waste from the journal boxes and setting it on fire, in an attempt to burn up the car."

The bureau had clearly asked Wendell to provoke violence that the public would then blame on radicals, especially the IWW. He could barely contain his pleasure. The second paragraph of his report begins, "The day was filled with excitement." Given his background as a private detective, he had most likely fought such battles before—on the side of strikebreakers. But for him the "excitement" seemed to be in the fighting itself.

Meanwhile, Attorney General Palmer was still fending off complaints that he had not yet found the perpetrators of the June bombings in eight cities, to one of which he had nearly fallen victim himself. But with the planned deportations, he and Hoover had bigger game in mind, which would distract the public from their failure to catch the bombers. Central to their plans was an organization called the Union of Russian Workers.

The *New York Times* published a story that had every sign of being planted by Hoover. Using information "from an official source in Washington," it quoted the fiery "constitution" of the Union of Russian Workers, filled with rhetoric about overthrowing "the parasitic rich." The group had no fewer than 500 organizers, the article claimed, infiltrated around the country. For Hoover and Palmer, the union was an ideal target for their strategy of mass deportations of leftists. The group was avowedly anarchist, many members were not naturalized, and the immigration laws now allowed the government to expel any noncitizens belonging to an anarchist organization. Other factors, as well, made the union a convenient target: its very name sounded foreign, and it lacked the network of influential friends and admirers of something like the NAACP or the Socialist Party.

The two men brushed aside, however, an inconvenient fact. Although the union's manifestos were radical, many of its members were not. Some who were illiterate could not even read its books and pamphlets. After the Bolshevik takeover in 1917, many of the union's anarchist founders had returned to Russia (where they soon discovered that the Soviets were as determined to stamp out anarchists as they were capitalists). The organization they left behind maintained a number of "People's Houses" in the cities of the Northeast. While these indeed stocked some political literature, they also offered adult education classes in English as well as in practical subjects like electricity, driving, and engine repair. Dozens of other immigrant groups had similar community centers.

Nonetheless, Palmer and Hoover were soon able to put their focus on the group to work. On top of the ongoing steel strike, the country's coal miners now walked off the job. Because it had tapped the telephones of the strikers' leadership, the Bureau of Investigation knew that the great majority of these miners were not anarchists or Bolsheviks, but men concerned with wages, hours, and dangerous and onerous working conditions, such as being required to push heavy rail carts of coal long distances underground by hand. Like so many others, these workers had lost ground to inflation, and at many rural mines there was nowhere to live but company housing and nowhere to buy food and clothing but the company store. To the delight of Palmer and Hoover, however, a small number of the striking coal miners were members of the Union of Russian Workers. In Hoover's words, these agitators were "leading astray the earnest laborers." Seizing Russian-born coal miners would both weaken the strike and provide a haul of candidates for deportation. Some 60 of them were soon arrested.

Someone else eager to take political advantage of the coal strike was General Wood, who rushed 800 soldiers with machine guns to West Virginia, the heart of coal country. The troops were to protect strikebreakers, or, as newspapers preferred to call them, "volunteer coal miners." Wood came to inspect his men, then traveled on to Virginia, Kansas, and other states as governors, the press, and coal industry moguls talked him up as a potential 1920 Republican presidential candidate. Although always claiming to be a simple military man above the political fray, he repeatedly voiced his plan for dealing with Reds: "S. O. S.—Ship or shoot!"

Not everyone in the Wilson administration, however, was con-

vinced that the United States was on the verge of revolution. Francis
Fisher Kane was a socially prominent Philadelphian who as a lawyer
had represented underdogs such as Ute Indians in Colorado fighting
a federal relocation plan. Attracted into government by Wilson's progressive promises, he had been US attorney for eastern Pennsylvania
since 1913. He now wrote to his boss, A. Mitchell Palmer, saying that
some of the most vocal left-wing agitators he saw were in fact private detectives "actively stirring up trouble" because "of course it is the
meat they feed on,—they know on which side their bread is buttered."
A similar report came in from a Bureau of Investigation official in Los
Angeles, who was convinced that four bombs that had just exploded in
the Southern California oil fields had been planted by "unscrupulous
detectives" who had "in view, possibly, employment by the companies
on whose property the bombs were found."

JUST OUTSIDE WICHITA, Kansas, an exhausted-looking Joe Tumulty
cryptically told the reporters aboard Woodrow Wilson's train that the
rest of the president's tour was canceled. They scrambled to invent ex-
planations. "In San Francisco, he expressed some annoyance, it is said,
upon hearing a loud orchestra piece in ragtime, giving evidence that his
nerves were affected," wrote the *New York Times* correspondent. "He
was unable to obtain sufficient exercise, and the result . . . was to send
the blood to his head at the expense of his stomach and other organs."
The train sped the Wilsons back to Washington, a lone locomotive
running ahead of it to be sure the track was clear.

On the very day the Mayflower crossed Missouri on this journey,
Emma Goldman was released from the women's penitentiary there. "I
had but one thing to regret," she wrote: "the friends I should have to
leave behind." She was happy to have finished her sentence, but apprehensive about what lay ahead. Palmer and Hoover had a list of people
they were eager to deport, and she knew she was on it. Hoover's venom
was even more intense than she could have known, for he had built up
a 70-page file of evidence against her.

On her way home, Goldman stopped in Chicago to see her former lover Ben Reitman, the man who had once been the "Great Grand Passion" of her life. She claimed to feel "serene" as she met his wife and child. Then it was on to Rochester, New York, to visit her 81-year-old mother and her sisters, one of whom was the mother of the boy whose death at the front in France Goldman had learned of in prison. The sister's "face was shrunken and ashy, unutterable despair in her hollow eyes. I held her close to me, her poor little body convulsed with sobs."

Finally Goldman arrived in New York, her home, where she "found destroyed what we had slowly built up through a long period of years." Albert Burleson had shut down the magazine she edited, and her long-time collaborator Alexander Berkman, also just released from prison, was waking up in cold sweats at night. He had spent more than seven months in solitary confinement, part of it in a two-and-a-half-foot by four-and-a-half-foot punishment cell, for protesting the killing of a Black convict shot in the back by a guard. "The large sums of money raised while we were in prison . . . had gone for appeals in cases of conscientious objectors, in the political-amnesty activities, and in other work," Goldman wrote. "We had nothing left, neither literature, money, nor even a home. The war tornado had swept the field clean."

Someone who did still have a home to return to was Woodrow Wilson. As his train neared Washington, Dr. Grayson ordered it slowed to 25 miles an hour, so the Mayflower would not rock from side to side and prevent his patient from sleeping. The window shades were drawn. As they watched the train slowly steam past, the crowds that lined the tracks remained silent. Daily headlines reported the story now doled out to the press by Tumulty: Wilson had wanted to give the remaining speeches on his schedule, but Dr. Grayson had forbidden it. Telegrams wishing the president well flowed in from as far away as Buckingham Palace.

Details released to the public remained scanty, but it was clear that the man who had just returned to the White House was seriously ill. Over tea, Edith Wilson told a group of journalists that the doctor had ordered "a complete rest" from official business. Beyond that, she revealed little.

On the morning of October 2, 1919, a week after his speech at Pueblo, Wilson woke up in pain, and his wife urgently ordered a car dispatched to fetch Dr. Grayson. But she took care not to make the call through the White House switchboard, for fear an operator might be listening in.

A few minutes later she found the president on the floor of his bathroom, unconscious.

IN NEW YORK, Emma Goldman was under close watch. The Bureau of Investigation was opening her mail, and an undercover agent briefly won the job of being her secretary. At a fund-raising dinner for her ($3 a plate, plus another $2.75 for beer), enjoying the food and drink were plainclothes spies from no less than three different agencies: the bureau, Military Intelligence, and the New York State Legislature's Lusk committee, whose operative reported of the guests, "the majority were Russian Jews and looked it." The threat of Goldman's deportation was on her supporters' minds. "With prohibition coming in and Emma Goldman going out," remarked one man at the banquet to Goldman's lawyer, "'twill be a dull country."

Even though J. Edgar Hoover had the proof of her lack of citizenship that he needed to deport Goldman, he remained so focused on her that he sent his star undercover man, Leo Wendell, from Pittsburgh to New York to see what else he could find out from his contacts among radicals there. Apparently still posing as a Pittsburgh Wobbly, Wendell attended a welcome-home party for Goldman organized by her niece. He reported that Goldman had "given up any considerable hope of being able to overcome the case of the government, but expects to be able to make a fight upon technicalities." He also claimed that she and Berkman were "very much dissatisfied with their attorney, Mr. Harry Weinberger, whom they think has taken all of their money and has not been able to produce any results." (Wendell may have been manufacturing news he thought would please Hoover, for in Goldman's autobiography, which does not stint on sharp judgments, she has nothing but praise for Weinberger.)

Goldman spoke at another gathering in New York, rallying supporters to lobby for Kate Richards O'Hare to be pardoned. Despite publicly scoffing at the government, she was quietly in despair at the prospect of being deported. She and Berkman made a whirlwind speaking tour to Chicago and Detroit with the foreboding "that it would be my last opportunity to raise my voice against the shame of my adopted land." In Chicago, journalists asked Berkman for a comment about the death of Henry Clay Frick, the antiunion steel executive whom he had unsuccessfully tried to assassinate 27 years earlier. Berkman's response was, "Deported by God."

IT WAS NOT God but Hoover who was engineering Berkman's and Goldman's troubles. At last, on October 27, 1919, Goldman, a figure known throughout the United States and Europe, came face-to-face with the still-obscure man less than half her age who was so determined to expel her from the United States. Along with several other officials and Goldman's lawyer, Weinberger, they met in a hearing room just to the side of the famous Great Hall of Ellis Island, the room through which millions of immigrants had entered the country.

"Miss Goldman, do you swear to tell the truth, the whole truth, and nothing but the truth, so help you God?" asked the presiding officer.

She answered only, "I affirm to tell the truth." Remembering this moment in her memoirs, she wrote, "I found the inquisitors sitting at a desk piled high with my dossier. . . . It was a farce I could not participate in, and I consequently refused to answer any questions."

Hoover had triumphed. He also enjoyed himself on this trip to New York in a way that he would never be able to do once his face became well known. With several other bureau officials, he blended in with the crowds at a left-wing rally at the Central Opera House, where, he noted, the 3,000 cheering participants were "mostly of foreign extraction." They also found a Harlem warehouse where some of Goldman's and Berkman's belongings were stored, and sifted through letters and scrapbooks. Hoover was delighted at the prospect of sending "these two notorious characters back to the colder climate of Russia."

Long-planned mass arrests by the Justice Department, centered on the Union of Russian Workers and gathering candidates for deportation, came only a few days after Goldman's hearing, on the night of November 7, 1919, the second anniversary of the Bolshevik coup in Russia. These arrests have gone down in history as the Palmer Raids, but they really should be called the Hoover Raids, because it was Palmer's determined deputy, quietly wielding an influence beyond his years, whose Radical Division had drawn up the lists and orchestrated the close coordination with local police departments.

Starting at 9:00 p.m. in each time zone, the raiders targeted offices and members of the Union of Russian Workers in more than a dozen cities in the Northeast and Midwest. Follow-up raids continued for several days. Altogether, 1,182 people were arrested, most without warrants. Raiders briefly detained, questioned, and sometimes roughed up a far-larger number, and then let them go.

In New York City, for instance, the union's "People's House" was surrounded by long black cars carrying agents led by the imposing Bureau of Investigation chief Big Bill Flynn himself, plus 30 city detectives under a sergeant of the bomb squad. That was clearly meant as a hint—although a totally misleading one—that the authorities were finally closing in on the June bombers.

Inside the building, union members were attending night-school classes in English, mathematics, and auto mechanics. The raiders roughly shoved them all downstairs, striking them with batons and blackjacks. When several women students objected, a detective shouted, "Shut up, there, you, if you know what's good for you." A man teaching algebra was amazed to see a raider enter his classroom brandishing a gun. The agent then "struck me on the head. . . . After I was beaten and without strength to stand on my feet, I was thrown down stairs and while I rolled down, other men . . . beat me with pieces of wood which I later found out were obtained by breaking the banisters."

After the raid the building looked "as if a bomb had exploded in each room," reported the New York *World*. "Desks were broken open, doors smashed, furniture overturned and broken, books and literature scattered, the glass doors of a cabinet broken, typewriters had apparently been thrown on the floor and stamped on," and there were "bloodstains over floor, papers, literature &c., and the washbowl was half full of bloody water." The *Times*, like most of the country's newspapers, editorially backed the arrests, but acknowledged that they had left many with "their heads wrapped in bandages." The raiders hit several dozen other left-wing and labor organizations around the city as well. Those among the arrested who were found deportable were marched through the streets of Lower Manhattan at dawn the next morning, with bandages and black eyes, to the ferry to Ellis Island.

Raids followed a similar pattern in other cities, where sometimes the authorities cast a wider net. In Detroit, agents interrogated all 1,500 theatergoers watching a Russian-language play. In Pennsylvania, 20 of the men arrested had been identified by company detectives as active in the steel strike. In Hartford, a man who came to a federal building to find out the fate of an arrested friend was surrounded by six interrogators whose chief "brought a rope and tied it around my neck, stating that he will hang me immediately if I do not tell him who conducts the meetings and who are the main workers in an organization called the Union of Russian Workers." Judges usually set bail at $10,000, a sum certain to keep anyone behind bars. Hoover was surely pleased when, after the raids, one informer reported that "these people appear to be afraid of everything now."

He clearly anticipated that many of those seized, like the men taking classes in New York, might not even be aware that the Union of Russian Workers was officially an anarchist organization. A telegram to his agents told them to make EVERY EFFORT TO OBTAIN FROM SUBJECTS STATEMENTS THAT THEY ARE MEMBERS OF ORGANIZATION AND BELIEVE IN ITS ANARCHISTIC TENDENCIES. THIS IS OF UTMOST IMPORTANCE.

Hoover invited along on the raids cameramen for the newsreels now popular in movie houses, calculating that the footage they captured, of officers wielding billy clubs and shoving around arrested leftists, would send the right message. A Justice Department press release declared that the Union of Russian Workers was "even more radical than the Bolsheviki" and that agents had found "red flags, guns, revolvers," and counterfeiting equipment on its premises. Many major papers dutifully repeated the claim. Some, prodded by Hoover or people working for him, went much further. The *New York Herald*, for instance, reported that the raids forestalled "a nationwide uprising" preparing "to spread a reign of terror." The *New York Times* spoke of "proof that Lenin himself had dictated the Bolshevist operations in this city."

A few weeks later, under a banner headline, the *New York Tribune* reported that in the Union of Russian Workers office "detectives and agents of the Department of Justice discovered a secret chamber in which were concealed explosives, chemicals and death-dealing devices." Oddly, raiders had not noticed this when they ransacked the building from top to bottom several weeks earlier. The news again left the impression that maybe this sinister-sounding organization was indeed responsible for the still-unsolved bombings of six months earlier. Although other newspapers took up the cry, curiously little came of the alleged discovery of the "death-dealing devices." No court ever convicted any group connected to the Union of Russian Workers of violence of any sort.

J. Edgar Hoover adroitly let his boss win credit for the raids, knowing that his own fortunes could rise still further if Palmer won higher office. "Mr. Wilson's political leadership is even now passing on to Attorney General A. Mitchell Palmer," wrote a *Washington Herald* columnist, "who is industriously reshaping Democratic policy." The *Providence Journal*, canvassing Democratic politicians about the upcoming 1920 presidential race, discovered that a "considerable number are known personally to favor Mr. Palmer." The month after the raids, Palmer set up his first campaign offices in three key states.

AFTER HIS WIFE had discovered him unconscious, an array of physicians who clustered at President Wilson's bedside found that he had suffered an ischemic stroke, a blood clot in the brain. His left arm and leg were paralyzed, his left eye's vision impaired, and part of the left side of his face was drooping. This was a much more severe version of the smaller strokes he had apparently experienced earlier in the year.

Over the following months the crucial decision-making troika of Edith Wilson, Dr. Grayson, and Joe Tumulty concealed the president's condition. None of the three publicly mentioned the words "stroke" or "paralyzed." No, he was merely suffering from "nervous exhaustion" and intestinal troubles, and needed rest. Sometimes they referred to "fatigue neurosis." Grayson claimed that Wilson was eager to work and had asked him to summon a stenographer but that he refused to do so—because it was a Sunday.

They insisted that the president's mind and speech were clear. Evidence on this is mixed. Within days of the stroke, Grayson claimed later, Wilson regained his sense of humor and recited one of the limericks he was fond of, although only in a whisper. Chief White House usher Ike Hoover, however, who was in and out of the presidential quarters frequently, later wrote that "he appeared just as helpless as one could possibly be and live. . . . There was never a moment during all that time when he was more than a shadow of his former self. He had changed from a giant to a pygmy."

Outside the White House where the stricken president lay, the country continued to boil, with strikes in critical industries, the worst racial violence in half a century, and ongoing combat in the war between the Right and Left. A stark reminder of the latter came some weeks after the president fell ill, when a furious gun battle broke out on the streets of Centralia, Washington, as local Wobblies found their meeting hall under attack from members of the American Legion. Many people were injured, the IWW hall wrecked and its contents burned, and six men were killed: four legionnaires, a deputy sheriff shot by accident by a member of his own posse, and a Wobbly who was seized from jail by a vigilante mob and thrown off a bridge with a noose around his neck. By some accounts, he was first castrated. Members of the mob stomped on his hands when he desperately tried to seize the edge of the bridge to save himself. No one was ever tried for the lynching, but seven Wobblies who had defended their hall were convicted of murder and would spend many years in prison, one dying there.

Domestic warfare like this had never particularly bothered Wilson, and there is no evidence anyone even told him about this episode. Even in his diminished state, however, he still cared passionately about the League of Nations. This hope, to his dismay, received a severe blow in mid-November when the Senate refused to ratify the peace treaty. There was still some hope that an amended version might pass if it could be negotiated, but the defeat was a painful setback for an already weakened man.

To add to his worries, the stock market crashed the same month, beginning a long downward slide that would see the Dow Jones Industrial Average lose nearly half its value over the next year and a half. The president was largely confined to his bedroom, his once clear and flowing handwriting now a mere scribble. Those around him faced the question: How should the country be governed? For at the time of his stroke Wilson still had 17 months of his term left to serve.

Even though everyone felt Vice President Thomas Marshall was a lightweight, Edith Wilson suggested that her husband resign and Marshall take over, as the Constitution prescribes. This proposal was rejected, she implausibly claimed, by one of the consulting physicians, the neurologist Francis X. Dercum. According to her, he said, "For Mr. Wilson to resign would have a bad effect on the country, and a serious effect on our patient." If he were to step down, "the greatest incentive to recovery is gone. . . . He has the utmost confidence in you." What, then, should she do? "Madam," Dr. Dercum supposedly declared, "it is a grave situation, but I think you can solve it. Have everything come to you; weigh the importance of each matter, and see if it is possible by consultation with the respective heads of the Departments to solve them without the guidance of your husband."

Can it really be that this doctor's suggestion determined how the country was to be run for months to come? Conveniently, Dercum was never able to dispute Edith Wilson's account, because by the time she published her memoir he was dead.

Wherever the idea came from, most likely from her, this is essentially what happened. It was she who decided, with the help of Tumulty and Grayson, which documents were brought to her husband's bedside and which visitors he could occasionally receive. These three insiders, each of whom had shown the absolute devotion to Woodrow Wilson that he so craved, would form an iron ring around him. Could he fully understand the papers they showed him? Not if we are to believe Ike Hoover, who declared that the president "was physically almost incapacitated; he could articulate but indistinctly and think but feebly." When the secretary of state also asked whether the vice president should take over, Tumulty furiously rebuffed him. Dr. Grayson assured him that the president's mind was "clear and acute."

Wilson's doctors would not speak to the press except in vague, upbeat terms, and the cabinet remained as much in the dark as everyone else. The president read no newspapers, and it would be six weeks before he was even shaved. No photographers, of course, were allowed anywhere near him. For a full month, Wilson saw no one except those in his inner circle. He had trouble even remaining upright in a wheelchair.

Finally, a month after the stroke, the ruling trio allowed him to have his first meeting with a cabinet officer, Attorney General Palmer, to discuss the coal strike, which was threatening the supply of the country's most essential fuel. It lasted only 20 minutes. Wilson lay in bed, still unshaven and looking very pale. Dr. Grayson was in the room the whole time. Did Palmer say anything about the massive raids to round up people to be deported? Did he mention the subject at a second meeting they had a short time later? We do not know. The president's State of the Union message sent to Congress several weeks after the first Palmer Raid—drafted by Tumulty, edited by Edith Wilson, and presumably at least read aloud to the ailing president for his approval— attacked radical "enemies of this country" who deserve "no leniency."

THE CONSTITUTION'S 22ND Amendment, limiting the president to two terms, was still decades away, so theoretically Wilson could again run for the White House in 1920, which he had hinted that he would like to do. But that now seemed inconceivable. Among the most prominent of those eyeing the office were the Democrat Palmer and the Republican Wood. Both were preparing to campaign on the promise of mass deportations.

Since his well-publicized November 7 raids, Palmer would have the advantage of being the man who actually set the expulsions in motion. But he and Wood were not alone in trying to ride a wave of nativism to the White House. Also thundering away about expelling aliens were two more men with their eyes on the Republican nomination.

One was President Nicholas Murray Butler of Columbia University, who declared, "Today, we hear the hiss of a snake in the grass and the hiss is directed at the things Americans hold most dear." He called for deporting "Reds" to the Philippines, the most distant US colony. More worrisome to Palmer was Senator Miles Poindexter of Washington State, who, months earlier, had called on the government "to deport every alien Bolshevist and to punish rather than protect those who practice their savage creed in this country." Poindexter now suggested that Palmer was failing to deport these savages: "The government had positively refused in many cases to allow them to go."

More such statements, resolutions, and petitions came from patriotic and business groups. Despite the sweeping arrests, in Chicago, the politically ambitious Cook County prosecutor attacked Palmer for his "petty, pusillanimous, and pussyfoot policy." The attorney general urgently wanted to show that he was using a firm hand against the Red hordes, and began planning a new and larger round of raids.

Although not running for president, someone delighted by all the talk about deportation was Congressman Albert Johnson. He was riding high: battling immigrants had been his prime cause for years, but now at last he could act on it, having just become chair of the House Committee on Immigration and Naturalization, an ideal pulpit. Offering no evidence but pandering to an enduring streak of American paranoia, he claimed wildly that "aliens were being smuggled across the Mexican border at the rate of 100 a day, a large part of them being Russian Reds who had reached Mexico in Japanese vessels."

To dramatize the threat the country faced, Johnson took members of his committee to hold hearings on Ellis Island. He put on a further bit of political theater for journalists by letting some detained anarchists awaiting deportation there hurl threats and insults at him through the bars of a large holding cell.

The always-garrulous congressman also told the reporters following him on this trip that he was outraged that wily radicals had outsmarted the Wilson administration. One group of Wobblies, for example, had been arrested in Seattle and sent in custody on a special train to New York. From there, they were to be expelled to Europe, but they foiled the plan. As Johnson explained, "It appears that some of the I. W. W.'s in that crowd took advantage of the Government to get a free trip to New York by declaring themselves aliens at Seattle, and then proving they were citizens on their arrival here."

Meanwhile, Emma Goldman's attempts to fight her deportation order failed, and in early December she found herself in detention on Ellis Island, sharing a room in the Baggage and Dormitory Building with two women arrested in the raid on the Union of Russian Workers. She quickly smuggled out to friends information about their miserable living conditions. The others awaiting deportation "were not permitted to mingle with us, but we managed to get from them notes that strained all our linguistic acquirements, almost every European language being represented." A photograph of the 50-year-old Goldman taken at this point shows her looking sober and wan, her usual pince-nez replaced by a pair of rimless spectacles, her face and neck a little puffy from nearly two years of prison food. She knew that it would be only a matter of days before she was expelled from the country that had been her home since the age of 16.

THESE FINAL MONTHS of 1919 seemed like the darkest period of repression that the nation had seen—at least so far. Mob behavior ruled. In Madison, South Dakota, a crowd of several hundred surrounded the family home of 30-year-old Ingmar Iverson, state chair of the Socialist Party and a conscientious objector just released from an army prison. When he failed to appear, members of the mob chopped their way through his roof with axes, tied his hands and feet, and prepared to paint him yellow. Police rescued him just in time, but the mob dispersed only when Iverson promised to leave town.

One peculiar incident even targeted a former member of Congress. Ernest Lundeen was a Republican who had represented Minnesota for one term in the House. But because he had voted against going to war in 1917, his party did not forgive or renominate him. On November 17, 1919, he was scheduled to give a speech at the opera house in Ortonville, Minnesota. But he got no further than "Ladies and Gentlemen" before the county sheriff and a group of American Legionnaires rushed on stage, grabbed him, and force-marched him out of the hall and onto a Chicago, Milwaukee and St. Paul Railway freight train that was slowly pulling out of town. The legion men shoved him into a refrigerator car and latched the door shut. During the train's journey, crew members heard his cries for help, rescued him, and invited the furious Lundeen into the caboose.

For him captivity was brief, but not so for others. Hundreds of Wobblies remained in jail. Hundreds more people, like Kate Richards O'Hare, were also behind bars, or, like Dr. Marie Equi, soon would be because they had objected to a war that had ended a full year earlier. Many conscientious objectors to that war were still suffering the particular cruelty of military prisons. Hundreds of people were awaiting deportation solely because most had been members of the Union of Russian Workers.

Even those who simply argued for such prisoners of conscience were sometimes themselves punished. In November 1919, three men in Syracuse, New York, published a leaflet with four drawings of prisoners being suspended by their wrists, beaten, chained up, or otherwise abused. "Mr. President," the leaflet said, "let our people go. . . . The war is over." When the three then tried to hold a public meeting, they were arrested, convicted under the Espionage Act, and sentenced to 18 months.

Albert Burleson continued to enthusiastically censor the nation's press, while back in March, in the *Schenck* decision, the Supreme Court had upheld—unanimously—the Espionage and Sedition Acts, the legal foundations for the national crackdown on dissent. And if that wasn't enough, so eager were politicians to show their toughness that they would introduce some 70 different additional sedition bills in Congress in late 1919 and early 1920.

In November 1919, however, something happened that didn't immediately change any of this, but offered a flicker of hope. A man was large enough to change his mind. It was Oliver Wendell Holmes Jr., the justice who had written that unanimous Supreme Court decision upholding the two acts. He didn't *say* he had changed his mind, but he showed it.

A new case, *Abrams v. United States*, had now come before the court. Jacob Abrams and several other young Russian Jewish immigrants had printed leaflets in English and Yiddish, which they had distributed at meetings—and scattered out the window of a Manhattan garment factory where a young woman in the group worked. The leaflets denounced President Wilson's sending troops to support the anti-Bolshevik forces in the Russian Civil War. The group was arrested and charged under the Espionage and Sedition Acts. From prison, Emma Goldman had written to her lawyer, Harry Weinberger, asking him to take on the case. He did, and argued eloquently for his clients. One died during the trial, his heart condition aggravated by pneumonia and a severe beating at the hands of New York police. The others received prison terms ranging up to 20 years.

When their appeal reached the Supreme Court, the majority of justices wanted to uphold the verdict. But Holmes, following some reading and discussions with legal colleagues over the summer, had been rethinking his position on free speech. He declared that he planned to dissent. Almost all his colleagues were shocked, for he was in no way sympathetic to the young radicals in the case. Three fellow justices were so dismayed that, most unusually, they came to his home to lobby him. According to Holmes's law clerk, who listened through an open door from the next room, the three reminded him of his service as a

Union infantry officer wounded in the Civil War (his sword still hung on the wall of the study where they were talking), and told him that "he should, like the old soldier he had once been, close ranks." In perilous times like these, they urged, the court should stick together, as it had in March, when Holmes had written for all of them. Politely defying them, the 78-year-old justice wrote his dissenting opinion, which Justice Louis Brandeis signed as well.

Supreme Court dissents, of course, do not make law in the way that majority opinions do. It would take several decades before the influence of this one was felt. But part of Holmes's dissent still echoes clearly, more than a century after he wrote it:

> When men have realized that time has upset many fighting faiths, they may come to believe . . . that the ultimate good desired is better reached by free trade in ideas—that the best test of truth is the power of the thought to get itself accepted in the competition of the market. . . . We should be eternally vigilant against the attempts to check the expression of opinions that we loathe.

Although little noticed by the public at the time, this passage would later become, in the words of a Holmes biographer, one of the "most-quoted justifications for freedom of expression in the English-speaking world." The dissent by Holmes and Brandeis was small comfort to the defendants in the case, one of whom was already awaiting deportation on Ellis Island, while another would soon join O'Hare in the women's penitentiary in Missouri. But to those who cared about civil liberties in America, Holmes's words were proof that the darkness was not total.

EMMA GOLDMAN AND Alexander Berkman, coal strikers from Appalachia, and people arrested in the New York classrooms of the Union of Russian Workers were joined at Ellis Island by prisoners who arrived from other parts of the country in shackles. There were 249 of them in all, who were to be deported to Russia on the *Buford*, an elderly, decrepit troopship, painted navy gray and known to its sailors as a heavy "roller" in rough seas. J. Edgar Hoover had borrowed it from the military. Around 2:00 a.m. on December 21, 1919, Goldman heard footsteps in the corridor. "There came the rattling of keys; the door was unlocked and noisily thrown open. Two guards and a matron entered. 'Get up now,' they commanded, 'get your things ready!'"

Dragging their belongings and an occasional musical instrument, she and the other deportees were herded into Ellis Island's Great Hall. "I felt tired and cold. No chairs or benches were about, and we stood shivering in the barn-like place." One man was on crutches; another, severely ill, had to be carried. "Some were still half-asleep, unable to realize what was happening." Berkman, who wore a sombrero in honor of the Mexican Revolution, led the group in singing the leftist anthem, "The Internationale," but could muster little enthusiasm from the others.

"It was noisy and the room was full of smoke," wrote another deportee, Ivan Novikov, in a letter intercepted and copied by the Bureau of Investigation. "Many with tears in their eyes were writing telegrams and letters. The officials promised to forward them. Whether they kept their promise—I do not know." Many were "in the clothes they had on at the time of the arrest. . . . There was no laughter." Then, as now, deportations severed families: "One left a mother, the other a wife and son, one a sweetheart." Novikov himself, a 37-year-old linotype operator who had arrived in the United States 10 years earlier, was leaving behind a wife and young son, who hoped to follow him to Russia later.

Journalists were told that the *Buford*'s departure would be only the beginning. "Another shipload is going out, perhaps this week," said the *New York Times*, as part of "a drive to cut down the Department of Justice's list of 60,000 radicals in the nation." To forestall any last-minute demonstrations by sympathizers at dockside, the ship, with 200 soldiers already on board as guards, had quietly slipped away from its wharf in Brooklyn, pushed through floating ice in the harbor and anchored near where the Verrazzano-Narrows Bridge is today. At 4:00 a.m., with the temperature in the twenties, shouting guards on Ellis Island ordered the captives outside and onto a path that led to the gangplank of a barge, attached to a tugboat, that was to take them across the harbor to the *Buford*.

"Deep snow lay on the ground," remembered Goldman. "The air was cut by a biting wind. A row of armed civilians and soldiers stood along the road. . . . One by one the deportees marched, flanked on each side by the uniformed men, curses and threats accompanying the thud of their feet on the frozen ground."

The Justice Department was so eager to make a public spectacle of ridding the country of this shipload of subversives that, besides mobilizing the press, it invited a delegation from Washington to witness the mass expulsion. Despite the hour, they joined the deportees on the tugboat, crossing the same harbor where Goldman had arrived as a teenager. The officials on hand included no fewer than five members of Congress. "Among those who had parting conversation with Miss Goldman was Representative Albert Johnson of Washington," wrote a reporter, "who did more listening than talking, however." The journalist, unfortunately, recorded no more about whatever piece of her mind Goldman unleashed on Johnson.

Shepherding the party of dignitaries on board the tugboat was the respectful, quiet, dark-haired 24-year-old with the unprepossessing round face who would soon wield far more power than any of them, J. Edgar Hoover.

The women deportees were separated from the others, and guards led them into the tugboat's galley. "A large fire roared in the iron stove," remembered Goldman, "filling the air with heat and fumes. We felt suffocating. There was no air nor water. Then came a violent lurch; we were on our way. . . . On the deck above us I could hear the men tramping up and down in the wintry blast. . . . Through the port-hole I could see the great city receding into the distance. . . . my beloved city."

There, in a tugboat kitchen, one of the greatest of American radicals and the man who would spend half a century hunting down such dissidents crossed paths one last time. We know what they said to each other because one of the congressmen was also present and later described the encounter to his colleagues in the House of Representatives. Goldman and Hoover were of similar stature, on the short side. She, a little heavier, would have stood nearly eye to eye as she looked at him through those rimless glasses of hers, with her defiantly outthrust chin. Personally, as well as politically, they could not have been more different: Goldman, the flamboyant prophet of sexual liberation, was a writer of earthy love letters, capable of great heights and depths of emotion. Whatever sexuality Hoover had was tightly closeted; he lived with his mother until her death when he was 43.

Goldman was wearing a black suit, under a long gray-and-black sealskin coat, which she probably had taken off in the stuffy galley. An admirer once described her as having "a face of fierce strength like a female pugilist." With her deportation, Hoover had won this particular match, but she did get in one last jab.

As the tug steamed through the harbor in the predawn darkness, Hoover asked, in the slightly rasping tone that would become familiar to millions of Americans over radio and television in the next five decades, "Haven't I given you a square deal, Miss Goldman?"

"Oh, I suppose you've given me as square a deal as you could," she replied, as she was ejected from the country where she had lived for 34 of her 50 years and found the voice that had won her admirers around the world. "We shouldn't expect from any person something beyond his capacity."

Men Like These Would Rule You

T HE DEPARTURE OF the *Buford* was, in the minds of Hoover and Palmer, just the beginning. Ten days later, on January 2, 1920, a second and larger set of night raids hit more than 30 American towns and cities to seize more candidates for deportation. Again, Hoover orchestrated everything, his office remaining open all night to take calls from agents reporting on the arrests. As they rounded up their targets, local police and vigilantes joined them. In Buffalo, for instance, a "citizens' committee" provided cars and drivers to help the raiders seize 250 people.

Hoover and Palmer cast a wide net. Raiders arrested 141 people attending a socialist meeting in Nashua, New Hampshire. In nearby Manchester, it was everyone dancing at the Tolstoi Club; in Lynn, Massachusetts, 39 Jewish bakers meeting to discuss forming a cooperative; in New Jersey, a group of Polish Americans raising money for a funeral; in Philadelphia, the members of the Lithuanian Socialist Chorus in midrehearsal. In Detroit, raiders entered a restaurant popular with socialists, arresting dancers, musicians, waiters, cooks, and everyone eating dinner.

More than 500 of those arrested in New York were jammed into quarters at Ellis Island, which ran out of cots and bedding. Several would die of pneumonia there. In Detroit, some 800 men and women were held, some for six days, in the narrow, windowless corridor of a post office building, with only a bare floor to sleep on and one toilet and one drinking fountain. Left without food for 20 hours, they could then eat only what families and friends brought them.

In Chicago, more than 100 arrested men appeared in court with bruises, black eyes, and cut lips after being attacked in the Cook County Jail by a group of prisoners led by a well-known thief. Guards waited until a number of "Reds" were knocked unconscious before stopping the beatings. In Boston, 140 prisoners in chains and leg irons were marched through the city's streets on their way to an unheated prison on an island in the harbor. A despairing inmate died by suicide there, jumping from a high window.

Palmer used the Justice Department publicity office like an arm of his undeclared presidential campaign. It issued press releases with headlines like "Warns Nation of Red Peril" and mug shots of prisoners—often showing the effects of their not being allowed to bathe or shave for days. The photos were tagged with numbers and captioned "Men Like These Would Rule You." Six days after the January raids, which cemented his position as the cabinet member most in the public eye, the attorney general drew more cheers than any other speaker at the annual Jackson Day dinner in Washington, an event often called the Democratic presidential candidates' debutante ball. Palmer's prospects were clearly on the rise.

There was little public criticism of the arrests, but one brave voice came from inside Palmer's own Justice Department. It was that of Francis Fisher Kane, the US attorney in Philadelphia, the man who some months earlier had told the attorney general he suspected private detectives were acting as agents provocateurs to create business for themselves. He had tried and failed to talk Palmer out of the plan for the massive January raids.

Ten days after they happened, Kane resigned his post. "By such wholesale raids the department is in danger of being made one of Injustice," he wrote Palmer, releasing his letter to the press. "It is one thing to debar an alien coming into this country . . . but it is quite another thing to deprive a man who has been in this country a long time, and who perhaps has a wife and children here, of what we are accustomed to think of as constitutional rights, irrespective of a man's citizenship." Instead, he said, the Justice Department should go after more important targets, such as "munition manufacturers and many other persons made rich by the war" who "are seeking to dodge the payment of their taxes."

Even beyond the mass arrests, progressive forces were having a rough time. The steel strike, the biggest of the torrent that had broken out in 1919, ended in January 1920 in humiliating defeat. The strikers had lost more than $100 million in wages; seen at least 18 workers killed in battles with police, militia, and soldiers; and won none of their goals. Few other strikes brought major improvements in working conditions or wages. The Red Scare showed no signs of abating. In Hammond, Indiana, a man went on trial for having shot dead a leftist who had said, "To hell with the United States." A jury took two minutes to find him not guilty.

The raids continued over the coming weeks, with Hoover personally leading one in Paterson, New Jersey, backed up by volunteers from the American Legion. He ordered some of those arrested taken directly to Ellis Island to await deportation. Included in the raiding party were half a dozen journalists, who rewarded Hoover with the kind of stories he liked. Adding to the excitement, the streets of Paterson were covered with snow, and, one newspaper reported, the raiders raced to at least one target in "a large bobsled drawn by two fast steeds."

There are no complete records of how many people were seized and interrogated in the raids of November 1919, January 1920, and the smaller roundups that followed, but several estimates place the total at about 10,000. Presumably excluding slavery, the historian Alan Brinkley calls the Palmer Raids "arguably the greatest single violation of civil liberties in American history." And Palmer promised that deportations by the tens of thousands would follow.

Those supporting the Bolsheviks in Russia had by now begun calling themselves Communists and—although the government net caught thousands of others as well—a major target of the latest wave of mass arrests were people who belonged to America's two Communist parties. The parties were squabbling with each other, and their combined membership may have numbered no more than 40,000, a minute percentage of the country's population. These members, however, were 90 percent immigrant, almost all from Russia or eastern Europe, which made them attractive deportation targets for Palmer and Hoover.

Others sounded the same themes about dangers facing the country. William J. Burns of the Burns Detective Agency, which of course had money to make off the Red menace, claimed there were 422,000 Communists in America. The chief of the business-backed National Security League set the number even higher: 600,000. Meanwhile, in the House of Representatives, Albert Johnson was promoting a bill that combined two of his lifelong passions: it would require any Wobbly who was a noncitizen to be deported.

That reliable barometer of Justice Department thinking, Leo Wendell, also signaled the rising importance of the Communists as a target. He joined the Pittsburgh branch of one of the parties and sowed discord and confusion, he reported happily, by telling a party meeting that it "was only a rendezvous for temperamental, hysterical radicals" and that members should leave and join the IWW instead. He then urged both Wobblies and Communists to wrest a local left-wing meeting hall out of the control of the "reactionary" Socialists. Soon afterward, perhaps to allay any suspicions that he was an agent provocateur, the authorities arrested him once more—supposedly for helping foment a strike of railway workers. To the pleasure of his handlers, no doubt, the seizure of this "well known I. W. W. agitator" again made the front pages of Pittsburgh's newspapers.

From agents like Wendell, from mailing lists and files confiscated in raids, and from information shared by private detectives and state government Red-hunters, J. Edgar Hoover was amassing a growing collection of information on those he considered subversive. Using the system that had intrigued him when he worked at the Library of Congress, his staff had recorded data on nearly 150,000 file cards; by two years later the total would be 450,000. He ordered up separate three-by-five-inch cards for individuals (who included elected officials he thought suspicious, such as Senator Robert La Follette); organizations; publications; places; and events, like demonstrations or meetings, with notes of who had taken part. Each card had on it the numbers of all bureau files mentioning its subject, and Hoover claimed that the system allowed all key information on a suspicious person or group to be gathered in two minutes. For decades to come, he would see such suspects everywhere.

ON JANUARY 7, 1920, five days after the latest round of Palmer Raids began, the New York State Assembly, the lower house of the state legislature, convened in Albany for a new session in its grand, pillared chamber, lit by daylight streaming in from high clerestory windows. For two hours it conducted routine business, electing a speaker and other officers. Then the five Socialist Party members of the assembly, all from New York City, were startled when the voice of the sergeant at arms rang out, summoning them to come forward. Four of the five were veterans of previous sessions, and none were tainted by scandal. However, the assembly's speaker, an ambitious conservative who hoped to run for governor, looked down at them and declared, "You have been elected on a platform which is absolutely inimical to the best interests of the State of New York and the United States."

Despite the astonished protests of the five, in short order the rest of the assembly, Republicans and Democrats alike—only two brave Democrats dissented—voted to declare the five seats vacant. When the five refused to leave the chamber, the sergeant at arms escorted them out, one by one. Socialist Louis Waldman was a garment union activist who had immigrated to the United States from Ukraine with, as he said, "the sounds of the pogroms" in his ears. As he was force-marched out of the chamber, he heard one of those who had voted to expel him say, "Sorry, Waldman, we just couldn't help it."

In angry speeches, press conferences, and prolonged hearings before the assembly's Judiciary Committee, the Socialists challenged their expulsion, but in vain. Exactly the same thing had already happened at the national level. Socialist Victor Berger of Wisconsin, who had once served in Congress some years previously, had been elected again to the House of Representatives in 1918. The House refused to let him take his seat, declaring it vacant. Wisconsin then held a special election to fill the seat, electing Berger again. On January 10, 1920, three days after the New York State Legislature ejected the Socialists, the House again expelled him.

That Berger was among his party's moderates, highly critical of what he saw as an emerging dictatorship in Soviet Russia, made no difference. The would-be congressman had other troubles as well: for newspaper editorials he had written, Judge Kenesaw Mountain Landis had recently sentenced him to prison under the Espionage Act. (His conviction would later be reversed on appeal.) "It was my great disappointment to give Berger only 20 years," Landis told an American Legion convention. "I believe the law should have enabled me to have him lined up against the wall and shot."

On such events, the man who had spoken of fighting a war to make the world safe for democracy had no comment. Indeed, Woodrow Wilson had no public comment on much of anything. He saw only a few visitors, and ventured no farther than the South Lawn of the White House in his wheelchair, letting Tumulty and others around him draft most of the statements issued in his name, although he sometimes dictated corrections. Only more than two months after his stroke had he recovered enough to take a few steps. Tumulty, Edith Wilson, and Dr. Grayson continued to filter all news reaching him.

HOW FULLY ABREAST the president was of Palmer's plan to arrest and deport tens of thousands of people, we do not know. But someone whose pedigreed heart was surely warmed by it was New York's aristocratic anti-immigrant crusader John B. Trevor. However, the cause Trevor cared about most was restricting people from coming into the country in the first place. Before long he realized that his most crucial ally in that fight would be the like-minded Albert Johnson, whose

House Committee on Immigration and Naturalization included other anti-immigration hawks as well.

They made an odd pair. Trevor was at home in places like New York's Harvard Club, with its dark wood paneling, oil portraits of dignitaries, and mounted heads of big game shot by the likes of Theodore Roosevelt. His five-story home on the Upper East Side was across the street from the even grander mansion of Andrew Carnegie. Johnson, by contrast, had grown up in Kansas, never went to college, and had first made his way in the world as a newspaperman, mostly in Washington State, enthusiastically joining the local "citizens' committee" that fought street battles with Wobblies.

Uncouth as Johnson might have seemed to the New York socialite, however, Trevor understood that he could be a crucial political ally, and so began spending considerable time with him. Trevor showed the congressman his color-coded ethnic map of New York, which, he claimed, Johnson declared "the most important piece of evidence we have ever had" about dangerous immigrants. As Daniel Okrent remarks in his history of the anti-immigration movement, "Trevor's xenophobia was ecumenical." He would tell Johnson that the prospect of more Polish Jews arriving in the United States gave him "convulsive shivers." He felt the same way about immigration by "Mexicans and Brazilians, who by the way, are rotten with various diseases." Trevor disapproved of Johnson's heavy drinking; he noticed that the congressman kept a bottle of whisky hidden on a bookshelf behind a multivolume compilation of immigration statistics. But for Trevor that was a minor issue.

Despite their differences in background, their relationship only grew closer, and Johnson began asking Trevor to join him at informal gatherings of members of his House committee—meetings that did not include two Jewish members. Johnson, still the small-town rube in his way, was awed that Trevor never balked at the expense of telephoning him long-distance. On at least one occasion he stayed at Trevor's mansion in Manhattan, Trevor hosting several dinner parties in Johnson's honor, with John D. Rockefeller Jr. among the guests.

Trevor gave Johnson books to read, among them Cécile Tormay's anti-Semitic tract, *An Outlaw's Diary*, a screed that blamed Jews for everything from troubles in Tormay's Hungary to the fall of the Roman Empire. The Jew, Tormay wrote, "penetrates the bodies of the nations. He invisibly organizes his own nation among alien peoples. . . . Orders are given in mysterious secrecy." Johnson, who never concealed his alarm at immigrants "of the Semitic race" coming into the United States, found the book "intensely interesting," reading parts of it aloud to traveling companions on a cross-country train trip back to his congressional district. He, in turn, recommended to Trevor a magazine piece, "The Jew and His Club."

Someone else who had immigrants in his sights, A. Mitchell Palmer, at last made the move everyone had been long expecting. On March 1, 1920, the attorney general formally announced that he was running for the Democratic nomination for president. On a quick speaking tour, he visited Kansas, Illinois, and Kentucky; opened up offices in other states; and appointed state and local campaign chairmen. He had many chits to call in, some from his time in Congress and some from his year as attorney general, when he had appointed US attorneys and other officials across the nation.

The most useful, however, came from an earlier wartime post in the Wilson administration as alien property custodian, when he had been in charge of confiscating and selling off German and Austro-Hungarian holdings in the United States. These included everything from breweries to a shipping line. The job was an ambitious politician's dream. Palmer had allowed some companies to find their way into influential hands at low prices, and had also appointed hundreds of people—most of them active in Democratic Party politics—to well-paid jobs managing these properties before then. The hundreds of sales also generated good fees for politically connected lawyers. Most of his presidential campaign contributors had either managed or purchased "alien property" once under Palmer's control.

His broad-shouldered, authoritative figure was much in the glare of photographers' flash powder as he issued statements and made speeches on the rights of labor, the responsibilities of capital, the virtues of women, and America's great role in the world.

Although a cabinet member and tied to Wilson's record, Palmer had the advantage of not being identified with the president's most conspicuous failure, the Senate's refusal to ratify the Paris peace treaty and the League of Nations. A second and final vote on the subject in early 1920, after some modifications of the treaty, failed again, leaving Wilson in the deepest despair. His half year in Paris, plus the exhausting monthlong tour of the country that had precipitated his stroke had all been, he now felt, in vain.

The first Democrat to announce his candidacy, Palmer appeared to have an excellent shot at the nomination. Once he won, it looked as if he might find himself up against another anti-immigrant bulldog, Leonard Wood. After a year of speechmaking in uniform, the general had finally declared his candidacy as a Republican. Wood promised that he would show the same firm hand in deporting aliens and radicals as he had in dealing with strikers: "like rats they should be exterminated or driven from the country."

If it was Palmer's jutting jaw up against Wood's army khaki, Palmer was determined not to be outdone in toughness. He was happy with the nickname the press came up with for him, "the Fighting Quaker," and impressed journalists with his decisiveness and presidential looks. One of them wrote:

A. Mitchell Palmer, in personal appearance, is every inch a statesman. Stalwart and tall, with no suggestion of fatness, he carries himself with a dignity that has in it nothing of pose, no trace of egotism. His face is calm, thoughtful, and strong in repose, lighting up with attractive animation. . . . He had emphatically the air of a man's man.

This man's man staked his campaign on deportations. In a long, fiery magazine article, he evoked every possible fear voters might have, from violent upheaval to uppity females ("hysterical neurasthenic women who abound in communism"). He claimed to have "private information" on "the plans for fomenting a nation-wide revolution in this country, prepared by Trotzky in Moscow." In his raids, he was only doing what Congress should have put in motion a year earlier, so congressional critics be damned. "Like a prairie-fire, the blaze of revolution was sweeping over every American institution. . . . It was eating its way into the homes of the American workman, its sharp tongues of revolutionary heat were licking the altars of the churches, leaping into the belfry of the school bell, crawling into the sacred corners of American homes, seeking to replace marriage vows with libertine laws."

Palmer was riding high. His long-planned presidential campaign was officially under way. More stories like the lavish press coverage of the *Buford*'s departure were sure to come. Thousands of the radicals rounded up in his raids and now filling overcrowded prisons were proving not to be American citizens. As soon as the paperwork was done, he and Hoover planned to deport them with all possible fanfare. Speaking in Manhattan, Palmer promised the people of New York that they would soon find a "second, third, and fourth" ship like the *Buford* "sailing down their beautiful harbor in the near future." The momentum from all this, he was confident, would carry him into the White House.

And then, abruptly, his plans ran up against an unexpected roadblock.

Seeing Red

T HE ROADBLOCK WAS, Palmer and Hoover first thought, only a temporary bureaucratic wrinkle. Although it was the Justice Department that was arresting people by the thousands, deportations had to be approved by the Immigration Bureau—which, to the exasperation of the two men, remained under the Labor Department. That department, however, had just seen a crucial change of leadership.

At the beginning of March 1920, Secretary of Labor William B. Wilson (no relation to the president) went on personal leave. Supposedly he had to care for his sick wife and dying mother, but also, possibly, he wanted to avoid having to make unpopular decisions about mass deportations. The deputy who might normally have taken his place, an ex-congressman from Alabama, had just resigned to run for the Senate. As a result, the department's third-ranking official, 70-year-old Louis F. Post, became acting secretary of labor. Post was the man who had once refused to sign a deportation order for Emma Goldman, and who had boldly written to Woodrow Wilson to suggest, unsuccessfully, a blanket pardon for opponents of the draft.

Post's wire-rimmed glasses, Vandyke beard, and thick head of dark hair combined to give him a striking resemblance to the commander now leading the Red Army to victory in the Russian Civil War, Leon Trotsky. In the eyes of Palmer and Hoover, he was just as dangerous.

The roots of Post's passion for justice ran deep. He was born on a

New Jersey farm in 1849 and, though too young to serve in the Civil War, was imbued with abolitionist zeal. As a boy, he talked to the free Black handyman who worked for his grandfather but noticed that the man had to eat at a separate table. Decades later, Post would become a founding member of the NAACP. As a young man, he spent two years working in the South during Reconstruction and saw how white southerners foiled any hope of racial equality. After serving as a court reporter in South Carolina in several trials that convicted Ku Klux Klansmen of murder, he was dismayed to see President Ulysses S. Grant pardon most of them several months later. Returning to the North, he became a federal prosecutor in New York City, work that left him disturbed at having to send people to prison for such offenses as selling cigars without paying the proper tax. In this job and in several years of private legal practice, however, he gained a keen knowledge of the law that he would one day put to extraordinary use.

Journalism, first on the side but eventually full-time, became his calling. While an editor at a lively pro-labor paper, the New York *Truth*, he supported the campaign that established Labor Day. As an editorial writer for the *Cleveland Recorder*, he crusaded against industrial monopolies. Along the way, he became a close friend of the writer Henry George and a leading figure in George's single-tax movement, which called for spreading the national wealth by treating all land as owned in common and taxing those who used it. Single-taxers were not socialists, but shared with them a passion for reducing the vast inequalities of the Gilded Age. As a young woman, Kate Richards O'Hare had been inspired by George's writings, and Emma Goldman found some single-taxers to have "integrity and moral strength." Post became a fluent and skillful lecturer as he carried the single-tax message to audiences throughout the country.

By the turn of the century, Post and his wife had started a Chicago-based magazine, *The Public*, whose concerns ranged far beyond the single tax. It denounced the American colonization of the Philippines, the unchecked power of big business, and racial discrimination, while supporting votes for women, free speech, and unrestricted immigration.

The magazine also favored government ownership of natural monopolies like streetcar and railway lines. Post was enthusiastic about all these issues, and loquacious; he was not a man to write a hundred words if he could write a thousand. If he was not writing, he was often sketching faces in a scrapbook.

Although others took over *The Public* after he joined the Labor Department in 1913, Post continued to write occasional articles for it and for other magazines. He was friends with progressives like Robert La Follette and the former Ellis Island supervisor Frederic Howe, who described *The Public* under Post's editorship as "fearlessly honest in opinion, keenly understanding in its reporting. . . . The best mirror of pre-war liberalism that we had."

Being in government did not tame Post. Nor was he intimidated by A. Mitchell Palmer and J. Edgar Hoover raging about the need to rid the country of Bolsheviks and anarchists. Unknown to Post, in January 1920 the Bureau of Investigation began compiling a file on him, hunting for connections to subversives. He was aware, of course, that some anarchists planted bombs, but he knew that their ranks also included "apostles of peace," like the followers of the novelist and pacifist Leo Tolstoy, who were "supremely harmless." It was "perverted," he wrote, to lump them all together as people to be deported.

Now in temporary charge of the Labor Department, where thousands of deportation cases needed approval, Post put his convictions into practice. He proved to be a shrewd investigator, a decisive administrator, and a master of the fine print of immigration law—on which he had recently published a carefully footnoted article in a scholarly journal. That combination of talents enabled him to accomplish some extraordinary feats during the mere six weeks that he served as acting secretary of labor.

First, he ordered department officials to send all deportation cases directly to him. Then he dispatched a trusted associate to make an inspection tour of the Immigration Bureau's prisons. Conditions in these overcrowded jails were even worse than Post had expected, with signs of the Palmer Raids' harshness visible everywhere. At the Deer Island prison in Boston Harbor was a three-foot-high pile of chains and shackles in which prisoners had been marched through the city's streets.

Then there was a key legal question. Membership in a group advocating violence against the government made someone lawfully deportable, which was why Palmer and Hoover had swept up thousands whom they claimed belonged to the Union of Russian Workers and the two Communist parties. But exactly what was membership? Post ruled that this had to mean *conscious* membership in a group whose policies you were fully aware of. He made this decision after learning that many people seized in the raids hadn't even known that one of the Communist parties listed them as members. These quarreling groups had split off from the Socialist Party, and sometimes a defecting Socialist had brought along the membership list of his or her entire chapter and signed everybody up in the new party without telling them. Furthermore, such members might have had only the haziest idea of what a party stood for if they did not speak English.

Then Post discovered that many of the agents making Palmer Raid arrests had done so without the deportation warrants that had to be issued by the Labor Department, or with warrants based on faulty information. He swiftly invalidated nearly 3,000 of those arrests, finding, for instance, one case in which a prisoner was held for two weeks *before* anyone even asked for a warrant for his arrest. And the raiders had not informed many of those seized that their answers could be used as evidence against them; nor were those arrested given access to lawyers. Even though such rights were not as protected then as they are today, Post was still outraged, and ruled that any noncitizen subjected to deportation proceedings was entitled to full constitutional safeguards. He knew the law and could cite court decisions backing him up.

He then ordered the release of many of those still held in squalid prisons like the one on Ellis Island and slashed the amount of bail for others. Out of 2,435 deportation cases of Communists forwarded by the Bureau of Investigation, Post allowed less than 20 percent of the people involved to be deported, threw out the majority of cases, and asked for further investigation of the remainder.

These actions, he knew, would infuriate Palmer, Hoover, and their allies in Congress—and they did. Probably after a nudge from Hoover, Albert Johnson, along with two other deportation enthusiasts from his House committee and the committee's sergeant at arms, appeared without warning at Post's office on April 1, 1920. They demanded to see all the paperwork for the deportation orders he had canceled. "Raiders Seize Federal Office . . . Much Laxity Alleged . . . Louis F. Post Chief Figure in Remarkable Episode" was how one newspaper headlined the story. The raiders found, however, that the files were far too bulky to carry away. Post told them that he had nothing to hide and that they were free to examine all the paperwork they wanted at the Labor Department. They left behind the sergeant at arms and another staff member, who spent several days doing so. As they were sorting through his books and papers, Post wryly noted, they classified works by Thomas Paine as "anarchistic."

"A raid on an executive department of the government is a new thing in Washington," wrote a newspaperman friend of Johnson's, clearly channeling the congressman's thoughts, "but in this case it is not surprising in view of the storm of criticism that has been rising for some time against the department of labor and its lenient, if not altogether friendly, attitude toward all brands of communists, bolshevists and anarchists."

As only an acting cabinet secretary, working for an incapacitated president, Post was vulnerable. "To defend himself," writes the historian Kenneth Ackerman, "Post knew his only chance would be to throw the first punch. . . . From his years in politics and journalism, he knew the best way was to find a single, clear, sympathetic case of some poor working stiff who never made trouble, never stole a dime, but who got caught up in this Red Scare dragnet by mistake, incompetence, or overkill, and to throw it in the public eye."

And so a 33-year-old Polish American dry cleaning worker named Thomas Truss found his life story described in the *New York Times*, the *Boston Globe*, the *Baltimore Sun*, and other newspapers around the country. To Post, here was the ideal case. Truss had a wife and three American-born children. He had been in the United States 13 years

and had applied for citizenship but the government had lost his paperwork. He had no police record. He was an elder at Saint Paul's Polish
Presbyterian Church in Baltimore, and church officials testified to his
good character.

His name had caught the eye of the Justice Department because
one of the Communist parties had mailed him a membership card. But
he had never been to a meeting. Agents arrested him with no warrant, questioned him with no lawyer present, told him no reason for
his arrest, and held him in jail for a week until he managed to produce
$1,000 bail. And now he was slated to be deported. "In a large propor-
tion of cases I have examined," Post told the press, "there is no better
reason for deportation than is disclosed in the present case."

Palmer and Hoover, conferring frequently in the attorney general's
corner suite in the Justice Department building on Vermont Avenue,
were furious that this impudent bureaucrat who looked like Trotsky
was foiling their blueprint for massive deportations. Seeing their plans
blocked, and with it, possibly, Palmer's hopes for the presidency, they
decided on a risky course of action: an all-out campaign to get Post fired.

Albert Johnson joined them, mocking Post on the House floor at
great length, saying that "the case of Thomas Truss is presumably the
least offensive" that Post could find, and that he was usurping power
that wasn't his, putting the country at great risk from "radicals, both
native and alien," who "connive day and night." Hoover quickly mobilized several more members of Congress. One called Post "a man
whose sympathies evidently are with the enemies of our Government."
Another accused him of having "flagrantly abused his power" and introduced a resolution to impeach him. Congress scheduled hearings on
the question.

Louis F. Post was clearly headed for an inquisition. And as these
tensions grew between rival departments of the Wilson administration,
the country's chief executive still remained invisible.

THE SECRECY SURROUNDING Wilson's condition was torn when one
of his doctors, a urologist, let the veil slip and revealed that the presi-

dent had had a stroke. Newspapers promptly began quoting physicians about what that might mean. The former head of the American Medical Association declared that a man in such a condition should not be in the nation's highest office.

Although Wilson had been hesitantly dictating a few letters a day, sometimes losing his train of thought, it was not until March 3, 1920, five months after the public had last seen him, that he could leave the White House for the first time, using a cane to hobble out the rear entrance to be taken for a drive. He had such trouble getting his left arm through the sleeve of an overcoat that he wore a cape instead. As the large car swept through Washington's streets, those who caught a glimpse of his pale figure in the front passenger seat did not know that he sat there, instead of in the rear, because its indented shape kept him from toppling over.

The League of Nations was now established, and would operate, toothlessly, from the shores of Lake Geneva in Switzerland for the next quarter century. But the United States would never join, and the president remained distraught that his country would never play the leadership role in the organization he had long imagined. "I feel like going to bed and staying there," he told Dr. Grayson. One of the few things that now cheered him, even briefly, was to watch old newsreels that showed the tremendous welcome he had received when he first arrived in Europe for the peace conference—days of glory that would not come again. With a full year still left in his term of office, Wilson, in the words of his biographer A. Scott Berg, was "residing more than presiding" in the White House "for the rest of his days there."

Despite his fragility, on April 14, 1920, Wilson called a cabinet meeting. It would be his first in more than seven months, and his first meeting of any sort with more than just one or two visitors. Cabinet members came to his White House study, where the president could remain seated behind his desk as they took their chairs. But they were startled when, as if they were unfamiliar guests at a reception, Chief Usher Ike Hoover announced each man by name as he entered the room. They wondered: Had Wilson forgotten who they were? Or, as sometimes happens with stroke victims, was he now partly blind?

"It was enough to make one weep to look at him," wrote Treasury Secretary David Houston. "One of his arms was useless. In repose, his face looked very much as usual, but, when he tried to speak, there were marked evidences of his trouble. His jaw tended to drop on one side, or seemed to do so. His voice was very weak and strained." Even more disturbing, he did not suggest an agenda or initiate conversation. "The President seemed at first to have some difficulty in fixing his mind on what we were discussing."

What they were discussing, very heatedly, was Louis F. Post. The dispute began with talk of the latest wave of strikes. Palmer tried to dominate the conversation with the same line he was taking in his presidential campaign: labor unrest was due to Bolsheviks and Wobblies. But he drew unexpected pushback from another cabinet member, Labor Secretary William B. Wilson, who was in his first day back in office after the six-week leave during which Post had taken his place.

Secretary Wilson, a former coal miner and union official who had himself on occasion beaten the Red Scare drum, was normally a laid-back, good-natured, even passive man who preferred negotiating to taking a strong stand. But Palmer's remarks somehow got under his skin, while the principled behavior of his own deputy, Post, strengthened his resolve. Wilson struck back at Palmer and blamed the strikes on "economic conditions" and what millions of Americans had been suffering for several years—wages that often lagged far behind the fast-rising cost of living.

It was then, according to the diary of Navy Secretary Josephus Daniels, that Secretary Wilson and Attorney General Palmer started arguing about Post. The labor secretary defended his deputy's actions during his own absence, backing him completely, while Palmer charged that Post had freed "alien anarchists who ought to be deported" and demanded his head. Secretary Wilson replied that the government had already expelled those who deserved deportation, and said of the remainder: "While they wished to change [the] government, they were not lawless & expected to compass [accomplish] change by legal ways." Then, Daniels recorded in his diary, "Palmer said that if Post were removed from office it would end the strike[s]." Secretary Wilson disagreed, claiming that would only "aggravate" the situation.

There is no record of what more Palmer said, but it is not unlikely that he told his cabinet colleagues the same thing he was now saying loudly in public: that only an untrammeled drive to deport dangerous radicals stood between the United States and a Communist uprising.

No one knew how much of this the president could follow. The cabinet meeting lasted only an hour and a half. "Doctor Grayson looked in the door several times, as if to warn us not to prolong the discussion," wrote Treasury Secretary Houston. The president waved him away each time. "Finally, Mrs. Wilson came in, looking rather disturbed, and suggested that we better go."

The only record of the president's reaction to the dispute that had taken place in front of him was, according to Daniels, that he "told Palmer not to let the country see red," a cryptic remark that apparently meant Palmer should back off from flamboyant Red-hunting. This seems to be confirmed by something the president told Dr. Grayson soon afterward. Sitting beside the fireplace in his bedroom, he said, "Mitchell Palmer talks too much. His ambition is to keep before the public."

In his foggy state, Wilson seemed to have forgotten that Palmer had already announced his candidacy for president, and instead thought he was preparing for a postcabinet career as a New York lawyer. He was certainly right, though, about Palmer wanting to "keep before the public."

In the two weeks after the cabinet meeting, Palmer, staking his presidential bid on maintaining the Red Scare at full throttle, had the Justice Department send out almost daily warnings of a nationwide Communist uprising scheduled for May Day. With Europe still in turmoil, the Communists near victory in the bloody civil war in Russia, and strikes continuing to erupt at home, he expected that traditional left-wing holiday to ignite the nation's tensions into revolutionary flame.

As May Day approached, the attorney general's alarm signals grew only more urgent, and the nation's daily newspapers obediently repeated them. "Palmer Reveals Red Plot to Slay High Officials" read one front-page headline. "Plots against the lives of more than a score of Federal and State officials have been discovered by the Department of Justice as part of . . . an industrial reign of terror," reported the Associated Press in a story that made front pages nationwide, quoting insiders who predicted "a saturnalia of violence" on the crucial day.

Other journalists revealed that the targets went beyond figures in government: "Included also in the list of marked men, Mr. Palmer stated, were prominent citizens in different parts of the country," said the *New York Tribune*. Palmer declared that the violence ahead could trigger "strikes in all the basic American industries." Headlines everywhere echoed his warnings: "Justice Dept. to Curb May Day Plot"; "Reds Plotting May Day Murders, Says Palmer"; "Radicals Plan Wholesale Assassination in U. S. May Day."

A Little Man, Cool but Fiery

THE IMMINENT COMMUNIST uprising in America was not the only thing Attorney General Palmer had on his mind. There was also his presidential campaign, and for that he had to appear not just tough but merciful. After Kate Richards O'Hare had been in prison for 14 months of her five-year term, Palmer suggested commuting her sentence to time served, and President Wilson agreed. "Mrs. O'Hare is the mother of four children," said the *Washington Times*, "and the President was informed that her family was suffering because of her imprisonment." Surely one political consideration behind Palmer's suggestion was that the upcoming presidential election he hoped to win would be the first in which all women could vote.

O'Hare's departure from the Missouri penitentiary was bittersweet. She had worked hard during her prison term—and not just in the clothing workshop. "I felt I should like to make my incarceration of social value . . . by making a detailed study of my fellow convicts." She took down their life stories, asking a long series of questions about their family and marital histories, education, work, and community ties. She believed deeply—contrary to popular opinion of the day—that criminal behavior was not a matter of heredity or bad character, but of social conditions. She planned a book that would combine her findings with chapters by a psychologist, a physician, and other specialists analyzing the data. Boldly going to the top, she had won permission to do her interviewing from the governor of Missouri. "I managed to get the case histories of about two hundred women." But when she looked for the bundle of transcripts to take with her on her departure, "I found that it was missing, and I was told that it had been destroyed."

Free, she faced a changed world. The Socialist Party, long the center of her political life, was hobbled by arrests, mounting legal bills, and the 10-year prison sentence of her close friend Eugene Debs. Some members had defected to the new Communist parties; many more, frightened by the Palmer Raids, had simply withdrawn from politics entirely. The Socialists now had less than a tenth of their peak prewar membership, and in some states were no longer an organized presence. Even so, 2,000 of O'Hare's admirers welcomed her back from prison with deafening cheers at a rally in St. Louis. Although she felt that "it seemed a crime against the children for me to leave home," she embarked on another of the marathon speaking tours on which she always felt most alive, her husband, Frank, accompanying her for the first few weeks.

O'Hare gave 90 speeches across the country over five months, demanding the release of the hundreds of political prisoners still behind bars. The 14 months she had spent there had left their mark: her hands were calloused, her voice weaker, and she had a scar where an electric sewing machine needle had pierced a forefinger. She stood as tall and erect as ever, but her famous head of red hair was now largely white. Her audiences continued to include undercover agents.

In Atlanta, she visited Debs in the federal penitentiary, but neither she nor anyone else succeeded in winning his freedom. Even though many prominent people publicly, and four members of Wilson's cabinet privately, advocated clemency for the ailing man who had once won 6 percent of the popular vote for president, Wilson was unbudgeable. When Palmer—no doubt with an eye on winning for himself the approval of some of that 6 percent—forwarded a recommendation to commute Debs's sentence, the president wrote across it, "Denied."

"I will never consent to the pardon of this man," he told Tumulty. Even though the war was long over, Wilson could not forgive those who opposed what he saw as a noble crusade.

Also without relief were those whose cases were still on appeal. Because of that drawn-out process, Dr. Marie Equi of Oregon would not even begin serving her sentence until October 1920, and the hapless Kentucky shoemaker Charles Schoberg and his two friends would not be imprisoned until December—more than two years after First World War's end.

Meanwhile, as the country awaited the great May Day uprising Palmer had warned of, the House Rules Committee opened hearings on Louis F. Post. Here, Palmer and Hoover expected, they would get their revenge on the man who had so stymied their deportation plans. Scrutiny of Post's misdeeds, they were certain, would end in his impeachment. Not only was the committee chaired by a Republican, who might enjoy the chance to make the Democratic administration look bad, but its ranking Democrat had lost a son at the front in France and might not feel kindly about Post's failure to deport antiwar radicals.

Around this time—the date is uncertain—Hoover privately expressed his confidence in Post's downfall. In a scrapbook he kept, he pasted a newspaper photo of the bearded Post, colored the background red, and placed a typed poem next to it. Whether Hoover wrote it himself or copied it from somewhere, we do not know. It began:

The "Reds" at Ellis Island
    Are happy as can be
For Comrade Post at Washington
    Is setting them all free. . . .
But Uncle Sam will clinch his fist
    And rise up mighty strong
Take hold of Comrade "Louie"—
    Send the "Reds" where they belong

When the hearings opened on April 27, 1920, in an atmosphere of wariness about the expected May Day upheaval, Hoover hoped that his enemy would receive that mighty blow from Uncle Sam's fist. Post himself did not attend, but he made sure his lawyers were present and taking careful notes of the arguments the Rules Committee was marshaling against him.

Although Albert Johnson was not a member of this committee, the hearings opened with a statement from him in his capacity as chair of the Committee on Immigration and Naturalization. Warming up the Rules Committee for the anticipated impeachment of Post, he declared that the United States "is seeing its laws violated by public officials in behalf of aliens who have contempt for this Government, who are here trying to overthrow it."

Other congressional deportation enthusiasts, including two who had been with Johnson on the tugboat taking deportees to the *Buford*, also testified about Post's perfidy. One Kansas congressman spoke darkly about "a widespread and carefully planned effort to Russianize this country. . . . The movement is not only against orderly government, but against the institution of marriage, the church, religion, and all the establishments of civilization." A colleague also evoked the sanctity of marriage, condemning Post as someone who "advocated, before he went into this high office, in his own books, the proposition of free love." Post had published a book in 1906 urging reform of the country's antiquated divorce laws, which often allowed marriages to end only on the grounds of proven adultery.

Several congressmen referred respectfully to J. Edgar Hoover, who had probably helped them prepare their statements. But they had not yet grilled Post himself. After several days of speechmaking, the committee adjourned for a week; when they next gathered, his inquisitors would meet the subject of their wrath face-to-face.

AS MAY DAY approached, cities began to look like military bases, armed and ready for the nationwide mayhem Palmer predicted. New York canceled all police leaves. Throughout the dread day itself and the night and the day to follow, all three shifts of the city's 11,000 officers and detectives were to be on duty. "Thus," said the *Times* on its front page, "the entire department could be mobilized and on the streets within a few minutes." Extra police protected possible targets, like the Public Library and Pennsylvania Station. The New York National Guard was on alert, ready to put 8,000 armed men on the streets within two hours.

The Post Office, continued the *Times*, was prepared "to guard against a repetition of last year's attempt to send infernal machines . . . through the mails," warning people not to open suspicious packages. Palmer had refused to name those whom the Communists supposedly were targeting for assassination on the crucial day, so the newspaper speculated on whom they might be: Judge Elbert Gary of US Steel? A district attorney here, a governor there? J. P. Morgan Jr. posted guards outside his Madison Avenue mansion.

Since New York was always a center of leftist activism, Big Bill Flynn, chief of the Bureau of Investigation, came to town and spent much of April 30 closeted with the heads of the bureau's local office and of the New York police bomb squad. The bureau even pulled 50 agents off its financial crimes unit to be "assigned to a special post for May Day work." The authorities were especially wary of attacks on a "loyalty parade" of boys, organized by the Rotary Club "as living proof of the younger generation's adherence to American principles. . . . Its route along Fifth Avenue will be bristling with uniformed policemen and detectives ready for instant action."

In Boston, trucks mounted with machine guns parked at seven key locations, and extra guards deployed around the state capitol and city jail. Court officials turned out for street duty to supplement the police. The most remarkable preparation for the uprising came in Chicago, where, the *Times* reported, "360 suspicious characters" were "under lock and key as a result of raids tonight [April 30], and agents of the Department of Justice [are] preparing to make additional roundups in the early hours of tomorrow." These preventive detentions were designed to foil the "reign of terror" planned for May 1.

Not only were the Bureau of Investigation and city police forces prepared to put down an insurrection, so was the army. After the ambitious Ralph Van Deman had stepped on too many toes and been kicked upstairs in 1918, domestic Military Intelligence and its huge network of agents were taken over by a brigadier general with the aristocratic name of Marlborough Churchill. (He was, in fact, a distant relative of Winston's.)

Churchill and his Military Intelligence colleagues portrayed their enemies as numerous beyond imagining, underlining their own role as a bulwark against this surging Red tide. In one later estimate, they calculated that the country contained, among other dangerous groups, 914,854 Socialists, 322,284 Red radicals, and an alarming 2,475,371 "unorganized Negroes," whatever that might mean. The number of Socialists they cited was approximately what Debs polled in his highest two presidential runs; where the other numbers came from, no one knows.

How was the country to defend itself against such a multifaceted menace? Following the First World War, the military began drawing up a series of contingency plans that ranged from Plan Brown, for putting down an insurrection in the Philippines, to Plan Green, for suppressing one in Mexico. Under the influence of Churchill's alarming reports, in the winter of 1919–20 work began on War Plan White—for suppressing insurrection in the United States.

The blueprint was extremely detailed. If an uprising disrupted normal trade, privately owned trucks would be commandeered for supply convoys of essential goods. The Army Corps of Engineers would step in to maintain water and power systems. If revolutionaries took over the commercial telephone and telegraph lines, the Signal Corps would connect the War Department with bases around the country.

As it expanded, War Plan White came to include drafts of various presidential proclamations to be issued as the need arose. One, for instance, provided wording for the president to declare an area to be "in a state of insurrection against the United States, and that all commercial intercourse between the said City (Counties) (State) (States) and the inhabitants thereof, and the citizens of other parts of the United States is unlawful."

War Plan White's creators were not thinking in terms of a "geographic" insurrection, another army document from this time makes clear, but an ethnic one. Interestingly, they were not worried about the "relatively large" Black citizenry in the South, because "this danger is well understood and the white population in these regions can be counted on to control the situation." Instead, it was Russians, eastern Europeans, and Jews who were the biggest source of "industrial and social unrest and danger, and . . . undoubtedly the most dangerous element of our population."

WHEN MAY DAY 1920 dawned at last, countless volunteer vigilantes buttressed the extra police who filled the streets. In New York, according to the *Tribune*, "there were more policemen in uniform and in plain clothes to the square inch than the city has ever before seen" and the Manhattan office of the Justice Department "bulged with special agents." Fifty of them alone kept watch over the route of the loyalty parade down Fifth Avenue. The police guard at the mayor's official residence was more than doubled, and bridges and ferry terminals were under close watch. Firemen stood by, ready to break up street demonstrations with their hoses. Anxious city officials took similar precautions across the country. Palmer was hunkered down in his Washington office, protected by armed guards, and let it be known that he kept a revolver in his desk.

Nothing happened.

There was no uprising, Communist or otherwise. Various left-wing meetings took place, as they had every May Day for decades, but all were peaceful. In New York, the only radical arrested was a man accused of violating an antilittering ordinance by stuffing pamphlets into apartment mailboxes. At a gathering of the Journeymen Bakers' Union, members wore red carnations, but threw no bombs. The Rotary Club parade of 40,000 boys, led by a 79-year-old Civil War veteran, passed down Fifth Avenue without interference. At the Amalgamated Clothing Workers May Day concert in Carnegie Hall, "there were no disturbances," reported the *Tribune*, "and so the policemen and agents of the Department of Justice, who were present in great numbers, had nothing to do but enjoy the music."

In San Francisco, the carpenters' union held a picnic and the Socialist Party a dance. In Chicago, police arrested a man seen carrying a book in Russian—which turned out to be the Bible. That city's clothing workers announced a one-day strike to support political prisoners, but manufacturers pointed out that union contracts already provided a May Day holiday. In Washington, DC, alarmed phone calls deluged the Justice Department and city police reporting a crowd marching behind a red flag. When officers rushed to investigate, they found a procession following the crimson banner of the Association of Harvard Clubs.

The stark failure of Palmer's May Day predictions put a humiliating dent in his presidential hopes, and also knocked the breath out of the campaign for a new sedition bill; none of the many proposed in Congress passed. The nation's daily newspapers, almost all of which had uncritically headlined Palmer's warnings without making any attempt to verify them, felt taken for a ride. Some broke ranks with the Red Scare for the first time.

The *Chicago Tribune* published a cartoon on its front page, captioned "A. Mitchell Palmer Out for a Stroll." It showed the attorney general's bulky, dark-browed figure, with a jowly face and pinstriped pants, looking down a street at an organ grinder, children jumping rope, a beggar, a boy with a catcher's mitt, a worker emerging from a manhole, and a mother wheeling a baby carriage. Every figure is adorned with a fierce beard and mustache and is labeled "Reds."

"We can never get to work if we keep jumping sideways in fear of the bewhiskered Bolshevik," said the *Rocky Mountain News*. "What Mr. Palmer is trying to do," declared the *San Francisco Examiner*, "is to distract public attention from his miserable failure to reduce prices and jail profiteers."

Profiteering was on people's minds thanks to recent congressional hearings. A few months previously, a particularly egregious example had come to light. It was at the giant Air Nitrates Corporation complex in Muscle Shoals, Alabama, where during the war workers processed ingredients for ammunition and explosives. Hearing reports that the company was inflating its costs in various ways, including multiplying the number of foremen and having higher-paid craftsmen and technicians do unskilled labor, the Bureau of Investigation sent 20 agents to look into the situation. The company then hired 40 private detectives to spy on the bureau's men—and, under its "cost-plus" contract, charged the government for their salaries.

Why was Palmer, instead of concentrating on such issues—which actually might have served him well politically—so obsessed by the certainty of a Communist uprising? He was, one writer comments, "a demagogue who believed his own demagoguery." In the end, he proved as blind as many would-be revolutionaries to the fact that most Americans have seldom dreamed of an armed left-wing revolution. Hoover's Radical Division had noticed a handful of anarchist and Communist leaflets and articles calling for a show of strength on May 1, and had warned Palmer that something might be afoot. In his eagerness to sound the alarm, that was all that Palmer needed. There is no record that he ordered any investigation into whether anyone was making the detailed preparations for such an uprising to actually happen.

For security operatives, from foot soldiers like Leo Wendell to chieftains like Hoover, it is, of course, always desirable to be seen as guarding against a dangerous threat. The illusion of a sinister radical menace guarantees big budgets. This pattern would continue until the very end of Hoover's long career, by which point 15 percent of the US Communist Party's tiny membership would consist of undercover FBI agents. Hoover, however, shrewder than Palmer, knew how to hint at an ominous Communist threat without making specific predictions that could fail to come true.

IT WAS ONLY a week after the non-uprising when the House Rules Committee reconvened in a room on the top floor of the Capitol. Beneath cut-glass chandeliers and oil portraits of long-dead congressmen, it resumed its investigation of Louis F. Post. And now here he was in person, complete with Trotsky beard and spectacles—"the short shaggy figure of the Accused," as the *New Republic*'s reporter put it. "But . . . he anticipated attack, he welcomed it, he ran to meet it with every weapon of fact, of humor, of legitimate pride. . . . A little man, cool but fiery, who set his belief in the Constitution of the country above all fears."

Post treated the committee as if they were students, and to teach them he used the full range of rhetorical skills he had developed as a traveling single-tax lecturer. During ten hours of testimony spread over two days, he gave the committee a graduate-level class in immigration law and the way the Justice Department had completely ignored constitutional protections for those it arrested.

He leavened all this with a needle-sharp wit, which none of the congressmen, almost all of them lawyers accustomed to making witnesses squirm, seemed to expect. When Post referred to something as being common knowledge, the committee's chair expressed skepticism, saying, "I am not impressed with the truth of everything I hear."

"Neither am I," Post shot back. "If I had been I would have deported every man that the detectives arrested."

Clearly enjoying the sparring, he repeatedly swatted off attempts by Johnson and other congressmen to interrupt him, and lost no chance to mock the Palmer Raids. These were based on "a vision of a great conspiracy to throw bombs. . . . In all these sweeping raids over the country, in which men were arrested at midnight and taken out of their beds at 3 o'clock in the morning in their homes, without warrant, in which their houses and their persons were searched without warrant," how many weapons were found? "Three pistols, two of them .22 caliber."

At this statement, according to the *Washington Times*, "laughter swept the room," and Post, seeing he had the audience with him, rubbed it in. "Now, I do not know whether a .22 caliber is for a homeopathic pill or a cannon ball. . . . I do not know anything about pistols. I never carried one in my life and never expect to." (In fact, raiders confiscated about three dozen firearms, still a small quantity for what may have been 10,000 people questioned. But it would take weeks for that information to emerge.)

Post lost no chance to mock Albert Johnson, suggesting to him that "your object is merely to get alien scalps to hang to [your] belt." And he talked of how "the mere expression of a thought" should not be a crime or cause for deportation. Here, he used a brilliant example. Judge Kenesaw Mountain Landis was "reported as having made a speech" saying that a group of Minnesota radicals "ought to be put up against a barn and shot. . . . Should Judge Landis be penalized because he used that expression in the heat of a speech?"

Toward the end of the hearing, the committee's ranking Democrat had become so charmed by Post that he told him, "I will give you an opportunity to say what your politics are, if you desire to do so." As someone who had been a political journalist for decades, Post was delighted, and held forth at length about his odyssey from boyhood admiration of Abraham Lincoln to the single-tax movement to his belief that free speech was almost holy. In response, the congressman told him that even though "I am probably not in sympathy with some of your views . . . I believe you have followed your sense of duty absolutely."

Newspaper editorials praised Post. He "gave a very good account of himself," said one, quoting him describing the Constitution as "a sacred document." "Some day, when the history of American liberty comes to be written," declared the liberal *Nation*, "the name of Louis F. Post will be given a high place, because he dared in a trying time to defy the forces of madness and hatred and greed that now threaten to overwhelm us."

Watching this masterful performance through the entire hearing, but saying nothing on the record, was J. Edgar Hoover. Was he someone the *New Republic* journalist had in mind when writing, "agitated gentlemen kept going into corners and emerging with a new question"? Perhaps.

The committee quietly abandoned its proceedings to impeach Louis F. Post. Hoover was furious. He had certainly lost this round of his battle against Post, but he did not abandon his fight, and made plans for a different kind of attack.

TWO ADDITIONAL EVENTS in the spring of 1920 gave many Americans second thoughts about the Red Scare. The first was a case before a federal court in Boston on petitions to release 18 noncitizens held in the notorious prison on Deer Island. The hearings before Judge George W. Anderson would turn out to greatly embarrass the Bureau of Investigation and Hoover, who was at the table with the government's lawyers.

Assisting the judge as amici curiae—friends of the court—were two Harvard Law School professors. One of them, Zechariah Chafee, the previous year, had helped persuade Supreme Court justice Oliver Wendell Holmes Jr. to change his mind and issue his landmark dissent in defense of free speech in the *Abrams* case. Two decades later, the other professor, Felix Frankfurter, would become a justice of that court himself. In their grilling of federal agents, Judge Anderson, Frankfurter, Chafee, and the other lawyers proved that Bureau of Investigation men had searched homes and arrested people without warrants, interrogated them without attorneys, set wildly excessive bail, accepted rides from some 20 nondeputized vigilantes, and corralled people who were US citizens as well as those who were not. "More lawless proceedings are hard to conceive," declared the judge.

The most shocking revelation was a letter, read aloud in court, from the Justice Department in Washington to the bureau chief in Boston, sent shortly before the Palmer Raid of January 2, 1920. "If possible," it said, "you should arrange with your under-cover informants to have meetings of the COMMUNIST PARTY and the COMMUNIST LABOR PARTY held on the night set. . . . This, of course, would facilitate the making of the arrests." People knew that the government had its spies, but the letter revealed that they had actually tried to convene Communist meetings to fit the raiders' schedule. It was a bombshell. "In these times of hysteria," commented Judge Anderson from the bench, "I wonder no witches have been hung."

Before long, Anderson set all the prisoners free. In a widely quoted passage from his excoriating 30,000-word decision, he declared that "a mob is a mob, whether made up of government officials acting under instructions from the Department of Justice, or of criminals, loafers, and the vicious classes."

A second pivotal event of the season was what became known as the "Twelve Lawyer Report." This document's signers were all eminent attorneys, many of them law professors. Besides Chafee and Frankfurter, who since the Boston trial was being shadowed by bureau agents, they included two law school deans, a former judge, and Francis Fisher Kane, the former US attorney in Philadelphia who had resigned in protest against the raids.

Precise, measured, and scrupulously documented, the report contained affidavits by people arrested in the Palmer Raids, their attorneys, and other investigators. It detailed how the victims had been kicked and punched by bureau agents, nearly starved in prison, thrown into solitary confinement for long periods, and had Justice Department personnel confiscate money from them and never return it.

The report's illustrations included a signature of one prisoner forged by department interrogators compared with his real signature, a photograph of a prisoner after a beating at the hands of the bureau, and another of the wreckage strewn on the floor of the Russian "People's House" in New York. The charges of unconstitutional actions by Palmer read almost like the counts of an indictment. To have a dozen of the country's most prominent jurists accusing its top law enforcement official of making "a deliberate misuse of his office" was virtually unprecedented. So was the revelation that he had prepared "an advertising campaign in favor of repression" by mailing press releases, photographs, and even cartoons to the nation's newspapers.

The Twelve Lawyer Report was widely distributed and had considerable impact in Congress. The press covered it respectfully, often on its front pages, and it would turn out to be something of a milestone in the history of American civil liberties; it is still cited in legal writings today. A furious J. Edgar Hoover immediately put his men to work searching for incriminating data on all the signers.

Together, the Boston trial and the release of the Twelve Lawyer Report greatly deflated the campaign for mass deportations and completely vindicated the actions of Louis F. Post. No journalist or politician, however, noticed clues suggesting that the same person had made both events happen: Post himself.

The Boston case had arisen in a curious way. A prominent civil liberties lawyer in that city received a memorandum from the Labor Department saying that the department "very greatly desired" that "a test case as to deportation . . . be brought at the earliest opportunity before a *friendly* judge." That judge, the memo urged, should be George W. Anderson—who had recently given a speech calling the Palmer Raids "appalling." The memo suggested several prisoners who would make good clients for the test case, and mentioned that Frankfurter and Chafee would be interested in helping out. In the files of the lawyer who received it, the memo is unsigned. But it bears every mark of being the work of Post. It was sent roughly two weeks after he had become the acting secretary of labor, and its recipient appears to have been a friend of Post's—as was Frankfurter.

Post's deft hand was similarly behind the Twelve Lawyer Report, whose signers also included Frankfurter. One of the 11 others who put their names to the report was Post's *own* lawyer. No less than four other signers were veterans of the single-tax movement in which Post had spent much of his political life. Unobtrusively, he himself had supplied much of the material in the report, and had quietly met at least once with its principal drafter—a man with whom he and his wife had been friends for years.

In a book he later wrote, *The Deportations Delirium of Nineteen-Twenty*, Post praised the "convincing and extremely able argument" of Judge Anderson's ruling and, as well, the report's "indictment of the Department of Justice by distinguished American lawyers." But he never mentioned his own role as mastermind of both, and he destroyed all correspondence that would have revealed it. Perhaps this is one reason why he is today so little known. He proved himself to be a rare combination: a master of quiet bureaucratic warfare and a man of high principle.

Policeman and Detective

ESPITE THE EMBARRASSING absence of the revolution he had predicted for May Day, A. Mitchell Palmer's chances for winning the Democratic nomination still seemed high. None of his rivals had a big popular base, and his years in politics had given him a network of influential friends. A majority of the Democratic National Committee, including its chair and vice-chair, supported him. He was confident he knew the pathway to victory. "I am myself an American," he declared, "and I love to preach my doctrine before undiluted one hundred percent Americans, because my platform is, in a word, undiluted Americanism." The journalist Heywood Broun wrote, tongue in cheek, "We assumed, of course, from the tone of Mr. Palmer's manifesto that his opponents for the nomination were Rumanians, Greeks and Icelanders." But then, Broun claimed, he wandered into a rival candidate's headquarters and was "astounded to discover that he, too, is an American."

Palmer was having trouble, however, gaining support from labor. His Red-hunting fervor had made even the moderate wing of that movement feel endangered. Many union members were disappointed that Palmer had not used his Justice Department to prosecute war profiteers and monopolists, after the wartime boom had left the United States a more unequal society than ever.

For any setback in his quest for the presidency, the attorney general blamed subversives. When he lost the Michigan primary, he knew whom to accuse: "Detroit is the largest city in America in population of alien reds or radicals and revolutionists." His campaign posters showed him raising an index finger above the legend "The Fighting Quaker—laying down the law." (His rivals were quick to call him the Quaking Fighter, the Fighting Quacker, or the Quaking Quitter.) He did much better in the next primary, Georgia, coming in a close second. "The drift has been decidedly toward Palmer," wrote the *Atlanta Constitution* two weeks before the 1920 Democratic National Convention.

Among Republicans, Leonard Wood still was in the lead. "General Wood is the choice of more Republicans to-day than any other candidate," wrote the *New York Tribune* six weeks before the Republican National Convention, adding, "He is the only Presidential aspirant with a chance of success on the first ballot." Other commentators agreed. On the campaign trail, he continued to wear his army uniform with combat ribbons on his chest and the two silver stars of a major general on his shoulders. Sometimes fellow officers flanked him on the platform. Wood won primaries in Minnesota, South Dakota, and Indiana, and in neighboring Ohio came within 15,000 votes of beating its own senator, Warren Harding.

In the general's national campaign office in Manhattan, a reporter found spirits high, and rhetoric that resembled Palmer's. "At the Wood headquarters . . . it is implied that General Wood was the original inventor of 100 per cent Americanism. . . . Energetic young men analyze and index and classify. There is the glint of efficiency, of super-efficiency, about the organization." An enthusiastic spokesperson gave the journalist an earful, confidently asserting that, as military governor of Cuba after the Spanish-American War, the general had already performed almost every job done by members of the American cabinet, not to mention having eradicated piracy, polygamy, and headhunting as a colonial official in the Philippines, and put rioters and Reds in their place in Omaha and Gary.

Wood turned openly to vigilante groups, saying that if "no other means . . . can be found," he would delegate to the American Legion "the task of suppressing the treasonable activities of the rabid alien."

Not surprisingly, among his biggest supporters were men who had been in the American Protective League. His strong hand in suppressing striking steelworkers and coal miners also impressed the wealthy, from John D. Rockefeller Jr. on down, who pitched in lavishly to finance his campaign.

That support backfired, however, when a Senate investigation showed that before the Republican National Convention had even begun, Wood had spent more than $1.7 million—the equivalent of nearly $60 million in purchasing power a century later—almost three times as much as all of his rivals for the nomination combined. In the days before expensive advertising on radio, TV, and the internet, spending such an amount in the primaries was almost unprecedented and provoked criticism. Some influential supporters began to worry about his chances, and urged Wood to moderate his calls for deporting radicals and to show more awareness that voters had down-to-earth economic worries. Still, he entered the June convention with more pledged delegates than any other Republican candidate.

The acerbic columnist H. L. Mencken compared Wood with Palmer, who appeared to be his principal rival among Democrats. The general, he wrote, "is the simple-minded dragon, viewing all human phenomena from the standpoint of the barrack-room. His remedy for all ills and evils is force. . . . One somehow warms to the old boy. He is archaic, but transparent. He indulges himself in no pishposh about ideals. He has no opinions upon any public question save the primary one of protecting property. His is a policeman's philosophy, and hence a good deal more respectable than that of Palmer, which is a detective's."

When the Democratic National Convention opened, the "detective" came in a close second on the first ballot. No candidate received a majority, but the hall was adorned with posters showing a stern, handsome, firm-jawed Palmer. Despite the damage to his reputation from the Twelve Lawyer Report and Judge Anderson's scorching denunciation of his raids, Palmer's hopes remained high. A large contingent of Justice Department staff members came to San Francisco for the first major party convention on the West Coast. As he circulated on the convention floor and in and out of Palmer's spacious headquarters in the Saint Francis Hotel, J. Edgar Hoover enjoyed his first trip to California.

At the Republican convention in Chicago, where the summer temperature soared to 102 degrees Fahrenheit, Leonard Wood's supporters cheered for more than 40 minutes when he was placed in nomination and from the balconies tossed down a cascade of red and green feathers lettered with his name. Although not gaining a majority, the general won the first four rounds of balloting.

Soon, however, he ran into trouble. No matter how erect and splendid he looked in his army khaki and well-polished boots and how fierce his denunciations of Reds, the nationwide wave of strikes had ebbed, and with it fears that something like the Russian Revolution would upend the United States. Republican leaders began to realize that the public no longer wanted a man on horseback to come to the country's rescue. They wanted a winning candidate atop their ticket, and for all his paeans to Americanism, Wood had distressingly little to say about anything else.

The general still had the largest number of pledged delegates, but it was not a majority. As the convention deadlocked, frantically negotiating candidates and their backers offered delegates' votes in return for everything from cabinet positions to an ambassadorship to access to federal oil reserves. The balance began to tip away from Wood.

The young journalist Walter Lippmann summed up why Wood's moment had passed:

> There were no end of Caesars after Julius as there are Roosevelts after TR. . . . His managers. . . . have tried to ride Wood to power behind the fiction that whatever you found in Roosevelt you would find again in Wood. But. . . . [Wood] was a prima donna capable only of singing soprano in a piece where there were no more prima donna parts left.

Wood's supporters, Lippmann added, were filled with "hatreds and violence . . . turned against all kinds of imaginary enemies—the enemy within, the enemy to the south, the enemy at Moscow, the Negro, the immigrant, the labor union." He concluded that "the real Wood nucleus is . . . too small to win an election" and, in the end, the Republican Party's kingmakers agreed with him.

After a long night of bargaining, the nomination finally went to the first choice of few but the second choice of many: the gregarious, conservative Senator Warren Harding from the crucial swing state of Ohio. With his resonant, baritone voice, handsome face, dark eyebrows, and full head of gray hair, he already looked presidential. And Harding had his law-and-order flank covered, since his vice-presidential running mate would be Massachusetts governor Calvin Coolidge, renowned for crushing the Boston police strike.

Palmer, it turned out, fared no better than Wood, largely for similar reasons, as people realized that the country did not need to be protected from a Communist revolution. But, like Wood, he had no other song to sing. As the Democratic convention ponderously held 44 rounds of balloting, his vote totals continued to diminish. The eventual nominee was the uninspiring Governor James M. Cox of Ohio.

In this political season, another party held its nominating convention, a far smaller one. Meeting in New York City, the Socialists had seen their ranks decimated by arrests, most of their newspapers and magazines shut down, and five of their members expelled from the New York legislature and one from the US Congress. There was no competition for the presidential nomination; it went, by acclamation, to Eugene Debs. But he was prisoner #9653 in the federal penitentiary in Atlanta, 13 months into a sentence of 10 years.

THE DEFEATS OF both Wood and Palmer were not the only indications of the country's changing mood. Similarly unsuccessful were two other contenders for the Republican nomination who had also bellowed about deporting aliens, Columbia University president Nicholas Murray Butler and Senator Miles Poindexter of Washington. Another sign of change: Congress made a substantial cut in funding for the Bureau of Investigation.

Wilson's cabinet, however, still had many months left in office, and did little to ease political repression. Postmaster General Albert Burleson continued to censor the press, a job he relished. One target was the nation's leading socialist daily, the *New York Call*. During the war, Burleson had first banned various issues from the mail, then canceled its second-class mailing privileges completely. More than two years later, the paper was still trying to get these restored. But Burleson ruled that, because the *Call* had violated the Espionage Act, it was not a bona fide newspaper and so was not entitled to second-class privileges.

"The preposterous claim of the Postmaster General," wrote the *New Republic*, "is as if the Pennsylvania Railroad were to refuse to sell [unseated Socialist congressman] Victor Berger a railway ticket, on the ground that having been convicted of violating the Espionage Law, he was no longer a 'person.'" Several other banned publications were fighting similar legal battles, and, when a lower court ruled against the postmaster general in one of them, with President Wilson's approval he appealed it to the Supreme Court as a test case. The high court upheld the ban, with only Justices Holmes and Brandeis dissenting.

Without waiting for any court decisions, J. Edgar Hoover continued to assume the right to remove from post offices anything that Burleson had overlooked. On May 10, 1920, for instance, a Bureau of Investigation agent in Los Angeles sent in a list of periodicals that "this office has sequestered" during the previous week: 100 copies each of three issues of the IWW's *Industrial Worker*, 50 copies of the same organization's monthly *One Big Union*, six copies of the Lithuanian-language *Proletaras*, and assorted other literature.

Five months later, Hoover sent a representative to a meeting at the Post Office about mailing privileges for *The Liberator*, the monthly started by Max Eastman and his sister Crystal to replace the banned *Masses*. He was apparently angling for a larger role for himself in censorship, and wanted to establish that precedent now, so that it would be firmly in place no matter who turned out to be postmaster general under the next president. He had long had his eye on *The Liberator*. His star agent, Leo Wendell, still posing as a Pittsburgh Wobbly, checked on the magazine while on a trip to New York and found it to be "in very serious financial straights [*sic*]. . . . Max Eastman and Crystal Eastman have suffered a large reduction in their salary from $200 to $80 per week. Both Max and Crystal are storming and screeching among their friends about this terrible indignity, but to no avail."

It was evidently on that same trip to New York that Wendell discovered a dangerous new organization, the American Civil Liberties Union. (In fact, it had been operating for several years, but had recently adopted a new name.) He informed Hoover that the group had "unlimited financial backing"—news that might have surprised its tiny staff—and that it was determined to support "free speech, free press, etcetera" for everybody, "no matter whether they be anarchists, IWW, Communists or whatever." Over the coming decades, Hoover's agents would compile more than 10,000 pages of documents about the ACLU.

Despite having lost the battle to have Louis F. Post impeached by Congress, Hoover now made one last attempt to take revenge. He worked behind the scenes with the American Legion, which at its annual convention in September 1920 made front-page news by calling Post a "serious menace to public security" and demanding that he be fired. Some newspapers promptly offered their editorial support: "That such an official should be allowed to remain in office," said the *New York Tribune*, "is an affront to patriotism."

Undaunted, Post tangled with the legion a few days later by refusing the group permission to conduct "Americanization" classes for immigrants arriving at Ellis Island and other ports of entry. Both the legion and Albert Johnson claimed that the island was now a sinister indoctrination center. Between people like Post and the subversive immigrants flooding the country, it was a "Dante's Inferno," Johnson warned his fellow House members, "a seething, struggling, volcanic mass of breathing human beings. Gentlemen, it is dangerous! Bolshevists and anarchists are made there overnight." By holding propaganda sessions for new arrivals, a legion official said, the organization hoped to "prevent them from falling under the rotten influences which contaminate so many immigrants." Post would have none of it.

When the legion presented a report attacking him to the largely paralyzed White House, it was handed off to Post's boss, William B. Wilson, who issued a ringing defense. The labor secretary said Post "ranks among the ablest and best administrative officers in the government service."

THE 1920 PRESIDENTIAL campaign fast became a rout for the Democrats. Their candidate, Governor Cox, valiantly logged some 22,000 miles traversing the country, but neither he nor his more glamorous vice-presidential running mate with a famous last name, the 38-year-old Franklin D. Roosevelt, lit the nation on fire. The genial Republican Warren Harding, sniffing victory in the air, mostly stayed home in Marion, Ohio, receiving well-publicized visits from delegations of farmers, workers, and veterans on a capacious, pillared front porch and a lawn almost large enough to seat a legislature. Most journalists could find no more weighty charge to assail him with than the rumor that somewhere in earlier generations he had a Black forefather. Although at this point in American history such an accusation could be damaging, Harding handled it lightly. "How do I know, Jim?" he cheerfully told one reporter who asked. "One of my ancestors may have jumped the fence." The issue evaporated.

Harding mounted his relaxed campaign on the theme "Back to Normalcy." (Although he is sometimes credited with inventing the word, it already existed.) Another slogan of his, "Let's be done with wiggle and wobble," crafted by an advertising man, was first used to attack Cox's ambivalence about the League of Nations, but was vague enough to stand for resoluteness in general. Early in the race Harding voiced a thought that would have been unimaginable coming from the mouths of either A. Mitchell Palmer or Leonard Wood: "Too much has been said about Bolshevism in America." The nation, Harding sensed, was tired of the Red Scare.

Harding was elected in a landslide of historic proportions, with more than 60 percent of the popular vote. After years of turmoil, the public did, indeed, want "normalcy." Before setting off on a vacation, the victor received the election results in an armchair at home in Marion, an unlit cigar between his lips. Ninety miles away in Dayton, Governor Cox, his own cigar alight, heard it in the office of a newspaper he owned, which, humiliatingly enough, issued an extra edition with word of his defeat. To put the election behind him, he made plans to go squirrel hunting.

For a third man, however, a vacation was out of the question. Eugene Debs won more than 900,000 votes, but the Socialist candidate heard that news while dressed in frayed and ill-fitting blue denim, sitting in the warden's office of his prison. When Clarence Darrow paid him a visit, in the cell he shared with six others, several of them bootleggers, he found Debs "loved and idealized by all the inmates." Darrow noticed that the cell's barred window looked out on a garden. Debs told him, "I look at that garden of flowers. . . . I never see the bars."

Darrow was only one of a stream of distinguished visitors calling on the 64-year-old prisoner. Debs often received twice as much mail as the rest of the inmates combined; prison censors worked overtime. Yet he had been allowed to campaign in his "jail house to the White House" run only by issuing one statement of 500 words each week. In one of them, for instance, he quoted President Wilson's revealing comments in a 1919 speech, when he asked, "Is there any child who does not know that the seed of war in the modern world is industrial and commercial rivalry?" The war just ended, Wilson declared, "was a commercial and industrial war. It was not a political war." Wasn't that saying, in different words, what socialists had contended for years: that the war was over profits, among rival capitalist powers? Debs and many others had gone to prison for saying exactly that.

His admirers had long hoped for his release. Now in its final months in office, the Wilson administration was quietly letting some other dissidents go free. At the end of November 1920, two full years after the war's end, a hunger strike finally prompted the release of the last remaining 33 conscientious objectors. Wilson had even freed a fellow inmate of Debs, a German undercover operative caught during the war trying to sabotage American freighters. When, some weeks after the election, the White House announced that the president had once again declined to pardon the Socialist leader, Debs declared, "It is he, not I, who needs a pardon."

Aftermath

MARCH 4, 1921, dawned brisk and cool. A gaunt Woodrow Wilson, beneath his overcoat dressed formally in gloves, gray trousers, and a cutaway, used a cane as Secret Service men helped him slowly ease each foot down a few steps under the White House portico. Warren Harding joined him in the back of an open car, both men in top hats, chatting uneasily on the short drive through applauding crowds to the Capitol. It was the first time outgoing and incoming presidents had ridden to an inauguration in an automobile and not a carriage.

Harding climbed the wide steps of the great building, but Wilson, in a wheelchair, went through a small door sometimes used for deliveries, and was taken upstairs by elevator. In the President's Room in the Senate wing, sitting behind a table, he received his cabinet, General Pershing, and other dignitaries. However, he declined Harding's invitation to witness his swearing in by Chief Justice Edward White, the man who had wept with joy at Wilson's call for war in this same building four years earlier. He knew he could not handle the many steps on the Capitol's east side, where the inauguration would take place.

As the Marine Band played "Hail to the Chief," all eyes focused on Harding. The Wilsons, accompanied by Dr. Grayson and almost unobserved, slipped away and into a limousine. It carried the couple to their new Georgian Revival home, equipped with wheelchair access and an electric elevator, in Washington's secluded Kalorama neighborhood. There they would remain quietly until Wilson died less than three years later.

Edith Wilson would live on in the house four decades more. In a memoir, a multivolume biography she authorized and partly financed, and even a carefully supervised Hollywood film—a lavish whitewash in Technicolor that won five Oscars—she assiduously crafted her husband's image as a president to rank with Washington and Lincoln. She also did her best to burnish the myth that, despite his stroke, he quickly recovered the ability to govern the country. She survived long enough to return to the Capitol for a VIP seat at the 1961 inauguration of John F. Kennedy.

Wilson's successor traditionally receives low marks. Americans associate Warren Gamaliel Harding with his fondness for poker and drink, his extramarital affairs (one of which produced a child), and some unsavory men he placed in high positions, one of whom would become the first former cabinet member jailed for crimes committed in office.

People have also mocked Harding for his language, which H. L. Mencken dubbed Gamalielese. "It reminds me of a string of wet sponges; it reminds me of tattered washing on the line; it reminds me of stale bean-soup, of college yells, of dogs barking idiotically through endless nights. It is so bad that a sort of grandeur creeps into it." A rival politician once called Harding's verbiage "an army of pompous phrases moving over the landscape in search of an idea. Sometimes these meandering words would actually capture a straggling thought and bear it triumphantly, a prisoner in their midst, until it died of servitude."

In the speeches he gave in his famously sonorous voice, Harding's nouns sometimes wandered into duty as verbs and often entire sentences were impenetrable, such as: "There was no American failure to resist the attempted reversion of civilization; there will be no failure today or tomorrow." Or "There is a public mandate in manifest understanding." Still, compared with the outright lies uttered by presidents before and since, these were minor sins.

Despite his flaws, Harding undid much of the harsh repression still in place from the war years and the Red Scare. His appointee as postmaster general stopped press censorship, limiting himself to distributing patronage jobs and to peripheral involvement in one of the administration's several corruption scandals. Harding also moved, although slowly, to set free more of the nation's remaining 147 federal political prisoners. Even before his election, he had privately acknowledged regrets about his own vote for war. "Why should we kid each other?" he told an Ohio newspaperman, off the record. "Debs was right. We shouldn't have been in that war." Many other Americans, not merely those on the left, had by then come to feel the same way.

Debs was then both living and working in the Atlanta penitentiary's hospital, which brought him closer to a dark side of life behind bars. One in five inmates suffered from syphilis, and at night he could hear the screams of morphine and heroin addicts experiencing withdrawal. A friend perished from an operation that went awry. The Socialist Party leader saw other inmates buried on prison grounds when no one claimed their bodies. Heart troubles made it hard for him to sleep and sometimes even to breathe.

Three weeks after the inauguration, with a promise from Debs not to escape, Harding's attorney general, Harry Daugherty, invited him to Washington for a visit. He traveled by overnight train, alone, unguarded, and in civilian clothes—something virtually unheard of for a prisoner serving a lengthy sentence. In Daugherty's office, according to the attorney general, they "talked freely for several hours." Despite their disagreements, Daugherty recalled, "I found him a charming personality, with a deep love for his fellow man. . . . I could understand why he was a man of influence and had polled a million votes."

By the time Debs returned to Atlanta, the news had gotten out. The American Legion and other right-wing groups were furious at the idea of his release. "He is where he belongs," declared the *New York Times*. "He should stay there." The president did, however, release a few prisoners, among them the three Kentuckians in the penitentiary at Moundsville, West Virginia, for their conversations in Charles Schoberg's cobbler's shop. Harding commuted their sentences to the six months they had served.

Kate Richards O'Hare continued to tour the country demanding freedom for Debs and the others who remained in jail. A few months after Harding took office, traveling with her 14-year-old daughter, she was scheduled to speak in Twin Falls, Idaho. The city council hastily passed an ordinance making her talk illegal. A local socialist telephoned her with the news, but O'Hare scoffed, "Barking dogs don't bite." After she ignored police warnings to leave town, three carloads of vigilantes, led by the local American Legion commander, grabbed her and shoved her onto the floor of one car. They drove her more than 150 miles before the car broke down during the night and she was able to escape—or was allowed to do so—outside a small town in Nevada. Shaken, she gave one more speech in Idaho, in a machine shop after being locked out of a lecture hall, and then suspended her tour for a month.

Finally, on Christmas Day 1921, her efforts, and pressure from many others, paid off. Eugene Debs walked free. Still in his convict's blue denim, the Socialist leader was first treated to a send-off breakfast at the home of the Atlanta penitentiary warden. Then he changed into a suit and shoes made in the prison workshop, and, with the $5 in his pocket issued to all convicts on their release, made his way slowly through the waiting crowd. He turned around to face the 2,300 prisoners crowded up against three floors of barred windows and shouting his name. Holding up his felt hat and cane, he wept. In the warden's car taking him to the station, he could still hear their cheers half a mile away.

As his train steamed north, groups of admirers boarded to greet him and ride on to the next stop. Instead of using the more expensive Pullman ticket the government had given him, Debs moved to coach and declared that he would donate the difference to victims of the famine now ravaging war-torn Russia. After the train arrived in Washington, he met again with Attorney General Daugherty, then walked the several blocks to the White House. In the Oval Office, Harding rose to shake his hand, saying, "I have heard so damned much about you, Mr. Debs, that I am now very glad to meet you."

They talked for half an hour. Soon afterward the president wrote to a friend: "He is of a very clean and lovable character, and I am sure I have heard men in Congress say things worse than the utterances upon which he was convicted." Debs joked to reporters that he had run for the White House five times, but this was the first time he'd actually gotten there.

From Washington's Union Station, he headed home to Terre Haute, Indiana, where festivities organized by Kate and Frank O'Hare awaited him. Debs was now free, but the president had only commuted his sentence to time served; he had not pardoned him—which would have restored all his rights, such as the ability to vote. Before his train pulled out, a journalist asked him how he felt about not regaining his full rights as a US citizen.

"Now," Debs answered, "I am only a citizen of the world."

ALBERT JOHNSON HAD not even waited for the new president to take office before arguing for further tightening of immigration laws. The bill he soon shepherded through Congress dramatically slashed the number of immigrants permitted to enter the country until a more permanent legal barrier could be put in place. His committee issued an alarmed report noting that "during the one month of October, 1920, it is estimated that of the 74,665 immigrants arriving at Ellis Island, more than 75 per cent were of the Semitic race."

Johnson was now infatuated with the new pseudoscience of eugenics, seeing in its elaborate hierarchy of races confirmation of a lifetime of prejudice. He repeatedly called a eugenics expert to testify before his committee, a man who showed slides with such images as "a typical American head," a "Filipino Girl with two extra limbs," and a chart of the "Approaching Extinction of Mayflower Descendants."

He also released documents he had obtained from the State Department, a stronghold of the country's WASP elite. These were statements from American consuls abroad describing those applying for visas to immigrate. From Athens: people "of the peasant class" who "represent a low form of unskilled labor." From Sicily: those who "are inimical to the best interests of the American government. . . . Their standard of living and their characteristics . . . render them unassimilable." And from Poland, where the applicants were largely Jews fleeing pogroms: "Ninety-five per cent of these persons are of the very lowest classes of the country. . . . They are filthy and ignorant and the majority are verminous."

Jewish organizations were furious. Accused of prejudice, the congressman shot back: "Not so. I care not whether the influx is Jewish, Moslem, Pagan, Buddhist, Christian or what not. . . . It brings too many who are antigovernment and anti-God." He raised the specter of the country being flooded with the most alien of aliens: "You will see ships coming into Ellis Island with immigrants hanging over the edges. Some ships today have established fourth-class steerage rates, and it is not much of an exaggeration to say that in the fourth class immigrants are fed from troughs like swine."

Many other luminaries took up this cry, including Wilson's former propaganda chief, George Creel, who wrote articles in the widely read weekly *Collier's* entitled "Melting Pot or Dumping Ground?" and "Close the Gates!" Johnson showed his fellow legislators the familiar color-coded map of "the situation in New York City," and introduced, as a witness, the map's creator (now long out of the army), "Captain Trevor."

EVEN THOUGH EUGENE Debs was now finally free, more than 100 political prisoners remained in federal penitentiaries. As 1922 began, Kate and Frank O'Hare, who each had a shrewd eye for how to appeal to the public, came up with a plan to head for Washington with members of the prisoners' families, as a "living petition." Twelve wives and 18 children departed with Kate from St. Louis. Filmed by a newsreel crew, "The Children's Crusade" traveled by train to more than a dozen towns and cities. Other women and children joined and left the caravan along the way. They held rallies in churches and union halls, parading down various Main Streets behind a boy holding a sign that said A LITTLE CHILD SHALL LEAD THEM.

The press loved it. In Terre Haute, a frail Debs left his sickbed to share a meal with the marchers and drop a $20 gold piece in their collection basket. In Chicago, Jane Addams saw off a contingent of women and children heading to join them. In Detroit, a Romanian children's choir sang for them and Finnish socialist women cooked for them. In Philadelphia supporters took the children to Independence Hall, and, in New York, to the circus.

As the marchers paraded along New York's Madison Avenue, the city police bomb squad followed them. A journalist recorded their banners: A HUNDRED AND THIRTEEN MEN JAILED FOR THEIR OPINIONS, IS THE CONSTITUTION DEAD? and I NEVER SAW MY DADDY. Among the marchers she found the wives of tenant farmers and Wobblies, oil-field hands and cotton pickers, a clothing worker and a pacifist preacher.

A young girl named Irene Danley carried a sign reading MY MOTHER DIED OF A BROKEN HEART. An Arkansas farmer and Christian socialist, Irene's father spent more than four years in Leavenworth. His wife died after his arrest, and various friends took in Irene and her four siblings. Small wonder that restaurant chefs cooked free dinners for the caravan and railroads transported them without charge.

Thirty-seven women and children finally arrived in Washington, moved into a house rented by supporters, tried to enter a church service the president was attending, and started picketing the White House with signs like NO PROFITEER WENT TO PRISON. Harding would not receive them, but by midsummer 1922, either his heart or his political instincts made him release 50 more federal political prisoners. A year later, only 36 were still left, including some convicted in the big show trial of Wobblies in Chicago that had ended five years earlier.

On August 2, 1923, midway through his presidential term, Warren Harding suffered a fatal heart attack and cerebral hemorrhage in a San Francisco hotel room. It was not until June 1924 that his successor, Calvin Coolidge, set the very last of the 36 prisoners free. For the first time in seven years, no American was in a federal prison because of something he or she had written, said, or believed.

How many political prisoners were there altogether? Restricting the total only to those jailed for a year or more by the federal government between 1917 and 1921 for their written or spoken words, the author Stephen Kohn, a lawyer, has counted 462 men and women. "The number of political dissidents who served less than a year in prison," he cautions, "is simply too great to document."

Also undocumented—a fact in itself shocking—is what appears to be an even greater number than those in federal custody: political prisoners incarcerated in county jails or state penitentiaries. A majority of states had passed copycat laws in the wake of the Espionage Act, and many cities, like Boston and New York, also rushed to do the same. No one has ever counted the total number of people jailed under such laws.

Only in a few states has anyone bothered to compile figures. In California, for example, which at that time was far from the nation's most populous state, more than 500 people were indicted under the state's criminal syndicalism law, one of many such measures around the country designed to silence the Left. Seventy-three of those Californians arrested were sent to prison for terms ranging from one to 14 years. In Montana, a 1918 sedition bill provided a prison sentence of up to 20 years and a $20,000 fine for any "disloyal, profane, violent, scurrilous, contemptuous, slurring or abusive" words directed against, among other things, the American form of government, the Constitution, or the flag. Forty men and one woman would serve a collective total of 63 years at hard labor, averaging 19 months each. After one defendant, Ray Rumsey, was imprisoned, his family farm failed, and his 12 children were put up for adoption. Before Montana governor Samuel Stewart left office in January 1921, he commuted the sentences of 50 prisoners, including seven rapists and 13 murderers—but not one person convicted under the state's sedition law.

WITH WILSON AND Palmer out of power, gradually some of the other actors also left the stage.

Robert La Follette was dismayed by the way both parties abandoned the progressive ideals he had fought for all his life. With his dramatically upswept forelock now a towering bush of gray, the diminutive senator ran as an independent candidate for president in 1924, garnering nearly five million votes, about one-sixth of the total. He carried only his home state of Wisconsin. For his disloyalty to his party, Senate Republicans stripped him of a committee chairmanship. He died the next year. More than 30 years later, a committee led by John F. Kennedy named him as one of the five most distinguished of all US senators.

After the Wilson administration ended, the slight, bearded figure of Louis F. Post took to the lecture circuit. He also wrote articles, pamphlets, and a long account of the successful battle with Palmer and Hoover to stop mass deportations. For the *Journal of Negro History* he described his experience as a young man seeing the old racist order triumph over Reconstruction in the South. He could not find a publisher, however, for a book that, counter to the mood of the day, backed an open-door immigration policy and denounced the idea that Anglo-Saxons were in any way superior to everyone else.

Ralph Van Deman, who built up his enormous Military Intelligence apparatus in 1917 and 1918, retired from the army in 1929. Settling in San Diego and supported by wealthy sympathizers, he opened a private intelligence bureau. With his own network of agents, he traded information with district attorneys, county sheriffs, police Red squads, the FBI, and employers eager to break unions. His vast collection of scurrilous data on subversives relied on the same system of file cards he had first developed to track Filipino nationalists. "It was a rare Red," declared the *San Diego Union* on the general's death in 1952 at 86, "whose appearance in this area was not duly noted." Van Deman did not hesitate to pass on the results of his surveillance to politicians who shared his suspicion of liberals and leftists of all kinds. One of those he helped was a young Californian running for the Senate in 1950, Richard M. Nixon, who won that race by smearing his opponent as a Communist sympathizer.

Another specialist in surveillance, Leo Wendell, enjoyed playing roles so much that he finally played too many, adopting at least four other aliases besides Louis Walsh. Finally, in 1924, a labor newspaper discovered who he was and blew his cover. He started a new life in Detroit, launching a detective and public relations agency that he called, with a triumphant flourish of his Pittsburgh alias, Wendell, Walsh, and Brown. There is no clue who Brown was—or if he even existed. Wendell did not, however, lose the love of violence that had been so visible when he reveled in beating senseless a strikebreaker on a Pittsburgh streetcar. He now worked for a time as a grand jury investigator, but he lost one such job, according to an account of the case, when "the special prosecutor learned that [Wendell's] methods of acquiring information included dangling recalcitrant witnesses by their heels from upper story hotel windows."

Such practices did not prevent Wendell from getting a commission in the intelligence branch of the Michigan State Troops, the predecessor to the Michigan National Guard, where he rose to the rank of lieutenant colonel. He died in 1945, leaving a tangle of debts and four children born to three different women, only one of whom he was married to at the time of the child's birth. His widow seized from a safe deposit box money he had set aside for his last lover, the mother of one of his children. She left her rival a note in the empty box reading, "Find what you were looking for?" Even after his death, Wendell left a trail of deception, for several obituaries declared that it was he who made the famous seizure of an attaché's briefcase on a New York City elevated train in 1915 that helped unravel Germany's wartime American spy network. All historians, however, credit another agent; Wendell was not even in New York at the time.

One more Red hunter, Major General Leonard Wood, greatly hoped to become secretary of war in the Harding administration. But the new president was in no mood to have a former rival with a passionate following anywhere near him. Instead, Harding sent Wood back to the Philippines, where he spent six frustrating years as governor general, fruitlessly trying to persuade Filipinos to abandon their dreams of eventual independence.

After being released from prison in 1921, Marie Equi resumed her medical practice. A heart attack slowed her down, but she lived long enough, as many other radicals of the era did not, to enjoy the complete pardon, restoring all rights, that President Franklin D. Roosevelt granted to 1,500 wartime dissenters on Christmas Eve 1933. She spoke in public for the last time the following year, supporting a longshoremen's strike.

Kate Richards O'Hare returned to the life she had known as a traveling speaker, now focusing on the horrendous conditions in America's prisons. Sometimes she even paced the lecture stage in the long dress of purple, black, and green stripes given to her in the Missouri penitentiary. "If I were ruler of the Universe," she wrote, she would "see to it that no judge ever sat on a criminal bench until he had served at least one year in prison." There is no record of how her children felt about her long absences from home, but perhaps it says something that none of them later made a career of political activism.

In her lectures O'Hare described a bleak world that had its own underground entrepreneurs: a trusty who for one dollar would leave your cell door unlocked all night; an older inmate who recruited young women to go to work for pimps when they were released. For years she also campaigned against the $43 million industry of prison contract labor, which manufactured goods like the garments she had herself sewn in the prison workshop, which in turn undersold clothing made by unionized workers. Thanks in part to her efforts, in 1929 Congress essentially banned the sale of such goods in interstate commerce.

Life was not easy for her. She wrote to Emma Goldman that she felt herself a "sort of political orphan now with no place to lay my head." She and her husband, Frank, divorced. Her last job was as assistant director of penology for a new reform-minded chief of the California state prison system. There, she was able to abolish flogging, close San Quentin State Prison's notorious dungeons, improve food and hygiene, and finally help establish the country's first major minimum-security prison for men. The *San Francisco Examiner* even referred to her as a "noted criminologist."

What happened, finally, to the three people in our story who, on a freezing December night in 1919, encountered each other in the kitchen of a tugboat crossing New York Harbor?

Emma Goldman, of course, had no choice but to board the steamship *Buford* when the tug arrived at the ship's anchorage. It carried her and 248 others on a journey that ended in Soviet Russia. Although she and Alexander Berkman had been curious to see the Communist experiment and had great hopes for it, they quickly became appalled by its violent suppression of all dissent. After two years, deeply disillusioned, they left Russia forever, and she spent the rest of her life in Europe and Canada. Although allowed into the United States for a brief lecture tour by Franklin Roosevelt's administration, it barred her from returning to live, despite her longing "for America like a woman for a man."

J. Edgar Hoover enjoyed one of the longest spans any American has spent in a position of great political power. In 1924, not yet 30, he became director of the Bureau of Investigation—which added "Federal" to its name in 1935—and would remain so for nearly fifty years. By midcentury, his stern, round face and hard-edged voice warning about Communist infiltration would become a familiar fixture of congressional hearings.

A master of public relations, he orchestrated the production of books with titles like *The FBI in Peace and War*, hagiographic movies like *The FBI Story*, and even a long-running TV series, *The FBI*. He had little interest in the thorny jobs of fighting the Mafia or white-collar crime, but relentlessly pursued a far easier target: members of the Communist Party and people he claimed were controlled by it, including Dr. Martin Luther King Jr. More than one president would have liked to see Hoover go, but his network of allies in Congress and his rumored store of damaging information about people in high places guaranteed that none of them dared fire him. He died in office in 1972.

Ironically, the least-known member of the trio in that tugboat kitchen had the greatest effect on twentieth-century America. Albert Johnson's decades-long crusade against immigrants climaxed in 1924, with the passage of the Johnson-Reed Act. Until it was abandoned more than 40 years later, the act placed the most severe restrictions on immigration in American history. It barred Asians from the country entirely, and it parceled out only a tiny quota of slots to other immigrants.

After an initial transition period of several years, these slots were allocated by a formula supposedly based on the "national origins" of the American population. This was a recipe for manipulation because, of course, so many Americans can trace their ancestry to more than one country or ethnicity. The entire scheme was the brainchild of Johnson's ally John B. Trevor, with its final formula allocating immigration slots influenced by an elaborate report Trevor helped compile. The report was full of figures that were impossibly precise, including a suspiciously large percentage of the US population whom he asserted were descendants of "old Colonial white stock."

Trevor and Johnson exchanged dozens of visits and hundreds of letters, Johnson sometimes addressing him as "My Dear Captain." They traded drafts of the immigration bill, Trevor at one point expressing anxiety about "undesirable mongrel immigration" from Latin America. As success neared, Trevor sent Johnson a monogrammed billfold from Cartier, and a telegram urging him, DO NOT YIELD on having a fingerprinting requirement in the new law.

"You can see the difference at Ellis Island," Johnson proudly declared after the act bearing his name passed. "Officials there say that the immigrants who come through look like our own people coming home from a vacation." And, of course, there were far fewer of them, and they were not of the sorts that Johnson and Trevor loathed. The Johnson-Reed Act reduced by nearly 95 percent the number of immigrants from southern and eastern Europe—in other words, Italians, Poles, and Jews. A young agitator in prison in Germany was impressed by the changes wrought by the law. "They refuse to allow immigration of elements which are bad from the health point of view," wrote Adolf Hitler in *Mein Kampf*, "and absolutely forbid naturalization of certain defined races."

Johnson was voted out of office in the Democratic sweep of 1932 and after that receded into well-deserved obscurity. But his work had been done. The law he and Trevor crafted would bar from the United States untold numbers of refugees from the Holocaust, leaving them to end their lives in Hitler's death camps. When a proposal was under discussion in 1939 that would have made an exception to the Johnson-Reed Act to allow 20,000 Jewish refugee children to enter the country, one of those who led the successful fight against it was Trevor, who declared that he wanted "to protect the youth of America from this foreign invasion." A product of the darkest period of America's twentieth century was precisely what stopped us from sheltering those trying to flee the nadir of the century in Europe.

AFTER THE EXTREME repression of 1917 to 1921 came to an end, Americans had plenty to distract them from politics. The automobile had decisively displaced the horse, and the Model T and Model A Ford also became illicit bedrooms on wheels. Those who could afford it held lavish parties like those of F. Scott Fitzgerald's Jay Gatsby, and those who couldn't still enjoyed the novelty of jazz, the radio, the phonograph, the new dial telephones, and the stardom of Babe Ruth. It would be comforting to say that the country had turned a page, decisively ending the conflicts that had riven it so deeply.

But had it? In some ways, an era did end, and its very excesses gave Americans a greater appreciation of the Bill of Rights, something gradually reflected over later decades in school curricula, Supreme Court decisions, and much more. No political mass arrests on the scale of the Palmer Raids happened again. Indeed, in early 1921, a Senate subcommittee subjected both Palmer and Hoover to a grilling about those raids so harsh that the attorney general feared he might be impeached. He never again ran for public office.

Never would the government censor news media and put publications out of business the way Albert Burleson had done. Most conscientious objectors of the Second World War and the Vietnam War did not endure the sadistic, sometimes fatal brutality suffered by their counterparts in 1917 and 1918. And a group founded to defend those very resisters became, over the following decades, one of the country's most influential civic organizations: the American Civil Liberties Union.

The legacy of the harsh crackdown of 1917–21, however, would prove long-lasting. First of all, it struck a shattering blow to the Socialist Party. Not only were most socialist newspapers and magazines barred from the mail, but enough Socialists were imprisoned that, had they all been in one place, they would have been able to hold a party congress behind bars. The long-term political prisoners of this era included not just rank-and-file party members, but former Socialist candidates for governor in South Dakota, Minnesota, and New Jersey. Other such prisoners included state Socialist Party secretaries in Minnesota, Washington, West Virginia, and South Dakota, and a former candidate for Congress in Oklahoma. And Kate Richards O'Hare, of course, had run for both houses of Congress, and Eugene Debs for president.

When Debs took to the road again after his release from prison, he often found that at the last minute he was denied the venues he had booked. In Cleveland, the City Club canceled its invitation, and in Los Angeles the only place he could speak was an outdoor rally at the city zoo. But Debs had it easier than the socialist writer Upton Sinclair, who, when he began giving a speech in San Pedro, California in 1923, was arrested while reading the First Amendment aloud. By the time Debs died in 1926, the party that had once elected 33 state legislators, 79 mayors, and well over 1,000 city council members and other municipal officials had shrunk to less than 10,000 members nationwide.

Socialism, of course, had never taken as deep root in the United States as it had in Europe, but for some years it was a significant force in American politics. The Republican and Democratic legislators who voted for early-twentieth-century reform measures like child labor laws and the income tax did so in part to stave off demands from the Socialist Party for bigger changes.

In 1911, for example, the Socialist congressman Victor Berger of Wisconsin introduced a bill for a national old-age pension, a goal that would be realized 24 years later as Social Security. In 1916, Socialist Meyer London of New York introduced a bill strikingly similar to one that would become law nearly a century later, the Affordable Care Act. He also advocated freedom for the Philippines, unemployment insurance, and paid maternity leave.

Typical of their governance of many other cities under their control, the Socialists who dominated Milwaukee for 38 years toughened building and factory regulation, curbed police power over strikers, provided free public concerts and lectures, raised the wages of city employees, and guaranteed them an eight-hour day. A state organization that was loosely allied with the Socialists, the Nonpartisan League, briefly controlled North Dakota, wresting power away from the big corporations that often put farmers in debt and creating what remains the country's only state-owned flour mill and state-owned bank.

The Socialist Party would never recover from the mass jailings and the crushing of its press that took place under Wilson. Had it not been so hobbled, even with a minority of voters, it might well have pushed the mainstream parties into creating the sort of stronger social safety net and national health insurance systems that people take for granted in Canada and Western Europe today. This is one of American history's most tantalizing "what if?" questions.

The Industrial Workers of the World were similarly shattered. Fearing a further round of prosecutions, Big Bill Haywood and eight other Wobblies, out on bail after they appealed their case, fled the country. As his ship left New York Harbor, Haywood claimed, he told the Statue of Liberty, "Good-bye, you've had your back turned on me too long." Their flight, however, dismayed some of the supporters who had put up the bail money, in one case by mortgaging a home—which was then seized by the government. Haywood would die in Russia in 1928 as a deeply unhappy exile, while the IWW shriveled at home. In later years, periodically some reporter would discover that the group still had a small office, and would do a story about the elderly men gathered there.

More far-reaching than the toll on the Wobblies was that on the labor movement. The country's courts, empowered by the slew of state criminal syndicalism laws enacted during the Red Scare, decisively turned against unions. Although labor militance was far lower after 1921 than in the few years before, courts issued as many injunctions against strikes during the 1920s as in the entire four decades starting in 1880. Even the resolutely moderate American Federation of Labor lost more than a million members between 1920 and 1923. In a country whose inequalities of wealth were rapidly increasing, the 1920s saw little significant social legislation. Labor unions would not regain their momentum until the shock of the Great Depression gave birth to the New Deal era in the mid-1930s.

In the eyes of those who presided over it, the repression of 1917–21 accomplished its purpose. James A. Finch, the longtime pardon attorney in the Justice Department, expressed this clearly when he wrote to Attorney General Daugherty in December 1923, after almost all the Espionage Act prisoners had finally been released: "It is exceedingly fortunate that the government has . . . kept a sufficient number of them in prison to set an example of firmness that will go down in history as a warning."

AS THE RED SCARE subsided, a warning of a more brutal sort was given to Black Americans who had hoped for a better life by leaving the Deep South. The Wilson administration had done virtually nothing to prosecute members of the white mobs who killed hundreds in the "Red Summer" of 1919, and such stark impunity bred more violence. One of the most horrific outbreaks came two years later in Tulsa, Oklahoma. This was the same city where, in 1917, the 16 Wobblies had been whipped, tarred, and feathered. What unfolded now, however, was infinitely worse.

The fateful chain of events began on May 30, 1921, with a rumor, probably spurious, that a Black man had threatened a white woman in an office building's elevator. Street fighting broke out and a white man was killed. Over the following two days, white mobs, including many veterans, roamed the city's streets, looting Black homes and businesses. They set scores of buildings on fire, sometimes from the top down by taking to the air in small planes to drop homemade incendiary bombs.

Signs of Black economic success have often provoked white resentment, and Tulsa had an unusually large Black business district, sometimes called Black Wall Street, that included shops, restaurants, hotels, and lawyers' and doctors' offices. More than 1,400 businesses and homes covering 35 blocks were left in charred, smoking ruins. A photograph W. E. B. Du Bois published in *The Crisis* looked like one of a city leveled to rubble by a carpet bombing. Some 8,000 people, almost all Black, were rendered homeless. The National Guard took 4,000 Blacks into custody, holding many for up to eight days. No whites were arrested. There was no accurate death count, but scholars now believe that some 300 people were killed, almost all of them Black. "Bolshevik propaganda," reported the *Los Angeles Times*, "was the principal cause of the race riot."

Two weeks after what he called "the late negro uprising," Tulsa's mayor announced that "everything is quiet in our city . . . this menace has been fully conquered." He promoted a plan for turning parts of the ruins into an industrial park and new railway terminal, to separate white and Black Tulsa. Blacks burned out of their homes would be allowed to rebuild "farther north and east." Zoning regulations were changed accordingly. That mayor, incidentally, was T. D. Evans, the same man who, as a judge four years earlier, had found the arrested Wobblies guilty because "these are no ordinary times."

Meanwhile, not just in the South but across the country, crosses flamed in the night as the Ku Klux Klan enjoyed a resurgence, reaching an estimated four million members by 1924. Many Klansmen, including the leading strategist of the group's rebirth, Imperial Wizard William Simmons, were former members of the American Protective League.

On Memorial Day 1927, a march of some 1,000 Klansmen through the New York City borough of Queens turned into a brawl with the police. Several people wearing Klan hoods were arrested, one of them a young real estate developer named Fred Trump. Ninety years later, his son, with similar feelings about people of color, would enter the White House.

During Donald Trump's presidency, the forces that had blighted the America of a century earlier would be dramatically visible yet again: rage against immigrants and refugees, racism, Red-baiting, fear of subversive ideas in schools, and much more. And, of course, behind all of them is the appeal of simple solutions: deport aliens, forbid critical journalism, lock people up, blame everything on those of a different color or religion. All those impulses have long been with us. Other presidents, both Republican and Democrat, have made dog-whistle appeals on the issue of race. The anti-Communist witch-hunting of Senator Joseph McCarthy and his imitators would prove far more influential in American political life than the country's minuscule Communist Party, putting people in prison, wrecking careers, and causing thousands to leave the country. The American tendency to blame things on sinister conspiracies has found new targets; instead of the villains being the pope or the Bolsheviks, in recent times they have included Sharia law, George Soros, Satanist pedophile rings, and more.

Vigilante superpatriots, sometimes violent, have cropped up again and again since the American Protective League prowled the streets looking for draft dodgers. Just as veterans of the Philippine War appeared in the political violence that surged after 1917, so veterans of later Asian counterguerrilla wars, in Vietnam, Iraq, and Afghanistan, have helped fill the ranks of new camouflage-clad armed militia groups.

Although the long battle between business and organized labor rarely again would become as violent as it was more than a century ago, it has not disappeared. With smooth-talking, social-media-savvy "union avoidance" consultants replacing National Guard troops and private detectives, that struggle continues to the present day.

America's version of democracy is far from perfect, and every generation or two we learn anew just how fragile it can be. Almost all the tensions that roiled the country during and after the First World War still linger today. It may be a sudden event that kindles them into flame, as did the nation's entry into that war, followed by the Russian Revolution, or it may be gradually mounting pressures. Some of those pressures are already here, such as the increasing northward flow of refugees fleeing global warming.

To keep these dark forces from overwhelming American society once again will require a lot from us. Knowledge of our history, for one thing, so we can better see the danger signals and the first drumbeats of demagoguery. Brave men and women both inside and outside the government, like those who spoke the truth and stuck to their principles more than a hundred years ago. A more equitable distribution of wealth, so that there will not be tens of millions of people economically losing ground and looking for scapegoats to blame. A mass media far less craven toward those in power than it was in 1917–21. And above all, a vigilant respect for civil rights and constitutional safeguards, to save ourselves from ever slipping back into the darkness again.

ACKNOWLEDGMENTS

As a writer I've been blessed in many ways, but none of them is greater than having friends and family members who have been willing to read my drafts and give me critical feedback. If I listed what I learned from each reader of this manuscript—a factual error here, a better way to organize a chapter there, a narrative kink or detour straightened out somewhere else—I could go on for pages. I won't, but let me just express my deep gratitude to all these readers: Georges Borchardt, Chuck Farnsworth, Elizabeth Farnsworth, David Hochschild, Michael Kazin, Cynthia Li, Scott Martelle, Michael Meyer, Barbara Sherman, Zachary Shore, Kathryn Kish Sklar, and a particularly low bow to Douglas Foster. My wife, Arlie Russell Hochschild, gets a special medal for reading and marking up the whole thing twice, taking time off to do so from working on a bold and extraordinary book of her own. It was a joy, as always, to share with her the people in these pages as I got to know them.

This book benefited greatly from the skilled pen of a superb freelance editor, my longtime friend Tom Engelhardt. Since he has worked on half a dozen previous books of mine as well, I've internalized more of his editorial skills than he will ever know. After Tom treated the book expertly on an outpatient basis, it then got superlative inpatient care from my Mariner Books editor Alex Littlefield. Editors at publishing houses are under such speed-up pressures these days that they often have little time for manuscripts, so the careful, sensitive reading Alex gave this book made me feel lucky indeed—all the more so when I received thoughtful comments, as well, from his colleague Jessica Vestuto. My thanks to Douglas Johnson for his admirably careful copyediting.

Several scholars of this period generously shared information, references, or documents with me: Bill R. Douglas, Aaron Goings, Julian Putkowski, Jonathan Rosenblum, John F. Sherman, and Kathryn Kish Sklar. Advice or help of other kinds came from Alexander S. Leidholdt, Nick Hiley, Marie Riley, and John Thiesen. I'm also indebted to the editors and fact-checkers of the magazines that published portions of this book when it was in progress: *The New Yorker*, *The New York Review of Books*, *The Washington Post Magazine*, and *Mother Jones*. Many thanks, too, to the institutions that let me try out some of this subject matter as lectures: Ashby Village, the National Council for History Education, and the American Academy in Berlin.

Most of the material here about Ralph Van Deman first appeared in my book *Lessons from a Dark Time and Other Essays*, and I have taken a few other details about this era from that volume as well. I have similarly stolen a few paragraphs from my *Rebel Cinderella: From Rags to Riches to Radical, the Epic Journey of Rose Pastor Stokes*, whose subject experienced the repression of the First World War years firsthand.

I was able to work in several archives before the COVID-19 pandemic made that impossible; after that, my requests for copies of materials or other help drew generous responses from the Abraham Lincoln Library and Museum, the Alkek Library at Texas State University, the Briscoe Center at the University of Texas, the University of Rochester, the Hudson River Museum, and the Bentley Historical Library at the University of Michigan. Vicki Killian retrieved some papers for me when COVID prevented a return visit to the National Archives.

I hope that my source notes and bibliography make clear the debts I have to other scholars of the years chronicled in this book. Some deserve special praise. Kenneth Ackerman's lively biography of J. Edgar Hoover's early years in office happened to be one of the first books I read about this period, and it was where I first met Louis F. Post. No one has studied Bureau of Investigation and FBI records as carefully as Regin Schmidt, and, before they became available, no one had examined court documents and newspapers as thoroughly as Gilbert Fite and H. C. Peterson. A. Scott Berg's biography of Woodrow Wilson was a constant reference for me, as was the monumental 69-volume collection of Wilson's papers superbly edited by Arthur Link and his colleagues. Alfred W. McCoy's writing introduced me to Ralph Van Deman and made me aware of how the violence of the Philippine War had come back to haunt the United States. And without the work of Charles H. McCormick, I would never have been aware of Leo Wendell. A grateful salute to them all.

SELECTED BIBLIOGRAPHY

Prefatory note: In the notes, I have generally not recorded the sources of items easily available from a variety of sources, both in print and online, such as debates in Congress or the speeches of Woodrow Wilson.

ARCHIVAL MATERIAL

Boehm, Randolph, ed. *U.S. Military Intelligence Reports: Surveillance of Radicals in the United States, 1917–1941*. Frederick, MD: University Publications of America, 1984. (34 microfilm reels.)

Kornweibel, Theodore, ed. *Federal Surveillance of Afro-Americans (1917–1925): The First World War, the Red Scare, and the Garvey Movement*. Frederick, MD: University Publications of America, 1986. (25 microfilm reels.)

Roscoe, Will. "The Murder of Frank Little: 'An Injury to One Is an Injury to All.'" Unpublished paper at the Montana Historical Society, 1973.

Trevor, John B. Papers. Bentley Historical Library, University of Michigan.

Van Deman, Ralph H. Papers. Hoover Institution Archives, Stanford University.

OG files, Record Group 65; Military Intelligence files, Record Group 165; US Army Overseas Operations and Commands, Record Group 395. National Archives and Records Administration (NARA), Washington, DC, and College Park, MD. At this writing, the OG file series, and some Military Intelligence files, are also available online at www.fold3.com.

CONGRESSIONAL HEARINGS

Investigation of Administration of Louis F. Post, Assistant Secretary of Labor, in the Matter of Deportation of Aliens. Hearings Before the Committee on Rules, House of Representatives, Sixty-Sixth Congress, Second Session, on H. Res. 522. Washington DC: US Government Printing Office, 1920. (Cited in notes as "Post hearings.")

DISSERTATIONS

Anderson, Adrian Norris. "Albert Sidney Burleson: A Southern Politician in the Progressive Era." PhD diss., Texas Technological College, 1967.

Candeloro, Dominic Lawrence. "Louis Freeland Post: Carpetbagger, Singletaxer, Progressive." PhD diss., University of Illinois at Urbana-Champaign, 1970.

Green, Martha Nesselbush. "Outspoken Woman: Gender and Free Speech in the Trial of Kate Richards O'Hare." PhD diss., Clark University, 1999.

Kim, Mee-Ae. "'It Is Time to Put Up the Bars': Albert Johnson and the Immigration Act of 1924." Master's thesis, Washington State University, 1995.

Mikkelsen, Vincent. "Coming from Battle to Face a War: The Lynching of Black Soldiers in the World War I Era." PhD diss., Florida State University, 2007.

OTHER

Link, Arthur, et al., editors. *The Papers of Woodrow Wilson*. Charlottesville: University of Virginia Press, Rotunda, 2017. (Cited in the notes as *PWW*.)

BOOKS AND ARTICLES

Ackerman, Kenneth D. *Young J. Edgar: Hoover, the Red Scare, and the Assault on Civil Liberties*. New York: Carroll & Graf, 2007.

Ameringer, Oscar. *If You Don't Weaken*. Norman: University of Oklahoma Press, 1983.

Anderson, Adrian. "President Wilson's Politician: Albert Sidney Burleson of Texas." *Southwestern Historical Quarterly* 77, no. 3 (January 1974).

Auerbach, Jerold S. "Woodrow Wilson's 'Prediction' to Frank Cobb: Words Historians Should Doubt Ever Got Spoken." *Journal of American History* 54, no. 3 (December 1967).

Avrich, Paul, and Karen Avrich. *Sasha and Emma: The Anarchist Odyssey of Alexander Berkman and Emma Goldman*. Cambridge, MA: Belknap/Harvard University Press, 2012.

Baker, Ray Stannard. *Woodrow Wilson: Life and Letters*. 8 vols. Garden City, NY: Doubleday, Doran, 1927–1939.

Barry, John M. *The Great Influenza: The Epic Story of the Deadliest Plague in History*. New York: Viking, 2004.

Bendersky, Joseph W. *The "Jewish Threat": Anti-Semitic Politics of the U.S. Army*. New York: Basic Books, 2000.

Berg, A. Scott. *Wilson*. New York: Putnam's, 2013.

Botkin, Jane Little. *Frank Little and the IWW: The Blood That Stained an American Family*. Norman: University of Oklahoma Press, 2017.

Bowles, Edmund A. "Karl Muck and His Compatriots: German Conductors in

America during World War I (And How They Coped)." *American Music* 25, no. 4 (Winter 2007).

Brandes, Stuart D. *Warhogs: A History of War Profits in America.* Lexington: University Press of Kentucky, 2015.

Brown, R. G., Zechariah Chafee, et al. *To the American People: Report upon the Illegal Practices of the United States Department of Justice.* Washington DC: National Popular Government League, 1920. (The "Twelve Lawyer Report")

Buckingham, Peter H. *Rebel against Injustice: The Life of Frank P. O'Hare.* Columbia: University of Missouri Press, 1996.

Capozzola, Christopher. *Uncle Sam Wants You: World War I and the Making of the Modern American Citizen.* New York: Oxford University Press, 2008.

Chapman, Lee Roy. "The Nightmare of Dreamland," *This Land*, 1 September 2011 (https://thislandpress.com/2012/04/18/tate-brady-battle-greenwood/).

Chester, Eric Thomas. *Free Speech and the Suppression of Dissent during World War I.* New York: Monthly Review Press, 2020.

———. *The Wobblies in Their Heyday: The Rise and Destruction of the Industrial Workers of the World during the World War I Era.* Santa Barbara, CA: Praeger, 2014.

Coben, Stanley. *A. Mitchell Palmer: Politician.* New York: Da Capo, 1972.

———. "A Study in Nativism: The American Red Scare of 1919–20." *Political Science Quarterly* 79, no. 1 (March 1964).

Conolly-Smith, Peter. "'Reading Between the Lines': The Bureau of Investigation, the United States Post Office, and Domestic Surveillance during World War I." *Social Justice* 36, no. 1 (2009).

Cooper, John Milton. *The Warrior and the Priest: Woodrow Wilson and Theodore Roosevelt.* Cambridge, MA: Belknap/Harvard University Press, 1983.

———. *Woodrow Wilson: A Biography.* New York, Knopf, 2009.

Cox, Mary Elizabeth. *Hunger in War and Peace: Women and Children in Germany, 1914–1924.* Oxford, UK: Oxford University Press, 2019.

Crosby, Alfred. *America's Forgotten Pandemic: The Influenza of 1918.* New York: Cambridge University Press, 2003.

Dalton, Brian J. "Wilson's Prediction to Cobb: Notes on the Auerbach-Link Debate." *Historian* 32, no. 4 (August 1970).

Daniels, Josephus. *The Cabinet Diaries of Josephus Daniels, 1913–1921.* Edited by E. David Cronon. Lincoln: University of Nebraska Press, 1963.

Dos Passos, John. *U.S.A.: The 42nd Parallel, 1919, The Big Money.* Edited by Townsend Ludington and Daniel Aaron. New York: Library of America, 1996.

Douglas, Bill. "Wartime Illusions and Disillusionment: Camp Dodge and Racial Stereotyping, 1917–1918." *Annals of Iowa* 57 (1998).

Drake, Richard. *The Education of an Anti-Imperialist: Robert La Follette and U.S. Expansion.* Madison: University of Wisconsin Press, 2013.

Dupuy, Ernest R. *Five Days to War: April 2–6, 1917.* Harrisburg, PA: Stackpole, 1967.

Ellis, Edward Robb. *Echoes of Distant Thunder: Life in the United States, 1914–1918.* New York: Coward, McCann, 1975.

Ellis, Mark. "J. Edgar Hoover and the 'Red Summer' of 1919." *Journal of American Studies* 28, no. 1 (1994).

Equal Justice Initiative. *Lynching in America: Targeting Black Veterans.* Montgomery, AL, 2017.

Falk, Candace Serena. *Love, Anarchy, and Emma Goldman.* New Brunswick, NJ: Rutgers University Press, 1990.

Feldman, Jay. *Manufacturing Hysteria: A History of Scapegoating, Surveillance, and Secrecy in Modern America.* New York: Pantheon, 2011.

Fischer, Nick. "The Committee on Public Information and the Birth of US State Propaganda." *Australasian Journal of American Studies* 35, no. 1 (July 2016).

Fite, Gilbert C., and H. C. Peterson. *Opponents of War, 1917–1918.* Madison: University of Wisconsin Press, 1957.

Fleming, Thomas. *The Illusion of Victory: America in World War I.* New York: Basic Books, 2003.

Foner, Philip S. *History of the Labor Movement in the United States.* 10 vols. New York: International Publishers, 1947–1994.

Freeberg, Ernest. *Democracy's Prisoner: Eugene V. Debs, the Great War, and the Right to Dissent.* Cambridge, MA: Harvard University Press, 2008.

Gillham, Lisa, with Bethany Richter Pollitt. "J. H. Kruse, War and the Terrible Threateners: Anti-German Hysteria in World War I Covington." *Northern Kentucky Views,* n.d., http://www.nkyviews.com/kenton/pdf/Kruse_Schoborg_Feldman.pdf.

Ginger, Ray. *Eugene V. Debs: The Making of an American Radical.* New York: Collier, 1977.

Goings, Aaron, Brian Barnes, and Roger Snider. *The Red Coast: Radicalism and Anti-Radicalism in Southwest Washington.* Corvallis: Oregon State University Press, 2019.

Goldman, Emma. *Living My Life: An Autobiography.* Salt Lake City: Gibbs M. Smith, 1982.

Goldman, Emma, and Alexander Berkman. *Anarchism on Trial: Speeches of Alexander Berkman and Emma Goldman Before the United States District Court in the City of New York, July, 1917.* New York: Mother Earth, [1917?].

Goldstein, Robert Justin. *Political Repression in Modern America from 1870 to 1976.* Urbana: University of Illinois Press, 2001.

Grayson, Cary T. *Woodrow Wilson: An Intimate Memoir.* New York: Holt, Rinehart and Winston, 1960.

Gregory, Ross. *Modern America, 1914 to 1945.* New York: Facts on File, 1995.

Gutfeld, Arnon. "The Murder of Frank Little: Radical Labor Agitation in Butte, Montana, 1917." *Labor History* 10, no. 2 (1969).

Hagedorn, Ann. *Savage Peace: Hope and Fear in America, 1919.* New York: Simon & Schuster, 2007.

Hamilton, John Maxwell. *Manipulating the Masses: Woodrow Wilson and the Birth of American Propaganda.* Baton Rouge: Louisiana State University Press, 2020.

Hanson, Ole. *Americanism versus Bolshevism.* Garden City, NY: Doubleday, Page, 1920.

Harries, Meirion, and Susie Harries. *The Last Days of Innocence: America at War, 1917–1918.* New York: Random House, 1997.

Hawkins, Michael Daly. "The Bisbee Deportation: There Will Be Ore." *Western Legal History* 31, no. 2 (2021).

Helquist, Michael. *Marie Equi: Radical Politics and Outlaw Passions.* Corvallis: Oregon State University Press, 2015.

Higham, John. *Strangers in the Land: Patterns of American Nativism, 1860–1925.* New Brunswick, NJ: Rutgers University Press, 2002.

Hodges, Adam. *World War I and Urban Order: The Local Class Politics of National Mobilization.* New York: Palgrave Macmillan, 2016.

Hoover, Irwin [Ike] Hood. *Forty-Two Years in the White House.* Boston: Houghton Mifflin, 1934.

Hough, Emerson. *The Web: The Authorized History of the American Protective League.* Chicago: Reilly & Lee, 1919.

House, Edward Mandell. *The Intimate Papers of Colonel House Arranged as a Narrative by Charles Seymour.* 4 vols. Boston: Houghton Mifflin, 1926–1928.

Houston, David F. *Eight Years with Wilson's Cabinet: 1913 to 1920, with a Personal Estimate of the President.* 2 vols. New York: Doubleday, Page, 1926.

Howe, Frederic C. *The Confessions of a Reformer.* New York: Scribner's, 1925.

Howlett, Charles F., Jeremy Kuzmarov, and Roger Peace, "United States Participation in World War One." United States Foreign Policy History and Resource Guide, 2018, http://peacehistory-usfp.org/ww1.

Interchurch World Movement. *Public Opinion and the Steel Strike: Supplementary Reports of the Investigators to the Commission of Inquiry.* New York: Da Capo, 1970.

Irons, Peter H. "'Fighting Fair': Zechariah Chafee, Jr., the Department of Justice, and the 'Trial at the Harvard Club.'" *Harvard Law Review* 94, no. 6 (April 1981).

Jaffe, Julian F. *Crusade against Radicalism: New York during the Red Scare, 1914–1924.* Port Washington, NY: Kennikat Press, 1972.

Jensen, Joan M. *Army Surveillance in America, 1775–1980.* New Haven: Yale University Press, 1991.

———. *The Price of Vigilance.* Chicago: Rand McNally, 1968.

Johnson, Donald. *The Challenge to American Freedoms: World War I and the Rise of the American Civil Liberties Union.* Lexington: University of Kentucky Press, 1963.

———. "Wilson, Burleson, and Censorship in the First World War." *Journal of Southern History* 28, no. 1 (February 1962).

Karp, Walter. *The Politics of War: The Story of Two Wars Which Altered Forever the Political Life of the American Republic (1890–1920)*. New York: Harper & Row, 1979.

Kazin, Michael. *American Dreamers: How the Left Changed a Nation*. New York: Knopf, 2011.

———. *War against War: The American Fight for Peace, 1914–1918*. New York: Simon & Schuster, 2017.

Keene, Jennifer. *Doughboys, the Great War, and the Remaking of America*. Baltimore: Johns Hopkins University Press, 2001.

Kellogg, Walter Guest. *The Conscientious Objector*. New York: Boni & Liveright, 1919.

Kendall, Paul. *Voices from the Past: Armistice 1918*. Barnsley, UK: Frontline, 2017.

Kennedy, David. *Over Here: The First World War and American Society*. New York: Oxford University Press, 1980.

Kennedy, Kathleen. *Disloyal Mothers and Scurrilous Citizens*. Bloomington: Indiana University Press, 1999.

Keynes, John Maynard. *The Economic Consequences of the Peace*. New York: Penguin, 1988.

Klingaman, William K. *1919: The Year Our World Began*. New York: St. Martin's, 1987.

Kohn, Stephen M. *American Political Prisoners: Prosecutions under the Espionage and Sedition Acts*. Westport, CT: Praeger, 1994.

Kornweibel, Theodore Jr. *"Investigate Everything": Federal Efforts to Compel Black Loyalty during World War I*. Bloomington: Indiana University Press, 2001.

———. *"Seeing Red": Federal Campaigns Against Black Militancy, 1919–1925*. Bloomington: Indiana University Press, 1998.

Krieger, Nancy. "Queen of the Bolsheviks: The Hidden History of Dr. Marie Equi." *Radical America* 17, no. 5 (September–October 1983).

Krugler, David F. *1919, the Year of Racial Violence: How African Americans Fought Back*. New York: Cambridge University Press, 2014.

Lansing, Robert. *War Memoirs of Robert Lansing, Secretary of State*. New York: Bobbs-Merrill, 1935.

Laurie, Clayton D. "The US Army and the Omaha Race Riot of 1919." *Nebraska History* 72 (1991).

Laurie, Clayton D., and Ronald H. Cole. *The Role of Federal Military Forces in Domestic Disorders, 1877–1945*. Washington, DC: Center of Military History, United States Army, 1997.

Leidholdt, Alexander S. "The Mysterious Mr. Maxwell and Room M-1: Clandestine Influences on American Postal Censorship during World War I." *American Journalism* 36, no. 3 (2019).

Levin, Phyllis Lee. *Edith and Woodrow: The Wilson White House*. New York: Scribner, 2001.

Lewis, David Levering. *W. E. B. Du Bois: Biography of a Race, 1868–1919*. New York: Holt, 1993.

Link, Arthur S. "That Cobb Interview." *Journal of American History* 72, no. 1 (June 1985).

Link, Arthur S., and Jerold S. Auerbach. Exchange of letters in "Historical News and Comments." *Journal of American History* 55, no. 1 (June 1968).

Lloyd George, David. *Memoirs of the Peace Conference*. Vol. 1. New Haven: Yale University Press, 1939.

Loerzel, Robert. "Blood in the Streets." *Chicago*, August 2019.

Lumpkins, Charles L. *American Pogrom: The East St. Louis Race Riot and Black Politics*. Athens: Ohio University Press, 2008.

McAdoo, William G. *Crowded Years: The Reminiscences of William G. McAdoo*. Port Washington, NY: Kennikat Press, 1971.

McCallum, Jack. *Leonard Wood: Rough Rider, Surgeon, Architect of American Imperialism*. New York: New York University Press, 2006.

McCormick, Charles H. *Seeing Reds: Federal Surveillance of Radicals in the Pittsburgh Mill District, 1917–1921*. Pittsburgh: University of Pittsburgh Press, 1997.

McCoy, Alfred W. *Policing America's Empire: The United States, the Philippines, and the Rise of the Surveillance State*. Madison: University of Wisconsin Press, 2009.

MacMillan, Margaret. *Paris 1919: Six Months That Changed the World*. New York: Random House, 2002.

McWhirter, Cameron. *Red Summer: The Summer of 1919 and the Awakening of Black America*. New York: Holt, 2011.

Mead, Gary. *The Doughboys: America and the First World War*. New York: Overlook, 2000.

Merriman, Scott A. "'An Intensive School of Disloyalty': The C. B. Schoberg Case under the Espionage and Sedition Acts in Kentucky during World War I." *Register of the Kentucky Historical Society* 98, no. 2 (Spring 2000).

Meyer, G. J. *The World Remade: America in World War I*. New York: Bantam Books, 2016.

Meyers, Christopher C. "'Killing Them by the Wholesale': A Lynching Rampage in South Georgia." *Georgia Historical Quarterly* 90, no. 2 (Summer 2006).

Miller, Sally M. *From Prairie to Prison: The Life of Social Activist Kate Richards O'Hare*. Columbia: University of Missouri Press, 1993.

Mills, Bill. *The League: The True Story of Average Americans on the Hunt for WWI Spies*. New York: Skyhorse, 2013.

Mock, James R. *Censorship 1917*. Princeton, NJ: Princeton University Press, 1941.

Morris, Edmund. *Colonel Roosevelt*. New York: Random House, 2010.

Murray, Robert K. *Red Scare: A Study in National Hysteria, 1919–1920*. Minneapolis: University of Minnesota Press, 1955.

National Civil Liberties Bureau. *The "Knights of Liberty" Mob and the I. W. W. Prisoners at Tulsa, Okla. (November 9, 1917)*. New York: 1918.

———. *What Happens in Military Prisons: The Public Is Entitled to Know the Facts*. New York: 1918.

Nielsen, Kim E. *Un-American Womanhood: Antiradicalism, Antifeminism, and the First Red Scare*. Columbus: Ohio State University Press, 2001.

Norwood, Stephen H. *Strikebreaking and Intimidation: Mercenaries and Masculinity in Twentieth-Century America*. Chapel Hill: University of North Carolina Press, 2002.

O'Hare, Kate Richards. *In Prison*. New York: Knopf, 1923.

———. *Kate O'Hare's Prison Letters*. Girard, KS: Appeal to Reason, 1919.

———. *Selected Writings and Speeches*. Edited by Philip S. Foner and Sally M. Miller. Baton Rouge: Louisiana State University Press, 1982.

———. *Socialism and the World War*. St. Louis: Frank P. O'Hare, 1919.

Okrent, Daniel. *The Guarded Gate: Bigotry, Eugenics, and the Law That Kept Two Generations of Jews, Italians, and Other European Immigrants Out of America*. New York: Scribner, 2019.

Pershing, John J. *My Experiences in the World War*. Vol. 1. New York: Frederick A. Stokes, 1931.

Persico, Joseph E. *Eleventh Month, Eleventh Day, Eleventh Hour: Armistice Day 1918, World War I and Its Violent Climax*. New York: Random House, 2004.

Pietrusza, David. *1920: The Year of the Six Presidents*. New York: Basic Books, 2007.

———. *TR's Last War: Theodore Roosevelt, the Great War, and a Journey of Triumph and Tragedy*. Guilford, CT: LP/Globe Pequot, 2018.

Polenberg, Richard. *Fighting Faiths: The Abrams Case, the Supreme Court, and Free Speech*. New York: Penguin, 1989.

Post, Louis F. *The Deportations Delirium of Nineteen-Twenty*. Chicago: Kerr, 1923.

———. "Living a Long Life over Again: A Memory Voyage across the Latter Half of the Nineteenth Century and the First Quarter of the Twentieth." Unpublished and undated autobiography in Louis F. Post Papers, box 4, Library of Congress, Washington, DC.

Preston, William, Jr. *Aliens and Dissenters: Federal Suppression of Radicals 1903–1933*. New York: Harper & Row, 1963.

Punke, Michael. *Fire and Brimstone: The North Butte Mining Disaster of 1917*. New York: Hachette, 2006.

Reed, John. *The Education of John Reed: Selected Writings*. New York: International Publishers, 1955.

Robertson, Stephen. "The Company's Voice in the Workplace: Labor Spies, Propaganda, and Personnel Management, 1918–1920." *Labor: Studies in Working-Class History of the Americas* 10, no. 3 (Fall 2013).

Rosenblum, Jonathan D. "Felix Frankfurter and the Bisbee Deportation." *Western Legal History* 31, no. 2 (2021).

Ross, Steven T., ed. *Peacetime War Plans, 1919–1935.* New York: Garland, 1992.

Sayer, John. "Art and Politics, Dissent and Repression: *The Masses* Magazine versus the Government, 1917–1918." *American Journal of Legal History* 32, no. 1 (January 1988).

Scheiber, Harry N. "What Wilson Said to Cobb in 1917: Another View of Plausibility." *Wisconsin Magazine of History* 52, no. 4 (Summer 1969).

Schmidt, Regin. *Red Scare: FBI and the Origins of Anticommunism in the United States, 1919–1943.* Copenhagen: Museum Tusculanum Press, University of Copenhagen, 2000.

Schrag, Peter. *Not Fit for Our Society: Immigration and Nativism in America.* Berkeley: University of California Press, 2010.

Sedgwick, Ellery. *The Happy Profession.* Boston: Little, Brown, 1946.

Sellars, Nigel Anthony. *Oil, Wheat, and Wobblies: The Industrial Workers of the World in Oklahoma, 1905–1930.* Norman: University of Oklahoma Press, 1998.

Slide, Anthony, ed. *Robert Goldstein and "The Spirit of '76."* Metuchen, NJ: Scarecrow Press, 1993.

Slotkin, Richard. *Lost Battalions: The Great War and the Crisis of American Nationality.* New York: Holt, 2005.

Smith, Page. *America Enters the World.* New York: McGraw-Hill, 1985.

Starling, Edmund W., as told to Thomas Sugrue. *Starling of the White House: The Story of the Man Whose Secret Service Detail Guarded Five Presidents from Woodrow Wilson to Franklin D. Roosevelt.* New York: Simon & Schuster, 1946.

Stoltzfus, Duane C. S. *Pacifists in Chains: The Persecution of the Hutterites during the Great War.* Baltimore: Johns Hopkins University Press, 2013.

Strang, Dean. *Keep the Wretches in Order: America's Biggest Mass Trial, the Rise of the Justice Department, and the Fall of the IWW.* Madison: University of Wisconsin Press, 2019.

Talbert, Roy Jr. *Negative Intelligence: The Army and the American Left, 1917–1941.* Jackson: University Press of Mississippi, 1991

Thomas, Louisa. *Conscience: Two Soldiers, Two Pacifists, One Family—A Test of Will and Faith in World War I.* New York: Penguin, 2011.

Thomas, Norman. *The Conscientious Objector in America.* New York: Huebsch, 1923.

Thomas, William H., Jr. *Unsafe for Democracy: World War I and the U.S. Justice Department's Covert Campaign to Suppress Dissent.* Madison: University of Wisconsin Press, 2008.

Thompson, J. Lee. *Never Call Retreat: Theodore Roosevelt and the Great War.* New York: Palgrave Macmillan, 2013.

Tumulty, Joseph P. *Woodrow Wilson as I Know Him.* Garden City, NY: Doubleday, Page, 1921.

Van Deman, Ralph H. *The Final Memoranda: Major General Ralph H. Van Deman, USA ret., 1865–1952.* Wilmington, DE: SR Books, 1988.

Vaughn, Stephen. *Holding Fast the Inner Lines: Democracy, Nationalism, and the Committee on Public Information.* Chapel Hill: University of North Carolina Press, 1980.

Villard, Oswald Garrison. *Fighting Years: Memoirs of a Liberal Editor.* New York: Harcourt, Brace, 1930.

Wagner, Margaret E. *America and the Great War: A Library of Congress Illustrated History.* New York: Bloomsbury, 2017.

Wallace, Mike. *Greater Gotham: A History of New York City from 1898 to 1919.* New York: Oxford, 2017.

Wawro, Geoffrey. *Sons of Freedom: The Forgotten American Soldiers Who Defeated Germany in World War I.* New York: Basic Books, 2018.

Weisberger, Bernard A. *The La Follettes of Wisconsin: Love and Politics in Progressive America.* Madison: University of Wisconsin Press, 2013.

Wexler, Alice. *Emma Goldman in America.* Boston: Beacon Press, 1984.

Williams, David. "The Bureau of Investigation and Its Critics, 1919–1921: The Origins of Federal Political Surveillance." *Journal of American History* 68, no. 3 (December 1981).

Wilson, Edith Bolling. *My Memoir.* Indianapolis: Bobbs-Merrill, 1939.

Work, Clemens P. *Darkest before Dawn: Sedition and Free Speech in the American West.* Albuquerque: University of New Mexico Press, 2005.

Zieger, Robert H. *America's Great War: World War I and the American Experience.* Oxford, UK: Rowman & Littlefield, 2000.

NOTES

PROLOGUE: NO ORDINARY TIMES

1   *"Most of them"*: "I.W.W. in Tulsa Raided by Police," *Tulsa Daily World*, 6 November 1917.

2   *"These are no"*: "Mob Violence in the United States," *Survey*, 27 April 1918.

2   *"You could see"*: Joe French, quoted in Sellars, *Oil, Wheat, and Wobblies*, 108.

3   *"The struggle of man"*: Milan Kundera, *The Book of Laughter and Forgetting* (New York: HarperCollins, 1999), 4.

4   *It banned hundreds*: Anderson, "Albert Sidney Burleson," 227, 229.

4   *"none of the policemen"*: "I.W.W. Members Flogged, Tarred and Feathered," *Tulsa Daily World*, 10 November 1917.

4   *"The first step"*: "Get Out the Hemp," *Tulsa Daily World*, 9 November 1917.

4   *"Any man"*: "Down the Agitators," *Tulsa Daily World*, 7 November 1917.

5   *"In the name of"*: "I.W.W. Members Flogged, Tarred and Feathered."

5   *"everything that we owned"*: National Civil Liberties Bureau, *The "Knights of Liberty" Mob*, 7.

5   *"were making no apparent"*: "I.W.W. Danger in Tulsa Not Ended," *Tulsa Daily World*, 11 November 1917.

6   *"The sound of"*: "Calls for Strict Ban on German Language," *New York Times*, 25 February 1918, and "German in Schools Must Go, Declares Defence Society," *New York Tribune*, 1 March 1918.

7   *"Educator Says"*: "Value of German Language Assailed," *New York Times*, 2 December 1917.

7   *"Masked Patriots"*: *New York Times*, 7 January 1918.

7   *"This is a nation"*: Thompson, *Never Call Retreat*, 245.

7   *"It is the Christian"*: "Dangerous Precept," *Atlanta Constitution*, 3 April 1918.

8   *"swarming"*: Henry James, *The American Scene*, ed. Leon Edel (Bloomington: Indiana University Press, 1968), 131–32.

8   *"If you don't like"*: Lyrics by Thomas Hoier, 1915.

10 *"has not been discovered"*: "Railroad Bridge Burned," *Tulsa Democrat*, 6 November 1917.

10 *"There are men"*: "Shoot Our Traitors at Home, Root Warns at Welcome Here from his Mission to Russia," *New York Times*, 16 August 1917.

11 *Two men*: L. A. Brown to Roger Baldwin, 25 March 1918, quoted in Chapman, "The Nightmare of Dreamland" (unpaginated).

CHAPTER 1: TEARS OF JOY

16 *"Oh, you beautiful doll!"*: Starling, *Starling of the White House*, 56, 62.

20 *"We created this Nation"*: Speech to the Grand Army of the Republic, Washington, DC, 28 September 1915.

20 *"peace without victory"*: Speech to the Senate, 22 January 1917.

21 *"The necessity of leading"*: Baker, *Woodrow Wilson: Life and Letters*, 6:505.

21 *"I'd never seen"*: John L. Heaton, *Cobb of "The World": A Leader in Liberalism: Compiled from His Editorial Articles and Public Addresses* (New York: Dutton, 1924), 268–70.

22 *"This was possibly"*: Cooper, *Woodrow Wilson: A Biography*, 443.

22 *The uncertainties only multiply*: For different views about this encounter, see Auerbach, "Woodrow Wilson's 'Prediction' to Frank Cobb"; Dalton, "Wilson's Prediction to Cobb"; Link, "That Cobb Interview"; and Scheiber, "What Wilson Said to Cobb in 1917."

23 *sermons in Washington's pulpits*: "War Tone in Sermons of Capital Ministers," *Evening Star* (Washington, DC), 2 April 1917.

23 *"Take my word"*: Thomas Gore of Oklahoma, in House, *Intimate Papers*, 1:93.

24 *"It was House"*: Lloyd George, *Memoirs*, 155.

24 *"My dear friend"*: House, *Intimate Papers*, 1:45.

24 *"This is the part"*: House to Wilson, 10 November 1915, in House, *Intimate Papers*, 2:92.

24 *"I thought it would"*: House, 2:467.

25 *"If he does not go"*: Baker, *Woodrow Wilson: Life and Letters*, 6:491.

25 *"National degeneracy"*: Ellis, *Echoes of Distant Thunder*, 320–21.

28 *"a small-calibre man"*: Berg, *Wilson*, 234.

28 *"He walked to"*: Sedgwick, *The Happy Profession*, 184–85.

28 *"Never had he"*: "Wilson's Plan Provides for Full Warfare," *New York Tribune*, 3 April 1917.

28 *"The public galleries"*: Lansing, *War Memoirs*, 239.

28 *Also with the White House*: "Happenings of Day in Capital Society," *Washington Times*, 3 April 1917.

29   "*His pale, immobile face*": Henry L. Stoddard, quoted in *The American Scrap Book: The Year's Golden Harvest of Thought and Achievement* (New York: Wm. H. Wise, 1928), 307.

29   "*Universal suffrage*": 19 June 1876, *PWW*, 1:143.

30   "*Slavery itself*": Woodrow Wilson, "Chapter XIII, State Rights (1850–1860)," in A. W. Ward, G. W. Prothero, and Stanley Leathes, eds. *The Cambridge Modern History* (New York: Macmillan, 1903), 7:441.

30   told "*darky stories*": See, for example, Daniels, *Cabinet Diaries*, 234 and 321.

30   "*There was more*": "Must Exert All Our Power," *New York Times*, 3 April 1917.

31   "*He was on his feet*": Houston, *Eight Years*, 1:254–55.

31   "*how they could be*": "Business Men Gather," *Washington Times*, 2 April 1917.

32   "*This sentence might*": "Must Exert All Our Power."

33   "*most alarming*": *Papers Relating to the Foreign Relations of the United States, 1917, Supplement 2, the World War* (Washington, DC: US Government Printing Office, 1932), 1:518.

33   "*A particularly vociferous:*" "Wilson's Plan Provides for Full Warfare," *New York Tribune*, 3 April 1917.

34   "*cheered him*": "Must Exert All Our Power."

34   "*pounding the arm*": Sedgwick, *The Happy Profession*, 186.

34   "*Bob, they'll crucify you*": The friend was International Seaman's Union leader Andrew Furuseth. Weisberger, *The La Follettes of Wisconsin*, 202.

35   "*Think what it was*": Tumulty, *Wilson as I Know Him*, 256–59.

35   "*and talked it over*": House, *Intimate Papers*, 2:470.

35   considered Tumulty "*common*": Berg, *Wilson*, 373.

CHAPTER 2: PLACE A GUN UPON HIS SHOULDER

37   *At 1:15 p.m.*: Josephus Daniels, *Our Navy at War* (New York: George H. Doran, 1922), 1. In a different version of the story, McCandless went to a window, in another to a White House side doorway.

38   "*America, I raised a boy*": Lyrics by Andrew B. Sterling, 1917.

38   "*The hopes of Missoula*": "High School Athletes Leave Sport for Army," *Daily Missoulian*, 11 April 1917.

40   *40 percent of its military budget*: Mead, *The Doughboys*, 6.

41   "*Let 'em shoot!*": Kazin, *War against War*, 25.

41   "*six men with nerve*": Dos Passos, *U.S.A.*, 317.

41   "*to an audience that dwindled*": Amos R. E. Pinchot, *History of the Progressive Party, 1912–1916* (Westport, CT: Greenwood, 1978), 128.

42   "*dangerous to the country*": Weisberger, *The La Follettes of Wisconsin*, 212.

42   "*a shadow Hun*": Kazin, *War against War*, 227.

42   "*I want to stand*": "House Passes Resolution," *Daily Missoulian*, 6 April 1917.

44   "*we let the cases*": David Kennedy, *Over Here*, 133.

44   *"War means autocracy"*: Baker, *Woodrow Wilson: Life and Letters*, 6:506n2.

44   *by a factor of 16:* David Kennedy, *Over Here*, 139.

44   *The American steel industry's:* Brandes, *Warhogs*, 166, 165, 136.

45   *doubled its president's salary:* Brandes, 169.

46   *"If you're going"*: "What Are You Going to Do to Help the Boys?" lyrics by Gus Kahn, 1918. This was the official song of the third Liberty Loan campaign.

46   *"The Kaiser will discover"*: "A Difference," *Alaska Daily Empire*, 25 April 1917.

46   *"country at peace"*: "What We Owe the President," *Goldfield News and Weekly Tribune*, 14 April 1917.

47   *"As a nation"*: Abraham Lincoln to Joshua F. Speed, 24 August 1855, quoted in Schrag, *Not Fit for Our Society*, 40.

48   *"Throughout the [nineteenth] century"*: Woodrow Wilson, *A History of the American People* (New York: Harper, 1918), 10:98–99.

49   *"bred, and . . . proud"*: "Text of President Wilson's Speeches at Columbus and Indianapolis," *Evening Star* (Washington, DC), 5 September 1919.

50   *a prominent eugenicist:* The eugenicist was Henry H. Goddard. Schrag, *Not Fit for Our Society*, 80–82.

50   *"You know what boys"*: "Riot Mars Funeral of Rabbi Joseph," *New York Times*, 31 July 1902.

51   *"best citizenry"*: "Some Reminiscences," *Grays Harbor Washingtonian*, 17 June 1934.

51   *"who tremble"*: "Congressman Johnson and Post Offices," *Grays Harbor Washingtonian*, 2 September 1913.

51   *"calling for the absolute"*: "Warns Eagles of National Dangers," newspaper name and date not visible; Johnson scrapbooks, Washington State Library (courtesy of Aaron Goings).

51   *"a system of codes"*: "Some Reminiscences."

52   *"supplied from every possible source"*: McCoy, *Policing America's Empire*, 78.

52   *To keep track:* NARA RG 395.

52   *"Now, this is the way"*: *Omaha World-Herald*, May 13, 1900, quoted in Paul Kramer, "The Water Cure," *New Yorker*, 15 February 2008.

53   *"one of the best known"*: Van Deman, *The Final Memoranda*, 22.

CHAPTER 3: THE CARDINAL GOES TO WAR

55   *"under a small, somnolent"*: Wawro, *Sons of Freedom*, 55

58   *"I love my flag"*: "A Patriot (Contributed by Salt Lake Local)," *Industrial Worker*, 14 April 1917.

60   *"Mr. Chairman, friends"*: Talbert, *Negative Intelligence*, 60

60   *"outlaw leaders"*: Kohn, *American Political Prisoners*, 8.

60 *"whole object"*: "Warns Eagles of National Dangers," newspaper name and date not visible; Johnson scrapbooks, Washington State Library (courtesy of Aaron Goings).

60 *"urging Negroes"*: Kohn, *American Political Prisoners*, 8.

61 *"Treason cannot"*: Drake, *Education of an Anti-Imperialist*, 188.

61 *"President Wilson today"*: "President Renews Plea for Press Censorship," *Evening Star* (Washington, DC), 23 May 1917.

61 *"has been called"*: Meyer, *The World Remade*, 275.

62 *"a menace to"*: "Opposes Postal Union," *Washington Post*, 6 December 1917.

62 *"over twenty negroes"*: Anderson, "Albert Sidney Burleson," 6.

62 *"a round, almost chubby"*: Anderson, "President Wilson's Politician," 347.

62 *"Burleson acted the part"*: McAdoo, *Crowded Years*, 180–81.

63 *"an extremely sly"*: Starling, *Starling of the White House*, 82.

63 *"those offensive negro papers"*: Kornweibel, *"Seeing Red,"* 90.

63 *"calculated to"*: Feldman, *Manufacturing Hysteria*, 35–36, 53.

64 *"a notorious exploiter"*: "Why America Entered the War!," *The Rebel*, 28 April 1917.

64 *First, it declared:* "Meitzen at the Federal Land Hearing," *The Rebel*, 10 April 1915.

65 *"slapdash gathering"*: Irving Howe, introduction to *Echoes of Revolt: The Masses, 1911–1917*, ed. William O'Neill (Chicago: Quadrangle Books, 1966), 5.

66 *"the wounded had lain"*: Sayer, "Art and Politics, Dissent and Repression," 69.

67 *"as friends of yours"*: 12, 13, and 16 July 1917, *PWW*, 43:165, 164, 187.

67 *"I would very much"*: 25 September 1917, in Baker, *Woodrow Wilson: Life and Letters*, 7:283.

67 *"the paper will henceforth"*: Conolly-Smith, "'Reading Between the Lines,'" 13.

68 *"cooperation of librarians"*: Conolly-Smith, 19

68 *"wholesale cripple-and-corpse factory"*: Andreas Latzko, *Men in Battle* (London: Cassell, 1918), 160.

68 *"with the full consent"*: "Ellen Key Pacifist Book under Ban," *The Sun* (New York), 31 May 1918.

68 *"contained seditious matter"*: NARA OG136944, 27 May 1918, 19 September 1918.

68 *"any news relating"*: NARA OG 291921, 14 August 1918. I learned of this document, as with so many other Bureau files, from the reference to it by McCormick.

69 *"You might just"*: "Demand for Expulsion of La Follette Cheered," *Evening Star* (Washington, DC), 28 September 1917.

70 *"on the ground of"*: Drake, *Education of an Anti-Imperialist*, 207.

CHAPTER 4: ENCHANTED BY HER BEAUTY

71   *"he strode along"*: Hutchins Hapgood, *A Victorian in the Modern World* (New York: Harcourt Brace, 1939), 302.

71   *He was a man*: Cooper, *Warrior and the Priest*, 69.

71   *"professional pacifists"*: McCallum, *Leonard Wood*, 263

71   *"a whole raft"*: "Colonel Denounces Traitors at Home," *New York Times*, 16 August 1917.

72   *"The bald fact"*: George E. Mowry, *Theodore Roosevelt and the Progressive Movement* (New York: Hill and Wang, 1960), 313.

72   *the volunteer force*: See *The Letters of Theodore Roosevelt*, ed. Elting E. Morison (Cambridge, MA: Harvard University Press, 1954), 8:1182, 1189, 1192–95, and Seward W. Livermore, *Woodrow Wilson and the War Congress, 1916–18* (Seattle: University of Washington Press, 1966), 19–31.

73   *"infernal skunk"*: McCallum, *Leonard Wood*, 263.

73   *"apothecary's clerk"*: Cooper, *Woodrow Wilson: A Biography*, 119.

73   *Wilson sometimes imitated*: Gene Smith, *When the Cheering Stopped: The Last Years of Woodrow Wilson* (New York: Morrow, 1964), 6.

73   *"I asked not only"*: "Mitchel Condemns Hylan at Garden," *The Sun* (New York), 2 November 1917.

73   *"the military situation"*: McCallum, *Leonard Wood*, 262.

74   *"full of intrigue"*: Talking to Dr. Grayson, 13 March 1919, *PWW*, 55:486.

74   *a cartoonist once showed*: *North American Review's War Weekly*, 14 December 1918, cover.

74   *"ashamed to sit"*: "Oust La Follette, Urges Roosevelt," *Los Angeles Times*, 25 September 1917.

74   *"old women"*: Morris, *Colonel Roosevelt*, 507.

74   *"That is an honorable"*: Fleming, *Illusion of Victory*, 151.

75   *"I have for the Goldman creature"*: Henry James [not the novelist of the same name], "With Entire Frankness," *San Francisco Call*, 1 May 1898.

76   *"the strongest and deepest"*: Emma Goldman, *Anarchism and Other Essays* (New York: Mother Earth, 1910), 242.

76   *"I for one"*: Charles Allan Madison, *Critics & Crusaders: A Century of American Protest* (New York: Holt, 1947), 229.

76   *"She is doing tremendous"*: NARA OG15446, 24 April 1917, quoted in Wexler, *Emma Goldman in America*, 168.

77   *"The head matron"*: Goldman, *Living My Life*, 629.

78   *"you have opened up"*: Falk, *Love, Anarchy, and Emma Goldman*, 4.

78   *"everyone in court"*: Goldman, *Living My Life*, 619–20.

78   *"'Reds' vs. U.S."*: 3 July 1917.

79   *"her influence is so"*: Kathleen Kennedy, *Disloyal Mothers*, 44, 45.

79   *"Gentlemen of the jury"*: Goldman and Berkman, *Anarchism on Trial*, 63.

79   *a bold official:* In 1919, when Goldman's deportation order landed on his desk again, the law had been changed and Louis F. Post, to his sorrow, had no choice but to sign it. Goldman was furious about this, and she seems to have been unaware that he had saved her from deportation two years earlier.

80   *"The watchful eyes"*: Goldman, *Living My Life*, 624.

CHAPTER 5: THOSE WHO STAND IN OUR WAY

81   *"Men, women, and children"*: Pershing, *My Experiences*, 58–59.

81   *"no recollection"*: Pershing, 93.

82   *"drowned out"*: "Until Prussianism Is Crushed Fight Must Be Continued," International News Service, *Austin American* (Texas), 15 June 1917.

84   *Karl Linderfelt:* See Scott Martelle, *Blood Passion: The Ludlow Massacre and Class War in the American West* (New Brunswick, NJ: Rutgers University Press, 2007), 103–119 passim, and elsewhere in this book.

84   *"In the Islands"*: Anthony Roland DeStefanis, "Guarding Capital: Soldier Strikebreakers on the Long Road to the Ludlow Massacre, (PhD diss., College of William and Mary, 2004), 263.

85   *"Plot for Revolt"*: *Wheeling Intelligencer* (West Virginia), 25 September 1917.

85   *"unhung traitors"*: "Root Scores Russian Reds," *New York Times*, 16 August 1917.

86   *"Upon close investigation"*: Robert L. Tyler, *Rebels of the Woods: The I. W. W. in the Pacific Northwest* (Eugene: University of Oregon Books, 1967), 10.

86   *"Wherever . . . there is"*: Reed, *Education of John Reed*, 181.

88   *joined a vigilante group:* Goings, Barnes, and Snider, *The Red Coast*, 79. See also "Work the Boycott on the Aberdeen Thugs," *Industrial Worker*, 21 December 1911, and "500 Thugs in Aberdeen," *Industrial Worker*, 30 November 1911.

88   *"we got hundreds"*: Robert Walter Bruere, *Following the Trail of the IWW: A First-Hand Investigation into Labor Troubles in the West—A Trip into the Copper and the Lumber Camps of the Inland Empire with the Views of the Men on the Job* (New York: Evening Post, 1918), 19, quoted in Aaron Goings, "Red Harbor: The IWW in Grays Harbor, Washington," IWW History Project, University of Washington, 2016, https://depts.washington.edu/iww/red_harbor.shtml.

88   *"had packed the strikers"*: "Some Reminiscences," *Gray's Harbor Washingtonian*, 29 July 1934.

88   *"Do you imagine"*: *Daily Washingtonian*, 4 February 1910, quoted in Goings, Barnes, and Snider, *The Red Coast*, 78.

88   *"immigrant with red"*: Goings, Barnes, and Snider, 79.

89   *Phelps, Dodge's after-tax income: Munitions Industry: Hearings before the Special Committee Investigating the Munitions Industry, United States Senate, Seventy-*

Third [-Seventy-Fourth] Congress, Pursuant to S. Res. 206, a Resolution to Make Certain Investigations Concerning the Manufacture and Sale of Arms and Other War Munitions (Washington, DC: US Government Printing Office, 1936), 6629.

89   *"enemy agents"*: 9 June 1917, quoted in Talbert, *Negative Intelligence*, 69.

89   *"I know of"*: 30 June 1915, online at Theodore Roosevelt Center, Dickinson State University. My thanks to Jonathan Rosenblum for letting me read an unpublished manuscript dealing with Roosevelt and Greenway.

90   *"No human being"*: Roosevelt to Felix Frankfurter, 19 December 1917, quoted in "Theodore Roosevelt on Mooney," *The Argonaut*, 23 April 1921.

90   *"the Sheriff of Bisbee"*: "Diversions of the I. W. W.," *New York Times*, 14 July 1917.

91   *"shadowed for months"*: "I. W. W. Members Being Held Here, Registered," *Pittsburgh Press*, 13 September 1918.

91   *"I. W. W. Plot Leader"*: "Prisoner Is Thought I. W. W. Plot Leader," *Pittsburgh Gazette Times*, 10 September 1918.

91   *"a nationally known radical"*: "Organizer for I. W. W. Is Arrested Here by Government Agents," *Pittsburgh Press*, 10 September 1918.

CHAPTER 6: SOLDIERS OF DARKNESS

93   *"gentle, soft-spoken man"*: Slide, *Robert Goldstein and "The Spirit of '76,"* xxiii.

93   *"one of the longest"*: "'Spirit of '76' Seen First Time in L. A. at Auditorium," *Los Angeles Evening Express*, 28 November 1917.

94   *"He shook like"*: "Ten Years for Film Producer," *Los Angeles Times*, 30 April 1918.

94   *"we are engaged"*: Slide, *Robert Goldstein and "The Spirit of '76,"* 209.

94   *"disloyalty among"*: Kohn, *American Political Prisoners*, 131.

94   *"the clergyman who"*: Fite and Peterson, *Opponents of War*, 115.

94   *"I wish Wilson"*: Fite and Peterson, 141.

95   *"or who takes"*: David Kennedy, *Over Here*, 106.

95   *"There is no excuse"*: Fite and Peterson, *Opponents of War*, 154.

95   *"all attempts, in Congress"*: "The Repression of Sedition," *New York Times*, 7 September 1917.

95   *"I hear the voices"*: State of the Union message, 4 December 1917.

96   *"I am physically unable"*: Hough, *The Web*, 483, 29.

97   *"Lieutenant Crockett, with Ilocano"*: *Annual Report of Major General Adna R. Chaffee, U.S. Army, Commanding Division of the Philippines* (Manila: 1901), 22 February 1901, 2:47.

97   *"please assist Mr. Briggs"*: A. Bruce Bielaski to All Special Agents and Local Officers, 22 March 1917, quoted in Mills, *The League*, 22.

98   *"If there were no suspects"*: Jensen, *Price of Vigilance*, 48.

99   *"The League has done"*: Hough, *The Web*, 163.

99   *more than 10,000 investigations*: Hough, 127–28.

99   *more than 2,000 cases*: David F. Forte, "Righting a Wrong: Woodrow Wilson, Warren G. Harding, and Espionage Act Prosecutions," *Case Western Reserve Law Review* 68, no. 4 (2018): 1127, says that of Espionage Act cases from 1917 to 1921, "2,168 came to trial. There were 1,055 convictions, 181 acquittals, 665 were allowed to lapse, and 135 were dismissed." The figure of "only ten" actual accused spies comes from Kazin, *War against War*, 189.

100   *"Three of us"*: Thomas R. Gowenlock, with Guy Murchie Jr., *Soldiers of Darkness* (Garden City, NY: Doubleday, Doran, 1937), 42–43.

100   *"the Ku Klux Klan"*: Hough, *The Web*, 414.

100   *"This work done"*: "Disloyalists Are Deported," *Decatur Herald*, 13 February 1918.

101   *"It seems to me"*: Wilson to Gregory, 4 June 1917, *PWW*, 42:446.

101   *"The most dangerous"*: John Lord O'Brian, April 1918, quoted in William H. Thomas Jr., *Unsafe for Democracy*, 4.

101   *"in which disloyal"*: *Report of the Attorney General*, 1922, p. 437, quoted in Fite and Peterson, *Opponents of War*, 36.

101   *"If I were of conscription"*: Fite and Peterson, 37.

102   *"A telephone"*: "Four Hours of Rioting on Common, 20,000 Mixing In," *Boston Daily Globe*, 2 July 1917.

102   *"the blackest month"*: John Reed, "One Solid Month of Liberty," *The Masses* 9, no. 11 (September 1917).

104   *"We have no interest"*: "Butte's Name Tarnished by the Stain of Lynch Law," *Anaconda Standard* (Montana), 2 August 1917.

104   *"make it so"*: "Treasonable Utterances May Have Provoked Butte Hanging," *Billings Gazette*, 3 Augusts 1917.

104   *"This is the first"*: Botkin, *Frank Little and the IWW*, 287.

104   *"Wait 'til I get"*: Punke, *Fire and Brimstone*, 207.

105   *"red-blooded American enough"*: Botkin, *Frank Little and the IWW*, 297.

105   *"Better start with"*: "Lynch-Law and Treason," *Literary Digest*, 18 August 1917.

105   *"I think the Company"*: Punke, *Fire and Brimstone*, 212.

105   *"A Little hanging"*: "At Home and Abroad," *Mother Earth Bulletin*, 1, no. 3 (December 1917).

CHAPTER 7: SHOOT MY BROTHER DOWN

109   *Ida B. Wells*: In later life, she was also known as Ida B. Wells-Barnett.

109   *Now, why should I*: "Bound for the Promised Land" by "Mr. Ward," 11 November 1916, reprinted in Steven A. Reich, ed., *Encyclopedia of the Great Black Migration* (Santa Barbara, CA: Greenwood, 2006), 398.

110 *"Something has got"*: US Congress, House of Representatives, Special Committee to Investigate the East St. Louis Riots, *Transcripts of the Hearings of the House Select Committee That Investigated the Race Riots in East St. Louis, Illinois* (Washington, DC: US Government Printing Office, 1918), 3635, quoted in Lumpkins, *American Pogrom*, 10.

110 *"Approximately 60,000 Negroes"*: "Statement by Gregory," *Chicago Tribune*, 4 November 1916.

111 *"I saw man after man"*: Carlos F. Hurd, "Post-Dispatch Man, an Eye-Witness, Describes Massacre of Negroes," *St. Louis Post-Dispatch*, 3 July 1917.

113 *"growing menace"*: "The Massacre of East St. Louis," *The Crisis*, September 1917.

114 *called it a "pogrom"*: "The East St. Louis Pogrom," *Survey*, 14 July 1917.

115 *"will not in fact"*: Wilson to Williams, 29 June 1917, *PWW*, 43:78.

115 *the hanging of three Black soldiers*: See Douglas, "Wartime Illusions and Disillusionment," for an excellent comprehensive view of this episode.

115 *"All were unarmed"*: Noah Leatherman, *Diary Kept by Noah H. Leatherman While in Camp during World War I* (Linden, Alberta: Aaron L. Toews, 1951), 26.

115 *"'God save my soul'"*: "Three Negro Soldiers Executed," *Evening Tribune* (Des Moines, IA), 5 July 1918.

115 *"Three negro soldiers"*: "Negroes Paid the Penalty," *Davenport Democrat and Leader* (Iowa), 5 July 1918.

115 *"close ranks"*: "Close Ranks," *The Crisis*, July 1918.

116 *"In the fall of 1917"*: Van Deman, *The Final Memoranda*, 33.

116 *"fortune tellers, supposed"*: Van Deman to Major W. H. Loving [his senior Black agent], 14 March 1918, NARA RG 165, Kornweibel microfilm, reel 19, p. 513.

116 *"several incidents of where"*: Kathryn S. Olmsted, *Right Out of California: The 1930s and the Big Business Roots of Modern Conservatism* (New York: New Press, 2017), 151.

116 *"German money"*: Report from Agent P. T. Rellihan, 28 July 1917, NARA RG 165, Kornweibel microfilm, reel 19, p. 523.

117 *"a protest against lynchings"*: Report from Agent Warren W. Grimes, 20 February 1918, NARA RG 165, Kornweibel microfilm, reel 19, p. 474.

117 *"repeated attacks"*: Van Deman to Major W. H. Loving, 3 May 1918, NARA RG 165, Kornweibel microfilm, reel 19, p. 617.

117 *"that he would be held"*: Loving to Van Deman, 10 May 1918, quoted in Theodore Kornweibel Jr., "'The Most Dangerous of All Negro Journals': Federal Efforts to Suppress the *Chicago Defender* during World War I," *American Journalism* 11, no. 2 (Spring 1994): 161.

117 *"presided over"*: Van Deman to A. Bruce Bielaski, 9 May 1918, NARA RG 165, Kornweibel microfilm, reel 19, p. 683.

117 *"to find out all"*: "Army Feared King, Secretly," *Commercial Appeal* (Memphis, TN), 21 March 1993.

CHAPTER 8: A WILY CON MAN; A DANGEROUS WOMAN

119 *"Together I am sure"*: NARA OG 67-40, 19 October 1917.

120 *"confined in a secret cell"*: "Two I. W. W. Leaders Compelled to Enroll for Army Service," *Pittsburgh Gazette Times*, 13 September 1918.

120 Leo M. Wendell: Even outside his undercover role, he sometimes referred to himself as Louis. But when operating aboveground in the last two decades of his life he called himself Leo.

120 *"an easy matter"*: McCormick, *Seeing Reds*, 45.

121 *"well received"*: NARA OG 360208, 2 May 1919.

121 *"We loafed together"*: NARA OG 67-40, 13 August 1917; NARA OG 67-40, 20 October 1917; McCormick, *Seeing Reds*, 51.

121 *"he owed his firing"*: McCormick, *Seeing Reds*, 54.

122 *"factional fight"*: NARA OG 67-40, 28 September 1917. Underlining in the original.

122 *"I have discouraged"*: NARA OG 67-40, 7 November 1917; NARA OG 67-40, 20 October 1917.

122 *"Attended a meeting"*: NARA OG 67-40, 20 October 1917.

122 *"prompt and courageous"*: Strang, *Keep the Wretches in Order*, 47, 53.

123 *"became necessary to procure"*: Steven Parfitt, "The Justice Department Campaign against the IWW, 1917–1920," IWW History Project, University of Washington, 2016, http://depts.washington.edu/iww/justice_dept.shtml#_edn1.

123 *"from a source of"*: "Sabotage and Arson Plotted by the I. W. W.," *New York Times*, 6 September 1917.

123 *"With financial records"*: Strang, *Keep the Wretches in Order*, 65.

124 *"Our purpose being"*: Kane to Gregory, 7 September 1917, quoted in Feldman, *Manufacturing Hysteria*, 52.

124 *"I want to see"*: "Marshall Hits Disloyal," *New York Times*, 2 December 1917.

125 employers' studies showed: Foner, *History of the Labor Movement*, 7:129.

125 *"the Link Belt Co."*: "Female Labor's Place in Automotive Industry," *The Automobile and Automotive Industries*, 27 September 1917, 528.

125 *"We wonder where"*: "Keep the Girls Off the Cars," *Motorman and Conductor*, 26 August 1918, quoted in Foner, *History of the Labor Movement*, 7:204.

125 *"spinsters can support"*: J. McKeen Cattell, "The School and the Family," *Popular Science Monthly* 74 (January 1909): 88, 92.

126 more than tripled: *100 Years of Marriage and Divorce Statistics, United States, 1867–1967* (Washington, DC: US Department of Health, Education, and Welfare, 1973), 22.

126 *"Women are successfully"*: Samuel Williams Cooper, "The Present Legal Rights of Women—II," *The American* 533 (25 October 1890).

127 *"The bitterness of it"*: O'Hare, *Selected Writings and Speeches*, 36, 42–43.

127 *"I heard heads"*: Miller, *From Prairie to Prison*, 55.

128 *"up and down"*: O'Hare, *Selected Writings and Speeches*, 123.

128 *"This is a bloody"*: O'Hare, *Socialism and the World War*, 12.

128 *"Never to me"*: Miller, *From Prairie to Prison*, 108.

129 *"blood-stained mire"*: O'Hare, *Socialism and the World War*, 16–19.

129 *"No Queen of"*: Military Intelligence agent John E. Harley, 13 April 1918, quoted in Green, "Outspoken Woman," 153.

129 *"a little, sordid"*: Green, 132.

129 *"if any young man"*: O'Hare, *Socialism and the World War*, 30.

129 *"the only way"*: Kathleen Kennedy, *Disloyal Mothers*, 19.

129 *"a dangerous woman"*: Green, "Outspoken Woman," 90, and Miller, *From Prairie to Prison*, 150. This is O'Hare's account of what the prosecutor said; the actual transcript of the case is incomplete.

130 *"American sons are"*: Kathleen Kennedy, *Disloyal Mothers*, 22.

130 *"the large number"*: Wawro, *Sons of Freedom*, 65, 70.

130 *"never selected advisers"*: Wawro, 70.

131 *"For God's sake"*: Fleming, *Illusion of Victory*, 121.

131 *"We shall be"*: Harries and Harries, *The Last Days of Innocence*, 215.

132 *"The years from"*: David Brion Davis, ed., *The Fear of Conspiracy: Images of Un-American Subversion from the Revolution to the Present* (Ithaca, NY: Cornell University Press, 1971), 205.

133 *"The war," one worried*: Robert Bullard, quoted in Harries and Harries, *The Last Days of Innocence*, 214.

CHAPTER 9: THE WATER CURE

135 *"Practically every taxicab"*: "President's Visit to Capitol Comes as Utter Surprise," *Washington Times*, 8 January 1918.

137 *"Out of this war"*: "The Black Soldier," *The Crisis*, June 1918, 60.

137 "Le bon Dieu": Morris, *Colonel Roosevelt*, 515.

137 *"He is in a belligerent"*: 11 February 1918, *PWW*, 46:327.

137 *Within less than*: A list in reel 6, folder 21 of the Burleson Papers at the University of Texas shows 44 periodicals barred from the mail as of 8 May 1918. At this point Burleson still had nearly three years of censoring ahead of him. Anderson, "Albert Sidney Burleson," 227 and 229, gives 75 as the eventual approximate total of barred publications, with "hundreds" of individual issues barred as well.

138 *some two million*: James Weinstein, *The Decline of Socialism in America* (New York: Monthly Review Press, 1967), 85.

138   *sentenced to two years:* Fred Carroll, *Race News: Black Journalists and the Fight for Racial Justice in the Twentieth Century* (Urbana: University of Illinois Press, 2017), 37.

138   *"Most Socialist papers":* Fite and Peterson, *Opponents of War,* 97.

139   *"If the reasons":* "Mr. Burleson, Section 481 1-2 B," *New Republic,* 17 May 1919.

139   *"You know I am not":* Villard, *Fighting Years,* 357.

139   *"Shall the Sentence":* Miller, *From Prairie to Prison,* 155.

139   *"Shall this family":* Green, "Outspoken Woman," 160.

139   *"to cast the evil eye":* "Mrs. O'Hare Tells of Trial and Sentence," *New York Call,* 17 February 1918.

140   *"bought our labor":* Goldman, *Living My Life,* 654.

140   *Marie Equi:* See Michael Helquist's thorough 2015 biography, *Marie Equi: Radical Politics and Outlaw Passions,* for most of the details of Equi's life.

141   *"her daughter was":* "Olympia Girl Tells Strange Tale of Intrigue and Conspiracy," *Oregon Daily Journal,* 28 May 1906.

141   *"is said to have grasped":* "Quarrel among Speckart Heirs," *Sunday Oregonian,* 27 May 1906.

141   *"If the police come":* Helquist, *Marie Equi,* 161.

141   *"Deputy Sheriff Downey":* *Oregonian,* 16 July 1913, quoted in Krieger, "Queen of the Bolsheviks," 59.

142   *"scampered around talking":* *The Autobiography of Margaret Sanger* (Mineola, NY: Dover, 1971), 206.

142   *"My arms are around you":* 2 October 1916, quoted in Helquist, *Marie Equi,* 151; 9 April 1921, quoted in Helquist, 151.

142   *"Here you poor fish":* Hodges, *World War I and Urban Order,* 98.

143   *"The police tried":* Helquist, *Marie Equi,* 143.

143   *"the most dangerous person":* Hodges, *World War I and Urban Order,* 96.

143   *"Teutons Are Still":* *Bridgeport Times* (Connecticut), 25 March 1918; *Seattle Star,* 26 April 1918; *Pueblo Chieftain* (Colorado), 10 May 1918; *Daily Star-Mirror* (Moscow, ID), 11 June 1918.

144   *"a higher percentage":* Kazin, *War against War,* 208–9.

144   *a determined core:* Five hundred and forty such resisters were court-martialed, according to Fite and Peterson, *Opponents of War,* 131; the more recent study by Stoltzfus, *Pacifists in Chains,* 92, uses a lower figure, 504. Walter Kellogg, a general who took part in an inquiry that made him more sympathetic to these men than he had expected, describes "an examination of over eight hundred objectors in twenty widely distributed military camps and posts" (Kellogg, *The Conscientious Objector,* v). Several hundred of those men, under great pressure, finally agreed to do the "alternative service" that would save a CO from prison.

144   *"I feel that only":* Fite and Peterson, *Opponents of War,* 132.

145   *"Men were forcibly":* Norman Thomas, *Conscientious Objector,* 144.

145   *"frightened little widow"*: Jane Addams, *Peace and Bread in Time of War* (New York: Macmillan, 1922), 125–26.

146   *"a garden hose"*: Charles Larsen describing an episode that happened on 25 August 1918, quoted in Norman Thomas, *Conscientious Objector*, 157.

146   *"noncommissioned officers"*: Sheldon Smith, quoted in Fite and Peterson, *Opponents of War*, 127.

146   *"This corporal had"*: Jesse Schwartzendruber describing what happened to George Miller, in Mary S. Sprunger, ed., *Sourcebook: Oral History Interviews with World War One Conscientious Objectors* (North Newton, KS: Mennonite Central Committee, 1986), 177.

146   *"Get the good old syringe"*: "The Water Cure in the P.I.," by Albert Gardner, Troop B, First US Cavalry, quoted in Paul A. Kramer, *The Blood of Government: Race, Empire, the United States, and the Philippines* (Chapel Hill: University of North Carolina Press, 2006), 141.

147   *"The air in the cell"*: Philip Grosser, *Uncle Sam's Devil's Island: Experiences of a Conscientious Objector in America during the World War.* (Boston: Excelsior Press, 1933), 12.

148   *"My dear wife"*: Stoltzfus, *Pacifists in Chains*, 159.

148   *"When we arrived"*: Stoltzfus, 159.

CHAPTER 10: NOBODY CAN SAY WE AREN'T LOYAL NOW!

149   *"every person who shall"*: Act No. 292, 4 November 1901, Section 8, *Punishments under Law Passed by the Philippine Commission* (Washington DC: US Senate, 1902), 3.

149   *the same tools*: Alfred W. McCoy makes this point in his brilliant *Policing America's Empire: The United States, the Philippines, and the Rise of the Surveillance State* (2009).

150   *"slumped down"*: Ameringer, *If You Don't Weaken*, 317.

150   *more than 1,000*: Schmidt, *Red Scare*, 312. It is remarkable that there yet exists no database of these victims, as there is, for instance, of lynching deaths in the United States, or First World War conscientious objectors in Britain.

150   *who was a lawyer*: Schmidt, 117. This is only one of Schmidt's remarkable discoveries in the Bureau of Investigation archives.

151   *"their assumed Constitutional rights"*: Post, "Living a Long Life over Again," 398–99.

151   *"My dear Mr. President"*: Post to Wilson, 8 February 1918, *PWW*, 46:289.

151   *"Your suggestion"*: Wilson to Post, 11 February 1918, *PWW*, 46:324–25.

151   *first "slacker raid"*: Mills, *The League*, 79–80; Jensen, *Price of Vigilance*, 191–92.

153   *"You and your brothers"*: Theodore Roosevelt to Theodore Roosevelt Jr., quoted in Morris, *Colonel Roosevelt*, 509.

153   *"I don't see how"*: Andrew Carroll, "World War I Letters Show Theodore

Roosevelt's Unbearable Grief after the Death of His Son," *At the Smithsonian* (blog), *Smithsonian*, 3 April 2017, https://www.smithsonianmag.com/smithsonian-institution/letters-unbearable-grief-theodore-roosevelt-death-son-180962743/.

153   *"part of the machine"*: Morris, *Colonel Roosevelt*, 536.

155   *"This is a damn war"*: Merriman, "'An Intensive School of Disloyalty,'" 188–89.

155   *"great generals"*: Merriman, 191.

155   *"will be over"*: Gillham with Pollitt, "J. H. Kruse, War and the Terrible Threateners," 24.

155   *"by disloyalty we mean"*: Gillham with Pollitt, 24.

156   *"Airship with Two Men"*: "On Dot, Raider Returns to Fly about Capital," *Independent-Record* (Helena, MT), 2 November 1917.

156   *The Boston Symphony*: See James J. Badal, "The Strange Case of Dr. Karl Muck, Who Was Torpedoed by *The Star-Spangled Banner* during World War I," *High Fidelity* 20, no. 10 (October 1970).

157   *Robert Prager*: See Peter Stehman, *Patriotic Murder: A World War I Hate Crime for Uncle Sam* (Lincoln, NE: Potomac, 1918).

157   *"In spite of"*: "Stamping Out Treason," *Washington Post*, 12 April 1918.

158   *"Well, I guess"*: "Jury Frees 11 in Prager Lynching," *New York Tribune*, 2 June 1918.

CHAPTER 11: CUT, SHUFFLE, AND DEAL

159   *largest civilian criminal trial*: Strang, *Keep the Wretches in Order*, xvii, 8, 75.

160   *"worthy of being"*: Wilson to Thomas Watt Gregory, 13 April 1918, quoted in Preston, *Aliens and Dissenters*, 130.

160   *"a face like"*: Patrick Renshaw, *The Wobblies: The Story of Syndicalism in the United States* (New York: Anchor Books, 1968), 31.

160   *"Big Bill Haywood was born"*: Dos Passos, *U.S.A.*, 87.

161   *"I've never read"*: Michael Cohen, "'The Ku Klux Government': Vigilantism, Lynching, and the Repression of the IWW," *Journal for the Study of Radicalism* 1, no. 1 (Spring 2007): 34.

161   *"The capitalist has"*: Bruce Watson, *Bread and Roses: Mills, Migrants, and the Struggle for the American Dream* (New York: Viking, 2005), 93.

162   *"upon the heights"*: Reed, *Education of John Reed*, 176.

163   *"whining and belly-aching"*: Strang, *Keep the Wretches in Order*, 104.

163   *"the danger that"*: Strang, 108.

163   *"Don't you know"*: David Pietrusza, *Judge and Jury: The Life and Times of Kenesaw Mountain Landis* (South Bend, IN: Diamond Communications, 1998), 126.

163   *"and then let"*: Ray H. Abrams, *Preachers Present Arms* (New York: Round Table Press, 1933), 217.

164   *"Where is your home?"*: Pierce C. Wetter, "The Men I Left at Leavenworth," *Survey* 49 (October 1922): 30.

164   *"They had cut"*: Strang, *Keep the Wretches in Order*, 145, 149–50.

164   *"no rich and no poor"*: *Evidence and Cross Examination of William D. Haywood in Case of Wm. D. Haywood, et al.* ([Chicago?]: Industrial Workers of the World, 1918), 109.

164   *at least three:* NARA OG 343013, 30 September 1919; NARA OG 343013, 18 October 1920; NARA OG 215915, 4 December 1920.

164   *a deliberate effort:* McCormick, *Seeing Reds*, 74–75, makes this speculation.

165   *"I asked him"*: NARA OG 18197, 9 July 1918.

165   *"With the arrest"*: "Prisoner Is Thought I. W. W. Plot Leader," *Pittsburgh Gazette Times*, 10 September 1918.

166   *"he objected strenuously"*: "Two I. W. W. Leaders Compelled to Enroll for Army Service," *Pittsburgh Post*, 13 September 1918.

166   *Across Van Deman's desk came reports:* Van Deman to Capt. Edward McCauley, 7 March 1918, in Boehm, *U.S. Military Intelligence Reports*, reel 1; Ralph E. Truman to Dept. of Intelligence Officer, 16 July 1917, in Boehm, reel 2; Van Deman to Bielaski, 10 July 1917, in Boehm, reel 1.

166   *"watery and neutral"*: Van Deman to Dr. F. D. Keppel, 1 March 1918, in Boehm, reel 5.

166   *"that it might be"*: Van Deman to Warden, 9 April 1918, in Boehm, reel 6.

167   *"is a seething"*: Samuel Stewart to Van Deman, 13 April 1918, in Boehm, reel 2.

167   *"tied up with form"*: *Hearings before the Committee on Military Affairs, United States Senate, Sixty-Fifth Congress, Second Session, on S. 4364,* 19 April 1918, p. 40.

167   *"wholly and unalterably"*: Wilson to Overman, 20 April 1918, *PWW*, 47:381. The letter was also quoted in the press: "President's Letter Which Sidetracked Chamberlain Bill," *New York Times Magazine*, 28 April 1918.

168   *"Their tall, straight"*: Vera Brittain, *Testament of Youth: An Autobiographical Study of the Years 1900–1925* (New York: Penguin, 1994), 420.

168   *"Whatever now befalls"*: Cooper, *Warrior and the Priest*, 328.

169   *"Retreat, hell!"*: Richard Suskind, *The Battle of Belleau Wood: The Marines Stand Fast* (London: Collier-Macmillan, 1969), 22.

170   *"if it would be"*: Strang, *Keep the Wretches in Order*, 166.

170   *"I am proud"*: Strang, 169.

170   *"The big game"*: Melvyn Dubofsky, *"Big Bill" Haywood* (New York: St. Martin's, 1987), 121.

CHAPTER 12: CHEERLEADERS

171   *"In this line"*: Hammer to Oscar Elsas, 14 February 1920, quoted in Robertson, "Company's Voice in the Workplace," 66.

171   *135,000 agents:* Sidney Howard with Robert Dunn, *The Labor Spy* (New York: Republic, 1924), 17.

172   *"The workers are careless":* 31 July 1918, quoted in Robertson, "Company's Voice in the Workplace," 61.

172   *who were "dissatisfied":* Robertson, 64.

173   *filing reports:* Most of Hammer's reports quoted here are in the Fulton Bag and Cotton Mills Digital Collection, Archives and Records Management Library and Information Center, Georgia Institute of Technology. At this writing they are posted online there.

173   *"advanced patriotic arguments":* 28 August 1918.

173   *"why was I":* Robertson, "Company's Voice in the Workplace," 69.

173   *"During the evening":* 20 September 1918.

173   *"benefitting the Kaiser":* Robertson, "Company's Voice in the Workplace," 67.

175   *"It became difficult":* Fischer, "Committee on Public Information," 58.

175   *"the absolute selflessness":* *Complete Report of the Chairman of the Committee on Public Information: 1917, 1918, 1919* (Washington, DC: US Government Printing Office, 1920), 1.

175   *"If ads could sell":* Wallace, *Greater Gotham*, 983.

176   *"Conference of Colored Editors":* Quotations about the conference, which took place from June 19 to 21, 1918, are from NARA, RG 165, Military Intelligence Negro Subversion file 154-Leland Harrison, DS to C, MIB. Re: Garden City RI. (The file title comes from an initial document that has nothing to do with the conference.)

176   *"German agents":* Reprinted in Mills, *The League*, xi.

177   *"complaints of even":* Fite and Peterson, *Opponents of War*, 20.

177   *"whether the man's heart":* Vaughn, *Holding Fast the Inner Lines*, 50.

178   *"Truth and Falsehood":* Arthur Bullard, "An Essay on the Beneficence of Fallacious Ideas," 6 (undated), Box 2, Bullard Papers, Princeton University, quoted in Vaughn, *Holding Fast the Inner Lines*, 3.

178   *"Have patriotic societies":* Creel to Lionel B. Moses, 22 August 1917, quoted in Fite and Peterson, *Opponents of War*, 76.

179   *"Albert Johnson under":* 17 November 1917.

179   *"Congressmen Face Death":* *Philadelphia Inquirer*, 18 November 1917.

180   *"the people will elect":* "Belgium to Be a Republic," *Spokesman-Review* (Spokane, WA), 31 December 1917.

CHAPTER 13: PEACE?

181   *"children used to flock":* Ameringer, *If You Don't Weaken*, 226.

182   *"far more ominous":* Roosevelt to Charles F. Gettemy, 1 February 1905, quoted in Ray Ginger, *Eugene V. Debs: The Making of an American Radical* (New York: Collier, 1949), 290.

183 *"outrageous utterances":* Wilson to Gregory, 29 October 1917, *PWW*, 44:463.

183 *"been very close":* Gregory to Wilson, 3 November 1917, *PWW*, 44:504.

184 *"on the streets":* "Dakota Ousts an Agitator," *Saturday News* (Watertown, SD), 31 January 1918.

184 *The historian Eric Chester:* See Chester, *Free Speech*, 162–66. In the spring of 1918, Debs made several ambivalent statements about the war. Like some other Socialists, he expressed reservations about the party's antiwar position when the armistice of Brest-Litovsk broke down and in February 1918 German troops began advancing into the infant Soviet Union, threatening the existence of what was seen as the world's first socialist country. But the following month the Germans and Soviets signed a more definitive peace treaty, and from that point on Debs moved back toward opposing the war.

184 *"Debs Asserts":* Indianapolis News, 18 June 1918.

185 *"Those prison bars":* Eugene V. Debs' Canton Speech (Chicago: Socialist Party of the United States, 1929), 3, 4, 7, 12, 14, 18. Other versions of the text differ slightly.

186 *"I have often wondered":* David Karsner, *Debs; His Authorized Life and Letters* (New York: Boni & Liveright, 1919), 28, 32, 42, 43.

187 *"Sometimes I wonder":* Weisberger, *The La Follettes of Wisconsin*, 224.

187 *"In my youth":* Pietrusza, *TR's Last War*, 3.

187 *"But," added:* James Amos, *Theodore Roosevelt: Hero to His Valet* (New York: John Day, 1927), 161.

187 *"that rabbit":* Thompson, *Never Call Retreat*, 232.

188 *"treasonable or seditious":* Jaffe, *Crusade against Radicalism*, 105.

189 *with the "invaluable":* Annual Report of the Attorney General of the United States for the Year 1918 (Washington, DC: US Government Printing Office, 1918), 15.

189 *"The red flag":* Helquist, *Marie Equi*, 176–77.

190 *"The 'officer of the day'":* National Civil Liberties Bureau, *What Happens in Military Prisons*, 3–6, 9.

191 *"require one severe":* Wood to Roosevelt, 23 July 1903, quoted in McCallum, *Leonard Wood*, 212

192 *"for the greater part":* Wood to William Howard Taft, 7 October 1903, quoted in McCallum, 216.

192 *"They are," he wrote:* Wood to Jacob Greenberg, 21 October 1918, quoted in Fite and Peterson, *Opponents of War*, 129.

192 *"exercised clemency":* "C.O.'s Get 25 Years," *Topeka State Journal*, 26 October 1918.

193 *"As terrifying as":* Barry, *The Great Influenza*, 335.

193 *"nothing more or less":* "Huns Ashore Here Seen as Cause of Epidemic of 'Flu,'" *Oklahoma City Times*, 19 September 1918.

196 *"It is urgent"*: Kendall, *Voices from the Past*, 154.

196 *6,750 men died:* Persico, *Eleventh Month*, 379.

196 *"absolutely no let-up"*: Meyer, *The World Remade*, 459.

197 *2,738 men:* Persico, *Eleventh Month*, 378.

197 *"near the front line"*: Kendall, *Voices from the Past*, 245.

197 *"Poor Negroes!"*: Persico, *Eleventh Month*, 204.

197 *"low in the scale"*: R. L. Bullard, "Among the Savage Moros," *Metropolitan Magazine* 24, no. 3 (June 1906).

198 *William Bird:* "Lynch at Will in State of Alabama," *New York Age*, 16 November 1918.

198 *"Send the niggers"*: The listener was Henry Johnson (quoted in Slotkin, *Lost Battalions*, 484).

198 *"the negroes were hit"*: Lieutenant Charles Fearing, quoted in Slotkin, 485.

198 *W. E. B. Du Bois:* "Confidentiel au sujet des troupes noires americaines," *The Crisis*, 18, no. 1 (May 1919). Du Bois published both the document's French original and his English translation.

198 *17 deaths:* Persico, *Eleventh Month*, 375–76.

CHAPTER 14: ANOTHER SAVIOR COME TO EARTH

201 *"On November 11"*: Goldman, *Living My Life*, 669–70.

201 *"The coming of peace"*: Norman Thomas, "Justice to War's Heretics," *The Nation*, 9 November 1918.

201 *"members of my family"*: Goldman, *Living My Life*, 672–73.

202 *"Well, Tumulty"*: Tumulty, *Wilson as I Know Him*, 335.

203 *"as a debutante"*: Macmillan, *Paris 1919*, 3.

204 *"to consider him"*: Hoover, *Forty-Two Years*, 79.

204 *"Mr. Wilson and his"*: Tumulty, *Wilson as I Know Him*, 340.

204 *"I was in favor"*: Klingaman, *1919*, 207.

205 *"About every second"*: Baker, *Woodrow Wilson: Life and Letters*, 8:577.

206 *"He does not seem"*: Jean Jules Jusserand, quoted in Levin, *Edith and Woodrow*, 298.

206 *"It was commonly believed"*: Keynes, *Economic Consequences*, 42–43.

206 *"There is a widespread"*: 3 August 1919, 12 November 1918, 27 December 1918, File: Correspondence, Letters Home, Van Deman Papers, Hoover Institution, Stanford University.

207 *"mush"*: 23 November 1918, quoted in Berg, *Wilson*, 516.

208 *"aghast at the outburst"*: Lloyd George, *Memoirs*, 147.

208 *"never believed nor"*: "General Wood's Tribute," *Weekly Kansas City Star*, 12 February 1919.

209 *"twelve minutes"*: "Wars Will Come, We Must Make Ready—Wood," *Chicago Daily Tribune*, 14 March 1919.

209   *"appears to think"*: "Burleson Pictured as Snoop, Trouble Maker, Disorganizer, Autocrat and Arch-Politician," *The World* (New York), 21 April 1919.

209   *"no longer performing"*: Wilson to Burleson, 27 November 1918, *PWW*, 53:214.

209   *"The President does not"*: 14 December 1916, *PWW*, 40:239.

210   *"I cannot believe"*: Wilson to Burleson, 28 February 1919, *PWW*, 55:327.

210   *"Continued to suppress"*: *PWW*, 55:327n1.

210   *"ought to make"*: Belle Case La Follette and Fola La Follette, *Robert M. La Follette, June 14, 1855—June 18, 1925* (New York: Macmillan, 1952), 2:939.

210   *"death has come"*: O'Hare, *Selected Writing and Speeches*, 129–30.

211   *"I entered quite"*: O'Hare, *Prison Letters*, 3.

211   *"Had we met"*: Goldman, *Living My Life*, 677.

211   *"Emma is very fine"*: O'Hare, *Prison Letters*, 4, 38–39, 63.

211   *"not for anything"*: Goldman, *Living My Life*, 706–7.

212   *"Kate was bringing"*: Goldman, 685.

213   *"extremity and recklessness"*: Merriman, "'An Intensive School of Disloyalty,'" 198.

213   *"If the Saviour"*: Cooper, *Woodrow Wilson: A Biography*, 548.

213   *"He was not accustomed"*: Lloyd George, *Memoirs*, 149.

215   *"unconquered from"*: Alex de Jonge, *The Weimar Chronicle: Prelude to Hitler* (New York: Paddington, 1978), 32.

215   *By 1918, each German*: David Welch, *Germany, Propaganda and Total War, 1914–1918* (New Brunswick, NJ: Rutgers University Press, 2000), 225.

215   *Starvation and malnutrition*: Cox, *Hunger in War and Peace*, 243, 182.

216   *"I have seen infants"*: "Germany Today," *The Nation* 108, no. 2804 (29 March 1919).

216   *"in secret behind"*: Drake, *Education of an Anti-Imperialist*, 271, 268.

217   *"a 600 horsepower motor"*: "Cary T. Grayson," *Collier's*, 13 March 1920.

217   *"Is Not Stricken"*: 5 April 1919.

217   *A 25-year-old*: Barry, *The Great Influenza*, 383–84.

217   *"One thing was"*: Hoover, *Forty-Two Years*, 99.

218   YOU CANNOT UNDERSTAND: 12 May 1919, *PWW*, 59:77.

CHAPTER 15: WORLD ON FIRE

219   *"We are running"*: Berg, *Wilson*, 566.

220   *"Russia! Russia!"*: Klingaman, *1919*, 294.

220   *From 1917 to 1920*: Gregory, *Modern America*, 125.

220   *"Lafayette, we are"*: Wagner, *America and the Great War*, 285.

220   *"If your home"*: "Keep Away from the 'Popular' Cities!," *Trench and Camp* 17, no. 3 (6 February 1919).

221   *"advise the unemployed"*: NARA OG 215915, 3 February 1919.

221 *first major general strike:* See the useful University of Washington website about the strike, the Seattle General Strike Project, http://depts.washington.edu/labhist/strike/.

221 *"to duplicate the anarchy":* Wagner, *America and the Great War*, 287.

222 *"Mayor Hanson and Nine":* Town Crier, 15 February 1919, quoted in Nielsen, *Un-American Womanhood*, 13.

222 *"two-fisted":* All quoted, not all sources specified, in Nielsen, 12.

222 *"You've got to grab":* Murray, *Red Scare*, 65.

222 *"bearded aliens":* Hanson, *Americanism versus Bolshevism*, 62, 283.

223 *A thousand people came:* Hodges, *World War I and Urban Order*, 133.

223 *the witch's broom:* Eliot Asinof, *1919: America's Loss of Innocence* (New York: Donald I. Fine, 1990), 186.

223 *"Red Scare praise":* Nielsen, *Un-American Womanhood*, 23–25.

224 *an unusual map:* Wallace, *Greater Gotham*, 1031–34.

224 *"If a man's love":* Louis Adamic, *My America, 1928–1938* (New York: Harper, 1938), 201.

225 *"Plans for the Protection":* Wallace, *Greater Gotham*, 1031.

226 *A far-right group:* The group in question was the American Defense Society.

226 *an elaborate fake:* Bendersky, *The "Jewish Threat,"* 65.

226 *were now "nationalized":* "Bolshevism Bared by R. E. Simmons," *New York Times*, 18 February 1919.

228 *"certified shorthand reporter":* Talbert, *Negative Intelligence*, 48.

228 *wrote a memorandum:* NARA, RG 165, Trevor to Director of Military Intelligence, 5 April 1919 and 2 May 1919, Military Intelligence 324-IO, New York.

230 *"deport these so-called":* "Deport Aliens Urging Treason, Says Gen. Wood," *New York Tribune*, 29 November 1919.

230 *American Legion demanded:* "Arrest Aliens, Legion Demands," *Los Angeles Times*, 12 May 1919.

230 *"a one-language nation":* "Half of Steel Men Not Americanized," *New York Herald*, 14 October 1919.

230 *be called "American":* 14 November 1919, quoted in Coben, "A Study in Nativism," 71.

231 *This joint effort:* See Leidholdt, "The Mysterious Mr. Maxwell and Room M-1," for a description of the origins of this operation and its control during the war by an American businessman with close ties to British intelligence.

231 *"tendencies looking toward":* Schmidt, *Red Scare*, 92.

231 *"was not an offensive":* NARA OG 334866, 12 September 1918.

231 *"keeping an eye":* Karp, *The Politics of War*, 328.

231 *"mere expression":* Berg, *Wilson*, 551.

231 *"a grave menace":* Berg, 551.

CHAPTER 16: SLY AND CRAFTY EYES

234 *"Sign or Starve"*: La Follette's Magazine 11, no. 6 (June 1919), 85.

235 *"Blow your nose"*: There are many versions, some with cruder lyrics.

236 *"a perfect jellyfish"*: Wilson, *My Memoir*, 252.

236 *"a tragic mystery"*: House, *Intimate Papers*, 4:518.

236 *"His audience wanted"*: Senator Henry Ashurst, quoted in Berg, *Wilson*, 607.

237 *"I never expected"*: Berg, 612.

237 *"There can seldom"*: Keynes, *Economic Consequences*, 43.

237 *"deal with the matter"*: Berg, *Wilson*, 617.

238 *"class war is on"*: The text was reprinted in a few newspapers and at this writing can be found online at https://www.historyisaweapon.com/defcon1/plainwords.html.

238 *"Wholesale Arrests"*: 3 June 1919.

238 *"Walsh," another paper*: "Officials Lay Blame for Blasts Here on New York Anarchists," *Pittsburgh Gazette Times*, 4 June 1919.

240 *"I never knew"*: Ackerman, *Young J. Edgar*, 13.

241 *"skim milk, weak"*: "Over There and Over Here," *The Agitator* (Wellsboro, PA), 7 May 1919.

241 *"Let there be"*: "Clean Up the Reds!," *Washington Post*, 4 June 1919.

241 *"I stood in"*: *Charges of Illegal Practices of the Department of Justice: Hearings before a Subcommittee of the Committee on the Judiciary, United States Senate* (Washington, DC: US Government Printing Office, 1921), 580.

242 *"Out of the sly"*: *Charges of Illegal Practices of the Department of Justice*, 27.

243 *"connected with Russian"*: Schmidt, *Red Scare*, 150.

243 *"on a certain day"*: Hagedorn, *Savage Peace*, 269.

243 *"we can round up"*: Francis P. Garvan, quoted in "Funds to Fight Reds," *Washington Post*, 27 June 1919.

244 *"It is hard"*: Ackerman, *Young J. Edgar*, 96–97.

244 *Radical Division*: Its name would be changed to the General Intelligence Division in mid-1920.

245 *"for spreading I. W. W. propaganda"*: "Dr. Mari Equi under Arrest," *Seattle Star*, 14 March 1919.

245 *"women who had disposed"*: O'Hare, *Prison Letters*, 4–5.

245 *"The dining room was"*: O'Hare, *In Prison*, 63–65.

245 *"I have volunteered"*: O'Hare, *Prison Letters*, 14, 7, 20, 24–25.

CHAPTER 17: ON THE GREAT DEEP

248 *"more concerned about"*: Woodrow Wilson, *The New Freedom: A Call for the Emancipation of the Generous Energies of a People* (New York: Doubleday, Page, 1913), 274.

248   *"moral passion"*: Howe, *Confessions of a Reformer*, 7, 253, 256, 271–73, 267, 280, 283–84.

251   *"unwise remarks"*: "Woman Lynched by Brooks Co. Mob," *Atlanta Constitution*, 20 May 1918.

251   *The mob included*: See Slotkin, *Lost Battalions*, 145, and Meyers, "'Killing Them by the Wholesale,'" for more detail.

251   *"It was right"*: "Returning Soldiers," *The Crisis* 18, no. 1 (May 1919): 14.

252   *"The incident is"*: "Nip It in the Bud," *True Democrat* (Bayou Sara, LA), 21 December 1918, quoted in Equal Justice Initiative, *Lynching in America*, 28.

252   *"crimes of this character"*: "White Men Should Organize to Prevent Necessity of Mob," *Vardaman's Weekly*, 15 May 1919.

253   *newcomers' "presence here"*: Loerzel, "Blood in the Streets," 1.

253   *Sunday, July 27, 1919*: Krugler, *1919*; McWhirter, *Red Summer*; Loerzel, "Blood in the Streets."

254   *"There's a nigger!"*: Roi Ottley, *The Lonely Warrior: The Life and Times of Robert S. Abbott* (Chicago: Regnery, 1955), 180–82.

255   *at least 103*: McWhirter, *Red Summer*, 225.

255   *"If it were possible"*: Jodi L. Rightler-McDaniels and Lori Amber Roessner, eds., *Political Pioneer of the Press: Ida B. Wells-Barnett and Her Transnational Crusade for Social Justice* (Lanham, MD: Lexington Books, 2018), 8.

255   *"kill any negro"*: Jerome Karabel, "The Ghosts of Elaine, Arkansas, 1919," *NYR Daily* (blog), *New York Review of Books*, 30 September 1919.

255   *"the race riots that have occurred"*: "President Planned to Ask Voiding of Police Unions," *Evening Star* (Washington, DC), 12 September 1919.

256   *"Brothers we are"*: "Let Us Reason Together," *The Crisis* 18, no. 5 (September 1919): 231.

256   *"Federal official"*: 28 July 1919.

257   *"Yes, he is the man!"*: Krugler, *1919*, 151.

258   *Most of the attackers*: Krugler, 148–50. See also Orville D. Menard, *Political Bossism in Mid-America: Tom Dennison's Omaha, 1900–1933* (Lanham, MD: University Press of America, 1989), 245.

258   *"was strong for"*: "What General Wood Says," *Evening State Journal* (Lincoln, NE), 8 October 1919.

258   *"the troops and the American Legion"*: "Trouble Here Laid to I. W. W.," *Omaha Daily Bee*, 6 October 1919.

CHAPTER 18: I AM NOT IN CONDITION TO GO ON

259   *"break the heart"*: Cooper, *Woodrow Wilson: A Biography*, 580.

259   *"He was obviously"*: Sir William Wiseman, quoted in Meyer, *The World Remade*, 545.

259   *"I promised our"*: Berg, *Wilson*, 619.

260 *"I cannot put"*: Grayson, *An Intimate Memoir*, 95.

260 *"Never have I seen"*: Tumulty, *Wilson as I Know Him*, 439.

260 *"With each revolution"*: Wilson, *My Memoir*, 280.

261 *"incensed and distressed"*: Tumulty, *Wilson as I Know Him*, 441.

261 *"The Red hysteria"*: Howe, *Confessions of a Reformer*, 327–28.

262 *"whether radical elements"*: NARA OG 372926, 12 September 1919.

262 *"Has Bolshevik Russia"*: "Unionism in Boston, Warning to Los Angeles," *Los Angeles Times*, 12 September 1919.

262 *"Lenin and Trotsky"*: Hagedorn, *Savage Peace*, 352.

262 *"at the mercy"*: "Wilson Denounces Police Strike That Left Boston a Prey to Thugs," *New York Times*, 12 September 1919.

262 *"To hell with football"*: "Harvard Organizing for Police Duty in Boston," *Boston Evening Globe*, 9 September 1919.

263 *"Several of the musical"*: "Broadway Dark as Actors' Strike Closes 12 Theatres," *Illustrated Daily News* (Los Angeles), 8 August 1919.

263 *"All the world's a stage"*: "The Conning Tower," 22 August 1919.

264 *"the poison of disorder"*: Speech in Des Moines, 6 September 1919.

264 *"incomparable consummation"*: Columbus, Ohio, 4 September 1919.

264 *"enterprise of divine"*: San Francisco, 18 September 1919.

264 *68.7 hours*: Commission of Inquiry, Interchurch World Movement, *Report on the Steel Strike of 1919* (New York: Harcourt, Brace and Howe, 1920), 12.

265 *14 percent of its stock price*: Meyer, *The World Remade*, 350.

266 *"Every one of us"*: Emerson Hough, "Round Our Town," *Saturday Evening Post*, 21 February 1920. Although Hough calls these vigilantes the Loyal Legion, other sources refer to them as the Loyal American League.

266 *"At Gary the trouble"*: "Wood Blames Reds for Gary Disorders," *New York Times*, 19 October 1919.

267 *"more fiction"*: Schmidt, *Red Scare*, 22.

267 *"Reds and I. W. W.'s Active"*: 9 October 1919.

267 *"Reds Fomenting"*: 16 October 1919.

267 *By one estimate*: Robert K. Murray, "Communism and the Great Steel Strike of 1919," in Richard O. Curry and Thomas M. Brown, eds., *Conspiracy: The Fear of Subversion in American History* (New York: Holt, Rinehart and Winston, 1972), 135.

267 *"there is a great deal"*: NARA OG 352037, 7 October 1919.

267 *"examined him"*: McCormick, *Seeing Reds*, 127.

267 *"I believe there is"*: Hoover to Burke, 10 February 1920, NARA OG 391485.

267 *"We want you"*: Interchurch World Movement, *Public Opinion*, 58–59.

268 *John Mach*: His real name was Michael Zierhoffer. See NARA OG 132509.

268 *"a man very much"*: Berg, *Wilson*, 628.

268 *"Block after block"*: "Pacific Fleet Is Reviewed by President," *New York Tribune*, 14 September 1919.

269 *"They stood in swarms"*: "President's Launch in Collision with Naval Whale-boat," *Vancouver Sun*, 14 September 1919.

269 *"looked flabbergasted"*: Louis Adamic, "The 'Assassin' of Wilson," *American Mercury*, October 1930.

270 *"the fatigue"*: Tumulty, *Wilson as I Know Him*, 439.

271 *"there was a single"*: Starling, *Starling of the White House*, 151.

271 *"A great wave"*: Tumulty, *Wilson as I Know Him*, 449

271 *"men and women were seen"*: "Wilson Gives Notice Time for Talk Is Up," *Boston Globe*, 26 September 1919.

272 *"asked to have"*: Grayson, *An Intimate Memoir*, 98.

272 *"upon the completion"*: Tumulty, *Wilson as I Know Him*, 447–48.

272 *"I am not in condition"*: Berg, *Wilson*, 636.

CHAPTER 19: IN A TUGBOAT KITCHEN

273 *"prominent Reds"*: NARA OG 36412, 6 September 1919.

274 *"from an official source"*: "Workers' Union Has 500 Agents Spreading Bolshevism in the United States—Constitution Proclaims War on Government," *New York Times*, 8 June 1919.

274 *the immigration laws now allowed*: Regin Schmidt, always the most astute reader of Justice Department records, explains this in *Red Scare* on pages 248–49.

275 *"leading astray"*: Schmidt, 87.

275 *"Ship or shoot!"*: See, for example, "'S.O.S., Ship or Shoot,' Wood's Motto for Reds," *Oshkosh Northwestern* (Wisconsin), 18 December 1919. Wood used the line in dozens of speeches.

276 *"actively stirring up trouble"*: Kane to Palmer, 16 July 1919, quoted in Schmidt, *Red Scare*, 34–35.

276 *"unscrupulous detectives"*: Special Agent Connell, 22 November 1919, NARA OG 376413.

276 *"In San Francisco, he expressed"*: "President Suffers Nervous Breakdown, Tour Canceled," *New York Times*, 27 September 1919.

277 *"face was shrunken"*: Goldman, *Living My Life*, 695, 700–701.

278 *"the majority were"*: Ackerman, *Young J. Edgar*, 111.

278 *"With prohibition coming in"*: Falk, *Love, Anarchy, and Emma Goldman*, 177.

278 *"very much dissatisfied"*: NARA OG 374217, 8 October 1919.

279 *"that it would be my last"*: Goldman, *Living My Life*, 708.

279 *"Miss Goldman"*: Ackerman, *Young J. Edgar*, 107.

279 *"I found the inquisitors"*: Goldman, *Living My Life*, 704.

279 *"mostly of foreign"*: Polenberg, *Fighting Faiths*, 166.

279 *"these two notorious"*: Hoover to Col. A. B. Cox, 2 January 1920, quoted in Schmidt, *Red Scare*, 262.

280 *"Shut up, there"*: "200 Caught in New York," *New York Times*, 8 November 1919.

280 *"struck me"*: Brown, Chafee, et al., *To the American People*, 18.

280 *"as if a bomb"*: Ackerman, *Young J. Edgar*, 116.

281 *"their heads wrapped"*: "200 Caught in New York."

281 *"brought a rope"*: Brown, Chafee et al., *To the American People*, 13–14.

281 *"these people appear"*: Schmidt, *Red Scare*, 271, 266, 273.

281 *"every effort to"*: Schmidt, 266.

282 *"even more radical"*: Schmidt, 273.

282 *"a nationwide uprising"*: "Department of Justice Men Seize Radicals on Second Anniversary of Soviet Rule," *New York Herald*, 8 November 1919, quoted in Schmidt, 273.

282 *"proof that Lenin himself"*: "Drastic Penalties Planned for Reds," *New York Times*, 12 November 1919.

282 *"detectives and agents"*: "Raid on 'Reds' Reveals TNT in Secret Laboratory," *New York Tribune*, 26 November 1919.

282 *"Mr. Wilson's political leadership"*: "Politics," *Washington Herald*, 9 November 1919.

282 *"considerable number"*: Ackerman, *Young J. Edgar*, 123.

283 *"he appeared just as helpless"*: Hoover, *Forty-Two Years*, 103.

284 *"For Mr. Wilson to resign"*: Wilson, *My Memoir*, 289.

285 *"was physically almost"*: Hoover, *Forty-Two Years*, 103.

285 *"clear and acute"*: Berg, *Wilson*, 645.

286 *"Today, we hear"*: "Nicholas M. Butler Cries 'War on Reds,'" *New York Tribune*, 13 November 1919.

286 *"to deport every alien"*: "Would Deport Bolshevists," *Washington Times*, 29 May 1919.

286 *"The government had positively"*: "Senator Poindexter Would Deport Reds," *Norwich Bulletin* (Connecticut), 18 November 1919.

286 *"petty, pusillanimous"*: "Raid Reds Here: Seize 150," *Chicago Daily Tribune*, 2 January 1920.

286 *"aliens were being smuggled"*: "Anarchists Flock Here from Mexico," *New York Times*, 24 November 1919.

287 *"It appears that some"*: "Send Reds Here for Deportation, Then Free Them," *New York Times*, 23 November 1919.

287 *"were not permitted"*: Goldman, *Living My Life*, 713.

287 *Ingmar Iverson*: "Mob at Madison Seizes Alleged War Objector, Forces Him to Get Out," *Daily Argus-Leader* (Sioux Falls, SD), 18 October 1919. I learned of this case from an unpublished manuscript by Bill R. Douglas.

288 *"Mr. President," the leaflet said:* Fite and Peterson, *Opponents of War*, 272.

290 *"he should, like":* Dean Acheson, *Morning and Noon* (Boston: Houghton Mifflin, 1965), 119. A college and law school classmate of Acheson's, Stanley Morrison, was Holmes's law clerk.

290 *"most-quoted justifications":* Liva Baker, *The Justice from Beacon Hill: The Life and Times of Oliver Wendell Holmes* (New York: HarperCollins, 1991), 539.

291 *"There came the rattling":* Goldman, *Living My Life*, 716.

291 *"It was noisy":* NARA OG 379190, 16 January 1920, to "Dear Friends."

291 *"a drive to cut down":* "249 Reds Sail, Exiled to Soviet Russia; Berkman Threatens to Come Back; Second Shipload May Leave This Week," *New York Times*, 22 December 1919.

292 *barge, attached to a tugboat:* There is some ambiguity about the nature of this vessel—perhaps because the trip took place in the middle of the night. Goldman refers specifically to a barge and tugboat. Congressman William Vaile, who was there, also calls it a tugboat. One newspaper refers to a "small army tender," and several to an "army tug," although a normal New York Harbor tugboat alone could not carry 249 prisoners plus their guards and assorted dignitaries, which suggests Goldman was right about the barge. A Bureau of Investigation agent refers to "the steamboat Emmigrant," and the *New York Times* to the *Immigrant*, with no description of the boat. There was, in fact, a vessel of this era called the *Immigrant*, variously described as a "cutter" and "a revenue cutter ferry," which sometimes made the run to Ellis Island. Apparently this was the craft involved, probably with a barge attached.

292 *"Deep snow lay":* Goldman, *Living My Life*, 717.

292 *"Among those who":* "Goldman Sorry to Leave U.S.," *Spokesman-Review* (Spokane, WA), 24 December 1919.

292 *"A large fire":* Goldman, *Living My Life*, 717.

293 *"a face":* Fenner Brockway, *Inside the Left: Thirty Years of Platform, Press, Prison, and Parliament* (London: George Allen & Unwin, 1942), 298.

293 *"Haven't I given you":* Appendix, *Congressional Record*, 66th Congress, Second Session, Extension of Remarks of the Hon. William N. Vaile of 20 December 1919, p. 8693, https://www.congress.gov/66/crecb/1919/12/01/GPO-CRECB-1920-pt9-v59-1.pdf.

CHAPTER 20: MEN LIKE THESE WOULD RULE YOU

296 *It issued press releases:* Schmidt, *Red Scare*, 295.

296 *"By such wholesale raids":* 12 January 1920, reprinted in *Survey*, 31 January 1920.

297 *"To hell with":* "Acquitted of Murder of Disloyal 'Red,'" *Evening Sun* (Hanover, PA), 20 February 1920.

297 *"a large bobsled":* "Criminal Anarchy Charge Is Made," *News* (Paterson NJ), 16 February 1920.

297   *about 10,000:* Schmidt, *Red Scare,* 178. Williams, "Bureau of Investigation and Its Critics," 561, uses a figure of 10,000 for the January raids alone, as does Preston, *Aliens and Dissenters,* 221.

297   *"arguably the greatest":* Alan Brinkley, "World War I and the Crisis of Democracy," in Daniel Farber, ed., *Security v. Liberty: Conflicts between National Security and Civil Liberties in American History* (New York: Russell Sage Foundation, 2008), 33.

298   *no more than 40,000:* Schmidt, *Red Scare,* 279. Some scholars give higher estimates, but Schmidt has studied Bureau of Investigation materials more thoroughly than anyone else I'm aware of.

298   *"was only a rendezvous":* NARA OG 379615, 27 February 1919.

298   *"well known I. W. W. agitator":* "Thousands of Radical Posters Are Seized," *Pittsburgh Post,* 16 April 1920.

299   *"You have been elected":* Jaffe, 145–46.

299   *"the sounds of ":* Jaffe, *Crusade Against Radicalism,* 146.

300   *"It was my great":* Strang, *Keep the Wretches in Order,* 104.

301   *"the most important":* Unpublished memoir, Trevor Papers, University of Michigan, box 1, p. 499. Unfortunately, all but a few dozen pages of this memoir have disappeared from the Trevor Papers.

301   *"Trevor's xenophobia":* Okrent, *The Guarded Gate,* 324.

301   *"convulsive shivers":* Trevor to Johnson, 18 February 1927, quoted in Okrent, 426.

301   *"Mexicans and Brazilians":* Trevor to Johnson, 18 February 1923, quoted in Okrent, 324.

302   *"penetrates the bodies":* Cécile Tormay, *An Outlaw's Diary: The Commune* (New York: Robert M. McBride, 1924), 22, 59.

302   *"intensely interesting":* Johnson to Trevor, 18 June 1924, Trevor Papers, University of Michigan, box 1.

303   *"like rats":* Emerson Hough, "Round Our Town," *Saturday Evening Post,* 21 February 1920.

303   *"A. Mitchell Palmer, in personal appearance":* Willis J. Abbot, "A. Mitchell Palmer, 'Fighting Quaker,'" *Literary Digest,* 27 March 1920.

303   *a long, fiery magazine article:* "The Case against the 'Reds,'" *Forum* 63, February 1920.

304   *"second, third, and fourth":* "Palmer Promises More Soviet Arks," *New York Times,* 29 February 1920.

CHAPTER 21: SEEING RED

306   *"integrity and moral strength":* Goldman, *Living My Life,* 712.

307   *"fearlessly honest":* Howe, *Confessions of a Reformer,* 195.

307   *"apostles of peace":* Post, *Deportations Delirium,* 14.

307 *a carefully footnoted article:* "Administrative Decisions in Connection with Immigration," *American Political Science Review* 10, no. 2 (May 1916).

309 *"Raiders Seize":* *Sun and New York Herald*, 2 April 1920.

309 *"anarchistic":* Post, *Deportations Delirium*, 224.

309 *"A raid on an executive department":* "Washington Men Raid L. F. Post," *Spokesman-Review* (Spokane WA), 6 April 1920.

309 *"To defend himself":* Ackerman, *Young J. Edgar*, 253.

310 *"In a large proportion":* "Scores Conduct of Communist Raids," *Boston Globe*, 10 April 1920.

310 *"a man whose sympathies":* Schmidt, *Red Scare*, 309.

311 *"I feel like going":* Berg, *Wilson*, 678.

311 *"residing more than presiding":* Berg, 679.

312 *"It was enough":* Houston, *Eight Years*, 2:68.

312 *"alien anarchists":* Daniels, *Cabinet Diaries*, 518.

313 *"Doctor Grayson looked":* Houston, *Eight Years*, 2:68.

313 *"told Palmer not":* Daniels, *Cabinet Diaries*, 518.

313 *"Mitchell Palmer talks":* 1 May 1920, *PWW*, 65:242.

314 *"Palmer Reveals Red Plot":* *Richmond Times-Dispatch*, 30 April 1920.

314 *"Included also":* "Reds Plotting May Day Murders, Says Palmer," *New York Tribune*, 30 April 1920.

314 *"strikes in all":* *Barre Daily Times* (Vermont), 30 April 1920.

314 *"Justice Dept. to Curb":* *Washington Times*, 30 April 1920.

314 *"Reds Plotting":* *New York Tribune*, 30 April 1920.

314 *"Radicals Plan":* *Bisbee Daily Review* (Arizona), 30 April 1929.

CHAPTER 22: A LITTLE MAN, COOL BUT FIERY

315 *"Mrs. O'Hare is":* "Wilson Frees Kate O'Hare," *Washington Times*, 29 May 1920.

315 *"I felt I should like":* O'Hare, *In Prison*, 182.

316 *"it seemed a crime":* Miller, *From Prairie to Prison*, 193.

316 *"I will never consent":* Tumulty, *Wilson as I Know Him*, 505.

317 *"The 'Reds' at Ellis Island":* Ackerman, *Young J. Edgar*, 275.

318 *"is seeing its laws":* Post hearings, 5, 16, 26.

318 *"a widespread and carefully":* Post hearings, 16.

318 *"advocated, before he":* Post hearings, 26.

318 *"Thus," said the* Times: "City under Guard against Red Plot Threatened Today," *New York Times*, 1 May 1920.

319 *"360 suspicious characters":* "Arrest 360 in Chicago to Forestall Radicals," *New York Times*, 1 May 1920.

320 *the country contained:* "MID Estimate of the Military Situation," 3 May 1921, NARA RG 165, File 242-13, quoted in Laurie and Cole, *Role of Federal Military*, 330.

320 *"in a state of insurrection"*: Ross, *Peacetime War Plans*, 60.

320 *another army document*: Summary of the Estimate on the United States, Course at General Staff College, 1919–1920, Intelligence, part IV, p.1; part III, pp. 4–5.

321 *"there were more policemen"*: "No May Day Outbreaks in U.S.; Three Killed, Many Hurt, in Paris," *New York Tribune*, 2 May 1920.

322 *published a cartoon*: 4 May 1920.

322 *"We can never get"*: Murray, *Red Scare*, 253.

322 *"What Mr. Palmer"*: "Only Danger of May Day Uprising Was in Palmer's Eye," *San Francisco Examiner*, 20 May 1920.

322 *a particularly egregious example*: Brandes, *Warhogs*, 170.

323 *"a demagogue who believed"*: John Braeman, "World War One and the Crisis of American Liberty," *American Quarterly* 16, no. 1 (Spring 1964): 109.

323 *15 percent of*: Curt Gentry, *J. Edgar Hoover: The Man and the Secrets* (New York: W. W. Norton, 1991), 442.

323 *"the short shaggy figure"*: "The Louis Post Case," *New Republic*, 26 May 1920.

324 *"I am not impressed"*: Post hearings, 70–71.

324 *"laughter swept the room"*: "House Report Lie, Says Post," *Washington Times*, 7 May 1920.

324 *"Now, I do not know"*: Post hearings, 71, 261, 242, 248.

325 *"gave a very good"*: "Post Self-Immolated," *Wilmington Morning Star* (North Carolina), 12 May 1920.

325 *"Some day, when"*: Henry Raymond Mussey, "Louis F. Post—American," *The Nation*, 12 June 1920.

325 *"agitated gentlemen"*: "The Louis Post Case."

326 *"More lawless proceedings"*: "Expose of Palmerism Means His Political End," *New York Call*, 26 April 1920.

326 *"If possible," it said*: Burke to Kelleher, 27 December 1919, quoted in Brown, Chafee, et al., *To the American People*, 39–40.

326 *"In these times"*: Ackerman, *Young J. Edgar*, 248.

326 *"a mob is a mob"*: Schmidt, *Red Scare*, 305.

327 *"a deliberate misuse"*: Brown, Chafee, et al., *To the American People*, 6–7.

328 *"very greatly desired"*: Memorandum to Lawrence G. Brooks, c. 21 March 1920, quoted in Irons, "'Fighting Fair,'" 1219.

328 *"appalling"*: Ackerman, *Young J. Edgar*, 206.

328 *"convincing and extremely able"*: Post, *Deportations Delirium*, 97, 297.

CHAPTER 23: POLICEMAN AND DETECTIVE

329 *"I am myself"*: Coben, *A. Mitchell Palmer*, 250.

329 *"We assumed"*: Pietrusza, *1920*, 246.

330 *"Detroit is the largest city"*: Coben, *A. Mitchell Palmer*, 257.

330 *His rivals were quick*: Ackerman, *Young J. Edgar*, 323.

330   *"The drift has been"*: 14 June 1920, quoted in Ackerman, *Young J. Edgar*, 322.

330   *"General Wood is the choice"*: "A National Candidate," *New York Tribune*, 27 April 1920.

330   *"At the Wood headquarters"*: "Storm Centre of the National Political Campaigns," *New York Times*, 2 May 1920.

330   *"no other means"*: "When the Government Fails to Do Its Duty," *New Republic*, 11 February 1920.

331   *"is the simple-minded"*: "A Carnival of Buncombe," *Baltimore Evening Sun*, 9 February 1920.

332   *"There were no end"*: Walter Lippmann, "Leonard Wood," in *Early Writings*, ed. Arthur Schlesinger Jr. (New York: Liveright, 1970), 157–66.

334   *"The preposterous claim"*: "Burleson and the Call," *New Republic*, 7 January 1920.

334   *"this office has sequestered"*: NARA OG 202600-282, 10 May 1920.

334   *Hoover sent a representative:* Hoover to James A. Horton, 27 September 1920, NARA OG 136944.

335   *"in very serious"*: 24 March 1920, NARA OG 136944.

335   *"unlimited financial backing"*: Woody Klein, ed., *Liberties Lost: The Endangered Legacy of the ACLU* (Westport, CT: Praeger, 2006), 133–34.

335   *"serious menace"*: "Legion Asks Dismissal of Louis F. Post," *New York Tribune*, 1 October 1920.

335   *"is an affront"*: "The Post Scandal," *New York Tribune*, 6 October 1920.

335   *"prevent them from falling"*: "Woods Amazed at Post's Legion Bar," *New York Herald*, 6 October 1920.

336   *"ranks among the ablest"*: "White House Issues Defense of Post," *Philadelphia Inquirer*, 21 January 1921.

336   *"How do I know"*: Robert K. Murray, *The Harding Era: Warren G. Harding and His Administration* (Minneapolis: University of Minnesota Press, 1969), 64.

336   *"Too much has been said"*: Sherman Rogers, "Senator Harding on Labor," *Outlook*, 18 August 1920, p. 670. The story was reprinted in some daily newspapers as well.

337   *"loved and idealized"*: Ginger, *Eugene V. Debs*, 421.

337   *"Is there any child"*: "President Wilson's Speeches Defending the Peace Treaty," *New York Tribune*, 6 September 1919.

338   *"It is he, not I"*: "Debs, Unrepentant, Denounces Wilson," *New York Times*, 2 February 1921.

CHAPTER 24: AFTERMATH

340   *"It reminds me of"*: "Gamalielese," *Baltimore Evening Sun*, 7 March 1921.

340   *"an army of pompous"*: "A Sort of Rehabilitation of Warren G. Harding," *New York Times*, 26 March 1972. The quotation is from William G. McAdoo, Wilson's secretary of the treasury. McAdoo was twice an unsuccessful candidate

for the Democratic nomination for president, and in the 1930s served a term
as US senator from California.

340   *"There was no American"*: Inaugural address, 4 March 1921.

341   *"Why should we kid"*: Freeberg, *Democracy's Prisoner*, 236.

341   *"talked freely"*: Harry M. Daugherty with Thomas Dixon, *The Inside Story of the
Harding Tragedy* (New York: Churchill, 1932), 118.

341   *"He is where"*: "Berger and Debs," *New York Times*, 2 February 1921.

342   *"Barking dogs"*: Miller, *From Prairie to Prison*, 196.

342   *"I have heard"*: Freeberg, *Democracy's Prisoner*, 299.

343   *"He is of"*: Harding to Malcolm Jennings, 6 January 1922, quoted in Ron Ra-
dosh, "Presidential Pardons and the Spirit of Clemency," *The Bulwark*, 14 July
2020.

343   *"Now," Debs answered*: Freeberg, *Democracy's Prisoner*, 299.

343   *"during the one month"*: *Emergency Immigration Legislation. Hearing before Committee on Immigrations, United States Senate, Sixty-Sixth Congress, Third Session,
on H. R. 14461*, p. 92.

343   *"a typical American"*: Okrent, *The Guarded Gate*, 276.

343   *"of the peasant class"*: "Parts of Report Jews Protested," *Boston Sunday Post*, 12
December 1920.

344   *"Not so. I care not"*: "To Vote Tomorrow on Alien Bar Law," *Washington Post*, 12
December 1920.

344   *"the situation in New York City"*: *Emergency Immigration Legislation. Hearing before Committee on Immigration, United States Senate, Sixty-sixth Congress, third
session, on H. R. 14461* (11 January 1921), p. 294.

345   *A journalist recorded*: Mary Heaton Vorse, "The Children's Crusade for Am-
nesty," *The Nation*, 10 May 1922.

346   *has counted 462:* These prisoners, as listed in chapter 12 of his book, total 465.
But I have reduced the number by three, because he includes Schoberg and
his two codefendants from Kentucky, whose imprisonment was delayed by
their appeal, and whose time behind bars was only some six months.

346   *"The number of"*: Kohn, *American Political Prisoners*, 3.

346   *No one has ever counted*: Kohn has a chapter about state-level prisoners in his
book, but many of the cases he lists are undated, and others are from the late
1920s, beyond the era under discussion here. And he lists only two cases from
Montana, when we know from Work's study, which I've cited, that the number
there was much larger.

346   *Seventy-three of those:* Woodrow C. Whitten, "Criminal Syndicalism and the
Law in California: 1919–1927," *Transactions of the American Philosophical Society*
59, no. 2 (1969): 52–53. These figures are from 6 May 1919 to 15 August 1924.

346   *Forty men:* Work, *Darkest before Dawn*, 182–83. The number convicted
under the state's sedition law may be particularly high because two key

federal officials in Montana, its district court judge and its US attorney, the later US senator Burton K. Wheeler, had an unusual regard for free speech. There were no federal wartime Espionage Act convictions in the state.

346 *not one person convicted*: "Silence Broken, Pardons Granted 88 Years after Crimes of Sedition," *New York Times*, 3 May 2006.

347 *"It was a rare Red"*: "Death Takes Van Deman, S. D. General," *San Diego Union*, 23 January 1952.

347 *One of those he helped*: "The Father of American Surveillance," in Adam Hochschild, *Lessons from a Dark Time and Other Essays* (Oakland: University of California Press, 2018), 49.

347 *a labor newspaper*: "Will Expose Labor Spies," *The Railroad Worker* 22, no. 6 (September 1924). The exposé apparently originally appeared in the *Pennsylvania Labor Herald*.

348 *"the special prosecutor learned"*: Bruce A. Rubenstein and Lawrence E. Ziewacz, *Three Bullets Sealed His Lips* (East Lansing: Michigan State University Press, 1987), 221.

348 *He died*: "Leo Wendell, Probe Aide, Dies at 55," *Detroit Free Press*, 12 July 1945; "Death Reveals Secret Agent's Many Services," *Times Herald* (Port Huron, MI), 12 July 1945.

348 *"Find what you were"*: Letter to the author from Marie Riley (Wendell's granddaughter), 18 March 2021.

349 *"If I were ruler"*: O'Hare, *In Prison*, 17.

349 *"sort of political orphan"*: Miller, *From Prairie to Prison*, 207.

349 *"noted criminologist"*: Director Says 'Rotten Food' Is Found in Prison," *San Francisco Examiner*, 8 June 1939.

350 *"for America"*: Falk, *Love, Anarchy, and Emma Goldman*, 5.

351 *"old Colonial white stock"*: Okrent, *The Guarded Gate*, 328.

351 *"undesirable mongrel immigration"*: 6 December 1923, Trevor Papers, University of Michigan, box 2.

351 DO NOT YIELD": 25 April 1924, Trevor Papers, University of Michigan, box 2.

351 *"You can see"*: "Immigration Again Becomes Big Problem," *St. Louis Daily Globe-Democrat*, 28 January 1927.

351 *"They refuse to allow"*: Adolf Hitler, *My Struggle* (London: Hurst & Blackett, 1936), 174.

352 *"to protect the youth"*: Okrent, *The Guarded Gate*, 374.

354 *"Good-bye, you've had"*: *Bill Haywood's Book: The Autobiography of William D. Haywood* (New York: International Publishers, 1929), 361.

355 *"It is exceedingly fortunate"*: Finch to Daugherty, 6 December 1923, quoted in Kohn, *American Political Prisoners*, 19.

356 *some 300 people"*: Allison Keyes, "A Long-Lost Manuscript Contains a Sear-

ing Eyewitness Account of the Tulsa Race Massacre of 1921," *At the Smithsonian* (blog), *Smithsonian*, 27 May 2016, https://www.smithsonianmag.com/smithsonian-institution/long-lost-manuscript-contains-searing-eyewitness-account-tulsa-race-massacre-1921-180959251/.

356　*"Bolshevik propaganda"*: "Blame Red Propaganda for Tulsa Race Riots," *Los Angeles Times*, 2 June 1921.

356　*"the late negro uprising"*: "Riot Statement Made by Mayor," *Tulsa Daily World*, 15 June 1921.

356　*Several people wearing*: Mike Pearl, "All the Evidence We Could Find about Fred Trump's Alleged Involvement with the KKK," *Vice*, March 10, 2016, https://www.vice.com/en/article/mvke38/all-the-evidence-we-could-find-about-fred-trumps-alleged-involvement-with-the-kkk.

abortion, 141
Abrams, Jacob, 289
Abrams v. United States, 289–90, 326
Ackerman, Kenneth, 244, 309, 360
Actors Equity, 263
Addams, Jane, 145, 227, 254, 345
Affordable Care Act, 353
African Americans. *See* Black Americans
agriculture, 124–25
Air Nitrates Corporation, 322–23
Alaska Daily Empire, 46
Albert I of Belgium, 180
Alien Enemy, An (movie), 177
"alien property," 302–3
Amalgamated Clothing Workers May Day
    concert, 321
American Bar Association, 95
American Brake and Shoe Foundry, 69
American Civil Liberties Union, 138, 335,
    352
American Defense Society, 6, 264
American Defense Vigilantes, 101
American Expeditionary Forces, 82
American Federation of Labor, 91, 221, 262,
    354–55
Americanism versus Bolshevism (Hanson),
    222–23
American Legion, 230, 255, 258, 283, 288,
    297, 300, 330, 335, 341, 342

American Legion Weekly, 230
American Library Association, 68
American Medical Association, 141, 311
American Protective League (APL), 97–100,
    126, 130, 231, 262, 356, 357
  move to Washington, DC, 132–33
  participation in raids of 1917, 123
  reorganization after the war, 227–28
  "slacker raids," 151–53, 185, 188–89
  Wood and election of 1920, 331
American Railway Union, 181–82
America's Answer, 176
Amsterdam News, 137–38
anarchism, 10, 75
anarchist bombings of 1919, 238–44
Anderson, George W., 326, 328, 331
Anti-Alien League, 230
anti-German feeling, 6–8, 33, 83, 153–58,
    176–77
anti-immigration agitation, 47–51, 86,
    88–89, 224–26, 229–31, 243, 247,
    286–87, 300–302, 343–44, 356–57
  Johnson-Reed Act of 1924, 350–52
anti-Semitism, 7–8, 27, 50, 172, 225–26,
    228, 301–2, 344, 351–52
Anti-Yellow Dog League, 101
Armistice of 1918, 195–97, 215
Army War College, 43
Arndt-Ober, Margarethe, 35

Ashurst, Henry, 122
Asinof, Eliot, 223
Atlanta Constitution, 330
Austro-Hungarian Empire, 17, 56, 57–58, 136, 195, 214–15, 234

Bach, Johann Sebastian, 157
Baker, Newton, 53, 115, 130–31, 145–46
Baker, Ray Stannard, 205, 217
Baltimore Sun, 309
Bannwart, Alexander, 25–26
Barry, John, 193
Beard, Charles, 227
Beast of Berlin, The (movie), 177
Becker, Maurice, 145
Belgium, 17, 18, 39, 56, 131, 136, 180, 188
Belleau Wood, Battle of 2, 168–69
Benedict XV, Pope, 203–4
Berg, A. Scott, 311, 361
Berger, Victor, 183, 300, 334, 353
Berkman, Alexander, 208
    arrest and trial of, 77–80
    Buford deportation, 290–93
    imprisonment of, 80, 102release from
        prison, 277, 278, 279
    in Russia, 350
Bethlehem Steel, 45
Bigelow, Herbert S., 178–79
Bird, William, 198
birth control, 76, 77, 126, 141–42, 142
Bisbee Deportation of 1917, 89–90
Black Americans, 107–17, 205
    Espionage Act and, 60–61
    discrimination against, 62, 107–109, 306
    Great Migration of, 108–10, 252
    lynchings of, 107–8, 114, 115, 138, 250–52
    surveillance of, 116–17
    Tulsa race massacre of 1921, 355–56
    white riots of 1919, 252–58
    during World War I, 59–60, 114–16, 197–98, 249–50
black-bag jobs, 99
blockade of Central Powers, 19, 20, 41, 58, 186, 215–18, 234

Bolsheviks, 10, 57–58, 131–32, 165, 220, 225–28, 264, 274–75, 280, 297–98
Bolshevism on Trial (movie), 227
Boni & Liveright, 68
Borah, William, 213
Boston
    Anti-Catholic agitation, 47
    May Day 1920, 319
    in Palmer Raids and aftermath, 296, 308, 326-328
    Police Strike of 1919, 261–63
    riots against leftists, 102, 229
    during World War I, 47. 156-157
Boston Globe, 102, 271, 309
Boston Symphony Orchestra, 156–57
Brady, W. Tate, 11
Brandeis, Louis, 27, 30, 212, 248, 290, 334
Brant, Joseph, 93
Brest-Litovsk, armistice of, 133
Brest-Litovsk, Treaty of, 214–15, 390nBriggs, Albert, 96–98, 132–33
Brinkley, Alan, 297
Britain
    post-war period in, 215
    during World War I, 16–19, 33, 37–38, 40–42, 55–56, 131, 168, 179
British colonialism, 41, 77, 102-103, 116, 136, 138, 216, 219–20, 236
British Mandates, 218, 233
Brittain, Vera, 168
Brooklyn Daily Eagle, 38
Broun, Heywood, 329
Brown, Will, 256–58
Buckingham Palace, 204, 277
Buford, USAT, 11, 290–93, 304, 318, 399n
Bullard, Arthur, 178
Bullard, Robert, 197
Bulletin for Cartoonists, 176
Bureau of Free Love, 226–27
Bureau of Investigation, 9, 68–69, 96, 97–98, 113, 122–23, 242, 268, 278, 308, 319, 333–34, 350
Burleson, Albert Sidney, 61–67
    anarchist bombings of 1919 and, 239
    background of, 61–62

Black Americans and, 62, 251
censorship by, 63–67, 137–39, 150, 159, 182–83, 209–10, 251, 277, 288–89, 334, 352
Burns, Ken, 2
Burns, William J., 298
Burns Detective Agency, 123, 298
Butler, Nicholas Murray, 69, 188, 286, 333
Butte, lynching in 1917, 103–5
Butte mining disaster of 1917, 102–4

Camp Dodge, 115, 145, 198
Camp Funston, 9, 146–47, 190–92, 201, 208, 245
Can Opener, The, 159–60
Canterbury Pilgrims, The (opera), 35
Cantigny, Battle of, 168
Capital (Marx), 161
Capone, Al, 2
Caporetto, Battle of, 131
Carnegie, Andrew, 301
Caruso, Enrico, 248–49
Catholic Register, 138
censorship, 4, 61, 63–69, 93, 130, 137–39, 209–10, 231, 258, 288–89, 334, 341
  Burleson and postal service, 63–67, 137–39, 150, 159, 182–83, 209–10, 251, 277, 288–89, 334, 352
Centralia massacre of 1919, 283–84
Central Intelligence Agency (CIA), 9
Chafee, Zechariah, 326-328
Champs-Élysées (Paris), 203, 214
Chaplin, Charlie, 46
Chaplin, Ralph, 123, 170
Château-Thierry, Battle of, 2, 168–69
Chester, Eric, 184
Chicago
  American Protective League in, 96-98, 100, 123, 132, 152
  Children's Crusade, 345
  May Day 1920, 319, 322
  Palmer Raids, 286, 296
  slacker raid of 1918, 152–53
  white riots of 1919, 252–55
  Wobblies in, 100, 123, 124

trial of 1918, 124, 132, 159–65, 169–70, 345
  during World War I, 83, 152-153
Chicago, Milwaukee and St. Paul Railway, 288
Chicago Defender, 109, 117, 138
Chicago Tribune, 150, 322
Children's Crusade, 344–45
Chinese Exclusion Act of 1882, 48
Churchill, Marlborough, 320
Churchill, Winston, 220, 320
Church of the Epiphany, 23
Ciro's (Paris), 168
Citizens Patriotic League, 154–55, 230
City, The (Howe), 248
Civil War, 25, 29, 30–31, 58, 62, 290, 306
Claws of the Hun, The (movie), 177
Clemenceau, Georges, 130–31, 137, 217–18, 236
Cleveland, 3, 152, 228, 229–30
Cleveland Recorder, 306
Coal and Iron Police (Pennsylvania), 84
Coalfield Strikes of 1913-1914 (Colorado), 84
Cobb, Frank, 21–22
Coeur d'Alene (Idaho) labor confrontation of 1899, 85
Colorado National Guard, 84
Columbia University, 69, 188, 224, 286, 333
Columbus, Ohio, 7, 187, 260
Committee of Thirteen, 228
Committee on Public Information (CPI), 175–79
Communism, 227, 297–98, 308, 323
Compiègne (France), 195
Conference of Christian Pacifists, 166
Congressional Medal of Honor, 198
conscientious objectors (COs), 9, 144–48, 190–92, 201. 245, 287-288, 338, 352
conscription. See draft
Constitution, US, 213, 285–86
Cook County Jail, 132, 159–60, 162, 164, 170, 296
Coolidge, Calvin, 262, 263, 333, 345
"cost plus" contracts, 45

Covington, Kentucky, 154–56

Cox, James M., 333, 336

Creel, George, 175–76, 178–79, 344

Crisis, The, 112–13, 117, 138, 224, 251, 356

Crockett, Thomas, 97, 100

Croix de Guerre, 250

Daniels, Josephus, 312–13

Danley, Irene, 345

Darrow, Clarence, 63, 237, 337

Daugherty, Harry, 341, 342, 355

Davis, David Brion, 132

Davis, Jefferson, 29

Daylight Saving Time, 43

Debs, Eugene V., 127, 181–82, 184–86, 227

  after prison, 341, 342, 345, 353

  antiwar sentiments of, 18, 64, 184–85, 237, 341

  background of, 181–82

  election of 1912, 91, 182, 316, 320

  election of 1920, 320, 337

  imprisonment of, 229, 237, 316, 333, 341

  release from prison, 337–38, 342

  trial of, 185–86

Declaration of Independence, 224

Deer Island Prison, 307–8, 326, 328

De Mille, Cecil B., 20

Democratic National Convention (1920), 330–33

Democratic Party, 3, 41, 109–10, 182

Dennison, Tom, 257–58

deportations, 3, 230, 238, 244, 248, 249, 261, 266, 274, 276, 285–88, 297

  Bisbee Deportation of 1917, 89–90

  in presidential campaign platforms (1920) 3, 230, 244, 266, 286, 303, 331, 333

  Post and Labor Department, 305–10, 312–13, 317–18, 323–25, 327–28

  USAT *Buford*, 11, 290–93, 304, 318, 399n

Deportations Delirium of Nineteen-Twenty, The (Post), 328

Dercum, Francis X., 284–85

Detective agencies, 9, 60, 104, 123, 155, 171–2, 267, 276, 323

Detroit, 98–99, 123

  Palmer Raids, 281, 295–96

Dial, The, 224

Dodge, Cleveland, 40

Dos Passos, John, 41, 160–61

draft, 8, 20, 21, 31–32, 43, 55, 58–60, 74, 83, 102–3, 130, 144–45

  Black Americans and, 114–15

  conscientious objectors (COs) and, 144–48, 190–92

  Selective Service Act, 58–59, 76–77, 144, 160

Du Bois, W. E. B., 251, 255–56, 356

  East St. Louis riots of 1917, 112–13

  Pan African Congress, 204, 251

  Wilson and, 137

  during World War I, 115–16, 117, 137, 198

Du Pont Company, 44

"Dynamite Express," 85

Eagle's Eye, The (Flynn), 242

Eastman, Crystal, 68, 334–35

Eastman, Max, 65–67, 68, 334–35

East St. Louis, 109–13

  riots of 1917, 111–13, 252, 255

Ebenezer Baptist Church (Atlanta), 117

Egypt, 41, 219

Eisenhower, Dwight, 239

Elaine, Arkansas, massacre of 1919, 254–55

election (presidential) of 1912, 73, 182

election (municipal) of 1917, 182–183

election (Congressional) of 1918, 204

election (presidential) of 1920, 3, 187, 285–86, 302–4, 329–33, 336–37

Ellis Island, 247–49, 261, 279, 287, 295, 297

  Buford deportations, 290–93

Elsas, Oscar, 171–74

Emergency Plan White, 320–21

Equal Rights League, 117

Equi, Marie, 140–43, 210, 288, 317

  aftermath, 348–49

  trial of, 189–90, 244–45

Erie Daily Times, 69

Espionage Act of 1917, 60–61, 63, 66, 67,
    69, 77, 83, 95, 99–100, 104, 129, 136,
    137, 149, 183, 231–32, 334, 346, 355
    Schenck v. United States, 212–13, 289
eugenics, 49–50, 343–44
Evangelical German Lutheran Church, 7
Evans, T. D., 2, 356
Everett (Washington) massacre of 1916, 141

Fairchild, Fred, 101
Family Limitation (Sanger), 142
Farewell to Arms, A (Hemingway), 131
Farrar, Frederic W., 123
FBI, The (TV series), 350
FBI in Peace and War, The (radio), 350
FBI Story, The (movie), 350
Federal Bureau of Investigation (FBI), 9,
    350. *See also* Bureau of Investigation
Feltman, Henry, 154–56
Finch, James A., 355
First Amendment, 353
First World War. *See* World War I
Fitts, William, 122
Fitzgerald, F. Scott, 352
Fiume, 207, 268
Flynn, William J. "Big Bill," 242–43, 280,
    319
Foch, Ferdinand, 195–97, 215
Ford, Henry, 98–99, 100
Ford Model A, 352
Ford Model T, 34, 111, 352
Ford Motor Company, 223
Fort Leavenworth, 147–48, 170, 201, 210,
    223, 345
Four Minute Men, 174–75
"Fourteen Points" speech of Wilson,
    135–37, 176, 187, 195, 203–6, 216
France, during World War I, 16, 18, 31, 33,
    37–38, 55–56, 81–82, 130–31, 168–69,
    188, 194–95
    Armistice, 195–97, 215
Frank, Leo, 8
Frankfurter, Felix, 326, 327, 328
Franklin, Benjamin, 93
Freedom of Information Act, 9

Freeman's Journal, 138
Freemasons, 132
French Foreign Legion, 18
Freud, Sigmund, 75
Frick, Henry Clay, 75, 79, 208, 279
Friendly Enemies (Hoffman), 163
Friendly Words to the Foreign Born
    (pamphlet), 177
Friends of Irish Freedom, 136
Fulton Bag and Cotton Mills, 171–74

Gaelic American, 138
Galleanists, 240–41
"Gamalielese," 340
Gandhi, Mohandas, 204–5
Garvey, Marcus, 109, 112, 205, 255
Gary, Elbert H., 265, 319
Gary, Indiana, 3, 265–66, 330
Gazeta, 248
Gellert, Ernest, 144–45
General Electric, 69
George, Henry, 306, 320, 348, 357
George III, 93
George Washington, USS, 202, 234, 235, 236
German-Bolshevik Conspiracy, The, 178
German Hospital and Dispensary, 7
German Savings Bank, 7
Germany. *See also* Nazi Germany
    Peace of Brest-Litovsk, 214–15
    post-war period in, 214–16, 218, 234
    during World War I, 16–17, 30, 56–57,
        131, 133, 168, 179–80, 186–87, 188,
        194–95
    Armistice, 195–97, 215
    Spring Offensive, 143–44
Geronimo, 39, 46–47
Gibson's Hotel (Pittsburgh), 119, 123,
    165
Gohl, William, 88
Goldfield News and Weekly Tribune, 46
Goldman, Emma, 74–80, 126
    aftermath, 350
    arrest of, 77–78
    assassination attempt of Frick, 75, 79
    background of, 75–76

Goldman, Emma (*cont.*)
  Buford deportation, 11, 248, 290–93, 350,
      399*n*
  deportation order, 79–80, 150–51, 248,
      278–79, 280, 287, 379*n*
  Hoover and, 278, 279, 291, 293
  imprisonment of, 80, 102, 139–40, 151,
      165, 166, 193, 201–2, 289
  Margolis and, 165
  O'Hare and, 130, 211–12, 245–46, 279,
      349
  release from prison, 276–79
  surveillance of, 278–79
  trial of, 78–80
Gold Star Mothers, 187
Goldstein, Robert, 93–94, 98
G.P. Putnam's Sons, 68
Grant, Ulysses S., 306
Grayson, Cary, 311, 339–40
  concealment of Wilson's health, 277–78,
      283, 285, 300, 313
  influenza of, 217
  Paris Peace Conference and, 217, 219,
      233, 235
  western tour of 1919, 249, 260, 270, 272,
      277–78
  during World War I, 15, 22, 26, 30
Great Depression, 355
Great Migration, 108–10, 252
Greenway, John, 89–90
Gregory, Thomas, 67, 96, 110, 183, 189, 231

Hammer, Grace, 171–74
Hanson, Ole, 221–23, 241
Hanson, Theodore Roosevelt, 222
Hanson, William Howard Taft, 222
Harding, Warren, 239, 339–43, 345, 348
  election of 1920, 330, 333, 336–37
Harlem, 77, 108, 116, 279
Harvard Clubs, 301, 322
Harvard University, 72, 224, 262–63
Haywood, William D. "Big Bill," 160–64,
      170, 354
Hearst, William Randolph, 64

Hemingway, Ernest, 131
Hill, Joe, 87
Hillquit, Morris, 182–83
Hindenburg, Paul von, 155
Hitler, Adolf, 215, 351–52
Ho Chi Minh, 205
Hofer, David, 147–48
Hofer, Joseph, 147–48
Hofer, Michael, 147–48
Holmes, Oliver Wendell, Jr., 212–13,
      280–90, 326, 334
Holocaust, 351–52
Home Defender, 51
Home Defense League, 101
Hoover, Ike, 217, 283, 285, 311–12
Hoover, J. Edgar, 11, 120, 334–35
  aftermath, 350
  background of, 244
  Goldman and, 278, 279, 291, 293
  Post and, 317–18, 325
  Radical Division and, 244, 256, 280,
      323
  raids. *See* Palmer Raids
  recordkeeping on radicals, 244,
      298–99
  Twelve Lawyer Report and, 327
  Union of Russia Workers and, 274–75,
      280
  Wood and, 267
House, Edward, 23–25, 30, 35, 135, 217,
      233, 235–36, 237
House Committee on Immigration and
      Naturalization, 51, 286, 300–302, 318
House Committee on Rules, 317–18,
      323–25
Houston, David, 312, 313
Howard University, 116–17
Howe, Frederic C., 247–49, 261, 307
Howe, Irving, 65
Howells, William Dean, 175
Hudson, George, 68
Hugo, Victor, 123
Hungarian American Wobblies, 119–20
Hun Within, The (movie), 177

Hurd, Carlos F., 111–12
Hutterites, 95, 147–48

Idaho labor confrontation of 1899, 85
Illuminati, the, 132
Illustrated Daily News, 263
immigration, 20, 33, 47, 48, 247–48, 261, 347
  opposition to. *See* anti-immigration
Immigration (Johnson-Reed) Act of 1924, 350–52
Immigration Bureau of Labor Department, 79–80, 123, 305, 307
Immigration Restriction League, 49
Indianapolis News, 184
Indian independence movement, 204–5, 219
Indian Wars, 11, 46–47
Industrial Worker, 87, 334
Industrial Workers of the World (IWW). *See* Wobblies
inflation, 110, 172, 220, 237, 275
Influenza pandemic of 1918, 192–94, 215, 217
Inter-Collegiate Socialist, 224
Internal Revenue Service (IRS), 123
Irish potato famine, 47
Irish War of Independence, 116, 216–17, 219–20, 236
Iron Cross, 34
Italian immigrants, 48, 50, 351
Italy
  Wilson's visit to, 203–4
  during World War I, 17, 38, 131
Iverson, Ingmar, 287–88

James, Henry, 8
Jefferson City Penitentiary, 80, 102, 139–40, 166, 193, 201–2
Jeffries, Jim, 108
Jewish Consumptive Sanitarium, 75
Jewish Daily Forward, 67–68
Jewish Educational and Charitable Association of St. Louis, 113–14
Jewish Labor Lyceum (Pittsburgh), 119

Jim Crow laws, 47, 107
Johnson, Albert
  aftermath, 343–44, 350–52
  anti-immigrant sentiments of, 50–51, 286–87, 298, 300–302, 343–44, 350–52
  background of, 50–51
  Goldman and, 292
  Post and, 309, 310, 318, 324–25, 335
  Wobblies and, 60, 88–89, 149, 287, 298
  during World War I, 179–80
Johnson, Henry, 250–51
Johnson, Jack, 108
Johnson-Reed Act of 1924, 350–52
Joint Address to Congress Leading to a Declaration of War Against Germany (1917), 26–34
Jordan, David Starr, 227
Journal of Negro History, 347
Joyce, James, 77
J. P. Morgan & Company, 31, 44
Julius Caesar (Shakespeare), 123

Kafka, Franz, 139
Kaiser, the Beast of Berlin, The (movie), 177
Kane, Francis Fisher, 276, 296–97, 327
Kansas City, 38, 74, 127, 208–9
Kazin, Michael, 144, 359
Kellogg, Walter, 385n
Kennedy, John F., 340, 347
Key, Ellen, 68
Keynes, John Maynard, 206, 237
King, Martin Luther, Jr., 117, 350
Kipling, Rudyard, 207
Kipps, Jack, 269–70
"kitchen soldiers," 43
Knights of Columbus, 142
Knights of Liberty, 1–5, 9, 10–11, 188
Know-Nothings, 47–48
Kohn, Stephen, 346, 404n
Kruse, J. Henry, 154–56
Ku Klux Klan (KKK), 11, 100, 108, 126, 177, 306, 356
Kundera, Milan, 3

labor movement, 84–90, 124–25, 354–55
labor strikes, 84, 86, 88–89, 91–92, 223–24,
    254, 263, 270–71
  Boston Police Strike of 1919, 261–63
  Seattle General Strike of 1919, 221–23,
    227–28
  steel strike of 1919, 264–68
  United Mine Workers coal strike of 1919,
    275–76
labor unions, 83–92, 107. *See also specific
    unions*
Ladino language, 231
Lafayette Escadrille, 18
La Follette, Robert, 216–17, 248, 255, 299,
    307
  aftermath, 346–47
  blockade of Europe and, 216–17, 234
  censorship and, 61, 210, 231
  Wilson's Fourteen Points speech, 137,
    187, 216
  during World War I, 34, 41–42, 58,
    69–70, 74, 186–87
Lakota Indians, 47
Lamar, William H., 139
Landis, Kenesaw Mountain, 162–63,
    169–70, 239, 300, 325
La Scala (Milan), 204Latzko, Andreas, 68
Lawrence of Arabia, 205
League of Nations, 12, 136–37, 205–9,
    213–14, 235–37, 303, 311
Lee, Robert E., 11, 30
Lenin, Vladimir, 57–58, 131–32, 133, 178
Lenon, Henry, 68–69
Lenox Hill Hospital, 7
Leonard, Oscar, 113–14
Leo XIII, Pope, 48
Les Misérables (Hugo), 123
Lewis, Charles, 252
Liberator, The, 68, 334–35
"Liberty Bond March" (song), 46
Liberty Bonds, 45–46, 69, 94, 95, 105, 117,
    149, 172, 183
Library of Congress, 244, 298
Life of Christ, The (Farrar), 123

Lincoln, Abraham, 43, 47–48, 69–70, 155,
    325
Lincoln Savings Bank, 7
Linderfelt, Karl, 84
Lippmann, Walter, 332–33
Lithuanian Socialist Chorus (Philadelphia),
    295
Little, Emma, 68
Little, Frank, 103–5, 108, 123, 162
Little Red Songbook, 87
Lloyd George, David, 24, 131, 207–8,
    213–14, 217–18, 236
Lodge, Henry Cabot
  anti-immigrant sentiments of, 49
  Wilson and Treaty of Versailles, 236–37,
    260–61, 272
  during World War I, 25–26, 27–28, 34
London, 17, 128, 204
London, Meyer, 353
Los Angeles Times, 85, 94, 262, 356
"Lost Battalion," 188
Lowe, Caroline, 170
Loyal American League, 228
Loyal Legion, 266
Lucas, Ed, 11
Ludendorff, Erich, 155, 195
Lundeen, Ernest, 288
Lusitania, 19, 40
Lusk, Clayton, 228–29, 278
lynchings, 8, 107–8, 138
  of Black Americans, 107–8, 114, 115, 138,
    250–52
  of Frank Little, 103–5, 107, 108
  of Robert Prager, 157–58
  of Will Brown, 256–57
  white riots of 1919, 252–58

McAdoo, William G., 40, 45, 62, 95
McCandless, Byron, 37
McCarthy, Joseph (McCarthyism), 3, 227,
    357
McCormick, Charles H., 120, 121, 361
Mach, John, 268
McKinley, Ada, 254

McKinley, William, 75
McNeil Island Penitentiary, 94
Magna Carta, 162
Mann, Louis, 163
Margolis, Jacob, 165
Marlatt, N. G., 170
Marshall, Thomas, 28, 105, 124, 204,
    284–85
Marx, Karl, 161
Masses, The, 65–67, 78–79, 334
May Day, 229–30
    strike of 1916, 91
    strike of 1919, 219, 229
May Day 1920, 313–14, 317, 321–23
    Palmer's predictions about, 314, 317, 318,
        322–23
    preparations for violence, 318–21
Menace, The, 48
Mencken, H. L., 331, 340
Men in War (Latzko), 68
Metropolitan Opera, 6, 35
Metropolitan Trust Company, 99
Mexican Revolution, 91
Mexican War of 1846-48, 69–70
Meyer, G. J., 61
Michigan State Troops, 348
Military Academy, US (West Point), 43,
    114
military draft. See draft
Military Intelligence, 9, 11, 59–60, 68, 166,
    167, 227, 319–20, 347
    New York City ethnic map, 224–25,
        228–29
Miller, A. F., 52–53
Miller, George, 189
Minneapolis slacker raid of 1918, 151–52
Morgan, J. P., Jr., 239, 319
Moro Rebellion, 191–92, 197
Mountain View Cemetery (Butte), 103
Mowry, George E., 72
Muck, Karl, 156–57

Nashville Banner, 41
Nation, The, 137, 201

National Association for the Advancement
    of Colored People (NAACP), 108,
    112–13, 117, 251, 306
National City Bank, 40
National Civil Liberties Bureau, 138
National Guard, 84, 152, 319, 348, 356, 357
National Rip-Saw, 127–28
National Security League, 68, 264, 298
nativism, 2–3, 10, 224–26, 229–31, 286–87
naval blockade of Central Powers, 19, 20,
    41, 58, 186, 215–18, 234
Nazi Germany, 215, 351–52
New Deal, 355
New Republic, The 323–24, 325, 334
New York City
    actors strike of 1919, 263
    anarchist bombings of 1919, 238–39
    anti-immigrant sentiments, 50
    Children's Crusade, 345
    May Day 1920, 318–21
    MI's ethnic map of, 224–25, 228–29
    nativism in, 224–26, 228–29, 230–31
    Palmer Raids, 280–81
    Victory Parade, 249–50
    vigilantism in, 101
    during World War I, 6–8
New York City Board of Education, 188
New Yorker, 65
New York Herald, 34–35, 282
New York National Guard, 319
New York Shipbuilding Company, 45
New York State Assembly, 183, 228,
    299–300
New York Stock Exchange, 40
New York Times, 7, 30, 32, 34, 90, 150, 230,
    256, 274, 276, 282, 291, 309, 318–19,
    341
New York Tribune, 184, 250, 263, 268–69,
    282, 314, 321, 330, 335
New York Truth, 306
New York World, 21–22, 34, 209, 280–81
New York Yankees, 39
Nicholas II, 57
Nielsen, Kim, 223–24

92nd Infantry Division, 115, 197–98
Nixon, Richard, 3, 347
No-Conscription League, 76–77
Nonpartisan League, 354
Northland College, 188
Novikov, Ivan, 291

O'Hare, Frank, 127, 139, 245–46, 343, 344, 345
O'Hare, Kate Richards, 126–30, 139, 227
   After prison, 316, 342, 343, 344–45, 349, 353
   background of, 127–28
   Goldman and, 130, 211–12, 245–46, 279, 349
   imprisonment of, 245–46, 288
   indictment of, 129–30, 139, 151
   release from prison, 315–16
   trial and sentencing of, 183, 185, 210–12
Okrent, Daniel, 301
Omaha, 3, 123, 124
   "Red Summer" of 1919, 256–58
One Big Union, 334
Open Shop Review, 223
Ottoman Turkey, 17, 195, 261
Outlaw's Diary, An (Tormay), 301–2
Overman, Lee, 225–26, 227, 239, 248

pacifism, 25–26, 101, 144
Paine, Thomas, 309
Palestine, 204
Palmer, A. Mitchell, 261, 276
   Alien Property Custodian, 302–3
   anarchists bombings of 1919 and, 239–44, 274
   appointment as Attorney General, 231–32
   background of, 232
   election of 1920, 282, 285–86, 296, 302–4, 310, 313, 329–33
   May Day predictions, 313–14, 317, 318, 322–23
   O'Hare and, 315
   raids. See Palmer Raids
   Union of Russian Workers and, 274–75

Palmer Raids, 280–82, 285, 286, 295–97, 300, 307–8, 310, 314, 316, 327, 352
Pan African Congress, 204, 251
Paris, during World War I, 81–82, 168, 186
Paris Peace Conference, 205–8, 213–20, 233–38
Patriotic American League, 228
Pearl Harbor, attack on, 39–40
Pennsylvania, USS, 202–3
People's Council of America for Democracy and Peace, 178–79
People's Counselor, 67
Pershing, John J., 2, 74, 81–82, 130, 168, 179, 196, 206, 339
Pettigrew, Richard F., 95
Phelps, Dodge & Company, 40, 89–90
Philadelphia Bulletin, 83
Philadelphia Inquirer, 194
Philippine War, 11, 47, 52–53, 60, 74, 84, 97, 129, 136, 149, 306, 357
   Moro Rebellion, 191–92, 197
Phillips, Wendell, 261
Phillips County, Arkansas, Elaine massacre of 1919, 254–55
Pickford, Mary, 175
Pinkerton National Detective Agency, 9, 60
Pittsburgh
   streetcar strike of 1919, 273–74
   strike of 1916, 90–92
   Wobblies in, 90–92, 119–24, 164–66, 221, 238–39, 267, 273–74, 298, 334–35
Pittsburgh Press, 91–92, 238
Plain Words (manifesto), 238
Poindexter, Miles, 286, 333
Poland, 218, 344
Pollak, Theodora, 124
Portland, Oregon, 141–43, 189, 221, 223, 230
Portland labor strike of 1919, 223
Portland Public Library, 230
Post, Louis F., 335–36
   aftermath, 347
   background of, 150–51, 305–7

deportations and Labor Department, 79–80, 150–51, 305–10, 312–13, 317–18, 323–25, 327–28
  Goldman's deportation and, 79–80, 150–51, 248
  House Rules Committee hearings, 317–18, 323–25
postal service. *See* Burleson, Albert Sidney
Prager, Robert, 157–58
presidential term limits, 285–86
press censorship. *See* censorship
Princeton University, 6, 29–30
profiteering, 44–45, 322–23, 329
Progressive Era, 27, 108, 265
Proletaras, 334
propaganda, 3–4, 17, 171–80
  Committee on Public Information, 175–79
Protocols of the Elders of Zion, 226
Providence Journal, 282
Prussian Cur, The (movie), 177
Public, The, 137, 306–7
Pueblo, Colorado, Wilson's speech of 1919, 270–72

racism, 2–3, 50–51, 108–9, 228, 356–57
  white riots of 1919, 252–58
Radical Division of Justice Department, 244, 256, 280, 323
Radical Library (Pittsburgh), 119, 121
Randolph, A. Philip, 144
Rankin, Jeannette, 26, 42, 144
rape, 115, 198, 250–51
Rebel, The, 64
Reconstruction, 29–30, 107, 108, 306, 347
Recruit, USS, 38
Red Cross, 6, 44, 82, 94, 101, 131
Red Scare, 2–3, 10, 222–24, 261, 264, 296–98, 325–28, 347, 354
Red Special (train), 182
"Red Summer" of 1919, 254–58
Reed, John, 65, 66–67, 78–79, 86, 102, 160, 162, 170
Reitman, Ben, 78, 276–77
Republican Guards (France), 203

Republican National Convention (1920), 330–33
Republican Party, 3, 41, 110
Revere, Paul, 38, 93
Roberts, Needham, 250–51
Rockefeller, Clarence, 208
Rockefeller, John D., Jr., 224, 239, 301, 331
Rock Springs, Wyoming, massacre of 1885, 48
Rocky Mountain News, 322
Rogers, Will, 204
Rome, Wilson in, 135–37, 176, 187, 195, 203–6
Roosevelt, Archibald, 153
Roosevelt, Eleanor, 240
Roosevelt, Franklin D., 28, 176, 240, 336, 349
Roosevelt, Kermit, 153
Roosevelt, Quentin, 72, 153, 168, 187, 207–8
Roosevelt, Theodore, 71–74, 237
  death of son Quentin, 168, 187, 207–8
  election of 1912 and, 73
  League of Nations and, 207–9
  Wobblies and Socialists, 85, 89, 182
  during World War I, 6–7, 25, 39, 42, 71–74, 82, 94, 153
Roosevelt, Theodore, Jr., 153, 168
Root, Elihu, 10–11
Rotary Club, 321
Rough Riders, 39, 71–72, 73, 89
Royal Navy, 18, 215, 219
Royal Vagabond, The (musical), 263
Rumsey, Ray, 346
Russia
  Peace of Brest-Litovsk, 214–15
  during World War I, 16, 38, 56–57, 131
Russian Civil War, 220, 264, 297–98, 305, 313
Russian Revolution, 10, 57–58, 131–32, 133, 136, 196, 264, 274–75, 280, 332, 357

Saar coalfields, 207, 218
St. Louis, 46, 316
  East St. Louis riots of 1917, 111–13, 252, 255
St. Louis Post-Dispatch, 111

Saint Paul's Polish Presbyterian Church
    (Baltimore), 310
Saint Regis Yacht Club, 225
Salem witches, 132
Salt Lake City, 160, 161, 270
San Antonio Inquirer, 138
San Diego Union, 347
San Francisco, 97, 156, 276, 322
San Francisco Examiner, 322, 349
Sanger, Margaret, 142
San Quentin State Prison, 349
Scarlett, Sam, 119, 123, 163–64
Schenck v. United States, 212–13, 289
Schimmel, E. A., 188
Schoberg, Charles, 154–56, 213, 230, 317,
    341
Schumann, Wilhelm, 94
"sealed train," 57, 131, 178,Seattle, 95, 99,
    132
    General Strike of 1919, 221–23, 227–28
    Wilson's stop in, 264, 268–70
    Wobblies in, 264, 268–70, 287
Second Army, US, 197
Secret Game, The (movie), 177
Sedition Act of 1918, 149–51
Sedition Slammers, 101
segregation, 59–60, 62, 107, 114, 197
Selective Service Act, 58–59, 76–77, 144, 160
Senate Committee on Foreign Relations, 237
Senate Committee on Privileges and
    Elections, 70, 216
sexism, 125–27, 226–27
Shakespeare, William, 123
Sherman Detective Agency, 171
Sherman Service, 171–74, 267–68
Signal Corps, 60, 320
Simmons, William, 356
Simons, George, 225–26
Sinclair, Upton, 237, 353
single-tax movement, 306, 324, 325, 328
Sisson Documents, 178
Slacker, The (movie), 177
"slackers," 8, 43, 151–53
"slacker raids," 151–53, 188–89
slavery, 29–30, 107, 108, 186, 261

Smart, William F., 228
Smith, Edward, 256–58
socialism, 64, 353–54
Socialist Party, 83, 119, 127, 181–86, 229,
    299–300, 308, 316, 341, 352–54.
    See also Debs, Eugene V.; *and specific
    members*
    antiwar sentiments of, 18, 25, 41, 60,
        64–65
    Black Americans and, 108–9
    O'Hare and, 127–30
Social Security, 353
Solidarity, 87
Somme, Battle of the, 16
Soper, Anson, 170
Soros, George, 357
Sousa, John Philip, 38, 46
"Soviet Ark" (*Buford*), 11, 290–93, 304, 318,
    399*n*
Soviet Union. *See* Russia
Spanish-American War, 25, 39, 47, 71, 152,
    330
"Spanish flu" epidemic of 1918, 192–94,
    215, 217
Speckart, Harriet, 141
Speculator Mine disaster of 1917, 102–4
Spirit of '76, The (movie), 93–94
Standard Steel Car, 45
Stanford University, 227
Statue of Liberty, 197, 202, 247, 354
steel strikes of 1919, 264–68, 297
Steffens, Lincoln, 79
Stewart, Samuel, 346
Strang, Dean, 164
streetcar strike of 1919, 273–74
Sunday, Billy, 163
surveillance, 9–10. *See also* detective agen-
    cies, Espionage Act of 1917, Sherman
    Service, and Wendell, Leo M.
    of Black Americans, 116–17
    Van Deman and World War I, 51–53,
        59–60, 116–17, 166–69

Tacoma Times, 179–80
Taft, William Howard, 239

Tea Party, 51

Thomas, Norman, 144

369th Infantry Regiment (Colored) ("Harlem Hellfighters"), 249–50

Togoland, 218

Tolstoi Club (Manchester), 295

Tolstoy, Leo, 307

Topeka State Journal, 184

Tormay, Cécile, 301–2

torture. *See* "water cure"

trade unions. *See* labor unions; *and specific unions*

trench warfare, 56, 143, 153, 179–80, 194

Trevor, John B., 224–29, 229, 300–302, 351–52

Trial, The (Kafka), 139

Trotsky, Leon, 178, 226, 262, 305, 310, 323

Truman, Harry S., 38

Trump, Donald, 3, 356–57

Trump, Fred, 356

Truss, Thomas, 309–10

Tulsa Daily World, 1, 4, 5

Tulsa Democrat, 10

Tulsa Outrage of 1917, 1–5, 9, 10–11, 85

Tulsa race massacre of 1921, 355–56

Tumulty, Joseph, 316
  concealment of Wilson's health, 277, 283, 285, 300
  Paris Peace Conference and, 202–3, 218, 235, 236
  western tour of 1919, 260–61, 271, 272, 276, 277
  during World War I, 22, 35–36

Turkey, 17, 195, 261

Turner, Hayes, 250–51

Turner, Mary, 250–51

"Twelve Lawyer Report," 327–28, 331

22nd Amendment, 285–86

unemployment, 40, 221, 237, 252

Union of Russian Workers, 274–75, 280–82, 287, 288, 290–91, 308

unions. *See* labor unions; *and specific unions*

Union Station (Washington, DC), 25, 259, 343

United Fruit Company, 166

United Kingdom. *See* Britain

United Mine Workers coal strike of 1919, 275–76

University of California, Berkeley, 25, 95, 150

University of Wisconsin, 42

U.S.A (Dos Passos), 160–61

US Steel Corporation, 44–45, 265–66, 319

Ute Indians, 276

Van Deman, Ralph, 51–53, 59–60, 89, 116–17, 166–69, 206–7, 319–20, 347

Vardaman, James K., 114, 252

Vatican, 203–4

Verdun, Battle of, 16

Vermont Avenue Christian Church, 23

Versailles, Treaty of, 218, 220, 234–38, 259–60, 303

Vietnam War, 9, 144, 352

vigilantism, 8–9, 97–101, 132–33, 229, 254–55, 266. *See also* American Protective League
  Tulsa Outrage of 1917, 1–5, 9, 10–11

Villa, Francisco (Pancho Villa), 91

Villard, Oswald Garrison, 139, 216

voter registration, 117

voter suppression, 47

Waldman, Louis, 299–300

Wallace, George, 3

Wall Street Journal, 262

War, Peace, and the Future (Key), 68

War Industries Board, 45

War Plan Brown, 320

War Plan Green, 320War Plan White, 320–21

Washington, Booker T., 109

Washington, DC, anarchist bombings of 1919, 239–43

Washington, George, 17, 43, 72, 93

Washington Evening Star, 61

Washington Herald, 282

Washington Post, 157, 217, 241

Washington Times, 135, 315, 324

"water cure," 52–53, 84, 97, 146, 149
Webster, Daniel, 69–70
Weinberger, Harry, 278, 279, 289
Wells, Ida B., 109, 112, 205, 255
Wells Fargo Express, 68
Wendell, Leo M., 323
  aftermath, 347–48
  Wobblies and "Walsh," 91–92, 119–22,
    123, 164–66, 221, 238–39, 267,
    273–74, 278, 298, 334–35
Wheeler, Burton K., 104, 105
White, Edward, 30–31, 32, 34, 339
white riots of 1919, 252–58
Why Freedom Matters (pamphlet), 138
Why War? (Howe), 248
Wilhelm II, 6, 46, 122, 143–44, 196
William I (the Conqueror), 49
Williams, A. D., 117
Williams, John Sharp, 32, 42, 114–15
Wilson, Edith
  aftermath, 340
  concealment of husband's health, 277–78,
    283, 284–85, 300
  Europe and Paris Peace Conference and,
    202–4, 217, 234, 236
  influenza of, 217
  western tour of 1919, 259–60, 260, 272,
    277–78
  during World War I, 15–16, 19, 24,
    35–36, 43–44
Wilson, Ellen, 15
Wilson, Joseph, 29
Wilson, William B., 305–6, 336
Wilson, Woodrow
  censorship and, 61, 66–67, 209–10
  concealment of ill health, 282–85, 300,
    310–13
  death of, 340
  Debs and, 184, 316, 337–38
  early life of, 29
  election of 1912, 6, 73
  election of 1916, 18, 65
  Europe trip of, 202–8
  House and, 23–25, 135, 217, 235–36, 237
  Howe and, 248–49, 261

  ill health of, 233, 237, 259–60, 272,
    282–83
  influenza pandemic and, 215, 217, 233
  League of Nations and, 136–37, 205–6,
    213–14, 259, 303
  Memorial Address at Suresnes, 233–34
  O'Hare and, 315
  Palmer and, 231–32, 243–44, 249, 276,
    312–13
  Paris Peace Conference, 205–8, 213–18,
    233–38
  Post and, 150–51
  presidency of Princeton, 6, 29–30
  presidential transition of 1921, 339–40
  Roosevelt and, 72–74
  strokes of, 16, 233, 237, 277–78, 282–85,
    284–85, 300, 310–13
  Van Deman and, 167
  western tour of 1919, 249, 259–61,
    263–66, 268–72, 276, 277–78
  white riots of 1919, 255
Wilson, Woodrow, during World War
  I, 15–16, 18–22, 26–27, 61, 82–83,
    135–36, 144
  address to Congress of 1917, 16, 20, 21,
    26–35
  declaration of war, 37–38, 40
  Flag Day speech of 1917, 82, 89
  "Fourteen Points" speech, 135–37, 176,
    187, 195, 203–6, 216
  mobilization efforts, 42–47
  opposition, 34, 41–42, 63–68, 69–70,
    76–77, 82–83, 95–96
  Zimmermann telegram, 19–20
Winchester Repeating Arms Company, 40
Windsor Castle, 179
Wobblies (Industrial Workers of the
  World), 85–92, 119–24, 132, 159–66,
    354–55
  American Protective League and,
    100–101
  Bisbee Deportations of 1917, 89–90
  Black Americans and, 108–9
  Butte lynching of 1917, 103–5
  Centralia massacre of 1919, 283–84

Chicago trial of 1918, 124, 159–64,
169–70, 345
Espionage Act and, 60–61
Everett massacre of 1916, 141
membership, 85, 86, 122
raids of 1917, 122–24, 142
Sacramento trial of 1919, 210
Seattle General Strike of 1919, 221–23
Tulsa Outrage of 1917, 1–5, 9, 10–11, 85
women in the workforce, 125–27
Women's Revolver League, 156
women's suffrage, 42, 126, 141, 205, 232
Wood, Leonard, 46, 258, 265–67
aftermath, 348
coal strike of 1919 and, 275
conscientious objectors and Camp Funston, 191–92, 208
election of 1920, 230, 286, 303–4, 330–33
League of Nations and, 208–9
during Philippine War, 191–92, 197
Roosevelt and, 74, 208–9
steel strike of 1919 and, 265–67, 275
during World War I, 39, 72, 73–74, 187
World War I, 2, 4, 10, 16–19, 130–31,
179–80, 186–89. *See also specific countries and persons*
anti-German sentiments in US, 6–8, 33,
83, 153–58, 176–77
Armistice, 195–97, 215
Black Americans in, 59–60, 114–16,
249–50

congressional vote for war, 41–42
conscientious objectors (COs), 144–48,
190–92
declaration of war of US, 37–38,
40
draft in. *See* draft
Lusitania sinking, 19, 40
mobilization efforts in US, 42–46
opposition in US to, 34, 41–42, 58–59,
63–68, 69–70, 76–77, 82–83, 93–96,
101–2
patriotism in US, 37–40, 46–47, 94, 96,
186
preparations for, 55, 58
"sealed train," 57, 131, 178,
Spring Offensive, 143–44
Van Deman and surveillance, 51–53,
59–60, 116–17, 166–69
war propaganda, 3–4, 171–80
Wilson and. *See* Wilson, Woodrow,
during World War I
Zimmermann telegram,
19–20
World War II, 351–52
Wounded Knee, Battle of, 47

York, Alvin, 188
Young, Charles, 114–15

Zapata, Emiliano, 91
Zimmermann, Arthur, 19–20

ABOUT THE AUTHOR

Much of Adam Hochschild's writing is about issues of human rights and social justice. Among his 11 books are *King Leopold's Ghost: A Story of Greed, Terror, and Heroism in Colonial Africa*; *Bury the Chains: Prophets and Rebels in the Fight to Free an Empire's Slaves*; *To End All Wars: A Story of Loyalty and Rebellion, 1914–1918*; *Spain in Our Hearts: Americans in the Spanish Civil War, 1936–1939*; and *Rebel Cinderella: From Rags to Riches to Radical, the Epic Journey of Rose Pastor Stokes*. As a journalist, he has reported for American magazines from five continents. Some of that work appears in his two collections of shorter pieces, most recently *Lessons from a Dark Time and Other Essays*. Michiko Kakutani of the *New York Times* called Hochschild's first book, *Half the Way Home: A Memoir of Father and Son* "an extraordinarily moving portrait of the complexities and confusions of familial love . . . firmly grounded in the specifics of a particular time and place, conjuring them up with Proustian detail."

Hochschild has won the PEN USA Literary Award, the Los Angeles Times Book Prize, and the Theodore Roosevelt–Woodrow Wilson Award of the American Historical Association. Two of his books have been finalists for the National Book Critics Circle Award and one for the National Book Award. His work has been translated into 15 languages. A lecturer at the Graduate School of Journalism at the University of California, Berkeley, he and his wife, the sociologist and author Arlie Russell Hochschild, have two sons and two granddaughters.